CONSUMER BEHAVIOR 2017-2018

12th Edition

RKMA MARKET RESEARCH HANDBOOK SERIES

By: Richard K. Miller and Kelli Washington

Published by:

Richard K. Miller & Associates
4132 Atlanta Highway, Suite 110
Loganville, GA 30052
(888) 928-RKMA (7562)
www.rkma.com

Richard K. Miller & Associates
since 1972

CONSUMER BEHAVIOR 2017-2018

12th Edition

RKMA MARKET RESEARCH HANDBOOK SERIES

ISBN Number (electronic edition): 9781577832430
ISBN Number (print edition): 9781577832355
ISSN 2380-8268 (online)
ISSN 2376-4988 (print)

Richard K. Miller & Associates
4132 Atlanta Highway, Suite 110
Loganville, GA 30052
(888) 928-RKMA (7562)
www.rkma.com

CONTENTS

PART I: THE AMERICAN CONSUMER

1

DEMOGRAPHIC OVERVIEW

1.1 Population Distribution

Census 2010 counted the U.S. population on April 1, 2010 at 308.75 million, a 9.7% increase over the count of 281.42 million from Census 2000.

The U.S. Census Bureau (www.census.gov) estimated the U.S. population as of July 2016 at 323.95 million.

There is in the United States, on average, one birth every 8 seconds, one death every 15 seconds, one international migrant (net) every 38 seconds, and a net population gain of one person every 14 seconds.

The U.S. population by gender at year-end 2015 was as follows:

- Male: 158,229,297
- Female: 163,189,523
- Total: 321,418,820

The U.S. population by age at year-end 2015 was as follows:

Age	Total	Male	Female
• 0	3,978,038	2,035,134	1,942,904
• 1	3,968,564	2,029,295	1,939,269
• 2	3,966,583	2,026,604	1,939,979
• 3	3,974,061	2,030,644	1,943,417
• 4	4,020,035	2,055,924	1,964,111
• 5	4,018,158	2,050,848	1,967,310
• 6	4,019,207	2,050,663	1,968,544
• 7	4,148,360	2,117,118	2,031,242
• 8	4,167,887	2,128,825	2,039,062
• 9	4,133,564	2,111,678	2,021,886
• 10	4,121,289	2,103,943	2,017,346
• 11	4,130,328	2,106,742	2,023,586
• 12	4,101,021	2,090,780	2,010,241
• 13	4,084,306	2,082,704	2,001,602
• 14	4,185,386	2,136,219	2,049,167
• 15	4,249,742	2,172,989	2,076,753
• 16	4,184,296	2,139,271	2,045,025
• 17	4,194,286	2,145,174	2,049,112
• 18	4,217,995	2,156,041	2,061,954
• 19	4,262,584	2,184,392	2,078,192
• 20	4,363,440	2,240,373	2,123,067

- 21 4,456,790 2,290,006 2,166,784
- 22 4,529,472 2,331,696 2,197,776
- 23 4,652,266 2,387,842 2,264,424
- 24 4,737,345 2,417,937 2,319,408
- 25 4,729,564 2,407,515 2,322,049
- 26 4,544,416 2,310,983 2,233,433
- 27 4,439,766 2,254,603 2,185,163
- 28 4,364,669 2,214,738 2,149,931
- 29 4,383,139 2,221,560 2,161,579
- 30 4,417,209 2,231,463 2,185,746
- 31 4,278,233 2,152,765 2,125,468
- 32 4,343,614 2,181,163 2,162,451
- 33 4,341,754 2,175,631 2,166,123
- 34 4,294,838 2,148,717 2,146,121
- 35 4,379,404 2,199,270 2,180,134
- 36 4,108,775 2,053,297 2,055,478
- 37 4,028,403 2,010,463 2,017,940
- 38 3,987,141 1,983,816 2,003,325
- 39 3,870,862 1,926,578 1,944,284
- 40 3,989,839 1,989,213 2,000,626
- 41 3,865,228 1,919,064 1,946,164
- 42 3,924,258 1,942,311 1,981,947
- 43 4,100,708 2,032,362 2,068,346
- 44 4,335,165 2,147,203 2,187,962
- 45 4,389,345 2,182,484 2,206,861
- 46 4,160,573 2,064,898 2,095,675
- 47 4,073,685 2,019,602 2,054,083
- 48 4,077,689 2,015,073 2,062,616
- 49 4,152,552 2,052,872 2,099,680
- 50 4,400,288 2,173,002 2,227,286
- 51 4,479,664 2,202,725 2,276,939
- 52 4,474,344 2,195,088 2,279,256
- 53 4,463,494 2,186,448 2,277,046
- 54 4,516,527 2,206,584 2,309,943
- 55 4,553,385 2,228,498 2,324,887
- 56 4,399,120 2,143,285 2,255,835
- 57 4,371,245 2,124,551 2,246,694
- 58 4,320,522 2,092,228 2,228,294
- 59 4,163,670 2,009,005 2,154,665
- 60 4,125,792 1,987,008 2,138,784
- 61 3,954,601 1,893,657 2,060,944
- 62 3,801,935 1,815,914 1,986,021
- 63 3,651,393 1,741,514 1,909,879
- 64 3,536,156 1,679,087 1,857,069
- 65 3,450,043 1,637,936 1,812,107

• 66	3,344,134	1,583,339	1,760,795
• 67	3,304,187	1,562,960	1,741,227
• 68	3,436,357	1,623,929	1,812,428
• 69	2,532,747	1,188,026	1,344,721
• 70	2,492,490	1,162,672	1,329,818
• 71	2,421,191	1,123,102	1,298,089
• 72	2,469,605	1,140,651	1,328,954
• 73	2,146,052	983,641	1,162,411
• 74	1,953,711	886,092	1,067,619
• 75	1,839,823	829,659	1,010,164
• 76	1,722,041	774,758	947,283
• 77	1,639,085	728,549	910,536
• 78	1,500,813	659,853	840,960
• 79	1,422,071	618,087	803,984
• 80	1,351,196	578,240	772,956
• 81	1,201,044	507,988	693,056
• 82	1,148,948	477,629	671,319
• 83	1,082,562	442,175	640,387
• 84	1,015,591	406,633	608,958
• 85	957,023	374,382	582,641
• 86	846,081	323,518	522,563
• 87	774,639	287,383	487,256
• 88	689,755	248,876	440,879
• 89	596,847	208,085	388,762
• 90	523,034	175,479	347,555
• 91	440,318	142,870	297,448
• 92	360,659	113,834	246,825
• 93	293,806	88,660	205,146
• 94	233,118	68,135	164,983
• 95	174,011	48,015	125,996
• 96	122,887	32,585	90,302
• 97	92,377	23,092	69,285
• 98	61,991	14,719	47,272
• 99	43,641	9,577	34,064
• 100+	76,974	15,088	61,886

"Overall, there are now more people in their 20s than in any other 10-year group. In 2010, those in their 40s were the largest group."

The New York Times

The U.S. Census Bureau defines four statistical regions, as follows:

- Region 1 - Northeast: Connecticut, Maine, Massachusetts, New Jersey, New York, New Hampshire, Pennsylvania, Rhode Island, Vermont
- Region 2 - Midwest: Illinois, Indiana, Iowa, Kansas, Michigan, Minnesota, Missouri, Nebraska, North Dakota, Ohio, South Dakota, Wisconsin
- Region 3 - South: Alabama, Arkansas, Delaware, Florida, Georgia, Kentucky, Louisiana, Maryland, Mississippi, North Carolina, Oklahoma, South Carolina, Tennessee, Texas, Virginia, Washington D.C., West Virginia
- Region 4 - West: Alaska, Arizona, California, Colorado, Hawaii, Idaho, Montana, Nevada, New Mexico, Oregon, Utah, Washington, Wyoming

In 2015, the population distribution by region was as follows:

- Northeast: 56.28 million (17.4% of total)
- Midwest: 67.91 million (21.1% of total)
- South: 121.18 million (37.7% of total)
- West: 76.04 million (23.6% of total)

1.2 Median Age

The median age of the U.S. population was reported by Census 2010 as follows:

- Female: 39.1
- Male: 36.1
- Both genders: 37.8

Overall the median age of the U.S. population is rising and will continue to do so for the foreseeable future.

"The country has been getting older. The median age of the population was 38 in 2015. The Census Bureau forecasts it will continue to rise, reaching 41 years old in 2059. In 1970, the median age was 27, just one year higher than it had been in 1930."

The New York Times

In 1950, just 8% of Americans were 65 or older. By 2015, the figure was 14% and it is expected to be 20% by 2030.

1.3 Births

According to the National Center for Health Statistics (www.cdc.gov/nchs), there were 3,977,745 births in the U.S. in 2015, slightly down from the 3,985,924 recorded in 2014 and 8% below the all-time high of 4,316,233 in 2007. The birth rate in 2014 was 12.5 per 1,000 population.

In 2015, the fertility rate fell to a new all-time low of 62.5 births per 1,000 women ages 15-to-44. This is 9% below the rate of 69.3 in 2007 and the lowest since World War II.. The fertility rates of females ages 15-to-19, 20-to-24, and 25-to-29 all fell to new record lows in 2015.

"Never before have young women had so few children. The first-birth rate also hit an all-time low in 2013, with the rate dropping for women in every age group under age 30. Clearly, young women are reluctant to have children, and the number of births is essentially unchanged only because older women are playing catch up before time runs out. The seeming stability in births belies the havoc wreaked by the Great Recession on the lives of young adults."

Demo Memo

1.4 Generational Demographics

Marketers typically categorize consumers into five generations, as follows:

	Year of Birth	Age (in 2016)	Population
• Seniors:	1945 and before	71 and older	29.19 million
• Baby Boomers:	1946-1964	52-to-70	72.88 million
• Generation X:	1965-1979	37-to-51	61.82 million
• Millennials (Gen Y):	1980-2000	16-to-36	92.21 million
• Generation Z:	2001-present	15 and younger	65.26 million

Generational assessments explore how the era in which people live influences their behavior. Many consumers who lived through the Great Depression of 1929, for example, remained frugal their entire lives because of the profound impact it had on them. Baby Boomers grew up without psychological scars from the Depression and generally spend more freely than their parents' generation. Subsequent generations have grown up in an age of abundance, easy credit, and a taste for luxury. Spending and lifestyles of Generation Z will likely be influenced by the Great Recession of 2008-2009.

Spending is also influenced by life cycles. Most members of Generation X are now in their peak earning and spending years. Baby Boomers, some looking toward retirement or semi-retirement, are beginning to spend less.

Generational demographics are further assessed in Part XI of this handbook.

1.5 Race/Ethnicity Distribution

The following is the U.S. population by race/ethnicity reported by Census 2010 and in July 2015 (source: Census Bureau):

	Census 2010	2015
• Hispanic	50,477,594	56,592,793
• White:	197,318,956	197,970,812
• Black or African American:	37,922,522	39,925,949
• Asian:	14,661,516	17,416,714
• American Indian or Alaska Native:	2,263,258	2,369,834
• Native Hawaiian or other Pacific Islander:	497,216	559,682
• Two or more races:	5,609,538	6,583,036
• Total:	308,745,538	321,418,820

As reported in Census 2010, 50.5 million people, or 16% of the total population, identify themselves as Hispanic or Latino. The Hispanic population increased from 35.3 million in 2000, when this group made up 13% of the total population. The Hispanic population increased 43.0% between Census 2000 and Census 2010, while the non-Hispanic population increased 4.9% during that period.

The ethnic composition of the U.S. population by generation is as follows:

	Caucasian	Hispanic	African American	Asian American	Other
• Baby Boomers:	72%	11%	11%	4%	2%
• Generation X:	62%	18%	12%	6%	2%
• Millennials (Gen Y):	58%	20%	14%	5%	3%
• Generation Z:	54%	24%	14%	4%	4%

Ethnic demographics are further assessed in Part IX of this handbook.

1.6 Overall Demographic Distribution

The following is the demographic distribution of U.S. adults in 2015 (source: Pew Research Center [www.pewresearch.org]):

Age

• 18-to-29:	21%
• 30-to-44:	25%
• 45-to-64:	34%
• 65 and older:	19%

Race/Ethnicity

• Caucasian:	65%
• Hispanic:	15%
• African-American:	12%
• Asian-American:	6%

Education

• Less than high school graduate:	12%
• High school graduate:	30%
• Some college/two-year degree:	28%
• Bachelor's degree or more:	30%

Family Status

• Married, no children at home:	24%
• Married, with children at home:	28%
• Unmarried:	48%

Nativity

• U.S. born:	84%
• Foreign born:	16%

1.7 Market Resources

U.S. Population Clock, U.S. Census Bureau; provides U.S. population estimate on a daily basis. (www.census.gov/main/www/popclock.html)

2

CONSUMER INCOME & WEALTH

2.1 Household Income

According to the U.S. Census Bureau (www.census.gov), real median household income in the United States in 2014 was $53,657, not statistically different in real terms from the 2013 median of $51,939. This was the third consecutive year that the annual change was not statistically significant, following two consecutive years of annual declines in median household income. In 2012, real median household income was 8% lower than in 2007, the year before the Great Recession.

Median household income has been as follows:

- 2000: $57,724
- 2001: $56,466
- 2002: $55,807
- 2003: $55,759
- 2004: $55,565
- 2005: $56,160
- 2006: $57,598
- 2007: $55,357
- 2008: $54,313
- 2009: $53,925
- 2010: $52,507
- 2011: $52,690
- 2012: $52,605
- 2013: $54,462
- 2014: $53,657

2.2 Income Distribution

In 2014, median household income of $53,657 was distributed as follows (source: Census Bureau):

Age of Householder

- Under age 25: $34,605
- 25-to-34: $54,243
- 35-to-44: $66,693
- 45-to-54: $70,832
- 55-to-64: $60,580
- 65 and older: $36,895

Race/Ethnicity

- African-American: $35,398
- Asian-American: $74,297
- Caucasian: $60,256
- Hispanic: $42,491

Household

- Married-couple family households: $68,426
- Non-family households: $32,047

Region

- Northeast: $59,210
- West: $57,688
- Midwest: $54,267
- South: $49,655

Community

- Inside metropolitan areas: $55,855
- Outside metropolitan areas: $45,482

Nativity

- U.S. born: $54,678
- Foreign born: $49,592

In 2014, the real median earnings of men and women who worked full time were $50,383 and $39,621, respectively. The 2014 female-to-male earnings ratio was 0.79, a figure that has not experienced a significant annual change since 2007.

2.3 Income By State

Median income by state in 2014 was as follows (source: Census Bureau):

- Alabama: $42,738
- Alaska: $62,855
- Arizona: $49,165
- Arkansas: $39,752
- California: $57,688
- Colorado: $60,729
- Connecticut: $66,481
- Delaware: $50,951
- District of Columbia: $63,435
- Florida: $47,313
- Georgia: $48,130
- Hawaii: $59,244
- Idaho: $50,193
- Illinois: $54,843
- Indiana: $48,691
- Iowa: $54,537
- Kansas: $51,107
- Kentucky: $41,921
- Louisiana: $39,637
- Maine: $49,997
- Maryland: $69,071
- Massachusetts: $63,772
- Michigan: $49,771
- Minnesota: $61,800
- Mississippi: $39,012
- Missouri: $50,399
- Montana: $44,938
- Nebraska: $53,364
- Nevada: $46,695
- New Hampshire: $70,063
- New Jersey: $64,722
- New Mexico: $43,091
- New York: $51,108
- North Carolina: $41,683
- North Dakota: $54,732
- Ohio: $45,709

- Oklahoma: $46,444
- Oregon: $54,417
- Pennsylvania: $53,305
- Rhode Island: $57,346
- South Carolina: $44,398
- South Dakota: $52,293
- Tennessee: $43,060
- Texas: $52,854
- Utah: $61,078
- Vermont: $55,616
- Virginia: $66,595
- Washington: $61,598
- West Virginia: $42,213
- Wisconsin: $54,554
- Wyoming: $57,024

2.4 Household Wealth

According to *Survey of Consumer Finances*, published every three years by the Federal Reserve (www.federalreserve.gov), median household net wealth, adjusted for inflation, has been as follows:

- 2007: $135,400
- 2010: $ 82,800
- 2013: $ 81,200

From 2007 to 2010, median inflation-adjusted net worth (e.g. wealth) fell 38.8% to $77,300, the same level as in 2001. This drop is attributed to the Great Recession.

Median household net worth continued to drift downward between 2010 and 2013, suggesting that most households were not recovering from the recession. Many households experienced double-digit declines in net worth between 2010 and 2013, after adjusting for inflation.

Following a 39% decline between 2007 and 2010, households headed by people ages 45-to-54 saw their net worth fall by an additional 17% between 2010 and 2013. Household segments headed by people without a high school diploma, with only some college, and the broad segment "nonwhites or Hispanics" also experienced double-digit declines in net worth between 2010 and 2013.

Overall, net household wealth, which mostly consists of home equity, stock portfolios, and other savings, was $81.5 trillion in June 2014, according to the Federal Reserve. Household wealth peaked before the recession at $67.4 trillion and reached a low of $55 trillion (inflation-adjusted) in early 2009, in the depths of the recession.

The distribution of wealth in the United States is as follows:

- The top 20% of Americans hold 84% of U.S. wealth
- The second 20% hold 11%
- The third 20% hold 4%
- The fourth 20% hold 0.2%
- The bottom 20% hold 0.1%

Twenty-five percent (25%) of American households have zero or negative net worth; 37% have a net worth of less than $12,000.

2.5 Poverty And Economic Insecurity

The U.S. poverty rate in 2014 was 14.8%, with 46.7 million people classified as living in poverty, according to the Census Bureau. This was an increase from 14.5% in 2013. The 2013 poverty rate was 2.3 percentage points higher than in 2007, the year before the Great Recession.

While Census Bureau figures provide an official measure of poverty, they are only a temporary snapshot and do not capture the makeup of those who cycle in and out of poverty at different points in their lives. That snapshot shows that 12.6% of adults in their prime working-age years of 25-to-60 live in poverty. But measured in terms of a person's lifetime risk, a much higher number – four in 10 adults – fall into poverty for at least a year of their lives.

According to an assessment by the Associated Press (AP), the risks of falling into poverty have been increasing in recent decades, particularly among people ages 35-to-55, and coinciding with widening income inequality. For instance, people ages 35-to-45 had a 17% risk of encountering poverty during the 1969-1989 time period; that risk increased to 23% during the 1989-2009 period. For those ages 45-to-55, the risk of poverty jumped from 12% to 18% over the two periods.

The AP study defines 'economic insecurity' as a year or more of periodic joblessness, reliance on government aid such as food stamps, or income below 150% of the poverty line. According to its assessment, the recent high rates of unemployment mean the lifetime risk of experiencing economic insecurity is 79%.

Poverty and economic insecurity cut across all ethnic and racial demographics. More than 19 million whites fall below the poverty line of $23,021 for a family of four, accounting for more than 41% of the nation's destitute, nearly double the number of poor blacks. Seventy-six percent (76%) of whites will experience economic insecurity by the time they turn 60.

"Hardship is particularly growing among whites, based on several measures. Pessimism among that racial group about their families' economic futures has climbed to the highest point since at least 1987. While poverty rates for blacks and Hispanics are nearly three times higher, by absolute numbers the predominant face of the poor is white."

Associated Press

Dynamics Of Economic Well-Being: Poverty, a study by the Census Bureau, reported that between 2009 and 2012, 31.6% of the U.S. population experienced poverty for at least two months.

Among Hispanics, 49.6% experienced poverty, the highest of all ethnic groups. By age, the percentage was 40.6% among children, 31.0% among adults ages 18-to-64, and 15.7% among the elderly. Among those without a high school diploma, 50.6% experienced poverty. Among those with some college education, 22.9% experienced at least two months of poverty.

The Census Bureau defines 'near poverty' as having a family income either below the poverty level or within 100% to 125% of the poverty level. In 2012, 61 million people, or 19.6% of the total U.S. population, were living in or near poverty. For a family of four with two adults and two children, this is an income of $29,104 or less. For someone who lives alone, it's an income of $14,931 or less. As a point of reference, a minimum-wage-earning, full-time worker has an annual income of $15,080, just above the near-poverty level.

According to *Living in Near Poverty in the United States*, a report by the Census Bureau, between 1966 and 2012, the percentage of Americans who live in or near poverty has fallen slightly – from 21.0% to 19.7%. The percentage in poverty increased from 14.7% to 15.0% during those years, while the percentage near poverty dropped from 6.3% to 4.7%. The poor and near-poor population expanded by more than 20 million between 1966 and 2012.

2.6 Market Resources

Household Income Trends, Sentier Research. (www.sentierresearch.com)

Income and Poverty In The United States, Census Bureau. (www.census.gov/hhes/www/income/income.html)

Institute for Research On Poverty, University of Wisconsin-Madison, 1180 Observatory Drive, Madison, WI 53706. (608) 262-6358. (www.irp.wisc.edu)

Panel Study of Income Dynamics, University of Michigan. (http://psidonline.isr.umich.edu/)

Survey of Consumer Finances, Federal Reserve. (www.federalreserve.gov/econresdata/scf/scfindex.htm)

3

CONSUMER DEBT

3.1 Household Debt

According to the *Quarterly Report On Household Debt and Credit*, by the Federal Reserve Bank of New York (www.newyorkfed.org), total U.S. household debt at year-end 2015 was $12.12 trillion, an increase from $12.07 trillion a year prior. Household debt was distributed as follows:

	2015	2014
• Mortgages:	$8.25 trillion	$8.36 trillion
• Student loans:	$1.23 trillion	$1.20 trillion
• Motor vehicle loans:	$1.06 trillion	$1.04 trillion
• Credit cards/revolving credit:	$ 733 billion	$ 731 billion
• Other:	$ 847 billion	$ 739 billion

In 2015, average household debt by category was as follows (source: Federal Reserve Bank of New York):

- Mortgages: $168,614
- Student loans: $ 48,172
- Auto loans: $ 27,141
- Credit cards: $ 15,762
- All types of debt: $130,922

Based on analysis of millions of credit records over a five-year period, a 2015 report by the Urban Institute (www.urban.org) reported U.S. household debt as follows (percentage of households):

- No debt: 29%
- Only credit card debt: 22%
- Only mortgage debt: 13%
- Only vehicle debt: 12%
- Vehicle and mortgage debt: 9%
- Only student loan debt: 4%

Debt profiles generally depend on lifestage. Mortgage debt, for example, peaks at 41% among consumers ages 48-to-52. Student loans peak at 23% among those ages 23-to-27.

3.2 Mortgage Debt

Mortgage debt accounts for 70% of total consumer debt. Sixty-six percent (66%) of adults have mortgages on their homes, according to The Harris Poll (www.theharrispoll.com).

The Federal Reserve Bank of New York reported that mortgage originations in Fourth Quarter 2015 were $437 billion. About 104,000 individuals had a new foreclosure notation added to their credit reports during the quarter.

In Fourth Quarter 2015, 2.2% of mortgages were 90 days delinquent.

According to The Federal Home Loan Mortgage Corporation (FHLMC), known as Freddie Mac (www.freddiemac.com), homeowners are shortening the terms of their mortgages. Since 2011, over one-third of refinancers paid off a 30-year loan and switched to a 20- or 15-year loan.

3.3 Credit Card Debt

According to the Federal Reserve Bank of New York, approximately 49% of households have credit card debt. Among those with credit card debt, the average was $15,762 per household at year-end 2015.

Credit card debt at year-end 2015 was $733 billion, an increase from $731 billion a year prior.

Credit cards are the only type of debt for 22% of U.S. households, according to the Urban Institute.

Many consumers have given up using credit cards entirely. According to the Federal Reserve, 30% of families have no credit cards.

3.4 Student Loans

About two-thirds of bachelor's degree recipients borrow money to attend college, either from the government or private lenders, according to the U.S. Department of Education (www.ed.gov).

Outstanding educational debt has been as follows (source: Federal Reserve):

- 2008: $ 731 billion
- 2009: $ 832 billion
- 2010: $ 912 billion
- 2011: $1.01 trillion
- 2012: $1.13 trillion
- 2013: $1.22 trillion
- 2014: $1.20 trillion
- 2015: $1.23 trillion

At year-end 2015, 11.5% of student loan balances were 90 or more days delinquent.

According to Pew Research Center (www.pewresearch.org), 19% of U.S. households owe student debt, more than double the share two decades earlier and a rise from the 15% that owed such debt in 2007, just prior to the onset of the Great Recession. Forty percent (40%) of households headed by someone younger than age 35 owe such debt. Among households owing student debt, the average outstanding balance is $26,682; 10% of student debtor households owe more than $61,894.

> **"While the overall level of student debt may not measure up to that of mortgages, it is highly concentrated among a small slice of people – those in their 20s and 30s – who are the engines of a great deal of economic activity. One of the crucial reasons the housing market has not expanded enough to support robust economic growth is that young adults are not setting up their own households at anywhere near the historical norm. Might higher student loan debt burdens be an important reason?"**
>
> *The New York Times*

An October 2015 Harris Poll found that 36% of U.S. adults are currently paying or have paid student debt in the past, a figure unchanged from 2013. Among these debtors, 39% say they have put off savings toward retirement, 30% have delayed buying or leasing a new car, and 30% have delayed buying a home.

3.5 Medical Debt

According to The Commonwealth Fund (www.commonwealthfund.org), 48 million people are paying off medical debt; an additional 27 million people report problems paying their medical bills.

FINRA Investor Education Foundation (www.usfinancialcapability.org) reports the percentages of adults with unpaid medical debt as follows:

- Millennials: 31%
- Gen Xers: 31%
- Baby Boomers: 22%
- Seniors: 10%

In 2015, 26% of adults ages 18-to-64 had problems paying medical bills, according to the Kaiser Family Foundation (www.kff.org). Among those with and without health insurance, these figures are 20% and 53%, respectively.

Hospitals write off about $25 billion, or 2.7% of revenue, as a result of consumer bad debt, according to the American Hospital Association (www.aha.org).

3.6 Market Resources

Detailed Tables On Debt, Census Bureau.
(www.census.gov/people/wealth/data/debttables.html)

Quarterly Report On Household Debt and Credit, Federal Reserve Bank of New York
(www.newyorkfed.org/medialibrary/interactives/householdcredit/data/pdf/HHDC_2015Q4.pdf)

Survey of Consumer Finances, Federal Reserve.
(www.federalreserve.gov/econresdata/scf/scfindex.htm)

4

HOUSEHOLDS & HOUSING

4.1 Households

The *Current Population Survey*, by the Census Bureau (www.census.gov), estimated there were 124.6 million households in the U.S. at year-end 2015. Distribution by race and ethnicity is as follows:

- Non-Hispanic white: 67.6%
- Black: 13.8%
- Hispanic: 13.0%
- Asian: 5.1%

Distribution by type of household is as follows:

- Family households, married couple: 48.3%
- Non-family households (a person living alone, unrelated people living together, or people in group settings): 33.8%
- Family households, husband or wife only present: 17.9%

Household composition has undergone significant shifts in recent decades. Distributions since 1970 have been as follows:

	1970	1980	1990	2000	2010
• Married couples with children:	40.3%	30.9%	26.3%	24.1%	20.9%
• Married couples without children:	30.3%	29.9%	29.8%	18.7%	28.8%
• Other family households:	10.6%	12.9%	14.8%	16.0%	17.4%
• Men living alone:	5.6%	8.6%	9.7%	10.7%	11.9%
• Women living alone:	11.5%	14.0%	14.9%	14.8%	14.8%
• Other non-family households:	1.7%	3.6%	4.6%	5.7%	6.2%

According to the *Current Population Survey*, households grew an average of about 500,000 per year from 2007 through 2014. This is less than half the annual pace of 1.2 million averaged 2000 through 2007, and lower than that averaged in the 1990s, when Generation X matured to become heads of households.

Between 2014 and 2015, the household count increased by 656,000. The change in number of households by age of householder is as follows:

- Under age 25: -282,000
- 25-to-34: 87,000
- 35-to-44: -43,000
- 45-to-54: -98,000

- 55-to-64: 114,000
- 65 and older: 877,000

"The decline in households headed by people ages 35-to-54 is due to the small Generation X population moving into those age groups. The increase in households headed by people aged 55 or older is due to the large Baby-Boom generation in those age groups."

Memo Demo, 10/17/15

Growth in the number of households headed by 25-to-34-year-olds had been declining since the end of the Great Recession, although the trend reversed slightly in 2015. The annual change in the number of these households has been as follows:

- 2010-2011: 315,000
- 2011-2012: 274,000
- 2012-2013: 171,000
- 2013-2014: -9,000
- 2014-2015: 87,000

The 25-to-34-year-old population is growing by more than half a million a year. But burdened by student debt, challenges in finding well-paying jobs, and rising rents, few in this age group can afford to live alone or head households.

4.2 Shared Households

The Census Bureau defines shared households as those with a household member ages 18 or older who is not in school nor the head householder, spouse, or cohabiting partner.

In 2014, there were 23.5 million shared households (19.1% of all households); 74 million adults (30.9% of all adults) lived in these households, according to the Census Bureau. This is a sharp increase from 2007, when there were 19.7 million shared households (17.0% of all households) housing 62 million adults (27.7% of all adults). In 1980, 12.1% of households were shared households.

Among shared households, the majority are multigenerational households, with adult children living with a parent or grandparent, or an elderly parent living with their adult children. According to *The Return of the Multi-Generational Family Household*, a report by the Social & Demographic Trends Project at Pew Research Center (www.pewsocialtrends.com), 16% of family households are multigenerational.

Young adults ages 25-to-34 are a major component of the growth in the shared-living population, especially since 2010. In 2014, 10.7 million adults in this age group were in a multigenerational household. This represents 25.2% of all 25-to-34 year olds. For comparison, 18.7% and 11.0% of 25-to-34 year olds lived in a multigenerational home in 2007 and 1980, respectively. In 2014 alone, 1.8 million young adults moved into a parent's home.

Stephanie Coontz, Ph.D., a family history professor at Evergreen State College, points out that there are a host of factors prompting families to combine expenses. Among them are higher housing costs and the struggling economy. Also, shared households are common among the country's growing number of immigrant families.

According to Amy Gover, a multigenerational issues expert at AARP (www.aarp.org), the most common multigenerational household is one with a grandparent as head of household with adult children that have moved in with their children, an arrangement usually spurred by the needs of one or both to combine resources and save money. The second most common arrangement is a grandparent moving in with an adult child's family, usually for caregiving reasons.

Roommates also account for an increasing number of shared households. Census 2010 reported 6.2 million households with non-relatives, including unmarried partners and roommates, an 8% increase from 2000.

4.3 Home Ownership vs. Renting

Annual Gallup Polls (www.gallup.com) have reported the percentages of adults who own or rent their primary residence as follows:

	Own	Rent
2001:	67%	29%
2002:	70%	28%
2003:	69%	27%
2004:	71%	26%
2005:	74%	24%
2006:	73%	22%
2007:	73%	22%
2008:	70%	26%
2009:	70%	26%
2010:	65%	30%
2011:	68%	28%
2012:	62%	34%
2013:	62%	34%
2014:	64%	32%
2015:	62%	35%

According to the Census Bureau, there were 74.41 million owner-occupied housing units and 42.88 million renter-occupied housing units in 2015; the home-ownership rate was 63.4%, a decline from 65.4% in 2012, and the all-time high of 69.0% in 2004.

Ownership rates by age in 2014 were as follows (percentage point change from 2004 in parenthesis):

- Under 25: 21.7% (-3.5%)
- 25-to-29: 32.7% (-7.5%)
- 30-to-34: 47.2% (-10.3%)
- 35-to-39: 56.0% (-10.2%)

- 40-to-44: 63.2% (-8.7%)
- 45-to-54: 70.7% (-6.5%)
- 55-to-64: 76.3% (-5.4%)
- 65 and older: 79.9% (-1.2%)

Ownership rates by region were as follows (percentage point change from 2004 in parenthesis):

	Ages 30-34	Ages 35-39
• Northeast:	42.1% (-9.8%)	53.9% (-8.0%)
• Midwest:	57.9% (-7.1%)	63.4% (-10.8%)
• South:	49.8% (-9.0%)	56.6% (-11.3%)
• West:	40.6% (-11.5%)	48.7% (-10.1%)

There were 18.5 million vacant housing units in 2015, or about 14% of the total.

4.4 U.S. Housing Inventory

American Community Survey, by the Census Bureau, reported median housing values as follows:

- 2007: $221,845
- 2008: $217,271
- 2009: $204,363
- 2010: $195,311
- 2011: $182,705
- 2012: $177,247
- 2013: $176,721
- 2014: $181,200

"The median value of owned homes in the United States increased in 2014 for the first time since the Great Recession."

Memo Demo, 12/16/15

4.5 New Homes And Multi-Family Units

The Census Bureau reports residential construction in 2015 as follows:

- Single-family homes completed: 648,000
- Multi-family units: 320,000
- Multi-family buildings: 14,000

The median size of a completed single-family house has been as follows:

- 1980: 1,570 sq. ft.
- 1990: 1,890 sq. ft.
- 2000: 2,077 sq. ft.
- 2010: 2,255 sq. ft.
- 2014: 2,506 sq. ft.
- 2015: 2,467 sq. ft.

The median size of multifamily units built in 2015 for rent was 1,057 sq. ft., while the median of those built for sale was 1,408 sq. ft.

Characteristics of new construction were as follows:

Single-Family Homes
- Four bedrooms or more: 282,000
- Two bedrooms or less: 66,000

Multi-Family Units
- In buildings with 50 units or more: 146,000
- Three or more bedrooms: 35,000
- Age-restricted: 3,000

Multi-Family Units
- Constructed using wood framing: 12,000
- One or two floors: 7,000

In 2015, 501,000 single-family homes sold. Characteristics were as follows:
- 453,000 were detached homes; 49,000 were attached homes
- 327,000 had a 2-car garage and 131,000 had a garage for 3 cars or more
- 200,000 had one story, 278,000 had two stories, and 24,000 had three or more

The median sales price of new single-family homes sold was $296,400 in 2015; the average sales price was $360,600.

4.6 Housing Affordability

The traditional affordability standard suggests that housing costs should be no more than 30% of household income. According to *State of the Nation's Housing 2016*, by the Joint Center for Housing Studies at Harvard University (JCHS, www.jchs.harvard.edu), the share of cost-burdened households (i.e., households exceeding the affordability standard) is at 35.3%, down from a record 37.2% in 2010. A full 28% of households are paying more than half their incomes for housing.

4.7 Vacation Homes

According to data by the U.S. Census Bureau, there are 5.33 million vacation, seasonal, or recreational homes in the United States. This represents 4.0% of the total U.S. housing stock. The following states have the highest concentration of vacation homes:

	No. Vacation Homes	Pct. of Total
• Maine:	125,000	17.2%
• Vermont:	50,000	15.4%
• New Hampshire:	69,000	11.2%
• Delaware:	45,000	11.0%
• Alaska:	32,000	10.2%
• Florida:	887,000	9.8%
• Montana:	40,000	8.2%

According to the *2016 Investment and Vacation Home Buyers Survey*, by the National Association of Realtors (www.realtor.org), 920,000 vacation homes were sold in 2015, down 18.5% from their most recent peak level of 1.13 million in 2014. The median vacation home price in 2015 was $192,000, a 28% increase.

Vacation-home sales accounted for 16% of real estate sales transactions in 2015.

4.8 Home Improvement

New homeowners are the most "home-improvement happy." According to JCHS, even though they represent only 13% of all homeowners, they typically account for 25% of home improvement spending. With home sales in decline, the home improvement market suffered during the economic downturn.

Home improvement spending has been on the rise since 2011. The Home Improvement Research Institute (www.hiri.org) assesses home improvement spending as follows (change from previous year in parenthesis):

- 2013: $289.7 billion (4.2%)
- 2014: $308.5 billion (6.5%)
- 2015: $330.2 billion (7.0%)
- 2016: $346.8 billion (5.0%)
- 2017: $363.4 billion (4.8%)
- 2018: $377.6 billion (3.9%)

4.9 Market Resources

Characteristics Of New Housing, Census Bureau. (www.census.gov/construction/chars/)

Current Population Survey, Census Bureau, 2016. (www.census.gov/cps/)

Home Improvement Research Institute, 10117 Princess Palm Avenue, Suite 575, Tampa, FL 33610. (813) 627-6770. (www.hiri.org)

Housing Vacancies and Homeownership, Census Bureau. (www.census.gov/housing/hvs/)

Joint Center for Housing Studies at Harvard University, 1033 Massachusetts Avenue, Fifth Floor, Cambridge, MA 02138. (617) 495-7908. (www.jchs.harvard.edu)

State of the Nation's Housing, Joint Center for Housing Studies at Harvard University, 2016. (www.jchs.harvard.edu/research/state_nations_housing)

5

COMMUNITIES

5.1 Where People Live

Metropolitan and micropolitan statistical areas, or metro and micro areas, are geographic entities defined by the U.S. Office of Management and Budget (www.omb.gov) for use by federal statistical agencies in collecting, tabulating, and publishing federal statistics. A metro area contains a core urban area population of 50,000 or more. A micro area contains a core urban area population of at least 10,000 but less than 50,000. Census 2010 reported the population distribution by core statistical area as follows:

- Metropolitan Statistical Area: 83.7%
- Micropolitan Statistical Area: 10.0%
- Outside core area: 6.3%

According to *Current Population Survey*, by the U.S. Census Bureau (www.census.gov), households are distributed by type of community as follows:

- Inside principal cities of Metropolitan Statistical Areas: 39.47 million (33% of total)
- Outside principal cities of Metropolitan Statistical Areas: 59.79 million (50%)
- Outside Metropolitan Statistical Areas: 19.42 million (16%)

There are 19,508 cities; they comprise 3.5% of land area in the U.S. *Population Trends In Incorporated Areas*, published in 2015 by the Census Bureau, reported that 62.7% of the U.S. population lives in a city.

5.2 Population Growth Trends

According to *City and Town Totals*, published in 2015 by the Census Bureau, the population of the nation's 749 largest cities (incorporated places with populations of 50,000 or more) increased 4.3% between 2010 and 2014 while the remainder of the United States grew by 2.4%.

Population growth between 2010-2014 by city size was as follows:

- 50,000 to 99,999: 4.0%
- 100,000 to 149,999: 4.2%
- 150,000 to 199,999: 3.9%
- 200,000 to 249,999: 4.2%
- 250,000 to 499,999: 4.3%
- 500,000 to 999,999: 5.0%
- 1 million or more: 4.2%

Among non-metropolitan areas of the U.S., two-thirds lost population between 2010 and 2014, according to a June 2015 report by the USDA's Economic Research Service (www.ers.usda.gov). A total of 1,310 non-metro counties had a declining population in the 2010-2014 time period. Population decline is caused by two factors: more people moving out than in and the number of deaths exceeding births. Among the 1,301 shrinking counties, 622 experienced a population decline because of both factors.

Demo Memo (http://demomemo.blogspot.com) assesses that the largest metropolitan areas, with a population of 1 million or more, grew 4.2% between 2010 and 2014. Smaller metropolitan areas grew 2.7%. Non-metropolitan counties as a whole lost 0.2% of their population during those years.

5.3 Most Desirable Places To Live

A survey by Pew Research Center's Social & Demographic Trends Project (www.pewsocialtrends.org) found that 46% of U.S. adults would rather live in a different type of community from the one in which they are presently living. There was no consensus, however, as to what is the ideal place to live. Survey participants responded as follows about their ideal community:

- Small town: 30%
- Suburb: 25%
- City: 23%
- Rural area: 21%

"Most city dwellers think the grass would be greener in a suburb, small town or rural area. But urbanites aren't alone in feeling mismatched with their surroundings. More than four-in-ten residents of suburbs, small towns and rural areas also report they would prefer to live in a different type of community."

Social & Demographics Trends Project
Pew Research Center

The following are other findings of the Pew study:

- By a ratio of more than three-to-one, Americans prefer living where the pace of life is slow. A similarly lopsided majority prefer a place where neighbors know each other well over one where neighbors generally are not acquainted.
- Over 60% of people prefer to live in a warmer climate.

- About seven-in-10 whites rate their current community as "excellent" or "very good"; only about half of Hispanics and four-in-10 blacks say the same. Rural and suburban residents rate their communities better than do residents of cities and small towns.
- People who live in a city – as well as people who wish to live in a city – are more open than others to the idea of living with neighbors who are of different races. They are also more open to living among immigrants.
- When it comes to community involvement, there is no difference among those who live in cities, suburbs, small towns, or rural areas. About half of the residents in each place say they are involved in their communities.

5.4 Satisfaction With Communities

A study by the Urban Land Institute (www.uli.org) assessed Americans' satisfaction with their communities, housing, and transportation and what they want for themselves and their families. The study was based on a survey of homeowners by Belden Russonello Strategists (www.brspoll.com). The following is a summary of the Urban Land Institute assessment:

Quality of Life

- Ninety percent (90%) of American adults are satisfied with their community's quality of life, and few worry that these communities are in danger of deteriorating. Groups who are least satisfied with where they currently live, such as Latinos and big-city residents, tend to be the ones who are the most optimistic and who think their communities are on the upswing.

Community

- About a third of the American public live in what they consider small towns, a third in middle-sized or big cities, 21% in suburbs, and 15% in rural areas. If given a choice, a quarter say they would like to be living in rural communities.

Satisfaction With Residence

- Be it single-family houses, apartments, or other structures, most adults like where they live. Nine in 10 adults report satisfaction with their current dwelling, and four in five are happy with the range of housing choices in their communities. Even among pockets of less contentment with housing, for example among Millennial adults (ages 18-to-34), Latinos, and big-city residents, dissatisfaction does not rise to high levels.

Home Ownership

- Seven in 10 believe that buying a home is a good investment for them, even in the aftermath of the housing and mortgage difficulties of the last few years. Two-thirds of survey respondents said they own their home and seven in 10 renters are hopeful that within five years they will join the ranks of home ownership.

Single-Family Homes

- Two-thirds of the survey participants say they live in detached single-family homes and the remainder live in apartments, duplexes, row houses, and manufactured homes. Among those who believe they will move in the next five years, the appeal of the single-family home is strong, with two-thirds expecting to move into or remain in a detached single-family home.

Mixed-Use Development

- Two groups have high interest in mixed-use development:
  - Young people and college graduates who are most enthusiastic about living in centers with shops and offices nearby.
  - Lower-income groups who would like to live in areas with more variety in housing type and economic diversity.
- Both of these groups share an interest in living close to where they work or go to school. They prefer to live in areas with public transit and would choose shorter commutes with smaller homes over longer commutes and bigger houses.

The Appeal of Compact Development

- While much of the public expresses a desire for single-family homes and rural and small town life, there are competing pressures and needs that make compact development more attractive. Proximity to jobs, schools, and medical services, as well as a community's walkability, are powerful draws for many Americans.

Commuting and Driving

- Most Americans travel by car, truck, or motorcycle nearly every day, and when the two-thirds who commute regularly go to their jobs or school 85% travel in a car.
- Travel times to work or school divide in relative thirds: fewer than fifteen minutes, fifteen minutes to half an hour, and over half an hour. Rural and suburban residents and African Americans have the longest commutes; about half need thirty minutes or more to travel to their job or school.

Public Transportation

- Overall, one in 10 commuters use public transit to get to school or work. Reliance on buses and trains is highest among people of color and, naturally, residents of urban areas. The public that is served by buses and trains say the quality of their public transit systems is satisfactory; however, half of those who do not have access to trains and buses are discontent with the lack of public transportation.

Walkability

- Americans place high priority on having communities that are walkable, and most are already at least somewhat content with this aspect of their own communities: 70% say their local sidewalks and crosswalks are satisfactory. One in five walk to a destination most days, and almost one-half do so at least once a week.

Job Market Dissatisfaction

- One area of some discontent with community life is the number and quality of job and career opportunities. More than two in five say this situation in their community is unsatisfactory. This is a problem most acutely felt by people of color and rural residents and, to a smaller degree, Millennials and Baby Boomers.

Migration

- Almost one-third of survey respondents said they moved to a different home in the last five years. The highest percentages of those who moved were young people, residents of large cities, and lower-income households. Most of those who moved did so because they sought larger homes. Two in five households anticipate moving within the next five years. Among Baby Boomers (ages 48-to-66), Caucasians, and Midwesterners anticipating a move, the majority say they would prefer moving to a rural location. Most Generation Yers, people of color, Westerners, and singles expressed an interest in urban living.

5.5 Generational Preferences

As Americans age and their incomes rise and then fall, their housing and community preferences vary.

Millennials (ages 18-to-34), half of whom are people of color, show the strongest preference for mixed-use communities. Most currently have an urban, apartment-living lifestyle. At the same time, Millennials are among the least satisfied with where they live and the most likely to be anticipating moving. They want walkable communities and use public transit more than others, although they are still very car dependent.

Many Generation Xers are in the child-rearing life stage and prefer single-family home ownership. While many members of Generation X are anticipating moving, they are not likely to be looking for mixed-use communities, nor to push for mass transit. This group has the largest percentages of high-income members, and if they move they will be seeking to buy single-family homes.

Baby Boomers, the middle ground on housing and transportation preferences and behaviors, live in a wide range of cities and towns. They are not as likely to move, but if they do Boomers will seek out smaller homes and shorter commutes. This cohort, as it eases into retirement, would like to be close to parks and apart from neighbors.

Seniors are the most likely to stay in their current homes. These older adults, who are mainly out of the workforce, are especially likely to want to be in walkable neighborhoods and close to health services, family and friends, and shopping and entertainment.

5.6 Important Community Attributes

When asked what attributes they considered important in a community, survey responses were as follows (percentage of respondents; source: Urban Land Institute):

- Neighborhood safety: 92%
- Quality of public schools: 79%
- Space between neighbors: 72%
- Walk or short drive to work or school: 71%
- Walk or short drive to doctors and hospitals: 71%
- Walkability: sidewalks/crosswalks: 70%
- Walk or short drive to shopping and entertainment: 66%
- Walk or short drive to parks or recreational areas: 64%
- Walk or short drive to family or friends: 63%
- Convenient public transportation: 52%

5.7 Market Resources

Better Cities & Towns, P.O. Box 6515, Ithaca, NY 14851. (607) 275-3087. (www.bettercities.net)

General Social Survey, National Opinion Research Center at the University of Chicago, 1155 E. 60th Street, Chicago, IL 60637. (773) 256-6288. (http://www3.norc.org/GSS+Website/)

Pew Research Social & Demographic Trends, 1615 L Street NW, Suite 700, Washington, DC 20036. (202) 419-4300. (www.pewsocialtrends.org)

The Demand Institute, 845 Third Avenue, New York, NY 10022. (212) 339-0220. (www.demandinstitute.org)

Urban Land Institute, 1025 Thomas Jefferson Street NW, Suite 500 West, Washington, DC 20007. (202) 624-7000. (www.uli.org)

6

URBAN & RURAL POPULATIONS

6.1 Overview

The U.S. Census Bureau (www.census.gov) identifies two types of urban areas, as follows:

- Urbanized Areas (UAs) of 50,000 or more people;
- Urban Clusters (UCs) of at least 2,500 and less than 50,000 people.

"Rural" encompasses all population, housing, and territory not included within an urban area.

6.2 Population Counts

Census 2010 counted the U.S. population as follows:

• Urbanized Areas:	219,922,123
• Urban Clusters:	29,331,148
• Rural:	59,492,267
• Total:	308,745,538

There were 486 UAs and 3,087 UCs.

The total population in 2010 and, for comparison, in 2000, was distributed as follows:

	2010	2000
• Urbanized Areas:	71.2%	68.3%
• Urban Clusters:	9.5%	10.7%
• Rural:	19.3%	21.0%

6.3 Suburbs And Exburbs

Suburban areas are outlying single-family housing areas that are surround larger cities and metropolitan areas. Typically, they don't have a system of politics; however, some do have medical services and smaller shopping areas.

The areas on the periphery of metropolitan areas, dubbed "exburbs," have been the fastest growing in recent years. While growth subsided in exburbs in the wake of the Great Recession, recent studies show that population migration to these areas has resumed.

"During the housing bubble, Americans moved in droves to the exurbs, to newly paved subdivisions on what was once rural land. Far-out suburbs had some of the fastest population growth in the country in the early 2000s, fueled by cheap housing and easy mortgages. And these places helped redefine how we think about metropolitan areas like Washington, pushing their edges farther and farther from the traditional downtown. In the wake of the housing crash, these same places took the biggest hit. Population growth in the exurbs stalled. They produced a new American phenomenon: the ghost subdivision of developments abandoned during the housing collapse."

The Washington Post, 3/26/15

A 2015 study by Brookings Institution (www.brookings.edu) found that for the first time since 2010 exurban counties were growing faster than inner urban core counties nationally. These locations, like Waller County in suburban Houston, Barrow County in suburban Atlanta, and Johnston County in suburban Raleigh, lie on the peripheries of large urban areas.

Recent suburbs accounted for roughly 43% of all U.S. residences in 2010. Between July 2013 and July 2014, core urban communities lost a net 363,000 people overall, according to Brookings, as migration increased to suburban and exurban counties. The biggest growth was in exurban areas. The reason is that more than 80% of employment growth from 2007 to 2013 was in the newer suburbs and exurbs. Between 2012 and 2015, as the economy improved, occupied suburban office space rose from 75% of the market to 76.7%, according to the real estate consultancy Costar (www.costar.com).

Potentially, the greatest source of exurban and peripheral revival lies with the maturation of the Millennial generation. According to demographer Wendell Cox at Demographia (www.demographia.com), roughly 90% of communities' population growth that can be attributed to Millennials since 2000 has taken place outside of the urban core.

According to a 2015 report by the Census Bureau, 529,000 Americans ages 25-to-29 moved from cities out to the suburbs in 2014, while 426,000 moved in the other direction. Among Millennials ages 24 and younger, 721,000 moved out of the city, compared with 554,000 who moved in.

"Exurbia is turning into something very different from the homogeneous and boring places portrayed in media accounts. For one thing exurbs are becoming increasingly ethnically diverse."

Forbes, 11/3/15

In the decade that ended in 2010 the percentage of suburbanites living in "traditional" largely white suburbs fell from 51% to 39%. According to a study by the University of Minnesota School of Law, 44% of residents in the 50 largest U.S. metropolitan areas now live in racially and ethnically diverse suburbs, defined as between 20% and 60% non-white.

7

WHERE PEOPLE WANT TO LIVE

7.1 Most Desirable States

A December 2015 Harris Poll (www.theharrispoll.com) asked adults the state they would most like to live in, not including the state where they currently live. Responses ranked as follows:

- Florida
- California
- Hawaii
- Colorado
- New York
- Texas
- North Carolina
- Arizona
- Oregon
- Tennessee
- Alaska
- South Carolina
- Georgia
- Washington
- Pennsylvania

By gender and generation, the most desirable states to live in are as follows:

Female

1. Florida
2. Hawaii
3. California
4. Oregon
5. Colorado

Male

1. (tie) California
1. (tie) Florida
3. Hawaii
4. (tie) Colorado
4. (tie) New York

Millennials (Ages 18-to-35)

1. California
2. Florida
3. New York
4. Hawaii
5. Colorado

Generation X (Ages 35-to-50)

1. California
2. Florida
3. Hawaii
4. Tennessee
5. North Carolina

Baby Boomers (Ages 51-to-59)

1. Florida
2. Hawaii
3. (tie) Arizona
3. (tie) California
5. Oregon

Seniors (Ages 70 and Older)

1. Hawaii
2. Florida
3. North Carolina
4. California
5. Arizona

When asked the state they would least like to live in, responses ranked as follows:

1. California
2. New York
3. Alaska
4. Mississippi
5. Texas
6. Alabama
7. Florida
8. Illinois
9. Michigan
10. District of Columbia
11. North Dakota
12. Arizona
13. Oklahoma
14. Kansas

15. (tie) Arkansas
15. (tie) Missouri

7.2 Most Desirable Cities

The Harris Poll asked adults the city they would most like to live in or near, not including the city where they currently live. Responses ranked as follows:

1. New York, NY
2. San Diego, CA
3. Denver, CO
4. Los Angeles, CA
5. Miami, FL
6. San Francisco, CA
7. Honolulu, HI
8. Atlanta, GA
9. Seattle, WA
10. Orlando, FL
11. Las Vegas, NV
12. Phoenix, AZ
13. Maui, HI
14. Portland, OR
15. Austin, TX

By gender and generation, the most desirable states to live in are as follows:

Female

1. New York, NY
2. San Diego, CA
3. Denver, CO
4. Honolulu, HI
5. Atlanta, GA

Male

1. New York, NY
2. San Diego, CA
3. (tie) Los Angeles, CA
3. (tie) Miami, FL
5. San Francisco, CA

Millennials (Ages 18-to-35)

1. New York, NY
2. Los Angeles, CA
3. Denver, CO

4. Miami, FL
5. San Francisco, CA

Generation X (Ages 35-to-50)

1. New York, NY
2. Seattle, WA
3. Denver, CO
4. (tie) Honolulu, HI
4. (tie) San Diego, CA

Baby Boomers (Ages 51-to-59)

1. San Diego, CA
2. New York, NY
3. (tie) Austin, TX
3. (tie) Denver, CO
5. Honolulu, HI

Seniors (Ages 70 and Older)

1. San Diego, CA
2. Honolulu, HI
3. Phoenix, AZ
4. New York, NY
5. (tie) Atlanta, GA
5. (tie) Miami, FL

When asked the city they would least like to live in, responses ranked as follows:

1. New York, NY
2. Detroit, MI
3. Los Angeles, CA
4. Chicago, IL
5. Dallas, TX
6. Miami, FL
7. San Francisco, CA
8. Houston, TX
9. Washington, DC
10. Las Vegas, NV
11. Anchorage, AK
12. Phoenix, AZ
13. St. Louis, MO
14. Atlanta, GA
15. Seattle, WA

7.3 Reasons For Wanting To Move

The Harris Poll asked adults the reasons they would consider moving to another state. Responses were as follows (multiple responses allowed):

- Better climate or better weather: 52%
- Job opportunity: 41%
- Proximity to family: 36%
- Health reasons: 25%
- Proximity to friends: 18%
- Proximity to significant other: 16%
- Educational opportunity: 14%
- An area where lifestyle is more accepted: 13%
- Where political views are more accepted: 11%
- To live in an area where recreational marijuana is legal: 11%
- Someplace where religious views are more accepted: 7%

Fifteen percent (15%) would not consider moving to another state for any reason.

8

POPULATION MIGRATION

8.1 Overview

According to the U.S. Census Bureau (www.census.gov), 36.7 million Americans moved in 2015.

About 5 million people, or 1.5% of the population, move to another state each year. These moves, which are typically job- or retirement-related, shift where billions of dollars are spent annually. Keeping abreast of population shifts can help businesses with expansion strategies.

8.2 Migration Trends

The rate of population migration, already in decline over several years, saw an even greater decline during the recession. According to the Census Bureau, the nation's mobility rates during the Great Recession were among the lowest since World War II.

The Census Bureau began tracking migration when the annual mover rate was 20.2%. Over time, the mover rate gradually declined. Rates hovered around 16% in the late 1990s and fell to around 14% by the early 2000s.

According to *Geographical Mobility*, a report by the Census Bureau, the mobility rate (i.e., percentage of people who moved) has been as follows:

- 2006-2007: 13.2%
- 2007-2008: 11.9%
- 2008-2009: 12.5%
- 2009-2010: 12.5%
- 2010-2011: 11.6%
- 2011-2012: 12.0%
- 2012-2013: 11.7%
- 2013-2014: 11.5%
- 2014-2015: 11.6%

According to the Census Bureau, 21 states and the District of Columbia had positive net domestic migration rates between 2014 and 2015. The following states had the highest rates of net domestic migration:

1. North Dakota
2. District of Columbia
3. Colorado

4. South Carolina
5. South Dakota
6. Montana
7. Florida
8. Nevada
9. Wyoming
10. Texas

New Mexico, New Jersey, Illinois, New York, and Alaska had the largest negative net domestic migration rates.

Mobility rates by age are as follows:

- Under 18: 13.1%
- 19-to-36: 20.4%
- 37-to-48: 10.6%
- 49-to-67: 5.9%
- 68 and older: 3.5%

"Mobility for young adults has fallen to the lowest level in more than 50 years as cash-strapped 20-somethings shun home-buying and refrain from major moves in a weak job market. Burdened with college debt or toiling in low-wage jobs, they are delaying careers, marriage and having children. They are staying put and doubling up with roommates or living with Mom and Dad, unable to make long-term plans or commit to buying a home, let alone pay a mortgage. Many understood after the 2007-2009 recession that times would be tough"

Houston Chronicle

By metropolitan area, Portland, Oregon; Austin, Texas; and Houston, Texas, experienced the highest gains in young adults, reflecting stronger local economies. Among college graduates 25 and older, Denver and Washington, DC, topped the list of destinations.

8.3 Reasons For Moving

Not only are Americans moving less than they once did, the reasons for moving are changing.

According to *Reason For Moving*, a report by the Census Bureau, people who move do so for the following reasons:

- Housing: 48%
- Family: 30%
- Employment: 19%
- Other: 2%

A study conducted at the Luskin School of Public Affairs at the University of California Los Angeles (http://luskin.ucla.edu/public-policy) compared the reason that people moved within their communities prior to and after the Great Recession. Primary reasons for moving before and during the Great Recession (2007-2009) were as follows:

	Pre-Recession	During Recession
• Demographic/life cycle:	28.2%	31.1%
• Own home/better neighborhood:	41.3%	30.4%
• Find cheaper housing:	20.8%	23.1%
• Look for work:	4.9%	7.8%
• Take a new job:	1.9%	2.3%
• Other:	2.8%	5.4%

"Typically, over the last couple of decades, when Americans moved, they moved to improve their lives. For the first time, Americans are moving for downward economic mobility. Either they lost their house or can't afford where they're renting currently or needed to save money."

Prof. Michael A. Stoll, Ph.D.
Chair, Public Policy
Luskin School of Public Affairs
UCLA

8.4 Moving In Retirement

The rate of migration typically increases as adults approach retirement.

According to The Demand Institute (www.demandinstitute.org), 40% of Americans ages 50-to-64 typically plan to move within five years of their retirement.

Consistent with the trend among the overall population, retirees are relocating less than in the past. According to the Census Bureau, among the nation's 74 million Baby Boomers, about 4 million move each year. Among those who move, 61% remain in the same county; only 15% move to another state. Only about 3.5% of Seniors (ages 70 and older) relocate each year.

> **"Many empty-nesters nowadays, unlike in the past, have opted not to pull up stakes and move to sunnier climes like Florida or Arizona. They want to continue to live near family and longtime friends. Others stay put because of the shaky economy or the difficulty of selling a home or getting a mortgage. Staying put dovetails with another big trend: the growing number of retirees continuing to do some paid part-time work."**
>
> *The New York Times*

8.5 Metropolitan Relocation

Surveys by International Demographics (www.themediaaudit.com) found that the migration of adults from metropolitan areas was half the rate prior to the Great Recession. The percentage of adults in metropolitan areas who moved outside that region dropped from 3.5% and 4.4% in 2007 and 2005, respectively, to 2.2% post-recession.

The Census Bureau reported the following metros attracted residents from other areas (population change from domestic migration):

- Austin, TX: 5.4%
- Raleigh, NC: 3.7%
- San Antonio, TX: 3.2%
- Denver, CO: 2.9%
- Charlotte, NC: 2.6%
- Nashville, TN: 2.6%
- Oklahoma City, OK: 2.6%
- Orlando, FL: 2.3%

- Houston, TX: 2.1%
- Dallas-Fort Worth, TX: 2.1%

The following metros lost residents to other areas:

- New York, NY: -1.9%
- Chicago, IL: -1.8%
- Detroit, MI: -1.6%
- Hartford, CT: -1.6%
- Cleveland, OH: -1.5%
- Los Angeles, CA: -1.1%
- Rochester, NY: -1.1%
- Providence, RI: -1.1%
- Virginia Beach, VA: -1.1%
- Memphis, TN: -1.1%

According to International Demographics, 61% of adults have lived within the same metro area for 20 years or more. The following are the metropolitan areas with the highest percentage of residents who have lived in the area for 20 or more years:

- Buffalo, NY: 84%
- Pittsburgh, PA: 81%
- Cleveland, OH: 79%
- Syracuse, NY: 77%
- Rochester, NY: 76%

"At the peak of the housing bubble in 2006, almost half a million people fled the country's 50 largest metro areas in search of less expensive places to live, many settling in distant suburbs. Then the recession put the brakes on all kinds of migration. Census data reveal that as Americans start moving around again, cities are seeing a different kind of urban flight. This time, hundreds of thousands of Americans who enjoy city living are abandoning major population centers not for suburbs but for more affordable, second-tier metropolitan areas."

Bloomberg Businessweek

8.6 Relocation Reports

Allied Van Lines (www.alliedvanlines.com), Atlas Van Lines (www.atlasvanlines.com), and United Van Lines (www.unitedvanlines.com), the three largest U.S. moving companies, report annually on migration activity in the United States.

48th Annual Magnet States Report, published in January 2016 by Allied Van Lines, reported the top inbound states as follows:

- Texas
- Florida
- Arizona
- Oregon
- South Carolina

Virginia, Illinois, Pennsylvania, New York, and New Jersey were the top outbound states.

The *2015 Migration Patterns* (24th edition), published in January 2016 by Atlas Van Lines, reported the states with the highest percentage of inbound moves as follows:

- Oregon
- Idaho
- North Carolina
- Alaska
- North Dakota

The following states had the highest percentage of outbound moves:

- Hawaii
- New York
- Illinois
- South Dakota
- Wyoming

The *39th Annual Migration Study*, published in January 2016 by United Van Lines, reported the top inbound states in 2015 were as follows:

- Oregon
- South Carolina
- Vermont
- Idaho
- North Carolina

The following were the top outbound states in 2015:

- New Jersey
- New York
- Illinois
- Connecticut
- Ohio

8.7 Market Resources

International Demographics, 10333 Richmond Avenue, Suite 200, Houston, TX 77042. (713) 626-0333. (www.themediaaudit.com)

Migration/Geographic Mobility, U.S. Census Bureau. (www.census.gov/hhes/migration/)

The Demand Institute, 845 Third Avenue, New York, NY 10022. (212) 339-0220. (www.demandinstitute.org)

9

PERSONAL LIFE

9.1 Satisfaction With Personal Life

Gallup Polls (www.gallup.com) periodically ask adults how satisfied they are with the way things are going in their personal life. Responses have been as follows:

	Very Satisfied	Somewhat Satisfied	Somewhat Dissatisfied	Very Dissatisfied
• 2002:	56%	29%	9%	5%
• 2005:	57%	28%	8%	5%
• 2008:	47%	33%	10%	8%
• 2011:	46%	32%	12%	8%
• 2013:	50%	29%	13%	7%
• 2016:	53%	32%	8%	6%

9.2 Personal Financial Situation

When asked by Gallup how they would rate their financial situation, responses were as follows:

	Excellent	Good	Fair	Poor
• 2002:	9%	43%	35%	13%
• 2003:	5%	45%	38%	12%
• 2004:	9%	42%	36%	13%
• 2005:	8%	44%	36%	12%
• 2006:	10%	41%	37%	12%
• 2007:	10%	45%	31%	14%
• 2008:	7%	38%	37%	17%
• 2009:	6%	36%	39%	19%
• 2010:	8%	33%	40%	19%
• 2011:	5%	37%	40%	18%
• 2012:	7%	34%	41%	18%
• 2013:	7%	38%	40%	14%
• 2014:	9%	39%	36%	16%
• 2015:	7%	39%	35%	17%
• 2016:	9%	41%	32%	17%

When asked to compare their current financial situation with that of one year prior, responses were as follows:

	Getting Better	Getting Worse	Same
• 2002:	52%	29%	19%
• 2003:	43%	35%	20%
• 2004:	53%	29%	18%
• 2005:	49%	35%	15%
• 2006:	47%	37%	15%
• 2007:	51%	32%	16%
• 2008:	32%	49%	17%
• 2009:	34%	43%	22%
• 2010:	39%	40%	19%
• 2011:	41%	41%	16%
• 2012:	42%	41%	16%
• 2013:	47%	36%	15%
• 2014:	43%	40%	16%
• 2015:	52%	33%	15%
• 2016:	47%	38%	14%

9.3 Economic Well-Being

Report on the Economic Well-Being of U.S. Households in 2015, published in May 2016 by the Federal Reserve (www.federalreserve.gov), reported financial well-being of U.S. households as follows:

- Sixty-nine percent (69%) of adults report that they are either "living comfortably" or "doing okay," compared to 65% in 2014 and 62% in 2013. However, 31%, or approximately 76 million adults, are either "struggling to get by" or are "just getting by."
- Individuals are 9 percentage points more likely to say that their financial well-being improved during the prior year than to say that their financial well-being declined.
- Twenty-two percent (22%) of employed adults indicate that they are either working multiple jobs, doing informal work for pay in addition to their main job, or both.
- Twenty-three percent (23%) of respondents expect their income to be higher in the year after the survey, down from 29% who expected income growth in the year after the 2014 survey.
- Sixty-eight percent (68%) of non-retired respondents saved at least a portion of their income in the prior year.
- Thirty-two percent (32%) of adults report that their income varies to some degree from month to month, and 43% report that their monthly expenses vary to some degree. Forty-two percent (42%) of those with volatile incomes or expenses say that they have struggled to pay their bills at times because of this volatility.
- Forty-six percent (46%) of adults say they either could not cover an emergency expense costing $400, or would cover it by selling something or borrowing money.
- Twenty-two percent (22%) of respondents experienced a major unexpected medical expense that they had to pay out of pocket in the prior year, and 46% of those who say they had a major medical expense report that they currently owe debt from that expense.

9.4 Happiness

Since 2008, The Harris Poll (www.theharrispoll.com) has conducted a happiness poll. The poll ascertains a Happiness Index based on survey responses relating to various aspects of their lives. The poll was annual prior to 2011 and biennial thereafter.

The median Happiness Index among all adults has been as follows:

- 2008: 35
- 2009: 35
- 2010: 33
- 2011: 33
- 2013: 33
- 2015: 34

By demographic, the Happiness Index in 2015 was as follows:

Gender

- Female: 36
- Male: 33

Age

- 18-to-24: 32
- 25-to-29: 31
- 30-to-39: 31
- 40-to-49: 30
- 50-to-50: 36
- 65 and older: 42

Race/Ethnicity

- African American: 36
- Caucasian: 34
- Hispanic: 28

Income

- Less than $35,000: 30
- $35,000 to $49,999: 35
- $50,000 to $74,999: 34
- $75,000 to $99,999: 35
- $100,000 or more: 38

Education:

- High school or less: 34
- Some college: 34
- College graduate: 36
- Post graduate: 37

According to a study by economist Angus Deaton, Ph.D., and Nobel Laureate Daniel Kahneman, Ph.D., at the Woodrow Wilson School of Public Affairs, Princeton University (http://wws.princeton.edu), income increases happiness only for those with annual incomes below $75,000. The lower a person's annual income falls below that benchmark, the unhappier he or she feels. But no matter how much above $75,000 people earn, they don't report any greater degree of happiness.

Researchers at Brookings Institution (www.brookings.org) have found a correlation between age and happiness. Happiness in most adults tends to diminish until age 50 or 55, then increases with age.

> **"The true causes of midlife dissatisfaction are not what you probably think. A growing body of research shows that they lie deep within our biology and that we reliably grow happier, regardless of circumstances, after our 40s have passed. The peak of emotional life may not occur until well into the seventh decade."**
>
> Jonathan Rauch, Senior Fellow
> Brookings Institution

9.5 Stress

The American Psychological Association (www.apa.org) has conducted the *Stress In America* survey since 2007. Adults participating in the survey have reported their stress on a scale of 1-to-10 (1 is little or no stress; 10 is a great deal of stress) as follows:

- 2007: 6.2
- 2008: 5.9
- 2009: 5.4
- 2010: 5.4
- 2011: 5.2
- 2012: 4.9
- 2013: 5.1
- 2014: 4.9
- 2015: 5.1

Stress In America 2015, published in March 2016, reported the stress index by demographic as follows:

Gender

- Female: 5.3
- Male: 4.9

Generation

- Millennials: 6.0
- Generation Xers: 5.6
- Baby Boomers: 4.3
- Seniors: 3.5

Race/Ethnicity

- African-American: 5.2
- Asian-American: 5.1
- Caucasian: 5.5
- Hispanic: 6.0

Community

- Rural: 4.7
- Suburban: 5.0
- Urban: 5.6

9.6 Personal Health

A November 2015 poll conducted by Gallup asked adults how they would describe their physical health. Responses were as follows:

- Excellent: 29%
- Good: 50%
- Fair: 16%
- Poor: 5%

When asked how they would describe their mental health or emotional well-being, responses were as follows:

- Excellent: 43%
- Good: 45%
- Fair: 8%
- Poor: 4%

The *National Adult Tobacco Survey*, by the Centers for Disease Control and Prevention (CDC, www.cdc.gov), reports that 21.3% of adults use tobacco.

9.7 Weight Control and Dieting

According to the CDC, 27% of adults are obese and an additional 36% are overweight. Being overweight increases the risk of diabetes, heart disease, cancer, arthritis, and other health problems.

Rand Corp. (www.rand.org) assessed that 6.6% of U.S. adults are severely obese, or more than 100 pounds above a healthy weight for their body type. Healthcare costs for those severely obese are more than double those of the general adult population.

A November 2015 poll conducted by Gallup asked adults how they would describe their personal weight situation. Responses were as follows:

- About right: 56%
- Overweight: 37%
- Underweight: 5%

According to Marketdata Enterprises (www.marketdataenterprises.com), consumers spend $62 billion each year on weight loss and weight control. Spending includes health club memberships, diet programs, diet drinks, and prepared foods. Annual spending for diet programs such as Jenny Craig, Nutrisystem, and Weight Watchers is $3.6 billion.

9.8 Exercise And Fitness

According to the CDC, 49% of adults engage in 30 minutes or more of moderate physical activity five or more days per week or vigorous physical activity for 20 minutes or more three or more days per week.

Americans who participate in sports, recreation, or exercise spend an average of 1.7 hours daily doing so – one-third of their leisure time is spent on these activities, according to the Bureau of Labor Statistics (www.bls.gov). But the vast majority of people are not so engaged in physical activities.

According to *The American Time Use Survey*, published by the Bureau of Labor Statistics (www.bls.gov), Americans, on average, spend 18 minutes per day participating in sports, exercise, or recreation. On average, teens are active 40 minutes a day; people ages 35 and above spend 15 minutes or less being active.

Survey of The American Consumer, by GfK MRI (www.gfkmri.com), reported in 2015 that 41% of adults exercise regularly. This percentage was the same as in the 2002 GfK MRI survey, however the number of adults who exercise at health and fitness clubs increased to 32% from 23% during that timeframe.

There are approximately 34,460 health and fitness clubs in the U.S., according to the International Health, Racquet & Sportsclub Association (www.ihrsa.org). Combined, they have approximately 54.1 million members. First Research (www.firstresearch.com) estimates 2016 spending for memberships and services at $25 billion.

9.9 Eating

According to the *Consumer Expenditure Survey*, by the Bureau of Labor Statistics, American households spend an average of $6,599 annually on food. The restaurant share of the food dollar is approximately 40.6%.

> **"Americans spend more at restaurants than they think they do. We know this because the *Consumer Expenditure Survey* asks respondents how much they usually spend at restaurants per week, and it also asks them to keep a daily diary of their expenditures. The results are not the same. The more precise diary method consistently shows restaurant spending to be 16% to 22% greater than the guesstimate. The opposite happens with grocery shopping. When asked how much they usually spend on groceries per week, households over-report their spending by about 21% in comparison with diary data on grocery purchases."**
>
> *Demo Memo*

Eating Patterns In America, by The NPD Group (www.npd.com), reported that households are eating at home more, but they are purchasing more prepared meals and are cooking less. Households eat eight of 10 meals at home.

> **"A decline in restaurant usage and an increase in meals from home is one of the single biggest changes in eating patterns in Americans in the last five years."**
>
> Harry Balzer, V.P.
> The NPD Group

According to The NPD Group, Americans purchased 190 restaurant or foodservice meals in 2015, a decline from 195 in 2013 and 206 in 2009.

According to the USDA Economic Research Service (http://ers.usda.gov/), 80.7% of adults get at least one prepared meal each week from a restaurant, grocery store deli, or vendor. The number of prepared meals are as follows:

- None: 19.3%
- 1 or 2: 24.1%
- 3 or 4: 21.6%
- 5 to 7: 15.4%
- 8 or more: 9.5%

Age is one of the most important determinants in how often people eat out. The percentages by age of those who do not eat out at all (or rarely do so) and those who eat out eight or more times per week are as follows:

	None/Rarely	**Eight or More**
• 20-to-39:	12.1%	16.0%
• 40-to-54:	20.0%	10.0%
• 55-to-64:	22.6%	9.1%
• 65 and older:	28.2%	4.4%
• All adults:	19.3%	9.5%

According to The Harris Poll, 86% of families with children have a family dinner at home at least once a week; 87% of families without children do so. The number of evenings families eat dinner at home per week is as follows:

- Once: 7%
- 2 or 3: 21%
- 4 to 6: 26%
- Every night: 33%

The percentages of families by age who have dinner together at least four times a week are as follows:

- 18-to-36: 52%
- 37-to-48: 50%
- 49-to-67: 62%
- 68 and older: 81%

When asked in the *National Health and Nutrition Examination Survey*, by the U.S. Department of Agriculture (www.usda.gov), how healthy is their overall diet, responses were as follows:

- Excellent: 9%
- Very good: 22%
- Good: 43%
- Fair: 22%
- Poor: 4%

A survey by The NPD Group found that while over 50% of adults say they eat healthful meals always or most of the time at home, only 25% say they eat healthy foods when they go out to eat.

In a recent Gallup Poll, 45% of adults said they actively try to include organic food in their diet. The figure was highest in the West (54%) and in metropolitan areas (50%). By age, the percentages who said they try to eat organic are as follows:

- 18-to-29: 53%
- 30-to-49: 48%
- 50-to-64: 45%
- 65 and older: 33%

Gallup polls have found the number of people who identify themselves as vegetarian has remained steady at about 5% since 1999.

9.10 Alcohol Consumption

A July 2016 Gallup Poll found that 64% of adults drink alcoholic beverages. Among those who drink alcoholic beverages, weekly consumption is as follows:

- Less than one drink: 37%
- 1-to-7 drinks: 48%
- 8 or more drinks: 13%

Among those who consume alcoholic beverages, the following are the beverages most frequently consumed:

- Beer: 42%
- Wine: 34%
- Spirits: 21%
- All same: 3%

The Harris Poll reports consumption of alcoholic beverages by adults as follows:

	Daily	At least once per Week	At least once a month	Less than once a month	Never
Gender					
• Female:	3%	21%	21%	33%	24%
• Male:	7%	38%	18%	24%	20%
Age					
• 21-to-34:	3%	33%	24%	21%	23%
• 35-to-46:	3%	30%	20%	32%	18%
• 47-to-65:	5%	29%	17%	31%	22%
• 66 and older:	11%	26%	18%	29%	27%
All	5%	29%	20%	29%	22%

9.11 Travel

Americans took 1.65 person-trips for leisure in 2015, according to the U.S. Travel Association (USTA, www.ustravel.org), spending $549.0 billion, or 67% of total U.S. travel spending.

The average household spends about $1,500 on travel each year, according to the *Consumer Expenditure Survey*.

Transportation for leisure travel is as follows (source: USTA):

- Automobile: 70%
- Van or small truck: 18%
- Airplane: 6%

The reported purposes of leisure trips are as follows (source: USTA):

- Personal leisure: 39%
- Visit friends or relatives: 36%
- Getaway weekend: 15%
- General vacation: 10%

According to the USTA, party composition for leisure travel is as follows (source: USTA):

- Solo travelers: 32%
- Adults only: 39%
- Adults with kids: 29%

Leisure travel is nearly evenly split between day trips and overnight trips, at 51% and 49%, respectively. Approximately 40% of leisure trips include a stay at a hotel, motel, or resort.

Twenty-seven percent (27%) of adults take a 'last-minute' trip at least once a year.

9.12 Charitable Giving

Based on data from over 4,000 nonprofit organizations, Blackbaud Inc. (www.blackbaud.com) reported charitable donations were $18.2 billion in 2015, of which $2.2 billion was given online.

According to The Harris Poll, 25% of adults feel that people have a personal responsibility to make the world a better place by being actively involved with various issues and causes. An additional 17% feel people should generally take part in things such as voluntary service, donating to charities, or getting involved in community activities because it is the right thing to do, and 48% feel people can get involved with different issues and causes if they want to, but shouldn't necessarily feel obligated to do so.

Ninety-one percent (91%) of adults have made contributions within the past three years. By age, those that have done so are as follows:

- 18-to-36: 86%
- 37-to-48: 92%
- 49-to-67: 93%
- 68 and older: 98%

Types of contributions were as follows:

- Used clothing: 73%
- Money: 66%
- Food: 53%
- Other used items: 45%
- Time/labor: 41%
- Blood: 18%

When asked what cause should be the biggest priority for charities to focus their resources, responses in the Harris Poll were as follows:

- Youth/families: 16%
- Education: 15%
- Human rights: 12%
- Medical research: 11%
- Disaster relief: 10%
- Environmental: 7%
- Global health: 7%
- Animals: 4%
- Other: 17%

9.13 Volunteering

Americans give their time to beautify neighborhoods, restore homes after disasters, mentor students, assist cultural organizations, and much more.

According to the Bureau of Labor Statistics, 61 million Americans, or 26% of those over the age of 16, volunteer at least once each year through or for an organization, volunteering a median of 52 hours. Among women, 29% engage in volunteer activities; 23% of men do so. The percentages by age who do volunteer work are as follows:

- 16-to-24: 21%
- 25-to-34: 23%
- 35-to-44: 31%
- 45-to-54: 30%
- 55-to-64: 28%
- 65 and older: 24%

The following are the most common activities, ranked by the percentage of adults engaged in various types of volunteer work (source: Bureau of Labor Statistics):

- Fundraising: 11%
- Tutoring/teaching: 10%
- Collecting/preparing/distributing/serving food: 9%
- General labor/supplying transportation: 9%
- Providing professional/management assistance: 8%
- Coaching/refereeing sports teams: 6%

According to the Corporation for National and Community Service (CNCS, www.nationalservice.gov), volunteers contribute about 8.2 billion hours a year.

While the perception may be that volunteers are primarily adults who are active in their communities or retirees with ample available time, many young adults also give their time. According to the CNCS, approximately 3.3 million college students, or 30% of all students, volunteer each year. Tutoring and mentoring are the most common activities.

9.14 Market Resources

Corporation for National and Community Service, 1201 New York Avenue NW, Washington, DC 20525. (202) 606-5000. (www.nationalservice.gov)

Stress In American, American Psychological Association. (www.apa.org/news/press/releases/stress/)

The Gallup Organization, 901 F Street NW, Washington, DC 20004. (202) 715-3030. (www.gallup.com)

The Harris Poll, a Nielsen Company, 60 Corporate Woods, Rochester, NY 14623. (585) 272-8400. (www.theharrispoll.com)

The NPD Group, 900 West Shore Road, Port Washington, NY 11050. (516) 625-0700. (www.npd.com)

10

PERSONAL WELL-BEING

10.1 Overview

Gallup (www.gallup.com) and Healthways (www.healthways.com) have been tracking personal well-being since 2008.

In 2015, Gallup surveyed 2.3 million adults asking how people feel about and experience their daily lives. A Well-Being Index® was computed for each state and major metropolitan area.

The Well-Being Index provides an assessment of well-being across five elements, as follows:

- Purpose: Liking what you do each day and being motivated to achieve your goals
- Social: Having supportive relationships and love in your life
- Financial: Managing your economic life to reduce stress and increase security
- Community: Liking where you live, feeling safe and having pride in your community
- Physical: Having good health and enough energy to get things done daily

Gallup found that compared with residents of low well-being communities, residents of high well-being communities have the following attributes:

- Purpose Well-Being: 12% more likely to learn new and interesting things
- Social Well-Being: 6% more likely to get positive energy from family and friends
- Financial Well-Being: 16% less likely to worry about money
- Community Well-Being: 18% more likely to be proud of their community
- Physical Well-Being: 25% less likely to have depression over their lifetime

---

"In communities with higher well-being, we have found that people live longer, happier lives and businesses and local economies flourish."

Gallup

10.2 Well-Being by State

The 2015 Well-Being Index score for the United States was 61.7.

The Well-Being Index and ranking for the five constituent elements are as follows:

Rank		Index	Purpose Rank	Social Rank	Financial Rank	Community Rank	Physical Rank
1.	Hawaii:	64.8	4	16	3	2	1
2.	Alaska:	64.1	5	5	1	7	6
3.	Montana:	63.8	21	37	9	1	4
4.	Colorado:	63.6	15	21	17	6	2
5.	Wyoming:	63.5	3	15	8	4	10
6.	South Dakota:	63.5	7	43	6	3	7
7.	Minnesota:	63.3	14	19	4	8	9
8.	Utah:	63.1	18	3	31	5	11
9.	Arizona:	63.0	6	7	23	16	8
10.	California:	62.7	10	18	21	29	3
11.	Texas:	62.7	2	11	35	18	20
12.	Florida:	62.4	9	4	36	27	16
13.	Wisconsin:	62.4	31	31	7	20	19
14.	Iowa:	62.4	20	35	5	11	30
15.	North Dakota:	62.3	11	48	2	19	37
16.	New Mexico:	62.2	19	13	32	31	14
17.	Virginia:	62.2	23	9	15	28	18
18.	Connecticut:	62.2	34	2	18	43	5
19.	South Carolina:	62.2	8	1	39	24	32
20.	Nebraska:	62.1	16	42	12	13	36
21.	New Hampshire:	62.1	48	17	20	14	21
22.	Maine:	62.1	28	36	22	10	33
23.	North Carolina:	62.1	17	8	44	17	29
24.	Washington:	62.0	42	23	11	26	24
25.	Kansas:	62.0	24	20	30	22	28
26.	Rhode Island:	61.9	36	14	19	38	15
27.	Delaware:	61.9	1	33	13	35	31
28.	Alabama:	61.8	13	12	42	21	41
29.	Vermont:	61.8	49	26	16	12	25
30.	Massachusetts:	61.8	47	28	25	34	12
31.	Oregon:	61.7	33	25	29	25	35
32.	New Jersey:	61.6	40	6	28	49	13
33.	Pennsylvania:	61.6	37	24	10	37	27
34.	Maryland:	61.6	29	10	14	48	26
35.	Illinois:	61.5	30	30	26	45	23
36.	Idaho:	61.5	43	40	48	9	40
37.	Tennessee:	61.5	26	38	40	15	42
38.	Nevada:	61.5	41	29	43	39	22

39.	Michigan:	61.3	38	34	24	33	38
40.	New York:	61.2	46	39	37	47	17
41.	Georgia:	61.2	27	27	49	41	34
42.	Louisiana:	61.1	12	22	46	42	39
43.	Mississippi:	60.9	22	32	50	40	43
44.	Arkansas:	60.9	25	49	38	23	47
45.	Missouri:	60.8	35	46	34	36	44
46.	Indiana:	60.5	39	41	33	44	46
47.	Ohio:	60.5	45	45	27	46	45
48.	Oklahoma:	60.4	32	47	45	32	48
49.	Kentucky:	60.3	44	44	41	30	49
50.	West Virginia:	58.5	50	50	47	50	50

10.3 Well-Being by Metro

The ranking for the five constituent elements of well-being for metropolitan areas is as follows:

Rank		Purpose Rank	Social Rank	Financial Rank	Community Rank	Physical Rank
1.	North Port-Sarasota-Bradenton, FL:	11	4	2	12	2
2.	Urban Honolulu, HI:	14	70	1	6	26
3.	Raleigh, NC:	9	6	13	3	24
4.	Oxnard-Thousand Oaks-Ventura, CA:	6	3	11	8	29
5.	El Paso, TX:	1	57	63	23	1
6.	Austin-Round Rock, TX:	12	37	37	4	21
7.	Provo-Orem, UT:	18	9	28	1	47
8.	San Jose-Sunnyvale, CA:	51	44	3	32	4
9.	Washington-Arlington, DC-VA:	27	12	5	35	9
10.	Winston-Salem, NC:	34	8	58	14	14
11.	Los Angeles-Anaheim, CA:	16	46	40	44	3
12.	San Francisco-Oakland, CA:	48	31	10	33	8
13.	Houston-The Woodlands, TX:	4	36	22	30	33
14.	Chattanooga, TN:	8	1	64	2	59
15.	Spokane-Spokane Valley, WA:	32	38	4	51	23
16.	San Diego-Carlsbad, CA:	41	53	25	18	15
17.	Minneapolis-St. Paul, MN:	53	58	7	16	22
18.	Omaha-Council Bluffs, NE:	38	47	6	10	72
19.	Cape Coral-Fort Myers, FL:	19	14	33	28	17
20.	San Antonio-New Braunfels, TX:	13	60	56	11	54
21.	Richmond, VA:	31	7	38	27	40
22.	Dallas-Fort Worth-Arlington, TX:	10	49	34	24	50
23.	Charleston-North Charleston, SC:	35	5	75	19	32
24.	Springfield, IL:	69	16	15	68	10
25.	Denver-Aurora-Lakewood, CO:	39	72	26	22	25

26.	Grand Rapids-Wyoming, MI:	52	35	8	17	61
27.	Boston-Cambridge-Newton, MA:	66	34	20	26	16
28.	Colorado Springs, CO:	30	54	87	25	27
29.	Tucson, AZ:	24	10	41	54	18
30.	Stockton-Lodi, CA:	17	20	21	93	13
31.	Albuquerque, NM:	22	69	71	59	7
32.	Charlotte-Concord-Gastonia, NC:	20	43	65	36	35
33.	Boise City, ID:	62	65	68	9	41
34.	Lancaster, PA:	71	93	9	13	43
35.	Miami-West Palm Beach, FL:	26	23	92	48	11
36.	Bridgeport-Stamford-Norwalk, CT:	63	88	43	58	5
37.	Hartford, CT:	61	30	18	62	20
38.	Phoenix-Mesa-Scottsdale, AZ:	33	40	48	50	37
39.	Milwaukee-Waukesha-W Allis, WI:	36	29	30	60	30
40.	Sacramento-Arden-Arcade, CA:	56	27	45	56	34
41.	Orlando-Kissimmee-Sanford, FL:	25	39	84	49	38
42.	Salt Lake City, UT:	60	64	74	29	36
43.	Wichita, KS:	29	41	16	46	74
44.	Nashville-Murfreesboro, TN:	49	84	61	31	53
45.	Bakersfield, CA:	3	2	99	96	31
46.	Fresno, CA:	5	89	85	90	12
47.	Palm Bay-Melbourne, FL:	70	75	66	37	28
48.	New Haven-Milford, CT:	47	48	50	91	6
49.	Atlanta-Roswell, GA:	37	42	77	67	42
50.	Greenville-Anderson, SC:	59	55	95	5	70
51.	Des Moines, IA:	90	74	23	7	88
52.	Augusta-Richmond County, GA:	46	11	90	39	65
53.	Jacksonville, FL:	45	45	52	70	45
54.	Baton Rouge, LA:	2	19	83	53	87
55.	New York-Newark, NY-NJ:	75	61	60	72	19
56.	Tulsa, OK:	7	22	59	21	95
57.	Riverside-San Bernardino, CA:	23	52	78	75	46
58.	Little Rock-Conway, AR:	15	28	55	47	83
59.	Allentown-Bethlehem-Easton, PA:	78	32	42	45	55
60.	Harrisburg-Carlisle, PA:	54	76	24	43	75
61.	Greensboro-High Point, NC:	57	62	91	42	73
62.	Seattle-Tacoma-Bellevue, WA:	84	66	36	55	58
63.	Portland-Vancouver, OR-WA:	91	73	57	41	51
64.	Chicago-Naperville-Elgin, IL:	50	77	39	79	44
65.	Madison, WI:	93	95	17	15	84
66.	Syracuse, NY:	44	13	27	78	67
67.	Ogden-Clearfield, UT:	92	83	97	20	56
68.	Albany-Schenectady-Troy, NY:	55	17	14	74	68
69.	Pittsburgh, PA:	81	68	12	61	71

70. Providence-Warwick, RI:	86	92	47	65	52
71. Jackson, MS:	21	63	88	95	63
72. Rochester, NY:	88	71	32	64	76
73. Oklahoma City, OK:	64	51	35	34	92
74. Philadelphia-Wilmington, PA-DE:	72	21	44	82	57
75. Columbia, SC:	43	33	100	92	39
76. New Orleans-Metairie, LA:	40	80	94	52	79
77. Kansas City, MO-KS:	68	56	49	57	85
78. Las Vegas-Henderson, NV:	79	87	69	84	49
79. Virginia Beach-Norfolk, VA:	76	50	54	85	62
80. Lakeland-Winter Haven, FL:	42	15	93	71	82
81. Tampa-St. Petersburg, FL:	67	59	79	63	69
82. Baltimore-Columbia-Towson, MD:	83	25	31	94	64
83. Memphis, TN:	28	24	98	89	78
84. Cleveland-Elyria, OH:	85	94	29	86	60
85. Akron, OH:	82	82	62	88	48
86. Louisville, KY:	74	97	89	40	89
87. Worcester, MA:	99	18	72	80	66
88. St. Louis, MO:	65	67	46	73	90
89. Buffalo-Niagara Falls, NY:	97	78	19	87	80
90. Birmingham-Hoover, AL:	58	90	81	66	96
91. Cincinnati, OH:	73	85	53	77	86
92. Detroit-Warren-Dearborn, MI:	87	86	70	97	81
93. Columbus, OH:	94	96	80	69	91
94. Scranton-Wilkes-Barre, PA:	89	91	51	98	77
95. Daytona Beach-Ormond Beach, FL:	80	26	82	83	94
96. Indianapolis-Carmel-Anderson, IN:	77	98	67	76	99
97. Dayton, OH:	95	79	73	81	98
98. Knoxville, TN:	98	99	96	38	100
99. Toledo, OH:	96	81	86	100	97
100. Youngstown-Warren, OH:	100	100	76	99	93

10.4 Well-Being Among Older Adults

The ranking by state among adults ages 55 and older for the five constituent elements of well-being is as follows:

Rank	Purpose Rank	Social Rank	Financial Rank	Community Rank	Physical Rank
1. Hawaii:	2	20	7	1	1
2. Montana:	15	38	11	5	3
3. South Dakota:	4	11	9	4	23
4. Alaska:	19	32	3	6	34
5. Iowa:	7	18	4	2	25
6. New Hampshire:	34	6	10	12	4

7.	Utah:	12	22	21	8	15
8.	Oregon:	22	4	12	18	10
9.	New Mexico:	1	39	25	27	5
10.	Connecticut:	21	8	13	42	2
11.	Minnesota:	20	23	5	19	19
12.	Colorado:	32	29	18	21	7
13.	Idaho:	36	17	15	9	20
14.	Nebraska:	11	33	16	7	38
15.	Florida:	8	1	31	26	8
16.	Delaware:	6	10	2	33	24
17.	Wisconsin:	23	34	6	16	18
18.	Arizona:	14	5	26	35	9
19.	Wyoming:	46	35	20	3	32
20.	Virginia:	16	7	27	17	33
21.	South Carolina:	5	3	47	11	28
22.	Texas:	3	12	38	20	36
23.	California:	18	27	34	38	6
24.	North Carolina:	9	2	43	13	29
25.	Pennsylvania:	25	33	8	37	11
26.	Washington:	38	24	14	36	31
27.	Kansas:	27	14	17	30	35
28.	Vermont:	49	45	19	31	12
29.	Massachusetts:	42	21	22	32	17
30.	Rhode Island:	37	41	40	25	13
31.	North Dakota:	44	49	1	28	39
32.	Michigan:	26	26	29	41	30
33.	Maine:	48	43	36	15	27
34.	Arkansas:	17	28	35	10	45
35.	New York:	39	30	32	45	14
36.	Maryland:	41	9	33	49	21
37.	Illinois:	33	36	23	50	22
38.	New Jersey:	45	15	39	46	16
39.	Missouri:	28	37	28	34	41
40.	Georgia:	24	16	49	44	37
41.	Louisiana:	13	25	50	24	43
42.	Mississippi:	10	19	48	22	42
43.	Tennessee:	31	46	44	14	44
44.	Alabama:	29	31	46	23	47
45.	Nevada:	50	48	45	48	26
46.	Indiana:	35	40	24	43	46
47.	Ohio:	43	42	30	47	40
48.	Oklahoma:	30	44	37	40	49
49.	Kentucky:	47	47	41	29	48
50.	West Virginia:	40	50	42	39	50

10.5 Market Resources

Healthways, 701 Cool Springs Boulevard, Franklin, TN 37067. (800) 327-3822. (www.healthways.com)

The Gallup Organization, 901 F Street NW, Washington, DC 20004. (202) 715-3030. (www.gallup.com)

PART II: SPENDING

11

CONSUMER SPENDING

11.1 Consumer Contribution to the GDP

According to the Bureau of Economic Analysis (www.bea.gov), real gross domestic product (GDP) – the output of goods and services produced by labor and property located in the United States – was $18.56 trillion in 2015, or $57,220 per capital. GDP growth was 2.4% in 2015. Consumer spending (i.e., personal consumption expenditures) was $12.90 trillion, or 69.5% of GDP.

11.2 Spending Assessment

According to the *Consumer Expenditure Survey*, published by the Bureau of Labor Statistics (BLS, www.bls.gov), average spending per consumer unit (which are similar to households) was $53,495 in 2014, a 4.7% increase from the previous year. Spending was distributed as follows (change from previous year in parenthesis):

- Housing: $17,789 (3.8%)
- Transportation: $ 9,073 (0.8%)
- Food: $ 6,759 (8.4%)
  - At home: $ 3,971 (-2.2%)
  - Away from home: $ 2,787 (6.2%)
- Personal insurance and pensions: $ 5,726 (3.6%)
- Healthcare: $ 4,290 (n/a
- Entertainment: $ 2,728 (9.9%)
- Cash contributions: $ 1,788 (-2.5%)
- Apparel and services: $ 1,786 (11.3%)
- All other expenditures: $ 3,548 (8.6%)

The BLS provides regional consumer spending surveys for the following metropolitan areas: Atlanta, Baltimore, Boston, Chicago, Cleveland, Dallas-Fort Worth, Detroit, Houston, Los Angeles, Miami, Minneapolis, New York, Phoenix, Philadelphia, San Diego, San Francisco, Seattle, and Washington, D.C., available online at www.bls.gov/cex/csxregreleases.htm.

11.3 Spending Trends

According to the *Consumer Expenditure Survey*, average annual household spending (in 2014 dollars) has been as follows:

- 2000: $52,303
- 2006: $56,833
- 2010: $52,230
- 2011: $52,312
- 2012: $53,042
- 2013: $51,929
- 2014: $53,495

> **"The average household spent $53,495 in 2014 – 3% more than in 2013, after adjusting for inflation. This is good news and it may signal an energized economy. Household spending reached an all-time high of $56,833 in 2006 (in 2014 dollars). In the years since, average household spending has fallen fairly steadily, reaching a low of $51,929 in 2013."**
>
> *Demo Memo*, 9/3/15

By householder demographic, household spending in 2014 was as follows:

Age

- Under 25: $32,179
- 25-to-34: $49,547
- 35-to-44: $62,512
- 45-to-54: $65,651
- 55-to-64: $56,267
- 65 and older: $43,635

Race/Ethnicity

- Asian-American: $62,784
- African-American: $38,543
- Hispanic: $45,561
- Caucasian: $57,403

Region

- Northeast: $57,027
- West: $55,460
- Midwest: $50,527
- South: $45,956

11.4 Consumer Price Index

The Consumer Price Index (CPI) is a measure of the average change in prices over time of goods and services purchased by households. The CPI assessment was initiated by the Census Bureau in 1977.

The CPI rose 0.7% in 2015 after a 0.8% increase in 2014. This is lower than the 2.4% average annual increase over the prior 10 years.

The overall CPI increased 1.0% for the 12-month period ending May 2016. Changes for select items were as follows:

- Apparel: 1.0%
- Energy: -10.1%
  - Gasoline (all types): -16.9%
  - Fuel oil: -23.6%
  - Electricity: -1.3%
  - Utility (piped) gas service: -4.7%
- Food: 0.7%
  - Food at home: -0.7%
  - Food away from home: 2.6%
- Medical care services: 3.5%
- Medical care commodities: 2.2%
- Shelter: 3.4%
- Transportation services: 3.2%
- Vehicles, new: -0.2%
- Vehicles, used: -2.3%

The BLS reports changes in the CPI on a monthly basis (www.bls.gov/cpi).

11.5 Market Resources

Bureau of Economic Analysis, 1441 L Street NW, Washington, DC 20230. (202) 606-9900. (www.bea.gov)

Consumer Expenditures, Bureau of Labor Statistics. (www.bls.gov/news.release/cesan.nr0.htm)

Consumer Price Index Summary, Bureau of Labor Statistics (www.bls.gov/cpi)

12

RETAIL SPENDING

12.1 The U.S. Retail Sector

The U.S. retail industry encompasses more than 1.6 million retail establishments and employs more than 24 million people (about 1 in 5 American workers), according to the National Retail Federation (NRF, www.nrf.com).

12.2 GAFO Spending

According to the Census Bureau (www.census.gov) of the U.S. Department of Commerce, total U.S. retail sales were $5.32 trillion in 2015, a 2.1% gain from 2014.

Sales at GAFO (general merchandise, apparel, furnishings, and other) stores were $1.26 trillion in 2015, a 1.6% gain from 2014.

Total retail and GAFO sales have been as follows:

	Total Retail	GAFO
• 2005:	$4.09 trillion	$1.06 trillion
• 2006:	$4.30 trillion	$1.11 trillion
• 2007:	$4.44 trillion	$1.15 trillion
• 2008:	$4.39 trillion	$1.14 trillion
• 2009:	$4.07 trillion	$1.09 trillion
• 2010:	$4.29 trillion	$1.11 trillion
• 2011:	$4.60 trillion	$1.16 trillion
• 2012:	$4.83 trillion	$1.19 trillion
• 2013:	$5.01 trillion	$1.21 trillion
• 2014:	$5.21 trillion	$1.24 trillion
• 2015:	$5.32 billion	$1.26 billion

GAFO sales were distributed by month in 2015 as follows:

- January: $ 89.9 billion
- February: $ 89.5 billion
- March: $100.2 billion
- April: $ 96.3 billion
- May: $105.0 billion
- June: $ 99.7 billion
- July: $102.0 billion
- August: $107.8 billion
- September: $ 98.2 billion
- October: $103.3 billion

- November: $115.3 billion
- December: $149.1 billion

Retail sales in 2015 for stores in the GAFO categories were as follows (change from previous year in parenthesis):

- General merchandise stores, including leased departments (NAICS 452): $673.0 billion (1.5%)
  - Superstores and warehouse clubs (NAICS 45291): $439.3 billion (-0.9%)
  - Discount department stores, including leased departments (NAICS 452112): $108.2 billion (-2.2%)
  - Variety stores and miscellaneous (NAICS 45299): $ 68.3 billion (10.2%)
  - Conventional and national chain department stores, including leased departments (NAICS 452111): $ 58.5 billion (0.5%)
- Apparel and accessories stores (NAICS 448): $254.2 billion (0.2%)
  - Family clothing (NAICS 44814): $ 97.8 billion (-1.6%)
  - Women's ready-to-wear (NAICS 44812): $ 46.0 billion (7.5%)
  - Shoe stores (NAICS 4482): $ 34.1 billion (10.4%)
  - Jewelry stores (NAICS 44831): $ 30.5 billion (-9.2%)
  - Men's and boy's clothing (NAICS 44811): $ 9.6 billion (6.7%)
- Sporting goods, hobby, book, and music stores (NAICS 451): $ 89.0 billion (1.5%)
  - Sporting goods stores (NAICS 45111): $ 46.5 billion (7.6%)
  - Hobby, toy, and game stores (NAICS 45112): $ 18.8 billion (-6.9%)
  - Book stores (NAICS 451211): $ 11.2 billion (-1.8%)
- Furniture and home furnishings (NAICS 442): $103.4 billion (2.7%)
- Electronics and appliance stores (NAICS 443): $103.8 billion (2.7%)
- Gift, novelty, and souvenir stores (NAICS 45322): $ 18.5 billion (-9.8%)
- Used merchandise stores (NAICS 4533): $ 17.2 billion (13.2%)
- Office supplies and stationary stores (NAICS 45321): $ 14.5 billion (-15.2%)

Retail sales in non-GAFO retail categories in 2015 were as follows:

- Motor vehicles and parts stores (NAICS 441): $1.107 trillion (4.7%)
- Food and beverage stores, not including restaurants (NAICS 445): $ 668.7 billion (3.0%)
- Restaurants and drinking places (NAICS 722): $ 622.6 billion (9.0%)
- Non-store retailers (NAICS 454): $ 486.1 billion (1.1%)
- Gasoline stations (NAICS 447): $ 432.6 billion (-18.9%)
- Building materials, home improvement and gardening equipment, and supplies dealers (NAICS 444): $ 332.1 billion (1.1%)
- Health and personal care stores, including pharmacies and drug stores (NAICS 446): $ 315.4 billion (5.7%)

12.3 E-Commerce

According to eMarketer (www.emarketer.com), 164.6 million U.S. consumers shopped online in 2015, spending an average of $2,973.

E-commerce buyer penetration has been, and is projected, as follows (source: eMarketer):

	2014	2015	2016	2017	2018	2019
• 14-to-17:	55.8%	57.2%	58.8%	59.8%	60.8%	61.5%
• 18-to-24:	71.0%	73.3%	75.6%	76.6%	77.3%	77.9%
• 25-to-34:	69.8%	71.6%	73.1%	75.1%	76.6%	77.7%
• 35-to-44:	71.6%	73.4%	75.6%	76.6%	77.5%	78.0%
• 45-to-54:	68.6%	70.8%	72.4%	75.4%	77.5%	79.5%
• 55-to-64:	64.4%	66.2%	68.6%	70.6%	72.5%	73.9%
• 65 and older:	38.8%	42.7%	45.9%	48.9%	50.3%	50.4%
• Total:	62.5%	65.0%	67.9%	68.9%	70.3%	71.1%

In a survey by the IBM Institute For Business Value (www.ibm.com), one-half of shoppers said they preferred shopping online.

"Shoppers are getting used to – and growing fond of – the online shopping experience. They enjoy the feeling of going to a favorite retailer's webpage and opening tabs of different items to compare as they scroll down the page. They like the 1-2-3 browse, click and purchase experience."

eMarketer

According to the U.S. Department of Commerce (www.doc.gov), e-commerce sales in the U.S. have been as follows:

	E-commerce Sales	Percent of Total Retail Sales	Growth
• 2005:	$ 86.3 billion	2.3%	25%
• 2006:	$114.6 billion	2.8%	33%
• 2007:	$132.8 billion	3.2%	16%
• 2008:	$132.3 billion	3.3%	no change
• 2009:	$134.9 billion	3.7%	2%
• 2010:	$167.7 billion	4.3%	24%

- 2011: $194.7 billion 4.7% 16%
- 2012: $225.5 billion 5.0% 16%
- 2013: $264.3 billion 5.7% 17%
- 2014: $304.9 billion 6.5% 15%
- 2015: $341.7 billion 7.3% 15%

"Despite all this growth, online purchases remain a very small portion of retail sales. Over 90% of all United States retail commerce still takes place in physical stores."

The New York Times

E-commerce sales by quarter in 2015 were as follows (change from same quarter in previous year in parenthesis):

- First quarter: $ 74.9 billion (14.4%)
- Second quarter: $ 78.8 billion (14.4%)
- Third quarter: $ 81.0 billion (15.1%)
- Fourth quarter: $107.1 billion (14.5%)

According to eMarketer, online retail spending in 2015 was distributed by product category as follows (change from previous year in parenthesis):

- Computer and consumer electronics: $76.1 billion (14.5%)
- Apparel and accessories: $59.7 billion (14.9%)
- Automotive and parts: $36.2 billion (14.6%)
- Books, music, and video: $31.5 billion (15.7%)
- Furniture and home furnishings: $23.1 billion (13.7%)
- Health and personal care: $19.6 billion (13.6%)
- Toys and hobby: $13.8 billion (14.2%)
- Office equipment and supplies: $ 9.3 billion (12.4%)
- Food and beverage: $ 7.9 billion (12.6%)
- Other: $70.1 billion (13.2%)

According to a survey by The Harris Poll (www.theharrispoll.com), the following percentages of adults have made select purchases online:

	Female	Male	Total
• Clothing:	75%	63%	69%
• Digital content (movies, music, e-books):	56%	62%	59%
• Shoes and accessories:	60%	47%	54%

• Personal electronics:	43%	55%	49%
• Household electronics:	37%	49%	43%
• Cosmetics and personal grooming:	41%	28%	35%
• Prescription medications:	24%	27%	26%
• Specialty food and beverages:	24%	27%	25%
• O-T-C medications:	19%	18%	18%
• Groceries:	15%	16%	15%

By age, consumers have made purchases online as follows:

	18-36	**37-48**	**49-67**	**68+**
• Clothing:	68%	77%	70%	61%
• Digital content (movies, music, e-books):	65%	72%	53%	38%
• Shoes and accessories:	58%	60%	52%	38%
• Personal electronics:	57%	57%	44%	26%
• Household electronics:	44%	49%	43%	27%
• Cosmetics and personal grooming:	39%	41%	32%	20%
• Prescription medications:	18%	26%	27%	40%
• Specialty food and beverages:	25%	32%	21%	27%
• O-T-C medications:	18%	19%	17%	18%
• Groceries:	18%	23%	11%	16%

12.4 Back-to-School

The back-to-school season typically is the second-biggest consumer spending event for retailers – behind the winter holidays – and can account for up to 15% of retailers' annual sales. It is sometimes used to gauge the health of the upcoming holiday shopping season.

According to NRF, back-to-school (K-12) and back-to-college spending have been as follows:

• 2009:	$17.4 billion	$30.1 billion	$47.5 billion
• 2010:	$21.4 billion	$45.8 billion	$67.2 billion
• 2011:	$22.8 billion	$46.6 billion	$69.4 billion
• 2012:	$30.3 billion	$53.5 billion	$83.8 billion
• 2013:	$26.7 billion	$45.8 billion	$72.5 billion
• 2014:	$26.5 billion	$48.4 billion	$74.9 billion
• 2015:	$24.9 billion	$43.1 billion	$68.0 billion
• 2016:	$27.3 billion	$48.5 billion	$75.8 billion

According to NRF's *2016 Consumer Intentions and Actions Survey*, conducted by Prosper Business Development (www.goprosper.com), students and parents reported average spending of $674 on back-to-school merchandise.

Back-to-school spending was distributed by category as follows:

	Avg. Per Student	Total Spending
• Apparel:	$235	$9.5 billion
• Electronics/computers:	$204	$8.3 billion
• Shoes:	$126	$5.1 billion
• School supplies:	$108	$4.4 billion

NRF's *2016 Consumer Intentions and Actions Survey*, reported average student and parent spending of $889 on back-to-college merchandise (excluding textbooks).

Back-to-college spending was distributed by category as follows:

	Avg. Per Student	Total Spending
• Electronics/computers:	$211	$11.5 billion
• Apparel:	$137	$ 7.5 billion
• Dorm/apartment furnishings:	$114	$ 6.2 billion
• Food, snacks and beverages:	$106	$ 5.8 billion
• Personal care items:	$ 78	$ 4.3 billion
• Shoes:	$ 70	$ 3.8 billion
• School supplies:	$ 65	$ 3.5 billion
• Gift cards/pre-paid cards:	$ 58	$ 3.1 billion
• Collegiate branded gear:	$ 49	$ 2.7 billion

12.5 Christmas Season Holiday Spending

According to the National Retail Federation, more than 90% of Americans celebrate either Christmas, Kwanzaa or Hanukkah.

> **"The holiday season generally accounts for 20% to 40% of a retailer's annual sales, according to the National Retail Federation, and Thanksgiving weekend alone typically represents about 10% to 15% of those holiday sales."**
>
> *The New York Times*

According to the Census Bureau, year-over-year growth of December retail sales has been as follows:

	Total Retail*	GAFO**
• 2005:	6.2%	4.6%
• 2006:	3.0%	3.7%
• 2007:	3.1%	-0.3%

• 2008:	-6.8%	-6.0%
• 2009:	5.6%	1.4%
• 2010:	6.4%	3.2%
• 2011:	5.6%	4.0%
• 2012:	1.6%	0.6%
• 2013:	3.7%	1.8%
• 2014:	3.9%	1.9%
• 2015:	2.1%	1.5%

* excluding motor vehicle and parts dealers
** GAFO: (general merchandise, apparel, furnishings, and other)

According to the National Retail Federation, total holiday (November and December) retail sales (excluding autos, gas and restaurant sales) increased 3.7% to $630.5 billion in 2015, significantly higher than the 10-year average of 2.5%. Holiday sales in 2015 represented approximately 19% of the retail industry's annual sales.

NRF's consumer spending survey found that the average shopper spent $805.65 in 2015, up from $802.45 in 2014.

Gift spending by recipient in 2015 was as follows:

- Family: $462.95
- Friends: $ 77.85
- Co-workers: $ 25.95
- Other, including pets: $ 28.05

Fifty-six percent (56%) of holiday shoppers purchased non-gift items for themselves and/or others, spending an average of $131.59.

Consumers also spent on decorations ($53.02), greeting cards/postage ($28.67), and food for holiday festivities ($107.80).

Holiday shopping by retail venue in 2015 was as follows:

- Discount stores: 55.9%
- Department: 55.6%
- Grocery stores: 44.1%
- Clothing or accessories stores: 33.4%
- Electronics stores: 30.8%
- Drug stores: 19.2%
- Craft and fabric stores: 18.8%

Forty percent (40%) of holiday shoppers began their holiday shopping before Halloween, 41% began their holiday shopping in November, and 19% began sometime in December.

Total holiday gift card spending was $25.9 billion in 2015. According to NRF's *Gift Card Spending Survey*, the average person buying gift cards spent $153.08, an 11.4% drop from 2014.

12.6 State-by-State Retail Spending

According to the National Retail Federation, retail sales in 2015 were distributed by state as follows:

	Pct. of National Total	Retail Sales
• Alabama:	1.50%	$ 48,849,750,000
• Alaska:	0.26%	$ 8,467,290,000
• Arizona:	2.24%	$ 72,948,960,000
• Arkansas:	0.91%	$ 29,635,515,000
• California:	11.90%	$387,541,350,000
• Colorado:	1.70%	$ 55,363,050,000
• Connecticut:	1.25%	$ 40,708,125,000
• District Of Columbia:	0.15%	$ 4,884,975,000
• Delaware:	0.37%	$ 12,049,605,000
• Florida:	7.30%	$237,735,450,000
• Georgia:	3.01%	$ 98,025,165,000
• Hawaii:	0.50%	$ 16,283,250,000
• Idaho:	0.51%	$ 16,608,915,000
• Illinois:	4.05%	$131,894,325,000
• Indiana:	1.99%	$ 64,807,335,000
• Iowa:	0.92%	$ 29,961,180,000
• Kansas:	0.79%	$ 25,727,535,000
• Kentucky:	1.26%	$ 41,033,790,000
• Louisiana:	1.33%	$ 43,313,445,000
• Maine:	0.51%	$ 16,608,915,000
• Maryland:	1.99%	$ 64,807,335,000
• Massachusetts:	2.34%	$ 76,205,610,000
• Michigan:	3.10%	$100,956,150,000
• Minnesota:	1.80%	$ 58,619,700,000
• Mississippi:	0.89%	$ 28,984,185,000
• Missouri:	1.97%	$ 64,156,005,000
• Montana:	0.36%	$ 11,723,940,000
• Nebraska:	0.62%	$ 20,191,230,000
• Nevada:	1.14%	$ 37,125,810,000
• New Hampshire:	0.67%	$ 21,819,555,000
• New Jersey:	3.12%	$101,607,480,000
• New Mexico:	0.62%	$ 20,191,230,000
• New York:	5.93%	$193,119,345,000
• North Carolina:	2.89%	$ 94,117,185,000
• North Dakota:	0.25%	$ 8,141,625,000
• Ohio:	3.39%	$110,400,435,000
• Oklahoma:	1.00%	$ 32,566,500,000
• Oregon:	1.27%	$ 41,359,455,000
• Pennsylvania:	4.07%	$132,545,655,000
• Rhode Island:	0.34%	$ 11,072,610,000

• South Carolina:	1.36%	$ 44,290,440,000
• South Dakota:	0.32%	$ 10,421,280,000
• Tennessee:	2.10%	$ 68,389,650,000
• Texas:	7.49%	$243,923,085,000
• Utah:	0.84%	$ 27,355,860,000
• Vermont:	0.25%	$ 8,141,625,000
• Virginia:	2.63%	$ 85,649,895,000
• Washington:	2.26%	$ 73,600,290,000
• West Virginia:	0.54%	$ 17,585,910,000
• Wisconsin:	1.80%	$ 58,619,700,000
• Wyoming:	0.21%	$ 6,838,965,000

12.7 Market Resources

Estimates Of Monthly Retail and Food Services Sales By Kind Of Business, U.S. Department of Commerce. (www.census.gov/retail/marts/www/marts_current.pdf)

National Retail Federation, 325 7th Street NW, Washington, DC 20004. (202) 783-7971. (www.nrf.com)

Quarterly Retail E-Commerce Sales, U.S. Department of Commerce. (www.census.gov/retail/mrts/www/data/pdf/ec_current.pdf)

Retail Business Market Research Handbook 2017-2018, Richard K. Miller & Associates, September 2016. (www.rkma.com/report-detail.cfm?report_id=132)

13

ENTERTAINMENT & LEISURE SPENDING

13.1 Expenditures On Leisure Activities

Richard K. Miller & Associates (RKMA, www.rkma.com) estimates the U.S. entertainment and leisure market at $2.6 trillion. For comparison: U.S. retail sales were $5.3 trillion in 2015, according to the U.S. Department of Commerce; national healthcare expenditures were $3.2 trillion in 2015, according to the Centers for Medicare & Medicaid Services.

The following are RKMA estimates of the major components of the leisure market:

- Adult entertainment: $ 26 billion
  (sources: *Forbes*, *U.S. News & World Report*, Associated Press)
- Art: $ 27 billion
  (source: TEFAF)
- Bars and nightclubs: $ 21 billion
  (source: National Restaurant Association)
- Bicycles: $ 6 billion
  (source: National Bicycle Dealers Association)
- Casino/parimutuel wagering: $ 68 billion
  (source: *Gaming & Leisure* and Jay Sarno & Associates)
- Collecting: $ 70 billion
  (source: *Investors Business Daily*)
- Consumer books: $ 23 billion
  (sources: U.S. Department of Commerce)
- Consumer electronics: $287 billion
  (source: Consumer Technology Association)
- Craft and hobby supplies: $ 31 billion
  (sources: Craft & Hobby Association)
- Cultural, the not-for-profit arts industry: $135 billion
  (source: Americans for the Arts)
- Dining out (casual and fine dining only): $220 billion
  (source: National Restaurant Association)
- Equestrian: $102 billion
  (source: American Quarter Horse Association)
- Event rentals: $ 3 billion
  (source: *The Wall Street Journal*)
- Fantasy sports: $ 2 billion
  (source: Fantasy Sports Trade Association)

- Festivals: $ 25 billion
(source: International Festivals & Events Association)
- Fishing: $ 42 billion
(source: U.S. Fish and Wildlife Service)
- Gardening: $ 30 billion
(source: National Gardening Association)
- Golf: $ 34 billion
(source: National Golf Foundation)
- Health and fitness clubs: $ 25 billion
(source: International Health, Racquet & Sportsclub Association)
- Hunting: $ 34 billion
(source: U.S. Fish and Wildlife Service)
- Lotteries: $ 27 billion
(source: North American Association of State and Provincial Lotteries)
- Motion picture and sound recording industries: $ 58 billion
(source: SRI International)
- Motorcycles: $ 18 billion
(source: Packaged Facts)
- Museums: $ 21 billion
(source: American Alliance of Museums)
- Music concerts: $ 7 billion
(source: Pollstar)
- Musical instruments and products: $ 7 billion
(source: *Music Trades*)
- National parks: $ 12 billion
(source: U.S. Park Service)
- Pets: $ 53 billion
(source: American Pet Products Association)
- Photography: $ 17 billion
(sources: Photo Marketing Association, Bureau of Economic Analysis)
- Premium video (pay TV, mobile video, DVD, broadband video, and theater/box office receipts): $182 billion
(source: iSuppli)
- Private clubs: $ 23 billion
(source: IBISWorld)
- Radio (ad-supported, not direct consumer spending): $ 17 billion
(source: Radio Advertising Bureau)
- Recreational boating: $122 billion
(source: National Marine Manufacturers Association)
- Recreation vehicles: $ 13 billion
(source: Recreation Vehicle Industry Association)
- Social caterers: $ 9 billion
(sources: National Restaurant Association, Technomic)
- Spas: $ 16 billion
(source: International Spa Association, PricewaterhouseCoopers)
- Specialty auto accessories: $ 29 billion
(source: Specialty Equipment Market Association)

- Spectator sports: $ 26 billion
  (source: *Sports Business Journal*)
- Sporting goods: $ 56 billion
  (source: Sporting Goods Manufacturers Association)
- State parks: $ 20 billion
  (source: National Association of State Park Directors)
- Swimming pools: $ 12 billion
  (source: IBISWorld)
- Tailgating: $ 15 billion
  (source: American Tailgaters Association)
- Television (ad-supported, not direct consumer spending): $ 68 billion
  (source: *Adweek*)
- Theme and amusement parks; family entertainment centers: $ 15 billion
  (source: International Association of Amusement Parks and Attractions)
- Travel and tourism (leisure travel only): $549 billion
  (source: Travel Industry Association)
- Video games: $ 24 billion
  (sources: NPD Group, Entertainment Software Association)
- Wildlife watching: $ 55 billion
  (source: U.S. Fish and Wildlife Service)

There is some overlap among the above expenditures. A few leisure activities are included in more than one category. This is somewhat offset by the fact that all types of leisure expenditures – hobby farming and wellness activities, for example – are not included in the list.

Based on published statistics by the U.S. government, leisure expenditures are significantly less than the $2.6 trillion figure assessed here. According to The Bureau of Economic Analysis (BEA, www.bea.gov), Americans spend $745 billion on leisure pursuits. This figure is significantly lower because the BEA classifies many leisure expenditures elsewhere. Travel and tourism, for example, is considered a separate category. Auto customizing and collecting, as another example, are classified as transportation expenditures. Collectible purchases, pets, videos, and various other leisure-related purchases are classified as retail expenditures.

13.2 Market Resources

Leisure Business Market Research Handbook 2017-2018, Richard K. Miller & Associates, September 2016. (www.rkma.com/report-detail.cfm?report_id=131)

PART III: ACTIVITIES

14

USE OF TIME

14.1 Americans' Use of Time

The *American Time Use Survey* (*ATUS*, www.bls.gov/tus/), first published in 2005 by the Bureau of Labor Statistics (BLS) of the U.S. Department of Labor and updated annually, is the most recognized source for data on use of time.

Use-of-time data is skewed because most people do not participate in all types of activities. *ATUS* accounts for this by quantifying for each type of activity the average amount of time spent both by all consumers and by only those who participate in an activity.

According to the 2015 *ATUS*, published by the BLS in June 2016, American adults' average 24-hour day, the percentage participating in various activities, and the average time spent among participants are distributed as follows:

	All Consumers	Pct.	Active Participants
• Sleeping and personal care:	9.64 hours	100%	9.64 hours
• Leisure and sports:	5.21 hours	96%	5.42 hours
• Working and work-related activities:	3.53 hours	43%	8.03 hours
• Household activities:	1.84 hours	76%	2.41 hours
• Eating and drinking:	1.18 hours	95%	1.24 hours
• Purchasing goods and services:	0.75 hours	44%	1.70 hours
• Caring for/helping household members:	0.51 hours	25%	2.06 hours
• Educational activities:	0.46 hours	8%	5.79 hours
• Organizational, civic, religious:	0.33 hours	15%	2.23 hours
• Caring for/helping non-household members:	0.19 hours	11%	1.66 hours
• Telephone calls, mail, email:	0.16 hours	21%	0.75 hours
• Other activities:	0.19 hours	14%	1.40 hours

By gender, adults' 24-hour day was distributed as follows:

	Men	Women
• Sleeping and personal care:	9.43 hours	9.85 hours
• Leisure and sports:	5.58 hours	4.86 hours
• Working and work-related activities:	4.18 hours	2.92 hours
• Household activities:	1.43 hours	2.23 hours
• Eating and drinking:	1.24 hours	1.13 hours
• Purchasing goods and services:	0.60 hours	0.88 hours
• Caring for/helping household members:	0.31 hours	0.70 hours
• Educational activities:	0.48 hours	0.45 hours

• Organizational, civic, religious:	0.29 hours	0.37 hours
• Caring for/helping non-household members:	0.16 hours	0.21 hours
• Telephone calls, mail, email:	0.12 hours	0.20 hours
• Other activities:	0.19 hours	0.20 hours

14.2 Older Americans

Among those ages 55 and older, time spent daily doing select activities is as follows:

	Ages 55-64	Ages 65-74	75 and Older
• Leisure and sports:	5.7 hours	7.2 hours	7.5 hours
• Working and related activities:	3.6 hours	1.2 hours	0.4 hours
• Household activities:	2.1 hours	2.4 hours	2.2 hours

By employment status, those ages 55 or older spent leisure time as follows:

	Not Employed	Employed
• Watching TV:	4.4 hours	2.8 hours
• Reading:	1.0 hours	0.7 hours
• Socializing and communicating:	0.7 hours	0.6 hours
• Relaxing and thinking:	0.7 hours	0.3 hours
• Other leisure:	1.1 hours	0.7 hours

14.3 Students

High school students spent the average weekday engaged in various activities as follows:

	Not Employed	Employed
• Sleeping:	8.8 hours	8.4 hours
• Education:	6.3 hours	5.6 hours
• Socializing, relaxing and leisure:	3.7 hours	3.0 hours
• Sports, exercise and recreation:	0.9 hours	0.6 hours
• Spiritual and volunteering:	0.2 hours	0.4 hours
• Working:	0.0 hours	1.6 hours

Full-time college and university students spent the average weekday engaged in various activities as follows:

• Sleeping:	8.3 hours
• Leisure and sports:	3.7 hours
• Educational activities:	3.3 hours
• Working and related activities:	3.1 hours
• Travel:	1.5 hours
• Eating and drinking:	1.0 hours
• Grooming:	0.8 hours
• Other:	2.3 hours

14.4 Market Resources

American Time Use Survey - 2015 Results, Bureau of Labor Statistics, June 2016. (www.bls.gov/news.release/atus.nr0.htm)

15

USE OF MEDIA & THE INTERNET

15.1 Time Spent Using Media

According to eMarketer (www.emarketer.com), the average time spent per day by U.S. adults using major media has been, and is projected, as follows (hours:minutes):

Digital Media	2012	2013	2014	2015	2016	2017	2018
• Mobile - non-voice:	1:28	2:15	2:37	2:53	3:06	3:15	3:23
- Audio/radio:	0:26	0:32	0:39	0:44	0:47	0:50	0:52
- Social networks:	0:09	0:18	0:23	0:26	0:29	0:32	0:34
- Video:	0:09	0:17	0:22	0:26	0:29	0:31	0:34
- Other:	0:44	1:08	1:14	1:16	1:20	1:22	1:24
• Desktop/laptop:	2:24	2:16	2:14	2:12	2:11	2:10	2:08
- Video:	0:20	0:22	0:23	0:24	0:25	0:25	0:24
- Social networks:	0:22	0:17	0:16	0:15	0:14	0:13	0:13
- Audio/radio:	0:07	0:06	0:06	0:06	0:06	0:06	0:05
- Other:	1:35	1:31	1:28	1:27	1:26	1:26	1:26
• Other connected devices:	0:18	0:17	0:19	0:23	0:26	0:28	0:30
• Total digital media:	4:10	4:48	5:09	5:28	5:43	5:53	6:01
Traditional Media							
• Television:	4:38	4:31	4:22	4:11	4:05	4:00	3:55
• Radio:	1:32	1:30	1:28	1:27	1:27	1:26	1:25
• Newspapers:	0:24	0:20	0:18	0:17	0:16	0:15	0:15
• Magazines:	0:17	0:15	0:13	0:13	0:12	0:11	0:11
• Other non-digital:	0:38	0:31	0:26	0:24	0:22	0:21	0:20
• Total traditional media:	7:29	7:07	6:48	6:32	6:22	6:14	6:07
Total	11:39	11:55	11:57	12:00	12:05	12:07	12:08

The time adults spend using digital media has surpassed the time spent watching TV since 2013.

"Thanks to media multitasking, U.S. adults will squeeze an average of 12 hours and 5 minutes per day of media usage into their waking hours this year – nearly an hour more than the average in 2011."

eMarketer, 6/6/16

15.2 Internet Access

American's Internet Access: 2000-2015, by Pew Research Center (www.pewresearch.org), reports adult use of the Internet as follows:

- 2000: 52%
- 2001: 55%
- 2002: 59%
- 2003: 61%
- 2004: 63%
- 2005: 68%
- 2006: 71%
- 2007: 74%
- 2008: 74%
- 2009: 76%
- 2010: 76%
- 2011: 79%
- 2012: 83%
- 2013: 84%
- 2014: 84%
- 2015: 84%

In 2015, Internet usage among adults was as follows:

Gender
- Female: 84%
- Male: 85%

Age
- 18-to-29: 96%
- 30-to-49: 93%
- 50-to-64: 81%
- 65 and older: 58%

Education
- Some high school: 66%
- High school graduate: 76%
- Some college: 90%
- College graduate: 95%

Income

- Less than $30,000: 74%
- $30,000 to $49,999: 85%
- $50,000 to $74,999: 95%
- $75,000 and higher: 97%

Race/Ethnicity

- African-American: 78%
- Asian-American: 97%
- Caucasian: 81%
- Hispanic: 85%

Residence

- Rural: 78%
- Suburban: 85%
- Urban: 85%

15.3 Home Broadband

Home Broadband 2015, by Pew Research Center, reports household use of home broadband for Internet access as follows:

- 2000: 1%
- 2001: 8%
- 2002: 11%
- 2003: 17%
- 2004: 25%
- 2005: 34%
- 2006: 42%
- 2007: 55%
- 2008: 56%
- 2009: 60%
- 2010: 62%
- 2011: 61%
- 2012: 65%
- 2013: 70%
- 2014: 68%
- 2015: 67%

Broadband use peaked in 2013. In 2015, 14% of households depended on a smartphone for Internet connectivity, an increase from 8% that did so in 2013.

In 2015, home broadband access among adults was as follows:

Gender

- Female: 67%
- Male: 66%

Age

- 18-to-29: 75%
- 30-to-49: 74%
- 50-to-64: 65%
- 65 and older: 45%

Education

- High school: 47%
- Some college: 75%
- College graduate: 87%

Income

- Less than $20,000: 41%
- $20,000 to $49,999: 63%
- $50,000 to $74,999: 80%
- $75,000 to $99,999: 88%
- $100,000 and higher: 90%

Race/Ethnicity

- African-American: 54%
- Caucasian: 72%
- Hispanic: 50%

Residence

- Rural: 55%
- Suburban: 70%
- Urban: 67%

15.4 Smartphone Use

U.S. Smartphone Use in 2015, by Pew Research Center, reports that 64% of adults own a smartphone. The demographics of smartphone owners are as follows:

Gender

- Female: 63%
- Male: 66%

Age

- 18-to-29: 85%
- 30-to-49: 79%
- 50-to-64: 54%
- 65 and older: 27%

Education

- High school: 52%
- Some college: 69%
- College graduate: 78%

Income

- Less than $30,000: 50%

- $30,000 to $49,999: 71%
- $50,000 to $74,999: 72%
- $75,000 and higher: 84%

Race/Ethnicity
- African-American: 70%
- Caucasian: 61%
- Hispanic: 71%

Residence
- Rural: 52%
- Suburban: 66%
- Urban: 68%

15.5 Online Activities

Since 2000, the Center for the Digital Future (www.digitalcenter.org) at the University of Southern California, Annenberg School for Communication has conducted the Digital Future Project. *2015 Digital Future Project* reported that 91% of Americans accessed the Internet, with an average of 21.5 hours per week spent online, 16.1 hours of which were at home.

According to the center, the following percentages of Internet users engaged in these online activities at least once a month:

- Email: 96%
- Internet surfing without a specific destination: 87%
- Look for news online: 79%
- Visit social networking sites: 74%
- Download/listen to music: 65%
- Download/watch videos: 64%
- Look for health information: 54%
- Play online games: 53%
- Search for humorous content: 52%
- Read blogs: 43%
- Listen to online radio stations: 38%
- Look for travel information: 37%
- Look for job/work: 29%
- Look at religious/spiritual content: 26%
- Gamble: 11%

15.6 Cross-Platform Access Of Content

According to comScore (www.comscore.com), time spent online with various types of content is distributed by platform as follows:

	Computer	Smartphone	Tablet
• Automotive:	76%	16%	8%
• Business/finance:	68%	29%	3%
• Entertainment:	50%	39%	11%
• Food:	56%	28%	16%
• Games:	18%	48%	34%
• Health:	54%	40%	6%
• Lifestyles:	50%	32%	18%
• News/information:	62%	31%	7%
• Radio:	8%	77%	15%
• Retail:	49%	35%	16%
• Social media:	33%	58%	9%
• Sports:	62%	31%	7%
• Technology:	20%	64%	16%
• TV:	68%	12%	20%
• Weather:	36%	55%	9%
• Total:	49%	39%	12%

15.7 Market Resources

2015 Digital Future Project, 13th Edition, Center for the Digital Future at the University of Southern California, Annenberg School for Communication & Journalism, 11444 West Olympic Boulevard, Suite 120, Los Angeles, CA 90064. (www.digitalcenter.org/wp-content/uploads/2013/06/2015-Digital-Future-Report.pdf)

comScore, 11950 Democracy Drive, Suite 600, Reston, VA 20190. (703) 438-2000. (www.comscore.com)

Digital Democracy Survey, 10th Edition, Deloitte, March 2016. (www2.deloitte.com/us/en/pages/technology-media-and-telecommunications/articles/digital-democracy-survey-generational-media-consumption-trends.html)

eMarketer, 11 Times Square, New York, NY 10036. (212) 376-5291. (www.emarketer.com)

Pew Research Center for Internet, Science & Technology, 1615 L Street NW, Suite 700, Washington, DC 20036. (202) 419-4500. (www.pewinternet.org)

16

CULTURAL ACTIVITIES

16.1 Public Participation In The Arts

Survey of Public Participation in the Arts, published once a decade and most recently in 2013 by The National Endowment for the Arts (www.arts.gov), asked U.S. adults which cultural and performing arts activities they had participated in during the prior 12 months. Responses were as follows:

	Percent	Number
Arts through electronic media:	71%	167 million
• Used TV, radio, or the Internet to access arts programming:	61%	144 million
- Music of any kind:	57%	135 million
- Programs or information about the visual arts:	14%	33 million
- Ballet, modern, or contemporary dance programs/shows:	11%	26 million
- Theater productions (e.g. a musical or stage play):	7%	16 million
- Books, short stories, or novels read aloud:	7%	16 million
- Opera:	4%	9 million
• Used a handheld or mobile device to access art:	38%	90 million
- Music of any kind:	34%	80 million
- Novels, short stories, or plays:	16%	38 million
- Visual artworks (e.g. painting, sculpture, graphic design, photography):	8%	19 million
- Theater or dance performances:	3%	7 million
• Used a DVD or CD player, record-player, or tape-player to watch or listen to music or to programs about theater, dance, visual arts, or literature:	27%	64 million
Moviegoing (excluding at-home viewing):	59%	139 million
Reading (excluding reading required for school or work):	58%	136 million
- Books:	54%	127 million
- Novels or short stories:	45%	106 million
- Poetry:	7%	16 million
- Plays:	3%	7 million

Visual and performing arts attendance:	49%	115 million
• Attended a visual arts event or activity:	39%	92 million
- Touring a park, monument, building, or neighborhood for historic or design purposes:	24%	57 million
- Attending a visual arts festival or a crafts fair:	22%	52 million
- Visiting an art museum or gallery:	21%	50 million
• Attended a live performing arts event:	37%	87 million
- Outdoor performing arts festivals:	21%	50 million
- Musical or non-musical plays:	18%	42 million
- Classical music, jazz, or Latin, Spanish, or salsa music:	17%	40 million
- Dance of any kind:	7%	16 million
- Opera:	2%	5 million
Art-making or art sharing:		
• Created, performed, or shared art through various activities:	50%	118 million
- Social dancing:	32%	76 million
- Weaving, crocheting, quilting, needlepoint, knitting, sewing:	13%	31 million
- Played a musical instrument:	12%	28 million
- Sang, either alone or with others:	9%	21 million
- Created leatherwork, metalwork, or woodwork:	8%	19 million
- Created pottery, ceramics, or jewelry:	5%	12 million
- Acting:	1%	2 million
• Performed or practiced in a specific art form:	10%	24 million
- Dance of any kind:	5%	12 million
- Choral singing or singing in a choir or glee club:	3%	7 million
- Classical music:	2%	5 million
- Latin, Spanish, or salsa music:	1%	2 million
- Jazz:	1%	2 million
- Musical or non-musical plays:	1%	2 million
- Opera:	<1%	1 million
• Emailed, posted, or shared artwork:	40%	94 million
- Photography:	26%	61 million
- Music of any kind:	21%	50 million
- Films or videos:	13%	31 million
- Other visual art (e.g. painting, sculpture, graphic design):	6%	14 million
- Dance of any kind:	5%	12 million
- Poetry, plays, or novels or short stories:	4%	9 million
• Created photography for artistic purposes or did photo editing:	18%	42 million
• Created other types of visual artworks, did scrapbooking, or creative writing:	14%	33 million

• Created, performed, recorded, edited, or remixed music, dance, film, or video:	10%	24 million
Arts learning through classes or lessons:	7%	16 million
- Voice training or playing a musical instrument:	3%	7 million
- Art appreciation or art history:	2%	5 million
- Creative writing:	2%	5 million
- Visual arts such as drawing, painting, pottery, weaving, or graphic or fashion design:	2%	5 million
- Dance of any kind:	2%	5 million
- Music appreciation:	1%	2 million
- Photography or filmmaking:	1%	2 million
- Acting or theater:	<1%	1 million

16.2 Performing Arts Activities

Survey of Public Participation in the Arts reported the following percentages of adults attending at least one performing arts function annually:

Musical

- Classical: 8.8%
- Jazz: 8.1%
- Dance other than ballet: 5.6%
- Latin, Spanish, or salsa: 5.1%
- Ballet: 2.7%
- Opera: 2.1%

Theater

- Musical play: 15.2%
- Non-musical play: 8.3%

16.3 Survey Of Metropolitan Areas

According to International Demographics (www.themediaaudit.com), 30% of U.S. adults living in metropolitan areas attended an opera, symphony, or theatre event within the prior 12 months. The following metropolitan areas have the highest percentage of adults who did so:

- Salt Lake City, UT: 41.1%
- Washington, DC: 38.4%
- Omaha-Council Bluffs, NE: 36.9%
- Ft. Myers-Naples, FL: 36.6%
- Madison, WI: 35.3%

16.4 Market Resources

Americans for the Arts, 1000 Vermont Avenue NW, 6th Floor, Washington, DC 20005. (202) 371-2830. (www.americansforthearts.org)

International Demographics, 10333 Richmond Avenue, Suite 200, Houston, TX 77042. (713) 626-0333. (www.themediaaudit.com)

National Endowment for the Arts, 400 7th Street SW, Washington, DC 20506. (202) 682-5400. (www.arts.gov)

17

LEISURE ACTIVITIES

17.1 Time Spent On Leisure Activities

The *American Time Use Survey* (ATUS, www.bls.gov/tus/), published June 2016 by the Bureau of Labor Statistics (BLS) of the U.S. Department of Labor, assessed leisure activities as follows:

- On an average day, 96% of people ages 15 and over engaged in some sort of leisure activity, such as watching TV, socializing, or exercising. Of those who engaged in leisure activities, men spent more time in these activities (5.8 hours) than did women (5.1 hours).
- Watching TV was the leisure activity that occupied the most time (2.8 hours per day), accounting for about half of leisure time, on average, for those ages 15 and over. Socializing, such as visiting with friends or attending or hosting social events, was the next most common leisure activity, accounting for nearly three-quarters of an hour per day.
- Men were more likely than women to participate in sports, exercise, or recreation on any given day – 23% compared with 18%. Men also spent more time in these activities than did women – 1.7 hours compared with 1.2 hours.
- On an average day, adults ages 75 and over spent 7.8 hours engaged in leisure activities – more than any other age group; 35-to 44 year-olds spent 4.0 hours engaged in leisure and sports activities – less than other age groups.
- Time spent reading for personal interest and playing games or using a computer for leisure varied greatly by age. Individuals ages 75 and over averaged 1.1 hours of reading per weekend day and 20 minutes playing games or using a computer for leisure. Conversely, individuals ages 15-to-19 read for an average of 8 minutes per weekend day and spent 1.3 hours playing games or using a computer for leisure.
- Employed adults living in households with no children under age 18 engaged in leisure activities for 4.5 hours per day, 1.1 hour more than employed adults living with a child under age 6.

According to the ATUS, Americans spend, on average, 5.21 hours per day engaged in leisure activities, which represents about ⅓ of their time. Daily leisure time is distributed by demographics as follows:

Gender

- Men: 5.58 hours
- Women: 4.86 hours

Age

• 15-to-19:	5.78 hours
• 20-to-24:	5.10 hours
• 25-to-34:	4.30 hours
• 35-to-44:	4.20 hours
• 45-to-54:	4.67 hours
• 55-to-64:	5.27 hours
• 65 and above:	7.16 hours

Education/work

• Less than high school education:	6.07 hours
• High school graduate:	5.37 hours
- Age 25+ and employed full time:	3.18 hours
• Bachelor's degree or higher:	4.30 hours
- Age 25+ and employed full time:	2.98 hours

17.2 Top 10 Leisure Activities in

Leisure Business Market Research Handbook 2017-2018 reports that the following were the Top 10 leisure activities in 2015:

Collecting

- Virtually everyone collects something. And for nearly every conceivable object, there are collectors. In 2015, 50 million collectors spent $70 billion purchasing items for their collections. Among the most popular collections: art, coins, dolls, and celebrity memorabilia.

Fitness Walking

- In 2015, 112 million Americans (ages six and older) walked as a fitness activity – walking ranked at #1 among all types of recreational activities.

Gardening

- Eighty million households, or 70% of all households, engaged in indoor/outdoor lawn and garden activities in 2015 and spent almost $30 billion in these activities.

Going to Movies

- Cinema box office attendance was approximately 1.32 billion in 2015; receipts were about $11 billion.

Going to the Beach

- When given a choice of destinations for leisure travel, 44% of adults pick one of America's 3,500 public beaches – this ranks #1 among all types of travel destinations.

Outdoor Activities in Public Parks

- Americans made more than 307 million visits to National Parks and 739 million visits to State Parks in 2015. Visits to city parks numbered in the trillions.

Reading

- 165 million adults, or 72% of all adults, read at least one book in 2015. Among those who read, the mean number of books read is 12. Women and seniors read the most.

Social Networking

- Among Internet users, 65% of adults and 81% of teens engaged in online social networking in 2015. On any given day, more than 40% of Americans – 128 million people – visit Facebook, the most popular social site.

Travel

- Americans took 1.5 billion trips for leisure in 2015 – spending an estimated $530 billion, which ranks it #1 in spending among all leisure activities. Over 40% of adults traveled on a summer vacation in 2015. Favorite activities for leisure travelers: dining out and shopping.

Watching Television

- Adults and teens spent an average 4.3 hours each day in 2015 watching television, with TV topping all media activities. Few, however, gave TV their undivided attention – three-quarters of viewers multitask while watching – going online, talking on mobile devices, or text messaging while also watching TV.

Other Popular Activities

- Over 40 million people participated in each of the following leisure activities in 2015:
  - Attended a college or professional sports event
  - Attended a fair or festival
  - Attended a music concert
  - Attended the theater/opera/symphony
  - Bicycled
  - Bowled
  - Exercised at a fitness club
  - Fished
  - Hiked and went camping
  - Hunted or went target shooting
  - Played a lottery
  - Played billiards/pool
  - Played video games
  - Visited a casino
  - Visited a museum
  - Visited a theme park

- Visited a zoo or aquarium
- Volunteered

17.3 Favorite Leisure Activities

The Harris Poll (www.theharrispoll.com) asked consumers what were their two or three favorite leisure-time activities. Responses by gender were as follows:

	Total	Female	Male
• Watching TV:	42%	42%	43%
• Reading:	37%	48%	24%
• Computer/Internet:	19%	18%	20%
• Time with family/friends:	18%	23%	13%
• Watching/going to movies:	11%	11%	11%
• Exercise/working out:	10%	10%	10%
• Video/computer games:	10%	8%	13%
• Walking/running/jogging:	8%	10%	7%
• Gardening:	7%	9%	5%
• Concerts/listening to/playing music:	7%	5%	10%
• Hobby-related activities:	5%	4%	5%
• Eating/going to restaurants:	4%	4%	4%
• Cooking/baking:	4%	5%	3%
• Sewing/needlework/quilting:	4%	7%	<1%
• Attending/watching sports events:	4%	2%	6%
• Shopping:	4%	6%	2%
• Sleeping/napping:	3%	4%	3%
• Relaxing/resting:	3%	2%	3%
• Fishing:	3%	2%	5%
• Crafts:	3%	5%	1%
• Swimming:	3%	3%	3%
• Golf:	3%	1%	7%
• Playing with pets:	3%	3%	2%

Responses by age were as follows:

	Total	18-to-36	37-to-48	49-to-67	68+
• Watching TV:	42%	38%	45%	42%	48%
• Reading:	37%	31%	35%	40%	42%
• Computer/Internet:	19%	16%	19%	21%	19%
• Time with family/friends:	18%	19%	19%	17%	20%
• Watching/going to movies:	11%	13%	13%	10%	5%
• Exercise/working out:	10%	13%	12%	7%	6%
• Video/computer games:	10%	16%	10%	8%	6%
• Walking/running/jogging:	8%	5%	11%	11%	7%
• Gardening:	7%	1%	4%	11%	14%
• Concerts/listening to/playing music:	7%	10%	9%	7%	2%

• Hobby-related activities:	5%	3%	1%	6%	9%
• Eating/going to restaurants:	4%	5%	3%	4%	7%
• Cooking/baking:	4%	5%	3%	4%	3%
• Sewing/needlework/quilting:	4%	2%	3%	6%	5%
• Attending/watching sports events:	4%	2%	5%	5%	2%
• Shopping:	4%	5%	7%	3%	2%
• Sleeping/napping:	3%	4%	4%	3%	1%
• Relaxing/resting:	3%	4%	3%	2%	1%
• Fishing:	3%	2%	4%	5%	2%
• Crafts:	3%	3%	3%	3%	4%
• Swimming:	3%	3%	1%	2%	6%
• Golf:	3%	3%	1%	4%	7%
• Playing with pets:	3%	3%	2%	2%	2%

The Harris Poll found that the number of leisure hours Americans have returned to 20 hours per week after dipping during the economic downturn. America's leisure time had fluctuated less than one hour annually between 1987 and 2007, consistently remaining between 19 and 20 hours, but dropped to an all-time low of 16 hours from 2008 through 2011. Leisure time was 20 hours per week for both men and women in 2013.

By age, the median time for leisure in 2013 was as follows:

- 18-to-36: 20 hours per week
- 37-to-48: 18 hours per week
- 49-to-67: 21 hours per week
- 68 and older: 30 hours per week

Among those with children in the household, leisure time averaged 15 hours per week. Those without children at home enjoyed 25 hours per week of leisure time.

17.4 Leisure Activities For Millennials

A survey by Urban Land Institute (www.uli.org) asked Millennials their favorite leisure activities; up to five activities could be listed. Responses were as follows:

	Total	Female	Male
• Watching TV:	56%	54%	58%
• Spending time with family:	48%	57%	38%
• Spending time with friends:	42%	43%	41%
• Listening to/playing music:	41%	39%	43%
• Reading:	38%	47%	29%
• Playing computer/video games:	32%	21%	42%
• Online social networking:	30%	33%	28%
• Cooking:	22%	29%	16%
• Exercise/go to the gym/indoor sports:	21%	17%	25%
• Shop in stores:	18%	24%	11%
• Shop online:	18%	21%	16%

17.5 Leisure Time For Seniors

The *American Time Use Survey* investigated leisure activities of Seniors, finding that this group spends their leisure time much differently than Seniors in years past.

> **"While individual retirees are probably as different as snowflakes, a deep dive into the demographic statistics of retirement shows that broader trends are shaping how retirees seek to enjoy the luxury of time – trends that confirm some popular assumptions about retirement while contradicting others."**
>
> *The New York Times*

The following is a summary of the ATUS leisure assessment for Seniors:

- Of the 42 million Americans age 65 or above, 18.7% remain in the labor force, a sharp increase from 13.9% a decade ago. Americans over age 65 who were still employed typically worked 6¼ hours a day.
- People over 65 devoted 6 hours and 40 minutes a day to socializing, relaxing, and at leisure – 2 hours and 45 minutes more than those ages 25-to-54.
- Forty-three percent (43%) of those over 65 read regularly for personal interest, devoting nearly two hours a day to reading. In contrast, only 15% of those ages 25 to 54 read regularly for personal interest, devoting about 80 minutes a day.
- About 20% of Americans over 65 said they participated in sports or performed other exercise regularly, about 90 minutes each occasion. Only 1.6% of Americans older than 65 played golf regularly, devoting 4 hours and 20 minutes on average to the sport on the days they played. Slightly more popular is running or walking on a treadmill or using other cardiovascular equipment – men for 30 minutes on average and women for 45 minutes.
- Almost 90% of older Americans said they regularly watched TV and movies at home, on average for 4 hours and 40 minutes a day. That compares with 3 hours and 10 minutes for Americans ages 25-to-54.
- Eleven percent (11%) of those 65 and over said they regularly played non-computer games, like bridge or Scrabble, averaging 1 hour and 52 minutes of play.

17.6 Vacations

PhoCusWright (www.phocuswright.com), a travel industry research firm, found that 65% of U.S. adults travel for leisure each year. The Harris Poll (www.theharrispoll.com) reported a similar finding, that 66% of U.S. adults plan at least one leisure summer trip each year.

Not taking time off burns people out and can wreak havoc on productivity. Vacation deprivation is one reason workers are reporting more mistakes, anger, and resentment at co-workers, according to the Families & Work Institute (www.familiesandwork.org), which recently found that those who vacationed experienced an 82% increase in job performance post-trip.

The now-popular micro-vacations – taking two or three days off – do not deliver the same stress-reduction benefits as vacations that last one and two weeks, research shows. Experts agree that a key ingredient in peak performance is a drastic change of scenery, coupled with shutting down for extended periods of time.

Vacations are also about health: At least two studies have correlated the stress-reducing benefits of annual vacations with lower rates of coronary heart disease.

"Research shows that vacations can reduce the risk of heart disease, depression, and a host of other ills, and even slow the aging process."

Condé Nast Traveler

17.7 Market Resources

American Time Use Survey - 2016 Results, Bureau of Labor Statistics, June 2016. (www.bls.gov/news.release/atus.nr0.htm)

Leisure Business Market Research Handbook 2017-2018, Richard K. Miller & Associates, September 2016. (www.rkma.com/report-detail.cfm?report_id=131)

18

SPORTS & RECREATION ACTIVITIES

18.1 Conditioning and Fitness

The *2015 Sports, Fitness And Leisure Activities Topline Participation Report*, published by the Sports & Fitness Industry Association (SFIA, www.sfia.org), reports total participation (at least once) and core participation (50 or more times) in conditioning and fitness activities among those ages six and older as follows (change from previous year in parenthesis):

	Total	Core
• Abdominal machine/device:	19.1 million (3.4%)	10.8 million (3.1%)
• Aerobics (high impact):	19.7 million (14.0%)	9.5 million (14.0%)
• Aquatic exercise:	9.1 million (7.5%)	3.2 million (0.6%)
• Barre:	3.2 million (10.3%)	638,000 (2.0%)
• Boot camp style cross-training:	6.8 million (-2.0%)	2.3 million (-3.2%)
• Calisthenics/bodyweight exercise:	22.4 million (n/a)	13.4 million (n/a)
• Cardio cross trainer:	7.5 million (37.8%)	3.2 million (18.9%)
• Cardio kickboxing:	6.7 million (6.9%)	2.2 million (-1.5%)
• Cross-training style workouts:	11.3 million (n/a)	5.6 million (n/a)
• Dance/other exercise to music:	21.5 million (n/a)	7.5 million (n/a)
• Elliptical motion trainer:	28.0 million (3.3%)	14.3 million (4.7%)
• Free weights (barbells):	25.6 million (-0.1%)	16.0 million (-0.3%)
• Free weights (dumbbells):	30.8 million (-4.5%)	19.1 million (-7.2%)
• Free weights (hand weights):	41.7 million (-3.5%)	24.8 million (-3.3%)
• Kettlebells:	10.2 million (n/a)	4.3 million (n/a)
• Pilates training:	8.5 million (5.4%)	3.4 million (2.6%)
• Rowing machine:	9.8 million (-3.6%)	4.2 million (-4.7%)
• Running/jogging:	51.1 million (-5.6%)	28.0 million (-6.0%)
• Stair climbing machine:	13.2 million (4.5%)	5.5 million (4.9%)
• Stationary cycling (group):	8.4 million (1.7%)	3.1 million (1.3%)
• Stationary cycling (upright/recumb.):	35.7 million (1.3%)	17.4 million (3.0%)
• Stretching:	35.6 million (-1.6%)	26.0 million (-1.7%)
• Swimming (fitness/competition):	25.3 million (-4.0%)	8.8 million (-6.3%)
• Tai Chi:	3.4 million (-0.7%)	1.4 million (-3.9%)
• Treadmill:	50.2 million (4.3%)	27.7 million (4.9%)
• Walking for fitness:	112.6 million (-4.1%)	76.9 million (-3.7%)
• Weight/resistance machine:	35.8 million (-1.2%)	21.2 million (-0.7%)
• Yoga:	25.3 million (3.9%)	10.4 million (2.7%)

18.2 Individual Sports

Total participation (at least once) and core participation (varies by sport) in individual sports were as follows (change from previous year in parenthesis):

	Total	Core #	Core Participation
• Adventure racing:	2.4 million (13.0%)	2+	1.3 million (14.3%)
• Archery:	8.4 million (10.3%)	26+	1.4 million (8.0%)
• Bowling:	46.6 million (0.9%)	13+	10.5 million (0.5%)
• Boxing for competition:	1.3 million (12.7%)	13+	204,000 (34.2%)
• Boxing for fitness:	5.1 million (-2.6%)	13+	2.7 million (-1.4%)
• Golf:	24.7 million (-0.1%)	-	n/a
• Ice skating:	10.6 million (-0.3%)	13+	1.7 million (5.3%)
• Martial arts:	5.3 million (0.9%)	13+	3.7 million (-0.4%)
• Mixed martial arts (comp.):	1.2 million (26.4%)	13+	257,000 (19.5%)
• Mixed martial arts (fitness):	2.5 million (8.8%)	13+	1.2 million (13.0%)
• Roller skating (2x2 wheels):	6.9 million (4.8%)	13+	1.3 million (-3.0%)
• Roller skating (inline):	6.1 million (-1.1%)	13+	1.9 million (-0.7%)
• Skateboarding:	6.5 million (3.7%)	26+	2.7 million (2.0%)
• Trail running:	7.5 million (10.9%)	-	n/a
• Triathlon (off-road):	1.4 million (1.5%)	2+	921,000 (-5.3%)
• Triathlon (traditional/road):	2.2 million (-2.6%)	2+	1.4 million (-5.4%)

18.3 Racquet Sports

Total participation (at least once) and core participation (varies by sport) in racquet sports were as follows (change from previous year in parenthesis):

	Total	Core #	Core Participation
• Badminton:	7.2 million (0.4%)	13+	2.1 million (-8.2%)
• Cardio tennis:	1.6 million (5.0%)	-	n/a
• Racquetball:	3.6 million (-6.0%)	13+	1.2 million (-7.6%)
• Squash:	1.6 million (12.9%)	8+	388,000 (16.7%)
• Table tennis:	16.4 million (-4.1%)	13+	4.6 million (-3.4%)
• Tennis:	17.9 million (1.3%)	-	n/a

18.4 Team Sports

Total participation (at least once) and core participation (varies by sport) in team sports were as follows (change from previous year in parenthesis):

	Total	Core #	Core Participation
• Baseball:	13.1 million (-1.0%)	13+	8.9 million (-2.5%)
• Basketball:	23.1 million (-2.5%)	13+	15.7 million (-5.5%)
• Cheerleading:	3.4 million (6.8%)	26+	1.6 million (3.1%)
• Field hockey:	1.6 million (5.6%)	8+	764,000 (2.3%)
• Football (touch):	6.5 million (-7.8%)	13+	2.8 million (-10.3%)

Football (flag):	5.8 million (-1.8%)	13+	2.6 million (-4.6%)
Football (tackle):	5.9 million (-3.0%)	26+	3.4 million (-4.9%)
Swimming (team):	2.7 million (4.1%)	50+	1.4 million (-1.4%)
Gymnastics:	4.6 million (-7.1%)	50+	1.7 million (-4.2%)
Ice hockey:	2.4 million (1.2%)	13+	1.3 million (-0.6%)
Lacrosse:	2.0 million (11.9%)	13+	1.0 million (12.3%)
Paintball:	3.4 million (-4.2%)	8+	996,000 (-5.0%)
Roller hockey:	1.7 million (33.7%)	13+	555,000 (21.3%)
Rugby:	1.7 million (7.9%)	8+	440,000 (3.0%)
Soccer (indoor):	4.5 million (-5.7%)	13+	2.6 million (-7.8%)
Soccer (outdoor):	12.6 million (-1.1%)	26+	6.0 million (-3.6%)
Softball (fast pitch):	2.4 million (-3.0%)	26+	1.3 million (-8.3%)
Softball (slow pitch):	7.1 million (3.0%)	13+	4.3 million (1.7%)
Track and field:	4.1 million (0.8%)	26+	2.3 million (2.0%)
Ultimate frisbee:	4.5 million (-10.8%)	13+	1.1 million (-20.6%)
Volleyball (beach):	4.6 million (-2.5%)	13+	1.5 million (-2.1%)
Volleyball (court):	6.3 million (-2.0%)	13+	3.5 million (-4.7%)
Volleyball (grass):	3.9 million (-4.6%)	13+	1.0 million (-2.9%)
Wrestling:	1.9 million (3.4%)	26+	950,000 (7.8%)

18.5 Outdoor Sports

Total participation (at least once) and core participation (8 or more times) in outdoor sports were as follows (change from previous year in parenthesis):

	Total	Core #	Core Participation
Backpacking (overnight):	10.1 million (11.4%)	-	n/a
Bicycling - BMX:	2.3 million (8.4%)	13+	1.1 million (10.2%)
Bicycling - mountain:	8.0 million (-5.8%)	13+	4.3 million (-9.5%)
Bicycling - road/paved:	39.7 million (-2.8%)	26+	20.5 million (-4.5%)
Birdwatching (>¼ mile):	13.2 million (-6.9%)	-	n/a
Camping (<¼ mile):	28.7 million (-2.1%)	-	n/a
Camping (RV):	14.6 million (0.5%)	8+	7.6 million (13.5%)
Climbing (sport/indoor):	4.5 million (-4.4%)	-	n/a
Climbing (traditional):	2.5 million (5.9%)	-	n/a
Fishing (fly):	5.8 million (-0.6%)	8+	2.2 million (4.1%)
Fishing (freshwater):	37.8 million (0.1%)	8+	18.0 million (1.4%)
Fishing (saltwater):	11.8 million (0.2%)	8+	4.8 million (1.9%)
Hiking (day):	36.2 million (5.4%)	-	n/a
Hunting (bow):	4.4 million (8.2%)	8+	2.1 million (12.2%)
Hunting (handgun):	3.1 million (-3.4%)	8+	1.1 million (-0.7%)
Hunting (rifle):	10.1 million (2.9%)	13+	2.8 million (2.2%)
Hunting (shotgun):	8.2 million (4.1%)	8+	3.4 million (11.1%)
Shooting (sport clays):	4.6 million (3.7%)	8+	1.5 million (4.0%)
Shooting (trap/skeet):	3.8 million (1.4%)	8+	1.4 million (5.7%)

• Target shooting (handgun):	14.4 million (0.4%)	8+	8.0 million (-0.2%)
• Target shooting (rifle):	13.9 million (0.1%)	8+	5.4 million (0.5%)
• Wildlife viewing (>¼ mile):	21.1 million (-1.2%)	-	n/a

18.6 Water Sports

Total participation (at least once) and core participation (8 or more times) in water sports were as follows (change from previous year in parenthesis):

	Total	Core
• Boardsailing/windsurfing:	1.6 million (18.0%)	285,000 (21.8%)
• Canoeing:	10.0 million (-1.1%)	n/a
• Jet skiing:	6.4 million (-0.9%)	1.8 million (-9.8%)
• Kayaking (recreational):	8.9 million (1.6%)	n/a
• Kayaking (sea touring):	2.9 million (8.1%)	n/a
• Kayaking (white water):	2.3 million (9.6%)	n/a
• Rafting:	3.8 million (-1.4%)	n/a
• Sailing:	3.9 million (0.2%)	1.2 million (-0.6%)
• Scuba diving:	3.1 million (-0.9%)	893,000 (8.5%)
• Snorkeling:	8.8 million (0.6%)	1.8 million (0.6%)
• Stand-up paddling:	2.8 million (38.1%)	n/a
• Surfing:	2.7 million (2.4%)	1.1 million (4.5%)
• Wakeboarding:	3.1 million (-5.8%)	926,000 (-8.4%)
• Water skiing:	4.0 million (-4.7%)	1.1 million (-3.3%)

18.7 Market Resources

Sports & Fitness Industry Association (SFIA), 8505 Fenton Street, Suite 211, Silver Spring, MD 20910. (301) 495-6321. (www.sfia.org)

19

AWAY FROM HOME

19.1 Overview

According to Nielsen (www.nielsen.com), the following are percentages of the U.S. population (age 12 and older) that visit various venues each month:

	Pct.	Number
• Airports:	21%	54 million
• Bars:	29%	65 million
• Coffeehouses or sandwich shops:	50%	130 million
• Convenience stores:	72%	187 million
• Drug stores:	69%	179 million
• Fast food or casual dining restaurants:	79%	204 million
• Gas stations:	88%	227 million
• Grocery stores:	90%	232 million
• Health clubs:	22%	86 million
• Large retail or department stores:	72%	186 million
• Movie theaters:	41%	107 million
• Public transportation (bus, taxicab, train):	27%	69 million
• Shopping malls:	65%	169 million
• Stadiums and arenas:	20%	51 million

The following sections provide a demographic profile of visitors to each of these outlets. (note: Education and Household Composition categories are based on adults ages 18 and older; other categories are based on those ages 12 and older.)

19.2 Airports

Gender

- Female: 45%
- Male: 55%

Age

- 12-to-17: 11%
- 18-to-24: 9%
- 25-to-34: 22%
- 35-to-44: 17%

- 45-to-54: 20%
- 55-to-64: 14%
- 65 and older: 8%

Race/Ethnicity
- African American: 14%
- Asian American/other: 10%
- Caucasian: 59%
- Hispanic: 17%

Annual Household Income
- Under $25,000: 11%
- $25,000 to $49,999: 16%
- $50,000 to $99,999: 46%
- $100,000 and above: 27%

Education
- Four-year college degree or higher: 63%

Household Composition
- Have children under age 18 living at home: 34%

19.3 Bars

Gender
- Female: 33%
- Male: 67%

Age
- 12-to-20: n/a
- 21-to-24: 21%
- 25-to-34: 26%
- 35-to-44: 26%
- 45-to-54: 13%
- 55-to-64: 9%
- 65 and older: 5%

Race/Ethnicity
- African American: 11%
- Asian American/other: 8%
- Caucasian: 62%
- Hispanic: 19%

Annual Household Income

- Under $25,000: 23%
- $25,000 to $49,999: 28%
- $50,000 to $99,999: 37%
- $100,000 and above: 14%

Education

- Four-year college degree or higher: 51%

Household Composition

- Have children under age 18 living at home: 39%

19.4 Coffeehouses And Sandwich Shops

Gender

- Female: 47%
- Male: 53%

Age

- 12-to-17: 14%
- 18-to-24: 16%
- 25-to-34: 20%
- 35-to-44: 19%
- 45-to-54: 13%
- 55-to-64: 12%
- 65 and older: 6%

Race/Ethnicity

- African American: 19%
- Asian American/other: 9%
- Caucasian: 55%
- Hispanic: 17%

Annual Household Income

- Under $25,000: 24%
- $25,000 to $49,999: 21%
- $50,000 to $99,999: 33%
- $100,000 and above: 22%

Education

- Four-year college degree or higher: 46%

Household Composition

- Have children under age 18 living at home: 44%

19.5 Convenience Stores

Gender

- Female: 43%
- Male: 57%

Age

- 12-to-17: 17%
- 18-to-24: 14%
- 25-to-34: 18%
- 35-to-44: 22%
- 45-to-54: 14%
- 55-to-64: 10%
- 65 and older: 6%

Race/Ethnicity

- African American: 16%
- Asian American/other: 6%
- Caucasian: 59%
- Hispanic: 17%

Annual Household Income

- Under $25,000: 29%
- $25,000 to $49,999: 26%
- $50,000 to $99,999: 33%
- $100,000 and above: 13%

Education

- Four-year college degree or higher: 41%

Household Composition

- Have children under age 18 living at home: 51%

19.6 Drug Stores

Gender

- Female: 54%
- Male: 46%

Age

- 12-to-17: 10%
- 18-to-24: 16%
- 25-to-34: 19%
- 35-to-44: 15%
- 45-to-54: 18%
- 55-to-64: 11%
- 65 and older: 11%

Race/Ethnicity

- African American: 19%
- Asian American/other: 4%
- Caucasian: 59%
- Hispanic: 18%

Annual Household Income

- Under $25,000: 29%
- $25,000 to $49,999: 28%
- $50,000 to $99,999: 30%
- $100,000 and above: 13%

Education

- Four-year college degree or higher: 43%

Household Composition

- Have children under age 18 living at home: 43%

19.7 Fast Food And Casual Dining Restaurants

Gender

- Female: 44%
- Male: 56%

Age

- 12-to-17: 13%
- 18-to-24: 15%
- 25-to-34: 17%
- 35-to-44: 19%
- 45-to-54: 16%
- 55-to-64: 11%
- 65 and older: 10%

Race/Ethnicity

- African American: 19%
- Asian American/other: 7%
- Caucasian: 60%
- Hispanic: 15%

Annual Household Income

- Under $25,000: 27%
- $25,000 to $49,999: 26%
- $50,000 to $99,999: 29%
- $100,000 and above: 17%

Education

- Four-year college degree or higher: 40%

Household Composition

- Have children under age 18 living at home: 42%

19.8 Gas Stations

Gender

- Female: 46%
- Male: 54%

Age

- 12-to-17: 13%
- 18-to-24: 13%
- 25-to-34: 18%
- 35-to-44: 21%
- 45-to-54: 19%
- 55-to-64: 10%
- 65 and older: 6%

Race/Ethnicity

- African American: 18%
- Asian American/other: 7%
- Caucasian: 59%
- Hispanic: 17%

Annual Household Income

- Under $25,000: 19%
- $25,000 to $49,999: 26%

- $50,000 to $99,999: 33%
- $100,000 and above: 22%

Education
- Four-year college degree or higher: 46%

Household Composition
- Have children under age 18 living at home: 50%

19.9 Grocery Stores

Gender
- Female: 49%
- Male: 51%

Age
- 12-to-17: 12%
- 18-to-24: 14%
- 25-to-34: 17%
- 35-to-44: 19%
- 45-to-54: 17%
- 55-to-64: 10%
- 65 and older: 11%

Race/Ethnicity
- African American: 14%
- Asian American/other: 8%
- Caucasian: 64%
- Hispanic: 14%

Annual Household Income
- Under $25,000: 26%
- $25,000 to $49,999: 29%
- $50,000 to $99,999: 30%
- $100,000 and above: 15%

Education
- Four-year college degree or higher: 40%

Household Composition
- Have children under age 18 living at home: 44%

19.10 Health Clubs

Gender

• Female:	51%
• Male:	49%

Age

• 12-to-17:	13%
• 18-to-24:	21%
• 25-to-34:	17%
• 35-to-44:	19%
• 45-to-54:	15%
• 55-to-64:	10%
• 65 and older:	7%

Race/Ethnicity

• African American:	12%
• Asian American/other:	10%
• Caucasian:	63%
• Hispanic:	15%

Annual Household Income

• Under $25,000:	9%
• $25,000 to $49,999:	16%
• $50,000 to $99,999:	47%
• $100,000 and above:	28%

Education

• Four-year college degree or higher:	67%

Household Composition

• Have children under age 18 living at home:	36%

19.11 Large Retail or Department Stores

Gender

• Female:	46%
• Male:	54%

Age

• 12-to-17:	11%
• 18-to-24:	16%
• 25-to-34:	16%

- 35-to-44: 22%
- 45-to-54: 16%
- 55-to-64: 9%
- 65 and older: 10%

Race/Ethnicity
- African American: 15%
- Asian American/other: 6%
- Caucasian: 65%
- Hispanic: 14%

Annual Household Income
- Under $25,000: 21%
- $25,000 to $49,999: 30%
- $50,000 to $99,999: 33%
- $100,000 and above: 17%

Education
- Four-year college degree or higher: 41%

Household Composition
- Have children under age 18 living at home: 42%

19.12 Movie Theaters

Gender
- Female: 46%
- Male: 54%

Age
- 12-to-17: 21%
- 18-to-24: 18%
- 25-to-34: 21%
- 35-to-44: 16%
- 45-to-54: 12%
- 55-to-64: 9%
- 65 and older: 4%

Race/Ethnicity
- African American: 15%
- Asian American/other: 8%
- Caucasian: 62%
- Hispanic: 15%

Annual Household Income

- Under $25,000: 19%
- $25,000 to $49,999: 27%
- $50,000 to $99,999: 39%
- $100,000 and above: 15%

Education

- Four-year college degree or higher: 50%

Household Composition

- Have children under age 18 living at home: 42%

19.13 Public Transportation (bus, taxicab, train)

Gender

- Female: 48%
- Male: 52%

Age

- 12-to-17: 4%
- 18-to-24: 20%
- 25-to-34: 23%
- 35-to-44: 17%
- 45-to-54: 17%
- 55-to-64: 11%
- 65 and older: 8%

Race/Ethnicity

- African American: 20%
- Asian American/other: 12%
- Caucasian: 50%
- Hispanic: 18%

Annual Household Income

- Under $25,000: 23%
- $25,000 to $49,999: 26%
- $50,000 to $99,999: 30%
- $100,000 and above: 21%

Education

- Four-year college degree or higher: 43%

Household Composition

- Have children under age 18 living at home: 43%

19.14 Shopping Malls

Gender

- Female: 47%
- Male: 53%

Age

- 12-to-17: 16%
- 18-to-24: 18%
- 25-to-34: 15%
- 35-to-44: 20%
- 45-to-54: 14%
- 55-to-64: 8%
- 65 and older: 9%

Race/Ethnicity

- African American: 20%
- Asian American/other: 7%
- Caucasian: 56%
- Hispanic: 17%

Annual Household Income

- Under $25,000: 23%
- $25,000 to $49,999: 25%
- $50,000 to $99,999: 33%
- $100,000 and above: 19%

Education

- Four-year college degree or higher: 43%

Household Composition

- Have children under age 18 living at home: 44%

19.15 Stadiums And Arenas

Gender

- Female: 41%
- Male: 59%

Age

- 12-to-17: 16%
- 18-to-24: 18%
- 25-to-34: 20%
- 35-to-44: 20%
- 45-to-54: 15%
- 55-to-64: 7%
- 65 and older: 5%

Race/Ethnicity

- African American: 11%
- Asian American/other: 10%
- Caucasian: 71%
- Hispanic: 8%

Annual Household Income

- Under $25,000: 14%
- $25,000 to $49,999: 26%
- $50,000 to $99,999: 35%
- $100,000 and above: 25%

Education

- Four-year college degree or higher: 56%

Household Composition

- Have children under age 18 living at home: 33%

20

WORK

20.1 The American Workforce

As of May 2016, the U.S. workforce count (ages 16 and older) was 151.03 million, according to the Bureau of Labor Statistics (www.bls.gov). By type of occupation, the workforce was as follows:

• Professional and related occupations:	34.71 million
• Sales and office occupations:	33.23 million
• Service occupations:	26.93 million
• Management, business, and financial operations occupations:	24.91 million
• Production, transportation, and material moving occupations:	17.87 million
• Natural resources, construction, and maintenance:	13.94 million

Ten occupations account for 21% of American workers. These occupations, ranked by number employed, are as follows (source: *Employment By Detailed Occupation*, BLS, April 2016):

• Retail salesperson:	4.62 million
• Secretary:	3.98 million
• Building cleaning workers:	3.84 million
• Laborer:	3.59 million
• Cashier:	3.43 million
• Food prep worker:	3.16 million
• Office clerk:	3.06 million
• Registered nurse:	2.75 million
• Customer service rep:	2.58 million
• Waitstaff:	2.46 million

Ranked by BLS's projected 2014-2024 job growth, the following are the fastest-growing occupations (source: *Fastest Growing Occupations*, April 2016)

	Growth	Median Annual Pay
• Wind turbine service technicians:	108.0%	$51,050
• Occupational therapy assistants:	42.7%	$57,870
• Physical therapist assistants:	40.6%	$55,170
• Physical therapist aides:	39.0%	$25,120
• Home health aides:	38.1%	$21,920
• Commercial divers:	36.9%	$50,470
• Nurse practitioners:	35.2%	$98,190
• Physical therapists:	34.0%	$84,020

• Statisticians:	33.8%	$80,110
• Ambulance drivers and attendants:	33.0%	$23,740

Median weekly earnings of the nation's 109.1 million full-time wage and salary workers were $830 in the first quarter of 2016. Median weekly earnings for men and women were $912 and $750, respectively, for men and women.

The federal minimum wage is $7.25 per hour. Nationally, 3.3 million workers are paid minimum wage or less. The following is a profile of minimum-wage workers:

- Percent who work full-time: 35.5%
- Percent with college experience: 42.2%
- Percent who live in the South: 46.4%
- Percent food prep workers: 46.7%
- Percent ages 25 or older: 49.6%

In 2015, 15.0 million people, or 10.1% of total U.S. workers, were self-employed. The self-employment rate – the proportion of total employment made up of self-employed workers – has trended down over the past two decades. In 1994, the self-employment rate was 12.1%.

20.2 Time Spent Working

The *American Time Use Survey* (*ATUS*, www.bls.gov/tus/), published by the Bureau of Labor Statistics (BLS) and assessed in Chapter 14 of this handbook, reported that 44% of adults of all ages worked. Those who worked spent an average of 8.03 hours per week working or engaged in work-related activities.

ATUS, published in June 2016, provided the following profile of workers:

- Employed persons worked an average of 7.6 hours on the days they worked.
- More hours were worked, on average, on weekdays than on weekend days, 8.0 hours compared with 5.6 hours.
- Far more people worked on weekdays than on weekend days: 83% of employed persons worked on an average weekday, compared with 34% on an average weekend day.
- On the days they worked, employed men worked 42 minutes more than employed women. This difference partly reflects women's greater likelihood of working part time. However, even among full-time workers (those usually working 35 hours or more per week), men worked longer than women, 8.2 hours compared with 7.8 hours.
- On the days they worked, 82% of employed persons did some or all of their work at their workplace, and 24% did some or all of their work at home. Workers spent more time working at the workplace than at home, 8.0 hours compared with 3.2 hours.
- Multiple jobholders were more likely to work on an average day than were single jobholders, 80% compared with 67%.
- Multiple jobholders also were more likely to work at home than were single

jobholders, 36% compared with 23%.

- Self-employed workers were nearly three times more likely than wage and salary workers to have done some work at home on days worked, 56% compared with 20%.
- Self-employed workers also were more likely to work on weekend days than were wage and salary workers, 43% compared with 31%.
- On the days they worked, 36% of employed people age 25 and over with a bachelor's degree or higher did some work at home, compared with only 7% of those with less than a high school diploma.

20.3 Job Satisfaction

Annual surveys by Gallup (www.gallup.com) ask working people about satisfaction with their job. In 2015, responses were as follows:

- Completely satisfied: 44%
- Somewhat satisfied: 42%
- Somewhat dissatisfied: 9%
- Completely dissatisfied: 4%

The percentages of workers somewhat or completely satisfied with their jobs has been as follows:

- 2005: 86%
- 2006: 90%
- 2007: 94%
- 2008: 90%
- 2009: 87%
- 2010: 87%
- 2011: 83%
- 2012: 89%
- 2013: 85%
- 2014: 89%
- 2015: 86%

Survey participants in August 2015 said they were satisfied with various aspects of their job as follows:

- Relations with coworkers: 92%
- Physical safety of workplace: 90%
- Job security: 84%
- Boss or immediate supervisor: 83%
- Flexibility of hours: 83%
- Amount of work required: 82%
- Amount of vacation time: 77%
- Recognition for work accomplishments: 76%
- Chances for promotion: 71%
- Compensation: 69%
- Health insurance benefits: 66%
- On-the-job stress: 63%
- Retirement plan: 62%

20.4 Workplace Flexibility

A survey by The Harris Poll (www.theharrispoll.com) assessed working adults on their perceptions and preferences around several work/life and flexibility issues. Findings were as follows:

- Seventy-five percent (75%) of working adults reported having "at least a little" flexibility at work.
- Seventy-three percent (73%) of working adults said that flexibility is one of the most important factors they consider when looking for a new job or deciding what company to work for.
- Sixty-eight percent (68%) of working adults agree that their company would be willing to accommodate them if they requested a flexible work schedule due to reasons like family care, personal work preferences, health issues, etc.
- Eighty percent (80%) of working adults agree that flexible work options are just as important for people who don't have children as they are for those who do, and interestingly, there is no significant difference in opinion between women (69%) and men (66%).
- When asked if they would be willing to give up a portion of their salary for more flexibility at work, 45% of working adults said they would be willing to relinquish at least some portion of their salary.
- Seventy-three percent (73%) of working adults believe it is possible to "have it all" when it comes to work/life balance.
- Thirty-nine percent (39%) of working adults say that they have considered leaving or have left a job because it wasn't flexible enough.

20.5 Working At Home

According to a recent study published in the *American Sociological Review*, nearly half of American workers bring work home with them regularly.

The U.S. Bureau of Labor Statistics estimates that 4.2 million adults are home-workers; about 65% of these people work full-time at home. Fifty-eight percent (58%) of stay-at-home-workers run their own business and 35% telecommute, working for private companies or nonprofits located elsewhere.

"As communication and information technologies advance, we are seeing that workers are increasingly able to perform work at home."

Peter J. Mateyka, Survey Statistician
U.S. Census Bureau

People who work exclusively from home have a median household income of $74,000, compared with $65,600 for on-site workers. Those who work both on-site and from home earn an average of $96,300.

Metropolitan areas in the southeast, southwest, and west have the largest share of home-workers, according to the Census Bureau. The following are the metropolitan areas with the highest share of people who work from home:

- Boulder, CO: 10.9%
- Medford, OR: 8.4%
- Santa Fe, NM: 8.3%
- Kingston, NY: 8.1%
- Santa Rosa, CA: 7.9%
- Mankato, MN: 7.7%
- Prescott, AZ: 7.6%
- St. Cloud, MN: 7.6%
- Athens, GA: 7.5%
- Austin, TX: 7.3%

The Harris Poll surveyed employed adults about working at home. Thirty-four percent (34%) said they worked at home at least part of the time. The extent of working at home was as follows:

- Work at home: 34%
  - Work primarily or exclusively from home: 9%
  - Spend about half of working time at home: 8%
  - Less than half my time working from home: 17%
- Do not currently work from home at all: 66%

Participants in the Harris Poll had the following opinions about working at home (multiple responses allowed):

- Working from home provides flexibility: 90%
- Working from home enables employees to balance work and family needs: 85%
- Working together in an office setting adds to team camaraderie: 84%
- Some of the best ideas and/or decisions can result from impromptu, in-person meetings and discussions: 83%
- The option of working from home is a significant job perk: 83%
- Working in an office setting improves communication/collaboration: 81%
- Working from home increases productivity and work output: 64%
- The option to telecommute has/would have an impact on my decision to take or stay at a job: 61%
- Working from home hurts speed and work quality: 35%

20.6 Market Resources

Bureau of Labor Statistics, U.S. Department of Labor, 2 Massachusetts Avenue NE, Washington, DC 20212. (202) 691-5200. (www.bls.gov)

Occupational Employment and Wages, Bureau of Labor Statistics. (www.bls.gov/oes/)

Work and The Workplace, Gallup. (www.gallup.com/poll/1720/work-work-place.aspx)

21

USE OF TECHNOLOGY

21.1 Market Assessment

The Consumer Technology Association (CTA; www.cta.tech) estimates the total retail consumer electronics (CE) market in 2016 at $287 billion, with wholesale revenue at $224 billion.

21.2 Technology Device Ownership

Digital Democracy Survey (2016 Edition), published annually by Deloitte (www.deloitte.com) since 2007, reported household ownership of technology products, by age, and devices as follows:

	14-18	19-25	26-32	33-49	50-68	69+	All HH
• Flat panel television:	80%	72%	81%	88%	87%	85%	84%
• Laptop computer:	90%	88%	84%	84%	80%	62%	82%
• Smartphone:	89%	84%	87%	78%	63%	53%	74%
• Desktop computer:	76%	57%	59%	68%	65%	77%	66%
• Tablet:	69%	62%	69%	59%	46%	44%	56%
• Gaming console:	80%	73%	72%	66%	32%	11%	54%
• Digital video recorder:	51%	36%	49%	57%	49%	50%	50%
• Streaming media box:	31%	28%	38%	27%	15%	10%	24%
• Fitness band:	17%	14%	27%	19%	8%	7%	15%
• Digital TV antenna:	13%	11%	14%	14%	15%	19%	14%
• Smart watch:	7%	8%	15%	9%	3%	1%	7%
• Virtual reality headset:	5%	6%	10%	4%	1%	0%	4%
• Drone:	2%	5%	7%	3%	2%	0%	3%

Technology Device Ownership: 2015, by Pew Research Center for Internet, Science & Technology (www.pewinternet.org), reported technology device ownership as follows:

	Millennials	All Adults
• Cellphone or smartphone:	98%	92%
• Desktop/laptop computer:	78%	73%
• Smartphone:	86%	68%
• Tablet computer:	50%	45%
• MP3 player:	51%	40%
• Game console:	56%	40%
• E-book reader:	18%	19%

21.3 Consumer Use Of CE Products

The *18th Annual Household CE Ownership and Market Potential Study*, published in April 2016 by the CTA, reported the technology devices experiencing the largest increase in household ownership from 2015 to 2016 include portable wireless speakers (up 10 percentage points to reach 35% household ownership); wearable fitness activity trackers (up 9 percentage points to 20% ownership); wireless headphones (up 9 percentage points to 36% ownership); and smart TVs (up 7 percentage points to 50% ownership).

The Internet-of-Things (IoT) continues to drive growth in emerging tech devices. Among the fastest-growing tech categories, wearable fitness activity trackers are now owned by 20% of U.S. households, almost double the number of households that owned the technology in 2015. Another 15% of households plan to purchase a device in 2016. Smart home devices (smart thermostats, lighting controls, motion sensors, etc.), led by smart thermostats, are now owned in 15% of households. Additionally, 8% of households currently own a smartwatch and another 8% are planning to buy one in 2016.

The following are the most-owned tech products in 2016:

Televisions

- Owned in 96% of households, market penetration is down by one percentage point from 2015. There are now almost as many TVs owned (320 million installed base) as the U.S. population (321 million). Twenty-two percent (22%) of consumers say they never intend to buy a TV, an increase from 18% in 2015. This is likely due to diffusion of video consumption across multiple device screens.

DVD/Blu-ray Players

- Owned by 77% of households, DVD/Blu-ray players are the second-most popular device, but ownership has experienced a downward trend over the last five years.

Smartphones

- Owned by 74% of U.S. households, smartphone ownership is up two percentage points from 2015. On average, Americans now own 2.4 smartphones per household, and the expected smartphone repeat purchase is 91%, comparable only to television ownership trends.

Laptop/Notebooks

- U.S. household penetration of laptops or notebooks is 68%, the same as in 2015.

Headphones

- Sixty-three percent (63%) of U.S. households own at least one pair of headphones, which replaced digital cameras in 2016 as the fifth-most owned tech device.

21.4 Category Assessment

CTA assesses consumer technology categories as follows:

3D Printing

- An expanding diversity of 3D printing capabilities will drive the sector's growth in 2016. CTA expects 3D printer sales to increase 64% from 2015, to reach 179,000 units sold, with total revenues of $152 million, a 38% increase.

Drones

- CTA expects U.S. sales of drones weighing more than 250 grams – the minimum for FAA-mandated registration – to reach one million units in 2016, a 145% increase from 2015's total. When adding drones weighing 250 grams or less to those totals, the total forecast for 2016 drone sales tops 2.8 million units (up 149% from 2015) and $953 million in shipment revenues (a 115% increase from 2015).

Laptops

- Unit shipments of traditional laptops are estimated to reach 27.6 million units in 2016, a 2% increase over 2015. Increasing sales of 2-in-1 computers (including both convertible laptops and detachable tablets) will drive this category's growth, with 11.7 million units sold in 2016 (48% growth over 2015) and $8 billion in revenue.

Smart Home

- CTA expects the smart home technology category – including smart thermostats, smart smoke and CO2 detectors, IP/Wi-Fi cameras, smart locks, smart home systems, and smart switches, dimmers and outlets – to reach 8.9 million units sold in 2016 (a 21% increase), with $1.2 billion in revenue.

Smartphones

- As the dominant sales category in the industry, smartphone unit shipments are projected to reach 183 million this year, up 5% from 2015. Smartphone revenues will reach $55 billion in 2016, a 4% increase from 2015.

Tablets

- After significant growth and wide adoption over the past five years, tablet sales will continue to decline in 2016. CTA projects unit sales to reach 60 million this year, a 9% decrease from 2015. Revenues are expected to hit $18 billion, down 12%.

Televisions

- After a banner year of sales growth in 2015 that saw LCD TV shipments climb 10% to top 39 million units, the TV market should reach a steady state in 2016. CTA projects revenues will reach $19 billion for all TV sets and displays in 2016, on par with 2015, as volumes drop 1% to just under 40 million units.
- Ultra high-definition (UHD) TVs: Driven in part by the market introduction of

next-generation technologies, shipments of 4K UHD displays are projected to reach 13 million units (an 83% increase). CTA expects revenue from 4K UHD displays in 2016 to top $10 billion, marking a 65% increase.

Video and Audio

- IoT connectivity is transforming core consumer tech categories. In video, sales of smart TVs are projected to top 27 million units in 2016, a 13% increase over 2015, and sales of streaming media players will hit 15.8 million units, a 5% increase.
- Connected speakers and wireless headphones are the standout categories in audio. Unit sales of Bluetooth/Airplay-capable speakers are expected to reach 17.4 million units in 2016 – a 40% increase – and $1.5 billion in revenue, while sales of wireless headphones will reach 3.9 million in unit sales (increasing 30%) and $623 million in revenue.

Virtual Reality (VR)

- With several notable VR headsets coming to market in 2016, CTA expects unit sales to increase by 500% over 2015, to reach 1.2 million units sold. Total revenues are projected to reach $540 million, a 440% increase.

Wearables

- Led by the popularity of fitness activity trackers and smart watches, unit sales among all wearables in 2016 are forecast to reach 38.4 million units. Fitness activity tracker volumes will hit 17.4 million units in 2016 – a 12% increase from 2015 – with revenues reaching $1.3 billion. Smart watches are expected to increase 28% to 13.6 million units, earning $3.7 billion in revenue, an increase of 22%.

21.5 Technology Impact

A November 2015 Harris Poll (www.theharrispoll.com) found adults are divided on how technology impacts the way we live our lives. On the one hand, 71% say that technology has improved the overall quality of their lives and 68% believe that it encourages people to be more creative. But at the same time, a strong majority of adults also believe technology is creating a lazy society (73%), has become too distracting (73%), is corrupting interpersonal communications (69%), and is having a negative impact on literacy (59%).

By generation, adults feel that technology has a positive affect on their lives in the following areas:

	Millennials	Gen Xers	Boomers	Seniors	All
• Ability to learn new skills:	72%	59%	60%	56%	63%
• Relationships with friends:	59%	46%	36%	34%	46%
• Ability to live life the way they want:	53%	43%	39%	40%	45%
• Happiness:	52%	42%	37%	38%	43%
• Social life:	57%	42%	30%	29%	42%
• Relationships with family:	46%	36%	33%	27%	37%

21.6 Market Resources

Consumer Technology Association, 1919 South Eads Street, Arlington, VA 22202. (866) 858-1555. (www.cta.tech)

22

USE OF TRANSPORTATION

22.1 Overview

According to the *Transportation Statistics Annual Report 2015*, published by the Bureau of Transportation Statistics (BTS, www.bts.gov), the average person travels about 17,000 miles per year using all modes of transportation, except bicycles and walking. Nearly four- fifths of person-miles were in cars or other personal vehicles, while domestic air travel accounted for 11%. U.S. residents and foreign visitors travel about 4.7 trillion miles within the United States each year.

According to the *American Time Use Survey* (www.bls.gov/tus/), published by the Bureau of Labor Statistics (BLS), working adults spend 0.77 hours their day traveling related to work. As of May 2016, the U.S. workforce count (ages 16 and older) was 151.03 million, according to the Bureau of Labor Statistics (www.bls.gov).

Travel to work is distributed as follows:

- Drive self: 76%
- Carpool: 10%
- Public transportation: 5%
- Walk: 3%
- Bicycle: 1%
- Other: 1%
- None (work at home): 4%

In 2015, 85.8% of American workers commuted by automobile; 76.4% drove to work alone; 9.4% carpooled. For comparison, these figures were 87.9%, 75.7%, and 12.2%, respectively, in 2000.

Personal travel not related to work accounts for about 74.8% of total daily person-miles of travel. People on average devoted about 30.3% of their person-miles of travel for social purposes and recreation. Another 29.6% of person-miles of travel were divided about equally between shopping and running family or personal errands. Travel related to school and church accounted for 6.2% of person-miles of travel.

The U.S. transportation infrastructure includes over 4 million miles of roads, nearly 139,000 miles of railroads, over 25,000 miles of navigable waterways, more than 5,000 public use airports, and 3,155 transit stations. The U.S. transportation infrastructure is valued at approximately $7.7 trillion, according to the BTS.

22.2 Driving

The Federal Highway Administration (FHWA, www.fhwa.dot.gov) estimates that Americans drove 3.15 trillion miles in 2015, a 3.5% increase from the previous year.

Auto travel is an integral part of the travel industry, with approximately 1.7 billion person-trips (84% of all U.S. domestic person-trips) being taken by car, truck, camper/RV, or rental car, according to the U.S. Travel Association (USTA, www.ustravel.org).

The Federal Highway Administration reported that the average American driver logs 13,476 miles each year. By age and gender, average mileage by licensed drivers was as follows:

	Men	Women	Avg. Total
• 16-to-19:	8,206	6,873	7,624
• 20-to-34:	17,976	12,004	15,098
• 35-to-54:	18,858	11,464	15,291
• 55-to-64:	15,859	7,780	11,972
• 65 and older:	10,304	4,785	7,646
• Average:	16,550	10,142	13,476

According to PIRG Educational Fund (www.uspirgedfund.org), 67% of Americans ages 16-to-24 have a driver's license, the lowest level in roughly a half-century. Among adults older than age 24, 87% have a driver's license.

Americans of all ages have reduced their driving. Since 2001, the total distance Americans drove fell by about 1% – the U.S. population grew by about 10% during those years. Among the lower percentage of youth and young adults who drive, a weak economy, growing urban populations, and rising fuel prices contributed to the decline.

According to International Demographics (www.themediaaudit.com), 15.8% of adults are high-mileage drivers, driving more than 350 miles in a typical week. Among high-mileage drivers, 45% earn more than $75,000 in household income, a figure that is 46% higher when compared to the typical U.S. adult. Further, 29.2% of high mileage drivers earn more than $100,000 in income, compared to 18.8% of all U.S. adults who fall into the same income category.

The following metropolitan areas have the highest percentages of high-mileage drivers:

- Charlotte, NC: 22.4%
- San Antonio, TX: 21.5%
- Columbia-Jefferson City, MO: 21.5%
- Little Rock, AR: 21.2%
- Columbia, SC: 21.0%

22.3 Vehicle Ownership

According to the Bureau of Transportation Statistics, there are 255.8 million personal vehicles – automobiles, SUVs, vans, and pickup trucks – in operation in the

United States. There are about 796 motor vehicles for every 1,000 people in the U.S., by far the highest per capita vehicle ownership in the world. There are 8.2 million motorcycles.

According to Pew Research Center (www.pewresearch.org), 88% of all households own or lease at least one vehicle, the same percentage as in 2001. However, among households headed by a person age 18-to-24, vehicle ownership dropped from 72% to 66%.

"Among most age groups, the level of ownership is similar to 2001. However, among households headed by those younger than 25, a decline is evident. The decline in vehicle ownership may be a reflection of declining preferences to drive among the young adult population."

Pew Research Center

According to the National Automobile Dealers Association (www.nada.org), dealerships sold or leased 17.4 million new cars and light trucks in 2015, a 5.8% increase from 2014. The average transaction price of a new car and light truck was $33,269 in 2015.

New vehicle purchases per 100 drivers, by age, are as follows (source: Edmunds.com):

- 18-to-24: 0.5
- 25-to-34: 2.9
- 35-to-44: 6.4
- 45-to-54: 6.8
- 55-to-64: 6.9
- 65-to-74: 6.7
- 75 and older: 3.8

Sport utility vehicles (SUVs) garner almost 27.8% of new vehicle sales, according to Edmunds.com.

The Bureau of Labor Statistics (BLS, www.bls.gov) reports average age of the nation's cars, vans, and SUVs is 11.3 years. Fifteen percent (15%) of the automobiles owned by American households are new-to-five-years-old, and 52% are at least 11-years-old. Owners spend an average of $437 a year maintaining new-to-5-year-old automobiles and $588 annually on 6-to-10-year-old vehicles.

22.4 Air Transportation

Bureau of Transportation Statistics reports the number of domestic and international passengers for scheduled flights (all carriers, all airports) into or from U.S. airports as follows:

- 2003: 704.1 million
- 2004: 767.2 million
- 2005: 804.4 million
- 2006: 811.7 million
- 2007: 838.4 million
- 2008: 812.3 million
- 2009: 770.6 million
- 2010: 790.2 million
- 2011: 804.6 million
- 2012: 815.5 million
- 2013: 827.3 million
- 2014: 853.1 million
- 2015: 895.5 million

Travel statistics for U.S. flights in 2015 were as follows (change from previous year in parenthesis):

- Number of flights: 9,526,000 (-0.3%)
- Revenue passenger miles: 1,289,000,000,000 (5.5%)
- Available seat-miles: 1,559,500,000,000 (5.5%)
- Load factor: 82.7 (no change)

22.5 Private Aviation

There are an estimated 2.7 million Americans with flying experience.

According to the Federal Aviation Administration (FAA, www.faa.gov), there were 590,039 active certificated pilots in the U.S. at year-end 2015. This number has been declining gradually over the past several decades, down from a high of over 827,000 pilots in 1980. One factor contributing to the decline in piloting is the expense of flight training and costs associated with operating and maintaining a plane. It can cost $8,000 to $10,000 for training and licensing, followed by $200 or more an hour for aircraft rental, according to Michael Miller, an aviation consultant for The Velocity Group (www.velocity-group.com).

The total number of pilots in 2015 included 170,718 private pilots, 122,729 student pilots, and 5,482 sport pilots. About 7% of pilots are female. The state of Alaska has the highest number of pilots per capita; out of an estimated 410,478 adult residents there were 7,933 pilots in 2015, a ratio of about 1:52.

According to the FAA, pilots log 28 million flying hours annually, approximately one-third of which are for recreation and personal use.

There are about 220,000 general aviation aircraft in the U.S., more that twice the total of all other nations combined.

22.6 Rail Transportation

Amtrak, the National Railroad Passenger Corporation (www.amtrak.com) provides intercity passenger rail services to more than 500 destinations in 46 states on a 21,000-mile route system. Amtrak reported the number of passengers, including commuters and long-distance travelers, as follows:

- FY2003: 22.3 million
- FY2004: 23.4 million
- FY2005: 24.0 million
- FY2006: 24.3 million
- FY2007: 25.8 million
- FY2008: 28.7 million
- FY2009: 27.2 million
- FY2010: 28.7 million
- FY2011: 30.2 million
- FY2012: 31.2 million
- FY2013: 31.6 million
- FY2014: 31.0 billion
- FY2015: 30.8 million

Amtrak revenue in FY2015 (October 1, 2014 - September 30, 2015) was $3.2 billion.

The most heavily used services, accounting for 17.6 million trips in FY2015, are those running on the Northeast Corridor, which serves Boston, New York City, Philadelphia, and Washington, DC.

22.7 Intercity Bus Transportation

Greyhound Lines, Inc. (www.greyhound.com), the largest provider of intercity bus transportation, operates a fleet of more than 1,735 active buses and serves about 3,800 destinations in North America. Greyhound logged 5.5 billion passenger miles in 2015.

Recent startups BoltBus (www.boltbus.com) and Megabus (www.megabus.com) appeal to budget-minded, urban-dwelling young adults by providing a hip image, technology (complimentary wi-fi and power outlets at every seat), and cheap fares. These companies hold costs down by providing city-center curbside pickup in lieu of service at bus terminals.

22.8 Public Transit

Public transit services include transit bus; commuter, subway, elevated, and light rail trains; and other kinds of public transit, such as ferry boats.

According to the National Transit Database of the Federal Transit Administration (www.fta.dot.gov), there are 729 urban transit agencies and 1,580 rural and tribal government transit agencies in the United States. Transit ridership includes over 10 billion unlinked transit trips on these systems each year.

Ridership by rail has grown rapidly in recent years due, in part, to considerable public investment. Still, buses account for the vast majority of transit routes and passengers.

"Americans are slowly warming to public transport, and used it for a record 10.7 billion trips last year. Even those living in the South and Southwest – home to some of the country's most sprawling cities – are getting more of a taste for it."

Art Guzzetti, Vice President
American Public Transport Association

22.9 Market Resources

American Public Transport Association, 1666 K Street NW, Suite 1100, Washington, DC 20006. (202) 496-4800. (www.apta.com)

Bureau of Transportation Statistics, U.S. Department of Transportation, 1200 New Jersey Avenue SE, Washington, DC 20590. (800) 853-1351. (www.bts.gov)

Federal Aviation Administration, 800 Independence Avenue SW, Washington, DC 20591. (202) 493-4305. (www.faa.gov)

Federal Highway Administration, 1200 New Jersey Avenue SE, Washington, DC 20590. (202) 366-4000. (www.fhwa.dot.gov)

National Automobile Dealers Association, 8400 Westpark Drive, McLean, VA 22102. (703) 821-7000. (www.nada.org)

Transportation Sustainability Research Center, 1301 S. 46th Street, Building 190, Richmond, CA 94804. (510) 655-3467. (http://tsrc.berkeley.edu)

U.S. Travel Association, 1100 New York Avenue NW, Suite 450, Washington, DC 20005. (202) 408-8422. (www.ustravel.org)

University of Michigan, Transportation Research Institute, 2901 Baxter Road, Ann Arbor, MI 48109. (734) 764-6504. (www.umtri.umich.edu)

PART IV: SHOPPING BEHAVIORS

23

IN-STORE SHOPPING

23.1 Preference For In-Store

The Harris Poll (www.theharrispoll.com) found that consumers generally report higher satisfaction with bricks-and-mortar stores than with online shopping.

> **"There are many reasons why a consumer would choose to visit a location-based retailer over its online counterpart, including convenience, selection, and immediate needs. Most of all, shoppers tend to want to interact with physical merchandise before purchasing it. Trend data shows that while consumers are increasingly shopping online, their brand experience when doing so tends to score lower than their in-store experience."**
>
> The Harris Poll

By age, a recent Harris Poll found adults prefer purchasing various retail categories in-person at a bricks-and-mortar store rather than online as follows:

	18-to-34	35-to-44	45-to-55	55 & older	Total
• Groceries:	68%	77%	85%	87%	78%
• OTC medications:	61%	62%	73%	79%	67%
• Clothing:	59%	62%	68%	79%	65%
• Prescription medications:	56%	57%	60%	57%	58%
• Cosmetics/personal grooming:	50%	49%	64%	72%	57%
• Specialty food and beverages:	55%	55%	58%	60%	57%
• Household electronics:	44%	51%	60%	74%	55%
• Shoes and accessories:	45%	49%	55%	69%	52%
• Personal electronics:	34%	39%	46%	61%	43%

In a survey by Synqera (www.synqera.com), 67% of adults said they prefer to shop in traditional, bricks-and-mortar stores than at commerce sites online. The survey found that 80% of shoppers are more likely to shop in a store that provides an overall customized shopping experience, and 66% are more likely to shop in a store where they receive personal suggestions while shopping.

23.2 Shopping Centers

According to *The State of the Shopping Center*, a report by The Nielsen Company (www.nielsen.com), traditional shopping centers have morphed into lifestyle centers which blend traditional retail with upscale leisure options that offer shoppers a place to gather and socialize as well as to shop. The lines between shopping, entertainment, and community are increasingly becoming blurred.

> **"Even in a world where consumers can connect with each other via text in an instant and do their shopping from their couches, people still crave a physical place to congregate, connect and engage. And more and more, shopping centers are a big part of fulfilling that need. No longer just a place to shop, shopping centers are key activity centers in the social fabric of communities, elevating their purpose beyond simply offering an outlet to buy groceries or pick up a new blouse."**
>
> Nielsen

23.3 How America Shops

Since 2004, WSL Strategic Retail (www.wslstrategicretail.com) has annually surveyed U.S. consumers about their shopping behaviors. The most recent assessment, *How America Shops*, provides insight into the behavior of today's retail shopper. The following are key findings from the study:

- Seventy-five percent (75%) of consumers say it is important to get the lowest price on everything they buy.

- Sixty-eight percent (68%) of shoppers say they regularly use coupons to reduce costs.
- Sixty-six percent (66%) of shoppers say they take a pause before buying to ask, "Is this a smart use of my money?" Among those with a household income of $150,000 or more, 47% do so.
- Fifty-eight percent (58%) of consumers say they manage their aspirations by sticking to brands and stores they can afford. Among those with a household income of $150,000 or more, 36% do so.
- Forty-eight percent (48%) of consumers say they are staying out of stores where they might be tempted to overspend. Among those with a household income of $150,000 or more, 28% do so.
- Forty-five percent (45%) of shoppers claim they only buy items that are on sale.
- Forty-three percent (43%) of consumers make a point to search online for store discounts before they shop.
- Twenty-six percent (26%) of shoppers admit that while they used to buy brand names they could not afford, they are no longer giving in to this indulgence.
- Fourteen percent (14%) of consumers say they use their mobile phones while in a store to see if they can find a lower price, before they buy.

WSL Strategic Retail identified the following trends in 2015:

- The American Dream today among shoppers is to be debt-free and it's influencing every buying decision. In addition, half of shoppers still struggle to afford the basics. Younger shoppers are using every tool to get what they want, how they want it, at the price they want to spend.
- Shoppers still prefer name brands, but in most categories 2 or 3 name brands are equally good enough. Which brand they choose often comes down to the lowest price at that moment.
- Fifty-six percent (56%) of shoppers make CPG brand decisions at the shelf ("first moment of truth"), but the future is Google's "zero moment of truth," where shoppers decide what to buy before the store. Of those who pre-shop, fewer than 15% change their mind in-store.
- Today, convenience drives retail choice, but there are so many options. Most shoppers expect low prices everywhere they shop and rarely need to compromise. Neither convenience nor price drives loyalty among shoppers today.
- Shoppers who connect with retailers digitally are more loyal to that retailer. For retailers who question investment in digital tools, this is a call to action.

23.4 The In-Store Experience

In a survey by Motorola Solutions (www.motorolasolutions.com), 74% of retail executives said they believe that developing a more engaging in-store experience will be critical to their business. Survey participants foresee the following technological developments occurring in the retail marketplace over the next five years:

- All transactions will be completed via mobile POS, self-checkout at terminal, or on shopper's mobile device: 56%
- Sales will come from online, mobile, and commercial sites: 42%
- Will send coupons based on customer location in the store: 42%
- Will provide personalized product details to shopper's smartphone based on previous behavior: 41%
- Will recognize customer in store with geofencing or presence technology: 35%

Consumers' cross-channel shopping behaviors will change retailers' marketing strategies. *Retail USA: 2016*, a study from Nielsen, forecasts the retail marketplace will change in the following ways:

- Store footprints either will get supersized for one-stop-shop convenience or downsized into smaller stores for quick grab-and-go trips.
- For people who view shopping as entertainment that engages all the senses, lifestyle outlets will blur the line of demarcation between traditional formats, merging restaurants with food markets, serving up food and wine tastings, providing live music and movies, and creating places for friends and co-workers to gather and socialize.
- Technology will bring consumers into the shopping experience via options such as touchscreen ordering, QR code advertising, mobile coupons, and shopping lists.
- Store brands will mushroom to include super premium offerings joined by an increasing number of restaurant and celebrity-chef brands, while a few consumer packaged goods brands will transition onto restaurant menus.
- The Big Four technology companies (i.e., Amazon, Apple, Facebook, and Google) will establish beachheads outside the tech world, challenging conventional players to re-think their business models and forge new alliances or chance seeing themselves become less relevant.
- Deep discounters will continue to keep the cap on operating costs in order to maintain their price edge, but low prices alone have not been enough to guarantee sales success.
- Retailers will expand designated stores-within-a store spaces, pulling together related items that fulfill a consumer need into a discrete space such as a cosmetics department complete with expert consultants, occasion-based home meal solution centers, or dedicated pet care areas.
- Mobile and online technologies will enable one-to-one marketing, customized shopping lists, menu plans, coupons, and other content to reflect user interests and consumption patterns.
- Online avatars and in-store service agents will assist consumers with meal management, entertainment, health and wellness monitoring, and fashion selections.
- In-store shelf-talkers will take on a new, interactive dimension with QR codes that connect directly to robust websites offering discounts and cross merchandising suggestions such as wine pairings.

- The chasm between income and wealth strata will enable retailers at both the high and low ends of the price spectrum to prosper by merchandising to niche audiences.

23.5 Self-Service

In the survey by Synqera, 73% of shoppers say they find waiting in the checkout line their least favorite aspect of in-store shopping.

A survey by Buzzback Market Research (www.buzzback.com) found that 66% of shoppers feel that self-service technology creates a more positive perception of the deployer's brand.

According to IHL Group (www.ihlservices.com), consumers made $312 billion in purchases through self-checkout lanes in 2015. Self-service transactions are growing at 7% per year.

A survey by Shapiro+Raj (www.ljs.com) found consumers divided on the benefits of self checkout. Only 43% said it shortens checkout time, while 38% feel it lengthens checkout. Still, given a choice, 39% say they prefer self-checkout over a cashier.

24

ONLINE SHOPPING

24.1 Why People Shop Online

A poll of Internet users by The Nielsen Company (www.nielsen.com) asking primary reasons for shopping online found the following:

- Able to shop 24 hours a day: 81%
- Saves time: 76%
- Able to comparison shop: 61%
- Easy to find what I am looking for: 56%
- Selection of items: 49%
- Can search by brands I like: 46%
- Available product information: 46%
- Low prices: 45%
- Items are in stock: 35%
- Low shipping costs: 24%
- Recommendations for items: 15%
- Customer service and communication: 12%
- Easy to return purchases: 11%
- Gift services such as cards, wrapping, or birthday/holiday reminders: 10%

A survey by Impulse Research (www.impulseresearch.com) found the primary reasons that Millennial adults, ages 18-to-34, shop online are as follows:

- Better prices: 37%
- Avoid shopping hassles and crowds: 29%
- Convenience: 18%
- Better selection: 13%
- Direct shipping to home: 3%

A survey by Accenture (www.accenture.com) found parents with children in school liked to shop online for the following reasons (percentage of respondents):

- Save money/find discounts: 70%
- To research products and prices: 63%
- Avoid going to many stores: 40%
- Avoid boring trips for kids: 28%
- Avoid kid pressure to buy items: 17%
- School works with e-retailers to ensure supplies are in stock: 7%

24.2 Characteristics Of Online Shopping

When asked how they typically find what they're shopping for online, responses were as follows (source: Nielsen; multiple responses allowed):

- Know the site by name: 69%
- Search engines: 62%
- Comparison shopping tools: 23%
- Subscribe to an e-newsletter from retailers: 15%
- Blogs/chat rooms/consumer reviews: 5%

Shopzilla (www.shopzilla.com) asked U.S. adults how they first saw the product they most recently purchased online. Responses were as follows:

- While surfing online: 29%
- Looking for something specific: 24%
- In email from store: 11%
- While "out and about": 8%
- In friend's house: 8%
- In a magazine: 7%
- In an ad: 6%
- On blog or other website content: 4%
- On Facebook: 2%
- On Pinterest: <1%
- On Twitter: <1%

24.3 Expectations Online

According to a survey by OneUpWeb (www.oneupweb.com), Internet users expect the following from e-commerce sites (percentage of respondents):

- Pricing/shipping information clearly stated: 96%
- Site looks credible and trustworthy: 76%
- Product displayed on homepage: 71%
- Visually appealing: 67%
- Total cost calculator: 59%
- Search function: 48%
- Privacy statement: 46%
- Onsite customer reviews: 41%
- Online customer service (live chat): 32%
- Links to social networks (Facebook, Twitter): 23%

According to a survey by A.T. Kearney (www.atkearney.com), the following attributes are important to consumers when shopping online (percentage of respondents):

- Finding specific products: 96%
- Free shipping: 93%

- Finding favorite brands: 92%
- Best price: 90%
- Ease of navigation: 88%
- Site security: 87%
- Special promotions: 78%
- Free samples: 67%
- Peer reviews: 59%
- New products: 55%

24.4 Selecting An Online Retailer

A survey by comScore (www.comscore.com) asked online shoppers the factors driving them to shop with an online retailer. Responses were as follows (two responses per survey participant):

- The ability to buy online and then make returns at the store: 62%
- The push of a coupon/promotion to my smartphone: 47%
- The ability to buy online and pick up in store: 44%
- The availability of an application designed specifically for a tablet: 41%
- The option to conduct one-click check-out online: 40%
- The ability to complete a purchase in store using mobile device: 37%
- The availability of a mobile application for a smartphone: 36%
- The availability of an in-store kiosk to browse products: 25%
- The ability to start a purchase online and then complete the purchase in store: 23%
- The ability to make an appointment for an in-store consult after researching online: 18%

When asked what factors have led them to recommend an online retailer to others, responses were as follows (multiple responses allowed):

- Free shipping: 68%
- Receiving my product when expected: 47%
- Free returns: 34%
- Easy returns and exchanges: 34%
- Tracking services: 29%
- Fast credits/refunds if I return products: 25%

24.5 Shopping On Social Sites

E-commerce transactions through storefronts on social media sites, dubbed social commerce, held great promise a few years ago with the rise in popularity of social networking. Consumers, however, have shown that they do not prefer to shop on social sites. A recent Harris Poll found that just 5% of U.S. adult Internet users had made a purchase on a social network such as Facebook, Twitter, or Pinterest.

"How many digital buyers in the U.S. actually take the final lead on a social platform? Not too many. Social media storefronts are now a relic."

eMarketer

Most social network storefronts have now closed. According to 8th Bridge (www.8thbridge.com), 62% of retailers with Facebook apps had product browsing in 2012. Now, less than 15% do so.

24.6 Buying Direct From Brands

For some product categories, consumers prefer to bypass third-party retailers and buy online directly from brands.

In a survey by BrandShop (www.brandshop.com), digital buyers said they prefer to purchase the following types of products directly from the brand (percentage of respondents):

- Apparel: 57%
- Electronics: 56%
- Household and consumer goods: 38%
- Food products: 37%
- Beauty and skincare: 30%

25

MOBILE SHOPPING

25.1 Overview

The use of a smartphone or tablet to assist in shopping, or even to make a purchase, continues to increase in popularity. Product research, price comparisons, and mobile coupon redemption are the most common uses of mobile devices by shoppers. Many smartphone users also have used their device to make a purchase, an activity typically referred to as 'mobile commerce' or 'm-commerce.'

A survey by Annalect (www.annalect.com) reported shopping-related activities conducted by mobile devices as follows (percentage of respondents):

	Smartphone	Tablet
• Compare/check prices:	67%	54%
• Look for coupons/discounts:	64%	44%
• Check reviews:	52%	45%
• Check product details:	49%	43%
• Check product availability:	47%	43%
• Make purchase:	40%	41%

eMarketer (www.emarketer.com) assesses the percentages of mobile buyers as a percentage of mobile shoppers as follows:

	Smartphone	Tablet	Total Mobile
• 2014:	51.9%	79.1%	69.7%
• 2015:	52.4%	80.9%	71.2%
• 2016:	53.0%	85.1%	73.9%
• 2017:	53.5%	86.8%	75.7%
• 2018:	53.7%	88.1%	76.0%
• 2019:	53.9%	88.3%	76.2%

The number of smartphone buyers and percentage of total digital buyers is assessed as follows (source: eMarketer):

	Number	Pct. of Digital Buyers
• 2014:	67.2 million	40.8%
• 2015:	78.3 million	45.6%
• 2016:	87.8 million	49.1%
• 2017:	95.1 million	51.2%
• 2018:	100.7 million	52.6%
• 2019:	105.6 million	54.1%

"For some consumers, the mobile screen is too small for frequently purchasing. Indeed, many mobile device users prefer to use a PC instead"

eMarketer, 2/5/16

comScore (www.comscore.com) reported that mobile accounted for 40% of time spent by consumers engaged in digital retail activities in 2015, but only 13% of spending.

25.2 Market Assessment

According to eMarketer, spending via mobile devices has been, and is projected, as follows:

	Sales	Pct. of E-commerce Sales
• 2012:	$ 24.78 billion	11%
• 2013:	$ 42.13 billion	16%
• 2014:	$ 56.67 billion	19%
• 2015:	$ 88.53 billion	26%
• 2016:	$123.13 billion	32%
• 2017:	$151.11 billion	35%
• 2018:	$178.27 billion	37%
• 2019:	$208.58 billion	39%
• 2020:	$242.08 billion	41%

The bulk of m-commerce spending is via tablets, which consumers tend to use more like a desktop than a phone. eMarketer assesses the percentage of total m-commerce sales that are via tablet as follows:

- 2014: 62.3%
- 2015: 53.8%
- 2016: 50.6%
- 2017: 48.7%
- 2018: 47.3%
- 2019: 46.4%
- 2020: 45.5%

"Mobile commerce had a breakthrough year in 2015. Smartphone retail m-commerce sales in the U.S. nearly doubled, driven by larger screens, smoother buying experiences, better mobile search and context-driven discovery. The same trend should continue throughout 2016. By 2020, smartphones will capture $129.44 billion of all retail m-commerce outlays in the U.S., a growth rate of 18.3%."

eMarketer, 5/4/16

25.3 Mobile-Deiven Retail Purchases

Smith Micro Software (www.smithmicro.com) estimates that mobile activities will drive $689 billion in retail sales in the U.S. in 2016.

BI Intelligence (https://intelligence.businessinsider.com) forecasts that beacon-triggered messages will drive $44.1 billion in retail sales in 2016.

25.4 Use Of Mobile Devices For Online Purchases

According to The Harris Poll (www.theharrispoll.com), the following percentages of adults have made select online purchases via cellphone or tablet (for comparison, using a laptop or desktop):

	Laptop/Desktop	Smartphone	Tablet
• Clothing:	65%	6%	10%
• Digital content (movies, music, e-books):	48%	12%	17%
• Shoes and accessories:	49%	5%	9%
• Personal electronics:	43%	5%	7%
• Household electronics:	38%	4%	5%
• Cosmetics and personal grooming:	31%	4%	5%
• Prescription medications:	21%	3%	4%
• Specialty food and beverages:	23%	3%	3%
• O-T-C medications:	15%	2%	2%
• Groceries:	12%	2%	2%

25.5 Customer Service For Mobile Shoppers

In a survey by Contact Solutions (www.contactsolutions.com), 75% of mobile shoppers said access to customer care impacts their shopping experience.

Fifty-five percent (55%) of survey respondents report that they struggle at least 20% of the time when using a mobile app to shop. Forty-three percent (43%) say they have come to expect no customer service at all from mobile apps.

Mobile shoppers respond to shopping difficulties via an app as follows (percentage of respondents):

- Close app and abandon cart: 51.3%
- Go to web using desktop or laptop: 36.9%
- Go to store and shop: 11.5%
- Call customer service: 8.2%

Ninety-five percent (95%) say that a great customer experience will make them more likely to do business again with a retailer.

Ninety-two percent (92%) of shoppers say it would be helpful to have customer care automatically provided within an app to help complete a task.

25.6 In-Store Mobile

A study by the Consumer Technology Association (CTA; www.cta.tech) found that 58% of shoppers prefer to look up information on their mobile devices while shopping in stores, rather than talk to a salesperson. Shoppers ages 25-to-44 and men were most likely to prefer to access their device for product information. Nearly two-thirds felt that the information they gather on their mobile devices is more helpful than in-store information from product displays or sales literature.

"One thing is clear: Consumers still value customer service, but the way they want it delivered is changing with their consumption habits. As the retail path to purchase changes – mobile is now a significant part of the process, especially for researching on the go and even in-store – so do consumers' preferences for how retailers connect with them."

eMarketer

By product category, mobile shopper use of devices for assistance when shopping is as follows (source: CTA):

- Electronics: 60%
- Groceries: 55%
- Apparel: 47%
- Shoes: 45%
- Health and beauty products: 39%

26

PEER-TO-PEER SHOPPING

26.1 Overview

The peer-to-peer (P2P) marketplace – which goes by a host of monikers such as collaborative consumption, communal consumption, asset-light lifestyle, the peer economy, and the sharing economy – lets individuals rent unused assets or sell goods and services to other individuals. The economic downturn was the impetus for growth of the concept.

Today there are numerous Internet-based services available to aggregate supply and demand.

"Why pay through the nose for something when you can rent it more cheaply from a stranger online? That is the principle behind a range of online services that enable people to share cars, accommodations, bicycles, household appliances, and other items, connecting owners of underused assets with others willing to pay to use them. Dozens of firms such as Airbnb, which lets people rent out their spare rooms, or RelayRides, which allows other people to rent your car, act as matchmakers, allocating resources where they are needed and taking a small cut in return."

The Economist

Time calls the sharing economy one of the 10 most important ideas that is changing the world.

26.2 Market Assessment

Forbes estimated the 2015 peer-to-peer marketplace at $5.5 billion and growth at an annual rate of over 25%.

Forrester Research (www.forrester.com) assessed the 2015 U.S. P2P market at $6.2 billion. Growth of 26% a year is projected by Forrester, with peer-to-peer spending reaching $17 billion in 2019.

26.3 Consumer Participation

According to a January 2016 survey by *Time*, in conjunction with Burson-Marsteller (www.burson-marsteller.com) and the Aspen Institute Future Of Work Initiative (www.aspeninstitute.org/programs/future-of-work/), 44% of adult Internet users have participated in the peer-to-peer marketplace, either as providers or users.

> **"More than 90 million Americans have played the roles of lenders and borrowers, drivers and riders, hosts and guests."**
>
> *Time*, 1/18/16

Time reported that 42% of adults had used peer-to-peer services or products; 22% have been providers. By category, users and providers are as follows (percentage of respondents in an online poll):

	User	Provider
• Ride sharing (e.g. Lyft, Sidecar, Uber):	22%	10%
• Accommodation sharing (e.g. Airbnb, HomeAway, VRBO):	19%	9%
• Service platforms (e.g. Care.com, Jandy.com, TaskRabbit):	17%	11%
• Car rental (e.g. Car2Go, Getaround, Zipcar):	14%	6%
• Food and goods delivers (e.g. Caviar, Instacart, Postmates):	11%	7%

Among peer-to-peer providers, 61% are male, 55% of members of an ethnic/racial minority, 51% are ages 18-to-34, and 41% reside in an urban area.

eMarketer (www.emarketer.com) assesses the number of U.S. adults that use the peer-to-peer marketplace, and that use transportation-sharing services, as follows:

	Any Peer-To-Peer	Transportation Sharing
• 2014:	15.4 million (6.3% of all adults)	8.2 million (3.4% of all adults)
• 2015:	21.7 million (8.8% of all adults)	12.4 million (5.0% of all adults)
• 2016:	27.0 million (10.8% of all adults)	15.0 million (6.0% of all adults)
• 2017:	30.9 million (12.2% of all adults)	17.0 million (6.7% of all adults)

- 2018: 34.0 million (13.3% of all adults) 18.2 million (7.1% of all adults)
- 2019: 37.3 million (14.5% of all adults) 19.4 million (7.5% of all adults)
- 2020: 40.0 million (15.3% of all adults) 20.4 million (7.8% of all adults)

26.4 Consumer Response

A 2015 survey by Vision Critical (www.visioncritical.com) asked adult Internet users if they would consider sharing-economy services and products if they provided a cost savings over traditional company providers. Responses by age and product/service were as follows:

Accommodations
- 18-to-34: 71%
- 35-to-54: 59%
- 55 and older: 54%

Car Rental
- 18-to-34: 62%
- 35-to-54: 51%
- 55 and older: 53%

Gifts
- 18-to-34: 60%
- 35-to-54: 47%
- 55 and older: 48%

Home Furnishings
- 18-to-34: 50%
- 35-to-54: 46%
- 55 and older: 36%

> **"While Internet users of all ages would consider using the sharing economy for the right mix of price, convenience, and other characteristics, Millennials are more interested across all use categories."**
>
> eMarketer, 10/13/15

26.5 Consumer Attitudes

In a May 2016 survey by AYTM Market Research (www.aytm.com), adults expressed the following opinions toward the sharing economy (percentage of respondents):

Good for Consumers

- Strongly agree: 11.7%
- Agree: 20.7%
- Somewhat agree: 27.4%
- Neutral: 30.0%
- Somewhat disagree: 6.6%
- Disagree: 1.6%
- Strongly disagree: 2.0%

Good for the Economy as a Whole

- Strongly agree: 11.0%
- Agree: 17.4%
- Somewhat agree: 26.8%
- Neutral: 34.7%
- Somewhat disagree: 6.2%
- Disagree: 1.7%
- Strongly disagree: 2.2%

Good for Business

- Strongly agree: 8.5%
- Agree: 14.2%
- Somewhat agree: 22.8%
- Neutral: 36.0%
- Somewhat disagree: 11.9%
- Disagree: 4.2%
- Strongly disagree: 2.4%

"The sharing economy is continuing to expand and many U.S. Internet users agree that it's not only good for them, but for businesses and the economy as a whole. However, there are also those that remain neutral about the sharing economy in general."

eMarketer, 5/27/16

26.6 Economic Impact

According to Arun Sundararajan, Ph.D., a professor at the Stern School of Business at New York University, the largest question for academics is whether the sharing economy simply replaces existing businesses or creates new value. People have purchased residential properties and automobiles solely to rent them out, for example, indicating the concept has an extended impact.

While the sharing economy clearly poses a competitive threat to traditional businesses, it also has a positive economic impact on cities. A study commissioned by Airbnb found that because peer-to-peer rentals tend to be cheaper than a hotel, people often stay longer and spend 31% more than those who stay in a comparable hotel. Among those who rented an Airbnb property in San Francisco, for example, 14% said they would not have visited the city at all without Airbnb.

> **"Of course established travel companies won't go out of business as a result of this sharing revolution, but the way we travel will almost certainly become more efficient. Put differently, your next 'hotel' may be someone's spare bedroom, your next ride to the airport might be n another person's car, and you might rent a stranger's vehicle when you arrive."**
>
> *USA Today*

Renting out underused assets can be profitable. Airbnb reports that hosts in San Francisco who rent out their homes do so for an average of 58 nights a year, earning a median $9,300. Car owners who rent their vehicles to others using RelayRides make an average of $250 a month; some make more than $1,000 monthly.

27

OMNICHANNEL SHOPPING

27.1 Overview

Omnichannel shopping allows consumers to shop across multiple channels – in-store, online, and on a tablet or cellphone – potentially at the same time. Shopping by catalog and by TV are also part of the omnichannel retail mix.

In the *17th Annual Customer Engagement Survey*, conducted in January 2016 by Boston Retail Partners (www.bostonretailpartners.com), 85% of retail executives reported that unified commerce was their leading priority. Similarly, retail executives said in a survey by KPMG (www.kpmg.com) that omnichannel strategies were their #1 priority.

Boston Retail Partners reported the following percentages of retailers offered select omnichannel options at year-end 2015:

- Returns accepted across all channels: 62%
- Inventory visibility across channels: 60%
- Special order from any channel: 49%
- Order visibility across channels: 47%
- Buy in-store and ship from digital channel, other store, or vendor: 44%
- Buy online, pick up in-store: 42%
- Buy anywhere, ship anywhere: 41%
- Buy online, ship from store: 38%
- Reserve online, pick up in-store: 38%

The State of Retail 2016, by TimeTrade (www.timetrade.com), reported that 51% of retail executives believe that retailers provide a consistent customer experience across all channels. According to the same study, however, only 26% of customers feel the same; 44% feel that the experience is somewhat consistent, and 20% believe that great improvement is needed.

27.2 Web-Influenced Retail Sales

Forrester Research (www.forrester.com) assessed web-influenced retail sales as follows:

	Non-web Influenced Off-line Sales	Web Influenced Off-line Sales	Online Sales
• 2012:	$1.61 billion	$1.16 billion	$231 billion
• 2013:	$1.57 billion	$1.29 billion	$261 billion
• 2014:	$1.55 billion	$1.41 billion	$290 billion
• 2015:	$1.49 billion	$1.55 billion	$319 billion
• 2016:	$1.47 billion	$1.67 billion	$345 billion
• 2017:	$1.44 billion	$1.80 billion	$371 billion

27.3 Customer Preference For Omnichannel Retail

A March 2016 survey by iModerate Research Technologies (www.imoderate.com), reported Internet users who believe it is important for e-commerce brands to operate physical stores as follows:

- Baby Boomers: 65%
- Generation Xers: 69%
- Millennials: 82%
- Generation Zers: 80%

According to *Omnichannel Preferences Study*, a report by A.T. Kearney (www.atkearney.com), 67% of consumers who purchase online use the physical store before or after the transaction.

Forrester Research (www.forrester.com) found that 71% of consumers expect to view in-store inventory online.

In the *Multichannel Consumer Survey*, by PricewaterhouseCoopers (PwC, www.pwc.com), 56% of U.S. adults said they are likely to spend more with multichannel retailers than with either online-only retailers or stores with bricks-and-mortar-only locations.

"Our research shows that when consumers use multiple channels, they spend more. That flies in the face of conventional wisdom that launching an online store steals sales from physical stores."

Lisa Feigen Dugel, Director
PwC Retail and Consumer Advisory Practice

In a survey of cardholders, VISA found that 83% of adults would choose a retailer based on how easy it is to transact across online, in-store, and mobile.

27.4 Cross-Channel Shopping

"Showrooming" is the practice where customers go to a bricks-and-mortar retail location, make a decision on what item to buy and, instead of heading to the check-out aisle, use a mobile device to find a better price online where they ultimately make their purchase. "Webrooming" occurs when consumers buy in a store after researching a purchase online.

GfK (www.gfk.com) reported that 28% of consumers engage in showrooming; 41% practice webrooming. By age, those who engage in these practices are as follows:

	Showrooming	Webrooming
• 18-to-24:	39%	34%
• 25-to-34:	32%	46%
• 35-to-49:	29%	43%
• 50-to-68:	18%	30%

Showrooming and webrooming are only two of the cross-channel shopping options used by today's consumers. Among those who said they had searched using one channel and made a purchase through another channel, a survey by Cisco Internet Business Solutions Group (www.cisco.com/web/about/ac79) found these consumers had engaged in the following cross-channel shopping activities (percentage of respondents):

- PC-to-store: 57%
- Store-to-online: 38%
- Mobile-to-PC: 26%
- Kiosk-to-store (immediate in-store sale): 24%
- Mobile-to-store: 24%
- Kiosk-to-store (delivery to location of choice): 15%

In a survey by comScore (www.comscore.com) conducted for UPS, consumers said their preferred method of access to multichannel retailers was as follows:

	Researching Products	Purchasing Products
• Online via desktop or laptop:	61%	44%
• In physical store:	13%	41%
• Online via tablet:	11%	7%
• Online via smartphone:	10%	4%
• With catalog, by phone, or email:	4%	4%

Gallup (www.gallup.com) found that use of a mobile device had increased retail store trips for 22% of consumers while decreasing store trips among 19%.

Deloitte (www.deloitte.com) reported that smartphone shoppers are 14% more likely than non-smartphone shoppers to convert in-store, even when those smartphone shoppers used a mobile app or site not belonging to the retailer. Seventy-two percent (72%) of shoppers who used their smartphone on their most recent in-store trip made a purchase while there, compared with 63% of shoppers who did not use a smartphone to assist in making a purchase during their last in-store trip.

27.5 Buy Online, Pick Up In-Store

A March 2016 survey by King Retail Solutions (www.kingrs.com) found that 54% of online consumers have purchased products online, picked up in-store, and said they like the option. By demographic, the percentages are as follows:

Gender

- Female: 50%
- Male: 58%

Generation

- Baby Boomers: 41%
- Generation Xers: 57%
- Millennials: 63%

In a survey by Blackhawk Engagement Solutions (www.bhengagement.com), 86% of adults who shop online said they would consider purchasing online and picking up in-store to save $10 to $50 per item; 78% said they would do so to receive an item three days earlier.

Slice Intelligence (https://intelligence.slice.com) reported the percentage of total e-commerce sales for select retailers that were picked up in-store in 2015 as follows:

- Sam's Club: 30.2%
- Kmart: 22.6%
- Toys "R" Us: 15.0%
- Best Buy: 11.8%
- Home Depot: 9.0%
- Walmart: 8.4%
- Target: 6.6%
- Bloomingdales: 3.1%

PART V: BEHAVIORAL ANALYSES

28

BRAND LOYALTY

28.1 Brand Preferences

Consumer brand preferences vary by product category. A survey by The NPD Group (www.npd.com) found brand names are relevant in some retail categories but of minimal importance in others. By category, shoppers look for a specific brand as follows:

	Always	Never
• Housewares/textiles:	4%	40%
• Furniture:	6%	44%
• Apparel:	14%	25%
• Food (grocery):	21%	12%
• Footwear:	23%	23%
• Cosmetics:	31%	22%
• Electronics:	31%	16%

The following are percentages of consumers willing to pay a lot more for premium brands:

- Electronics: 11%
- Footwear: 9%
- Cosmetics: 8%
- Furniture: 8%
- Food (grocery): 6%
- Housewares/textiles: 4%

Retailing Today, in conjunction with Shapiro+Raj (www.ljs.com), surveyed consumers on their brand preferences. The following is a ranking of retail product categories for which consumers are most brand sensitive, based on the percentage of consumers with a brand preference:

- Beverages: 90%
- Snacks: 88%
- Health and beauty aids: 87%
- Cosmetics: 81%
- Cameras/film: 79%
- Candy: 78%
- Groceries and canned foods: 72%
- Consumer electronics: 65%

- Men's apparel: 64%
- Intimate apparel: 63%
- Toys: 58%
- Computer/entertainment software: 56%
- Greeting cards: 54%
- Women's apparel: 52%
- Children's apparel: 51%
- Domestics: 37%

In a survey by comScore (www.comscore.com), the following percentages of consumers said they buy their preferred brand of these select consumer packaged goods regardless of cost:

- Toothpaste: 57%
- Canned soup: 52%
- Shampoo: 52%
- Laundry detergent: 47%
- Pasta sauce: 45%
- Mouth rinse: 44%
- OTC medications: 43%
- Fruit juice: 40%
- Facial tissue: 39%
- Jeans: 39%
- Paper towels: 35%
- Small appliances: 34%

28.2 Brand Attributes

When asked in a 2015 survey by Sprong (www.sprongpr.com) the brand attributes they considered most important, consumers, by age, responded as follows (percentage of respondents):

	18-to-34	35-to-54	55 and Older
• Overall quality of product or service:	63%	71%	75%
• Value of the product/service for the money:	62%	69%	71%
• Customer service:	38%	43%	42%
• How well they treat their employees:	17%	13%	11%
• The quality of their management:	14%	7%	4%

"Research from Sprong ... found that when evaluating brands, consumers put far greater value on their own personal experience and that of their close friends than what brands themselves say."

The Center for Media Research, 10/26/15

28.3 Store Brands

The influence of cost on brand loyalty increases as consumers are impacted by economic conditions. In a survey by Accenture (www.accenture.com), 39% of consumers said they increased their purchases of store brands or private label brands in recent years because of the economy. The study reported the following attitudes toward private label products (percentage of respondents):

- Buy because they are cheaper: 66%
- Quality is just a good: 50%
- Better variety: 48%
- Trust: 42%
- Just another brand: 36%
- Prefer store brands: 28%
- Buying private label for many years: 28%
- Don't buy/not as good: 9%
- Embarrassed to buy: 4%

Private label revenue and marketshare in 2015 was distributed by retail channel as follows (source: The Nielsen Company [www.nielsen.com]):

	Revenue	Unit Share	Dollar Share
• Supermarkets:	$ 62.0 billion	23.1%	19.5%
• Drug stores:	$ 8.3 billion	17.3%	16.5%
• All retail channels	$115.3 billion	21.0%	17.7%

The Nielsen assessment did not include private label sales in baby care, consumer electronics, convenience stores, dollar store retailers, hardware and home improvement, health and beauty, home decor and domestic goods, office supplies, personal care, pet care, and specialty retail.

"In response to consumer demand, retailers across the country are freshening and extending existing private label offerings and rushing to their shelves whole new lines of store brands to leverage evolving lifestyles and desirable product attributes and to stay competitive with the rival down the street and its own popular store brands."

The Nielsen Co., 3/4/16

For several years department stores have been creating stronger private labels while also eliminating underperforming or over-distributed supplier brands to increase their consumer appeal and reduce pervasive sameness. In 2007, the percentage of sales at Macy's in exclusive or limited-distribution brands, including its private label lines, was 35%. By 2015, store brands increased to 45% of sales. The percentage is even higher at Kohl's and JCPenney, where private label brands represent 48% and 50% of sales, respectively.

28.4 Brand Loyalty In Travel

A survey by Deloitte (www.deloitte.com) found that only 14% of travelers say they are loyal to a particular airline; just 8% say they are loyal to any hotel brand.

Price, comfort and service drive decisions more than loyalty programs. When picking airlines, most travelers say they look first at safety, value, and whether flights are on time. When choosing hotels, they look at price, whether there is free parking, comfort, and location. Loyalty programs rank near the bottom of influencing factors.

28.5 Increasing Brand Loyalty

Various studies point to convenience, customer service, loyalty programs, price, and social network connections as influences on customer loyalty.

Convenience

- According to Brand Keys (www.brandkeys.com), convenience increases product and service consideration, adoption, and loyalty by 19%.

Customer Service

- Few things can affect customer loyalty like customer service. According to a survey by Accenture, in assessing loyalty related to retailers of technology products, over 80% of customers who rated their service below average said they would buy from a different company next time. Merely average service dropped customer purchasing loyalty from 51% to 27%.

Customer Surveys

- Many customers feel more loyal to a brand if it takes the time to find out their opinion. In a survey by Cint (www.cint.com), 62% of customers said they were more likely to purchase a brand's product if their opinion has been sought by the brand.

Price

- A survey by Acxiom (www.acxiom.com) found that 53% of adults would change to a new auto insurance carrier to save $300 annually.

Social Network Connections

- Studies have shown that a company's social followers are more likely to buy the brand's products. In a survey by Chadwick Martin Bailey (www.cmbinfo.com), more than half of Facebook users said they are likely to purchase at least a few brands they are social friends and followers of; 67% of Twitter followers indicated the same. Also, 60% of respondents claimed their Facebook fandom increased the chance that they would recommend a brand to a friend; among Twitter followers, that percentage rose to almost 80%.

In the *Brand Loyalty Survey* by ClickFox (www.clickfox.com), survey respondents identified the following as the best ways companies can build brand loyalty (percentage of respondents):

- Providing exceptional customer service: 34%
- Rewarding purchases, feedback, and referrals: 20%
- Sending exclusive and/or relevant offers and specials: 13%
- Providing personalized products or services: 12%
- Knowing the customer when they visit or call: 10%

29

BUYING AMERICAN-MADE

29.1 Preference For U.S.-Made Products

In a recent Harris Poll (www.theharrispoll.com), 61% of adults said they are more likely to purchase something when an ad touts it is 'Made in America,' and 3% said they are less likely to buy it; 35% said they are neither more nor less likely to purchase a product when an ad emphasizes it is Made in America.

Those who are more likely to purchase a product that is Made in America, by age and region, are as follows:

Age	**Much More Likely**	**Somewhat More**	**Neither**	**Less Likely**
• 18-to-34:	15%	29%	52%	4%
• 35-to-44:	20%	42%	37%	1%
• 45-to-54:	29%	37%	30%	4%
• 55 and older:	39%	37%	22%	3%
Region				
• East:	22%	38%	36%	3%
• Midwest:	32%	35%	31%	2%
• South:	25%	35%	36%	4%
• West:	26%	32%	38%	5%
Overall	26%	35%	35%	3%

When asked about factors influencing their decision to buy American-made products in a Harris poll, survey participants said the following were important (percentage of respondents):

- Keeping jobs in America: 90%
- Supporting American companies: 87%
- Safety concerns with products produced outside the U.S.: 82%
- Quality concerns with products produced outside the U.S.: 83%
- Patriotism: 76%
- Human rights issues with products produced outside the U.S.: 76%
- Decreasing environmental impact since products don't need to be shipped as far: 71%

Other surveys have found preference for U.S.-made to be even higher. In a survey by Boston Consulting Group (BGC, www.bcg.com), 80% of adults said they preferred U.S.-made goods and that they are willing to pay more for them.

Interestingly, BCG also found that many consumers in other countries also prefer U.S.-made goods. When the same question was asked of Chinese consumers, 47% said they preferred Made in America.

A poll by *The New York Times* had findings consistent with the Harris Poll.

> **"Two-thirds of Americans say they check labels when shopping to see if they are buying American goods, according to a *New York Times* poll taken early this year. Given the example of a $50 garment made overseas, almost half of respondents – 46% – said they would be willing to pay from $5 to $20 more for a similar garment made in the United States."**
>
> *The New York Times*

29.2 Buying American By Product Type

When asked about various categories of products in a Harris Poll, the following percentages of adults said it is important to buy American-made products:

- Major appliances: 75%
- Furniture: 74%
- Clothing: 72%
- Small appliances: 71%
- Automobiles: 70%
- Sports/exercise equipment: 66%
- Home electronics/TVs: 66%
- Smartphones/tablets: 66%
- Jewelry: 63%
- Motorcycles: 59%
- Novelty/gift items: 59%

By gender, responses were as follows:

	Female	Male
• Major appliances:	79%	71%
• Furniture:	78%	71%
• Clothing:	77%	67%
• Small appliances:	76%	66%

• Automobiles:	74%	65%
• Sports/exercise equipment:	69%	64%
• Home electronics/TVs:	72%	60%
• Smartphones/tablets:	71%	61%
• Jewelry:	67%	58%
• Motorcycles:	61%	58%
• Novelty/gift items:	66%	51%

By generation, responses were as follows:

	Millennials	**Gen Xers**	**Baby Boomers**	**Seniors**
• Major appliances:	57%	74%	86%	85%
• Furniture:	54%	76%	86%	84%
• Clothing:	56%	76%	80%	80%
• Small appliances:	53%	72%	81%	81%
• Automobiles:	58%	72%	76%	75%
• Sports/exercise equipment:	50%	70%	76%	71%
• Home electronics/TVs:	49%	69%	74%	76%
• Smartphones/tablets:	46%	69%	76%	76%
• Jewelry:	47%	67%	69%	70%
• Motorcycles:	46%	62%	67%	61%
• Novelty/gift items:	45%	64%	66%	61%

By demographic region, responses were as follows:

	Urban	**Suburban**	**Rural**
• Major appliances:	72%	74%	81%
• Furniture:	71%	73%	79%
• Clothing:	70%	72%	73%
• Small appliances:	72%	68%	76%
• Automobiles:	71%	67%	75%
• Sports/exercise equipment:	64%	65%	73%
• Home electronics/TVs:	69%	63%	71%
• Smartphones/tablets:	66%	64%	71%
• Jewelry:	62%	60%	68%
• Motorcycles:	55%	58%	63%
• Novelty/gift items:	57%	56%	61%

29.3 Market Resources

Made In USA Foundation. (http://madeusafdn.org)

Maker's Row, an online directory of U.S.-manufactured products. (www.makersrow.com)

The Made In America Movement. (www.themadeinamericamovement.com)

30

BUYING LOCAL

30.1 Buying Local

According to the Institute for Local Self-Reliance (www.ilsr.org), for every $100 spent at a locally owned store, $45 remains in the local economy, compared with about $13 per $100 spent at a national chain retailer.

"Locally owned businesses create more jobs locally and, in some sectors, provide better wages and benefits than chains do. Compared to chain stores, locally owned businesses recycle a much larger share of their revenue back into the local economy, enriching the whole community."

Stacy Mitchell, Senior Researcher
Institute for Local Self-Reliance

Civic Economics (www.civiceconomics.com) estimated that if San Francisco Bay Area consumers shifted 10% of their spending from national chains to local businesses, the impact would be $192 million in increased economic activity for the region and almost 1,300 new jobs.

According to *Time*, 82% of consumers actively support local or neighborhood businesses.

30.2 Locally Sourced Food Products

There has been a trend of increased demand for locally sourced foods at restaurants, farmers' markets, and groceries among patrons. While locally grown foods are not necessarily healthier, consumers are comforted by knowing the source of their food items. As concerns about food safety rise, the number of locavores – those who eat locally produced foods when available – is also increasing.

In an October 2015 Harris Poll (www.theharrispoll.com), 50% of adults said it is important when they are purchasing in a grocery that food is locally grown or sourced. Those that believe local sourcing is important are as follows:

Gender

- Female: 53%
- Male: 47%

Age

- 18-to-35: 54%
- 36-to-50: 49%
- 51-to-69: 47%
- 70 and older: 53%

Household

- Children: 56%
- No children: 47%

"When it comes to perusing the grocery store, there's a plethora of different factors that can lead to picking one item over another. One factor that's been getting its fair share of media attention and in-store callouts is 'local.' "

Harris Poll, 12/8/15

In a survey by the National Restaurant Association (www.restaurant.org), 64% of adults said locally sourced menu items are important when choosing a full-service restaurant (FSR). For comparison, 43% said organic or environmentally friendly food was important. In choosing a quick-service restaurant (QSR), locally sourced and organic menu items were cited as an important consideration by 63% and 45% of adults, respectfully. By gender and age, those placing a priority on locally sourced, and for comparison, organic menu items are as follows:

	Locally Sourced		Organic/Environmentally Friendly	
	FSR	**QSR**	**FSR**	**QSR**
Gender				
• Men:	59%	60%	38%	40%
• Women:	69%	65%	47%	50%

Age

• 18-to-34:	58%	58%	46%	48%
• 35-to-44:	68%	67%	37%	40%
• 45-to-54:	63%	63%	44%	46%
• 55-to-64:	67%	64%	44%	45%
• 65 and older:	68%	65%	41%	43%

Opinions vary as to what constitutes 'local' food products. In a survey by The Hartman Group (www.hartman-group.com), consumers defined 'local product' as follows:

- Within 100 miles: 50%
- Within my state: 37%
- Within a region: 4%
- In the United States: 4%

In a survey by A.T. Kearney (www.atkearney.com), the following percentages of adults said they are willing to pay more for local foods:

- Single urban households: 95%
- Young couples w/o kids: 78%
- Affluent families: 71%
- Senior citizens: 68%
- Middle income families: 67%
- Low income families: 57%

A.T. Kearney found that grocery shoppers largely embrace local food options because they believe it helps local economies (66%), delivers a broader and better assortment of products (60%), and provides healthier alternatives (45%). Some shoppers say they buy local food to improve the carbon footprint (19%) and to help increase natural or organic production (19%).

When asked about the availability of local food at their preferred supermarket, 65% say their supermarket offers at least some kind of locally sourced food. Almost 30% of grocery shoppers say they consider purchasing food elsewhere if their preferred store does not carry local foods. Only 5% indicate they shop for local foods at big-box retailers, 15% at national supermarkets. Overwhelmingly, respondents say their main source for local food is the local farmers market and farm stores.

30.3 Buy Local Initiatives

Most states have programs that encourage residents to buy local. The following is a selection of programs:

- Alabama: www.fma.alabama.gov/buy_fresh.htm
- Alaska: www.buyalaska.com
- Arizona: http://localfirstaz.com

- Colorado: www.coloradolocalfirst.com
- Hawaii: http://hdoa.hawaii.gov/add/md/buy-local-it-matters/
- New York: www.ny.gov/programs/buy-ny
- Utah: www.localfirst.org
- Virginia: www.buylocalvirginia.org
- Wisconsin: http://datcp.wi.gov/Business/Buy_Local_Buy_Wisconsin/

Similarly, some cities have launched initiatives to encourage residents to shop at locally owned businesses. The following are some example programs:

- Buffalo, NY: www.thepartnership.org/buylocal
- Gainesville, FL: www.gainesvillechamber.com/member-services/buylocal/
- Pasadena, CA: http://cityofpasadena.net/Pasadena_First/
- Philadelphia, PA: www.sbnphiladelphia.org/initiatives/
- Portland, ME: www.portlandbuylocal.org
- Portsmouth, VA: www.portsmouthva.gov/buy-local.aspx
- Scarborough, ME: www.buylocalscarborough.org
- Steamboat Springs, CO: www.steamboat-chamber.com/info/buy.local.asp

31

CONSUMER CONFIDENCE

31.1 Overview

In general, the more confident people feel about the economy and their job and income, the less likely they are to avoid making purchases. When confidence is trending down, consumers are likely to slow their spending, thus the rate of economic growth slows. Conversely, when consumer confidence is trending up, the economy typically grows with increases in consumer spending.

There are several recognized measurements of consumer confidence. This chapter provides a review of various assessments.

31.2 Consumer Comfort Index

The Consumer Comfort Index, which began in 1985, is announced weekly by Bloomberg (www.bloomberg.com/consumer-comfort-index/).

The following three questions are used to calculate the index:

- Would you describe the state of the nation's economy these days as excellent, good, not so good, or poor?
- Would you describe the state of your own personal finances these days as excellent, good, not so good, or poor?
- Considering the cost of things today and your own personal finances, would you say now is an excellent time, a good time, a not so good time, or a poor time to buy the things you want and need?

The index is derived from telephone interviews conducted by Langer Research Associates (www.langerresearch.com). The margin of error is ±3 percentage points.

31.3 Consumer Confidence Index

The Consumer Confidence Index is calculated each month by The Conference Board (www.conference-board.org) based on a survey of consumers' opinions on present conditions and future expectations of the economy. The Consumer Confidence Index was started in 1967 and is benchmarked at a reference of 100 for 1985, a year chosen because it was neither a peak nor a trough. Opinions on current conditions make up 40% of the index, with expectations of future conditions comprising the remaining 60%.

Each month The Conference Board surveys 5,000 U.S. households. The survey consists of five questions that ask respondents' opinions about the following:

- Current business conditions
- Business conditions for the next six months
- Current employment conditions
- Employment conditions for the next six months
- Total family income for the next six months

Survey participants are asked to answer each question as 'positive,' 'negative,' or 'neutral.' The relative value is calculated for each question separately and compared against each relative value from 1985. This comparison of the relative values results in an index value for each question. The index values for all five questions are then averaged together to form the Consumer Confidence Index. The data is calculated for the United States as a whole and for each of the country's nine census regions.

The results from the Consumer Confidence Survey are posted at www.conference-board.org/data/consumerconfidence.cfm on the last Tuesday of each month at 10:00 a.m. EST.

31.4 Consumer Sentiment Index

The Consumer Sentiment Index is one of the most recognized among several consumer confidence measures. It was devised in the late 1940s by Prof. George Katona at the University of Michigan. The index is calculated monthly based on 500 telephone household interviews conducted by the University of Michigan's Institute for Social Research (www.sca.isr.umich.edu/). Thomson Reuters publishes the Consumer Sentiment Index.

The University of Michigan releases three related figures each month: the Index of Consumer Sentiment (ICS, or MCSI), the Index of Current Economic Conditions (ICC), and the Index of Consumer Expectations (ICE). The ICE is an official component of the U.S. Index of Leading Economic Indicators.

31.5 Current Economic Conditions

The *Current Economic Conditions* report, commonly known as the Beige Book, is published by the Federal Reserve Board eight times per year. Each Federal Reserve Bank gathers anecdotal information on current economic conditions in its district through reports from bank and branch directors and interviews with key business contacts, economists, market experts, and other sources. The Beige Book summarizes this information by district and sector.

The *Current Economic Conditions* reports are available online at www.federalreserve.gov/monetarypolicy/beigebook/default.htm.

31.6 Economic Confidence Index

The Gallup Organization (www.gallup.com) continuously monitors consumer confidence with a two-question survey. The percentage of Americans classifying economic conditions as positive, negative, and mixed is reported daily based on a three-day rolling average of surveys of approximately 1,500 adults.

The poll, which guides the determination of Gallup's Economic Confidence Index, consists of the following questions:

- How would you rate economic conditions in this country today: as excellent, good, only fair, or poor?
- Right now, do you think that economic conditions in the country as a whole are getting better or getting worse?

Gallup reports on its website the Economic Confidence Index on a daily, weekly, monthly, and quarterly basis. The data is posted at www.gallup.com/Search/Default.aspx?s=&p=1&q=economic+confidence+index&b=Go.

32

CUSTOMER SATISFACTION

32.1 Overview

Surveys by Service Management Group (SMG, www.smg.com) assess various aspects of customer satisfaction at retail stores. The surveys query customers based on their most recent retail visit and compare various factors that relate to customer satisfaction.

32.2 Factors Contributing To High Customer Satisfaction

The following are findings from recent SMG surveys:

Corporate Headquarters Markets

SMG research found chain retail stores don't have an advantage with locations in the same city as corporate headquarters. Customers rated their satisfaction at chain locations as follows:

	Overall Satisfaction	Likely To Return
• Corporate headquarters market:	71%	74%
• All other markets:	72%	75%

"Customers visiting retail stores in the same city as the brand's corporate headquarters are actually slightly less satisfied than customers visiting locations in other cities. Customers may have slightly higher expectations of brands that are headquartered close to their home."

Service Management Group

First-Time vs. Returning Customers

SMG found that first-time customers are generally more difficult to satisfy than returning customers. Survey results are as follows:

	Highly Satisfied	Highly Likely to Return	Highly Likely to Recommend
Returning customers:	70%	67%	72%
First-time customer:	67%	59%	57%

"Across retail segments, first-time customers are generally less satisfied overall than returning customers. Loyalty to a brand is generally built up over time – one experience is often not enough to create a loyal customer."

Service Management Group

Large vs. Small Stores

Based on the size of the store, customers rated their satisfaction with retail locations as follows:

	Overall Satisfaction	Likely To Return
• Smallest footprint:	64%	65%
• Smaller footprint:	63%	64%
• Larger footprint:	63%	64%
• Largest footprint:	62%	63%

"Customers in the smallest footprint stores are slightly more satisfied. As stores increase in size, customers are somewhat less satisfied and less likely to recommend the store to their friends and family. These findings support the recent move by retailers to create smaller footprint locations in order to deliver better experiences. Most typically, customer issues in larger stores center on locating products and finding assistance."

Service Management Group

Mall vs. Freestanding Locations

Based on store location, the following percentages of customers said they likely would return to or recommend a retail location:

	Likely To Return	Recommend
• Freestanding:	75%	73%
• Mall:	75%	71%

"Customers visiting a mall location of a retailer are less likely to return and recommend than customers visiting other store formats. Free-standing locations don't share brand equity or customer experience with mall properties or adjoining retailers."

Service Management Group

Newer vs. Older Locations

Based on the age of the store, the following percentages of customers said they likely would return to or recommend a retail location:

	Likely To Return	Recommend
• Store under two years old:	78%	74%
• Store 2-to-5 years old:	75%	68%
• Store 5-to-10 years old:	74%	66%
• Store more than 10 years old:	73%	65%

"Customers visiting stores more than two years old report lower scores on loyalty metrics. Infusing capital into stores is a solid investment toward improving the customer experience. By doing so, operators can showcase the latest in store design and product enhancements."

Service Management Group

Returning Merchandise

Comparing customers with returns with those not returning merchandise, those highly satisfied with their most recent shopping experience are as follows:

	Overall Satisfaction	Friendliness	Speed
• No return:	57%	56%	47%
• Return:	57%	56%	44%

"Customers with returns are equally satisfied with their visit when compared with those who did not return an item. Returns are an unglamourous part of the retail world and stores seem to be doing a nice job handling returns."

Service Management Group

Rural vs. Urban Locations

Based on market population, the following percentages of customers said they likely would recommend a retail location based on their most recent shopping experience:

- Population more than 50,000: 63%
- Population 10,000-to-50,000: 66%
- Population less than 10,000: 67%

"Rural customers are slightly more satisfied overall with their retail concepts. Rural shoppers may have a smaller number of options to shop and, as a result, a smaller frame of reference when comparing experiences."

Service Management Group

32.3 Market Resources

Service Management Group, 1737 McGee Street, Kansas City, MO 64108. (800) 764-0439. (www.smg.com)

33

ETHICALLY CONSCIOUS CONSUMERISM

33.1 Trust In Business

Since 2001, Edelman (www.edelman.com) has published the *Edelman Trust Barometer*. In the 2016 survey, 51% of U.S. adults said they generally trust business as an institution, a figure that was unchanged from the prior year.

Consumers report engaging in the following behaviors for trusted companies:

- Choose to buy products/services: 68%
- Recommend to a friend/colleague: 59%
- Shared positive opinions online: 41%
- Defend company: 38%
- Paid a premium for products/services: 37%
- Bought shares: 18%

Consumers engage in the following behaviors for distrusted companies:

- Refused to buy products/services: 48%
- Criticized companies: 42%
- Disagreed with others: 35%
- Shared negative opinions: 26%
- Paid more than wanted: 20%
- Sold shares: 12%

33.2 Corporate Social Responsibility

2015 Millennial CSR Study, by Cone Communications (www.conecomm.com), reported the following actions and views on corporate social responsibility (CSR):

	Millennials	All Adults
• Would switch brands to one associated with a cause:	91%	85%
• Purchase products with a social or environmental benefit:	87%	83%
• Pay more for a product from a CSR company:	70%	66%
• Volunteer for a cause supported by a company they trust:	74%	56%
• Sharing products rather than buying:	66%	56%
• Take a pay cut to work for a responsible company:	62%	56%
• Use social media to address or engage with companies around social and environmental issues:	66%	53%
• Share positive information about companies and issues they care about:	38%	30%

• Share negative information about companies and issues they care about:	26%	21%
• Directly communicate with companies around issues:	18%	14%
• Contribute directly to an effort led by a company:	17%	12%

> **"From buying products associated with a cause they care about to using their online networks to amplify social and environmental messages, Millennials are universally more engaged in corporate social responsibility (CSR) efforts."**
>
> Cone Communications, 9/23/15

33.3 Use Of Products With An Environmental Benefit

The following are findings of Cone Communications' *Green Gap Trend Tracker* survey related to the use of products with an environmental benefit:

- Ninety percent (90%) of adults say they believe it's their responsibility to properly use and dispose of products with an environmental benefit, but their actions do not align with intent. Only 30% say they often use products in a way that achieves the intended environmental benefit; 42% say they dispose of products in a way that fulfills the intended environmental benefit.
- Eighty-five percent (85%) of adults say they want companies to educate them on how to properly use and dispose of products.
- Seventy-eight percent (78%) say they will boycott a product if they discover an environmental claim to be misleading.
- Seventy-one percent (71%) of consumers say they wish companies would do a better job helping them understand environmental terms.
- Seventy-one percent (71%) of adults say they regularly read and follow instructions on how to properly use a product, 66% read proper-disposal instructions, and 41% say they perform additional research to determine how best to utilize and discard a product for maximum benefit.
- Although more than 60% of respondents say they understand the environmental terms companies use in their advertising, the majority continue to erroneously believe common expressions such as "green" or "environmentally friendly" mean a product has a positive (40%) or neutral (22%) impact on the environment. Fewer were able to correctly identify these terms as meaning the product has a lighter impact than other similar products (22%) or less than it used to (2%). Despite the

attention given to product development and environmental marketing, consumer misunderstanding of "green" claims has remained flat at around 60% since 2008.

33.4 Ethical Influence On Purchase Decisions

According to *The Ethical Consumer U.S.*, a November 2015 report by Mintel (www.mintel.com), 23% of adults say their purchase decisions are always or often influenced by a company's ethics; an additional 47% say that their decisions are influenced sometimes.

Actions taken when they believe a company is ethical or unethical are as follows (percentage of respondents):

Ethical

- Buy products/services: 45%
- Tell others: 34%
- Neither of these: 34%

Unethical

- Stop buying products/services: 56%
- Tell others: 35%
- Neither of these: 26%

"More than half of adults stop buying products from unethical companies."

eMarketer, 12/10/15

34

GIFT GIVING

34.1 Overview

The percentages of consumers giving gifts for holidays and occasions are as follows (sources: National Retail Federation [NRF, www.nrf.com] and VoiceQuilt [www.voicequilt.com]):

- Christmas: 96%
- Birthdays: 95%
- Religious holidays: 89%
- Valentine's Day: 72%
- Mother's Day: 71%
- Father's Day: 66%

Gifting Report 2015, by Unity Marketing (www.unitymarketingonline.com), assesses the annual U.S. gifting market at $131 billion.

> **"While the annual year-end holiday gifting season receives the lion's share of marketer and retailer attention when it comes to the gifting market, the reality is that gifting represents a significant marketing opportunity throughout the whole year. Out of the typical gifters' annual gifting budget, Christmas accounts for slightly less than half of the total. The majority of gift purchases are made the rest of the year."**
>
> Unity Marketing, 5/15

34.2 Characteristics of Gift Giving

According to VoiceQuilt, 47% of all U.S. women buy gifts for 10 or more occasions throughout the year; 25% say they give gifts for 15 or more events, and 19% give gifts for 20 or more occasions over a 12-month period. The vast majority of U.S. women spend less than $50 on gifts regardless of the occasion.

Women have the following motivations behind their gift giving (source: VoiceQuilt):

- To say "I love you:" 65%
- Because they love giving gifts: 52%
- To surprise the gift receiver: 48%
- Because the occasion required a gift: 39%
- To thank someone: 35%
- Because it was the right thing to do: 27%
- To reciprocate: 10%
- To say "I'm sorry:" 4%
- Felt peer pressured: 1%
- To outdo someone else's gift: 1%

The following are the most important attributes of gifts (source: VoiceQuilt):

- Original: 78%
- Sentimental: 77%
- Make recipient feel its "just for them:" 74%
- Unique: 70%
- Heirloom: 54%
- Expensive: 19%

A survey by Research Now (www.researchnow.com) found that people find the most challenging aspect of holiday shopping as follows (percentage of responses; two responses allowed per survey participant):

- Finding the right gift: 60%
- Staying within budget: 56%
- Long lines and traffic: 50%

People consider the following to be the most difficult to buy gifts for (source: Research Now):

- Someone who has everything: 68%
- Unclassified love interest (not an official significant other or ex): 33%
- Frenemies (a friend who is also a rival): 26%

34.3 Gift Cards

CEB TowerGroup (www.cebglobal.com/financial-services/tower-group.html) assessed that consumers spent $124 billion on gift cards in 2015, a figure that was unchanged from the prior year. Seventy-seven percent (77%) gave a gift card during the year.

The *Gift Card Spending Survey*, by the National Retail Federation, reported spending on gift cards for the 2015 Christmas holiday season were $25.9 billion. Among those purchasing gift cards, average spending was $153.08, an 11.3% drop from the prior year.

When asked in the 2015 survey by the NRF the reasons they were giving gift cards, responses were as follows:

- Gift cards allow the recipient to select their own gift: 50%
- Gift cards are easier and faster to buy than traditional gifts: 25%
- It is easier to mail/ship a gift card to out-of-town recipients: 6%

A survey by Bizrate Insights (www.bizrateinsights.com) found that 61% of adults hoped to receive a gift card during the 2015 holiday season; 46% planned to give one. By generation, the percentages were as follows:

	Hope to Receive	Plan to Give
• Millennials:	72%	43%
• Generation Xers:	66%	52%
• Baby Boomers:	54%	47%
• Seniors:	42%	40%

Not only are gift cards used as gifts for all occasions, they are also used to transfer money. Parents and family gave $2.9 billion worth of gift cards to students for back-to-college in 2015, according to the National Retail Federation.

CardHub (www.cardhub.com) estimates that some $44 billion in unredeemed gift-card value has been accumulating since 2008.

34.4 Responsible Gift Giving

The Responsible Giving Survey, conducted by Ketchum Global Research Network (www.ketchum.com), studied the intent behind giving and examined how attitudes and culture shape gifting decisions and shopping habits. The survey found that 78% of adults give gifts during the holiday season because they want to and not out of a sense of obligation.

The following are other findings of the survey:

- Eighty-one percent (81%) of adults appreciate charitable donations given on their behalf in lieu of a gift; 74% would volunteer their time to charity as a gift if they thought others would value this type of responsible giving.
- Fifty-nine percent (59%) of adults prepare alternative gifts such as homemade gifts and make donations of time or money to charities during the holiday season.
- Forty-nine percent (49%) of married men say their spouse takes full responsibility for purchasing holiday gifts; 75% of married women say they take full responsibility for purchasing holiday gifts.

- Thirty-three percent (33%) of married men say they and their spouse share the responsibility of purchasing holiday gifts, but only 20% of married women say the same.
- Forty percent (40%) say that giving a homemade gift is better than giving a store-bought gift.
- Parents are more likely than adults without children to say they will make gifts rather than purchase some gifts (40% of parents vs. 29% of non-parents).
- Fifty-seven percent (57%) of those employed gave a gift to coworkers; 42% gave their boss a gift.
- Women are more likely than men to give a holiday gift or tip to people at work.
- Older adults ages 65 and above are more likely than adults overall to give a holiday gift or tip to people whose services they employ, such as a hairstylist (59% vs. 41% overall), a gardener or housekeeper (57% vs. 41% overall), or a mail or newspaper carrier (54% vs. 40% overall).

Fifty-nine percent (59%) of adults say that they have never re-gifted, though a similar number of adults say that re-gifting is socially acceptable. Among those who say that re-gifting is not socially acceptable, 22% admit that despite that belief, they have re-gifted.

The majority of adults agree that it's important to set an agreed-upon spending limit for gifts between family members or friends. Half agree that you should consider how much someone else can afford to spend when purchasing a gift for them.

Thirty percent (30%) of adults think someone is being irresponsible if they do not send a note of thanks for a gift. Older adults ages 50 and above are more likely than younger adults ages 18-to-29 to agree that someone is being irresponsible if they do not send a note of thanks for a gift (44% of older adults vs. 20% of younger adults).

34.5 Wedding Gift Giving

A survey by Claria Corporation (www.claria.com) reported that 75% of adults attend one to three weddings each year. Eighty percent (80%) buy gifts from the bride and groom's registry; 34% purchase wedding gifts through online retail channels.

Sixty-five percent (65%) typically buy gifts for all couples who invite them to a wedding, 30% only purchase gifts for weddings they attend. Sixty percent (60%) of respondents reported spending $26 to $75 for a wedding gift.

Ninety-four percent (94%) of engaged couples are registered.

34.6 Graduation Gift Giving

According to the National Retail Federation, 30% of consumers purchase a graduation gift, spending collectively approximately $4 billion each year. The average consumer buying graduation gifts gives to two graduates and spends an average of $90 on gifts.

Fifty-nine percent (59%) of those who give graduation gifts give cash, a higher percentage than for any other occasion. Additionally, 32% give gift cards.

34.7 Returning Gifts

The downside to gift-giving and -receiving is gifts that are unwanted. According to a Western Union survey, 75% of Americans have pretended to like a gift they received.

The National Retail Federation estimates that 10% of holiday purchases are returned. A survey by *Consumer Reports* found that about half of Americans include receipts with their gifts to help with returns and exchanges. A survey by HomeGoods found that 54% of adults had re-gifted presents; 36% had done so on several occasions.

35

LOYALTY PROGRAM PARTICIPATION

35.1 Participation

According to *2015 Colloquy Loyalty Census*, by Colloquy (www.colloquy.com), there are 3.3 billion loyalty memberships in the United States. The average American household holds memberships in 29 loyalty programs spread among the retail, financial services, travel, and various other sectors – but is active in only 12 of them. The number of memberships by sector are as follows:

Retail

- Specialty retail: 433.5 million
- Drug store: 267.6 million
- Department store: 229.6 million
- Grocery: 169.7 million
- Mass merchant: 164.3 million
- Fuel & convenience store: 24.5 million

Travel & Hospitality

- Airline: 355.9 million
- Hotel: 288.7 million
- Gaming: 156.5 million
- Restaurant: 54.8 million
- Cruise and car rental: 44.9 million

Financial: 577.9 million

2015 Loyalty Report, by Bond Brand Loyalty (https://bondbrandloyalty.com), reported that U.S. consumers participate in an average of 6.7 loyalty programs.

"Consumers have a finite capacity in terms of the number of programs and brands with which they can actively engage."

2015 Loyalty Report
Bond Brand Loyalty

Promo Magazine estimates annual spending for loyalty program development and implementation at $2.0 billion. This figure does not include the value of program rewards.

35.2 Customer Incentives

Technology Advice (www.technologyadvice.com) found in its survey of loyalty program members reasons for participation as follows (percentage of respondents):

- Save money: 58%
- Receive rewards: 38%

When asked their preference for type of program, responses were as follows:

- Card-based: 37%
- Digital: 33%
- Either: 30%

Pulse Of The Online Shopper, published in 2015 by UPS (www.ups.com), reported the most valuable loyalty benefits as follows (percentage of respondents):

- Free product, gift certificate, or cash back for frequent purchases: 61%
- Product discounts: 58%
- Free shipping: 57%
- Exclusive access to sales, promotions, and new products: 30%
- Low-cost one- or two-day shipping: 15%
- Convenience or higher priority service: 8%
- Elevated status: 7%
- Personalization - knowing customer upon sign-on: 7%
- Customized recommendations based on shopping preferences: 6%

An August 2015 survey by Colloquy reported reasons that people continue to participate in a loyalty program as follows (percentage of respondents):

- The program is easy to understand: 81%
- Relevant rewards and offers: 75%
- Supports lifestyle/personal preferences: 54%
- Provides lots of ways to earn rewards faster: 50%
- Has a smartphone app: 48%

In a July 2015 survey by LoyaltyOne (www.loyalty.com), 62% of respondents said they would pay to join a rewards program if their favorite retailer had a paid loyalty program; among those ages 25-to-34, the figure was 77%.

35.3 Effectiveness

According to Bond Brand Loyalty's *2015 Loyalty Report*, 86% of consumers feel that loyalty programs are worth participating in. Eighty-three percent (83%) say that programs make them more likely to continue doing business with certain companies and 49% say they spend more with brands than before their loyalty program membership.

In a survey by the Chief Marketing Officer Council (www.cmocouncil.org), 69% of respondents said most of their experience with loyalty programs has been "pretty good," and 10% said they've been "very satisfied." Half said a program membership either "strongly motivates my repeat business or visits" (21%) or is "usually a big factor in my decision-making" (30%). The survey also found that 32% of respondents felt that program participation held little to no value, and 37% felt individual rewards had even less to offer by way of value.

> **"Without a great experience, loyalty programs are less valuable to customers and abandoned early even if they promise discounts."**
>
> eMarketer, 2/3/16

Loyalty Programs: A Cross-Industry Analysis of Usage and Effectiveness, a report by the Direct Marketing Association (www.the-dma.com), provides the following assessment of loyalty programs:

- Seventy percent (70%) of loyalty programs offer free enrollment to their customers; 16% tier their fee structure and rewards program.
- The use of loyalty programs in the financial services sector is on the rise, due in part to the expanded range of premium reward card products designed to build loyalty among affluent consumers. These card products provide extensive experiential reward benefits and are often co-marketed with other luxury brands.
- Among retail and department store loyalty programs, member upgrades are the rewards most likely to be redeemed.
- Seventy-four percent (74%) of supermarket and grocery store loyalty programs use face-to-face interactions to invite customers into loyalty programs, making it the most used channel in that segment.
- Sixty-five percent (65%) of hotel and restaurant loyalty programs have a proprietary loyalty program in place, rewarding customers with their own products/services.
- Sixty-seven percent (67%) of catalog merchants offer their loyalty programs for free; one quarter charge different membership fees depending on the level of the program, and less than 10% charge a one-time nominal fee to customers who join.

Among the most popular loyalty programs is Amazon Prime, which guarantees free two-day shipping on most orders with no purchase minimum and streamed access to tens of thousands of TV shows and movies. *Money* estimates that about one-half of U.S. households have an Amazon Prime membership (Amazon does not disclose membership numbers). Annual membership is $99. While Amazon does not release Prime membership numbers, Consumer Intelligence Research Partners (www.cirpllc.com)
estimated that Amazon Prime had 54 million U.S. members as of January 2016, spending on average about $1,100 per year, compared to about $600 per year for non-members.

35.4 Sector Assessment

By sector, Bond Brand Loyalty's *2015 Loyalty Report* reported the following percentages of members were very satisfied with loyalty programs:

- Casual dining restaurant: 52%
- Retail: 45%
- Entertainment: 45%
- Quick-service restaurant: 41%
- Consumer packaged goods: 31%

According to WSL Strategic Retail (www.wslstrategicretail.com), loyalty programs targeting high-income consumers see greater participation. Compared with 58% of those with incomes below $50,000, 93% of shoppers with household incomes above $100,000 participate in loyalty programs.

Many retailers are restructuring their loyalty programs with tiered membership levels. By exceeding spending thresholds members achieve elite status and associated perks. The highest reward level for Sephora's Beauty Insider program, for example, gives free shipping, early access to new products and sales, and VIP event invites for shoppers who spend $1,000 or more in a year. At Nordstrom, making it into the upper tiers requires $2,000, $5,000, or $10,000 in annual spending. At Best Buy, Premier Silver status goes to those spending at least $2,500 in a year.

36

PAYMENT PREFERENCES

36.1 Comparison Of Payment Methods

According to a study by Bankrate (www.bankrate.com) and Princeton Survey Research Associates (www.psrai.com), U.S. adult consumers primarily used the following methods for their holiday shopping in 2015:

- Debit cards: 38%
- Credit cards: 37%
- Cash, check, and other: 24%
- Proximity mobile payments: 1%

The primary reason consumers said they did not use mobile payments were as follows:

- Not secure enough: 36%
- Other payment methods are more convenient: 31%
- Don't know how to use: 12%
- Do not own a phone that allows them: 11%
- Favorite stores do not accept them: 3%
- Other: 7%

36.2 Credit and Debit Cards

According to The Nilson Report (www.nilsonreport.com), spending for goods and services on American Express, Discover, MasterCard, and Visa brand consumer and commercial credit, debit, and prepaid cards issued in the U.S. generated $4.79 trillion in purchase volume in 2015, up 7.8% from 2014. Credit cards accounted for 59% of spending in 2015 compared to 41% for debit cards.

Payment card purchase volume in the U.S. in 2015 was as follows (change from previous year in parenthesis):

- Visa debit cards: $1.374 trillion (7.9%)
- Visa credit cards: $1.344 trillion (10.8%)
- American Express: $ 717 billion (4.8%)
- MasterCard credit cards: $ 653 billion (7.4%)
- MasterCard debit cards: $ 580 billion (8.0%)
- Discover: $ 118 billion (-6.9%)

Merchants paid $71 billion in fees to have payments processed in 2015.

36.3 How Americans Pay Their Bills

According Javelin Strategy & Research (www.javelinstrategy.com), Americans made $3.5 trillion in payments for seven common types of bills in 2015. Methods used for bill payment were as follows:

- Financial institution online: 37%
- Biller online: 31%
- Check payment by mail: 10%
- Biller mobile: 9%
- Financial institution mobile: 9%
- Walk-in location: 6%
- Call-in: 4%
- Third-party bill-pay service: 3%
- Other: 1%

36.4 Point-Of-Sale Payments

Traditional paper-based payments (cash and check) have increasingly lost favor with consumers and merchants for point-of-sale (POS) retail transactions and are quickly being replaced by plastic cards and alternative payments. Cash POS transactions have been, and are forecast, as follows (source: Javelin Strategy & Research):

- 2012: $874 billion
- 2013: $788 billion
- 2014: $775 billion
- 2015: $760 billion
- 2016: $746 billion
- 2017: $732 billion
- 2018: $717 billion
- 2019: $711 billion

"For many years, cash and paper checks dominated consumers' wallets, with consumers using cash for smaller dollar-value transactions and selecting checks for big-ticket items. This trend has taken a dramatic turn, as consumers increasingly abandoned their traditional paper-based payments for card payments. "

Javelin Strategy & Research, 5/21/16

Cash is still the most commonly used payment option for in-store purchases, with 65% of all consumers using cash to make a purchase in the past seven days. Despite the regular use of cash, debit and credit dominate total POS spending.

36.5 Online Retail Payments

In 2015, consumers spent a total of $341.7 billion online, according to the U.S. Department of Commerce.

Online retail payments are distributed as follows (source: Javelin Strategy & Research):

- Major credit card: 41%
- Debit card: 32%
- Online alternative payments: 15%
- Prepaid/gift card: 6%
- Store-branded credit card: 5%

> **"Do not be deceived by the use of 'alternative' in online alternative payments, as these payment options have clearly become mainstream for online retail payments. Over 80% of online shoppers report that they have used an online alternative payment service (such as PayPal, Amazon Payments, or Google Wallet) for an online purchase. And the reach does not stop there. Increasingly, platforms that were once exclusive to e-commerce are moving into physical stores. PayPal is now an accepted payment method at 18,000 physical stores."**
>
> Javelin Strategy & Research

36.6 Proximity Mobile Payments

Proximity mobile payments – point-of-sale transactions that use mobile devices as a payment method via tapping, waving, and similar functionality – are growing in popularity in the U.S., although the growth has been somewhat less than forecast.

eMarketer (www.emarketer.com) assesses the number of proximity mobile payment users and total transactions as follows:

	Users	Transactions
• 2014:	16.4 million	$ 3.68 billion
• 2015:	23.2 million	$ 8.71 billion
• 2016:	37.5 million	$ 27.05 billion
• 2017:	50.2 million	$ 61.75 billion
• 2018:	58.8 million	$114.63 billion
• 2019:	69.8 million	$210.45 billion

"Mobile payments will triple in the U.S. in 2016. Several factors will drive the growth. Mobile wallets like Apple Pay, Android Pay, and Samsung Pay will become a standard feature on new smartphones. Also, more merchants will adopt point-of-sale systems that can accept mobile payments, and incentives like promotions and loyalty programs will be integrated to attract new users."

eMarketer, 10/26/15

36.7 Market Resources

Javelin Strategy & Research, 4301 Hacienda Drive, Suite 550, Pleasanton, CA 94588. (925) 225-9100. (www.javelinstrategy.com)

The Nilson Report, 1110 Eugenia Place, Suite 100, Carpinteria, CA 93013. (805) 684-8800. (www.nilsonreport.com)

37

PRICING

37.1 Overview

Along with product, promotion, and place, pricing is one of the Four Ps of the classic marketing mix.

Most customers consider pricing the most important aspect of shopping. A recent survey by The NPD Group (www.npd.com) asked consumers what factors they considered extremely important in deciding where to shop. Responses were as follows (percentage of respondents):

- Price: 85%
- Sales and special deals: 75%
- Convenience of location: 60%
- Ease of shopping: 60%
- Customer service: 56%

"Price trumps sales and special deals, customer service, and convenience as a factor in deciding where to shop for the majority of U.S. consumers. Eighty-five percent of consumers say the price needs to be right before they shop."

The NPD Group

Retailers must strike a balance between offering prices that are attractive to customers, yet still provide themselves with a reasonable margin. Underpricing can drastically cut into a company's bottom line.

> **"Companies leave millions of dollars on the table every year through sub-optimal pricing practices. The current abundance of customer data, in the context of increased global competition and the instant information sharing made possible by the Internet, requires companies to not only set the right prices, but to continually monitor and refine pricing."**
>
> UC Berkeley Pricing for Profitability

37.2 Dynamic Pricing

Dynamic pricing, also called market-based pricing and variable pricing, adjusts prices based on demand. It was introduced by airlines in the 1980s when carriers began shifting capacity by offering discounts on full fare prices. Most travelers today are aware that fares fluctuate with demand.

The dynamic pricing model is also popular in professional sports ticketing. Most MLB, NBA, NFL, and NHL teams adjust single-game ticket prices – up or down – as late as game day. Software by Digonex Technologies (www.digonex.com), Qcue (www.qcue.com), and Veritix (www.veritix.com) is used by teams to guide variable pricing based on past ticket sales, team matchups, day and time of the game, player injuries, weather, and the going rate on ticket resale websites. Qcue reported that its MLB clients that implemented dynamic pricing increased season revenue by an average of $900,000 by adjusting the price in each section of the ballpark for each game.

Dynamic pricing is also practiced in the retail sector. Many online retailers have regularly adjusted prices on a daily basis for several years. Bricks-and-mortar retailers have recently caught up by using electronic shelf tags.

"Dynamic pricing may be the future of retail. The retail industry, following in the footsteps of travel and hospitality, knows that real-time price shifts online will not only buffer against showrooming – shoppers can't rely on prices online to be cheaper or quantities more abundant – but also maximize revenues. Prices rise and fall based on customer traffic, demand, weather, the time of day, loyalty card data, and more."

eMarketer

A host of monitoring services and software tools is available to guide online retailers in their pricing. Providers of these services and tools include the following:

- 360pi (www.360pi.com)
- CommerceHub (www.commercehub.com)
- Competitor Monitor (www.competitormonitor.com)
- PriceManager (www.pricemanager.com)
- Profitero (www.profitero.com)
- Upstream Commerce (www.upstreamcommerce.com)
- WiseCommerce (www.wiser.com)

37.3 Price-Matching

While not a new practice, price-matching has increased since 2011, when Walmart rolled out its Ad Match Guarantee. Big-box retailers Best Buy, Home Depot, Target, and Toys "R" Us, among others, also use price-matching programs to better compete with rivals.

While retailers dislike price-matching, once one retailer offers to do it, rivals feel compelled to follow. Because price equivalencies are not always simple to ascertain, matching policies vary. Best Buy, for instance, lets customers match prices if the rival store is within a 25-mile radius, while Walmart lets store managers decide how far and wide price-matching applies.

"Price-matching is a necessary evil today. Although price-matching promotions have been around for years, they've become a key marketing tool to attract shoppers squeezed by stagnant wages and 7%-plus unemployment. It can be a risky strategy. Not only are the programs hard to manage, they're often left to the discretion of an individual cashier. Price-matching can backfire if shoppers don't get the deal they expect and leave confused or angry."

Bloomberg Businessweek

An assessment by DealScience (www.dealscience.com), a company that ranks online deals from thousands of retail brands, discovered that at least 20% of big-box retailers had price-matching policies, though many do not advertise them. The practice is commonplace for home and sporting goods and electronics retailers, but even higher-end merchants like Nordstrom have price-matching guidelines. Some retailers, including Best Buy, Home Depot, and Lowe's allow managers to go a step better than price matching by offering 10% below a competitor's price.

Recognizing that their strongest competition is online retailers, not nearby stores, some retailers have expanded their price-matching. During the 2013 holiday season, for example, Best Buy matched the prices of any online competitor if customers showed proof of the lower price. With such bold policies, price-matching morphed into pricing negotiations with customers.

The New York Times reported that when a shopper asked at Nordstrom and Bloomingdale's if the retailers were open to bargaining, sales representatives and managers at both stores said yes without hesitation. And, at Kohl's, when a shopper asked for a 15% discount, the answer was yes.

"Armed with increasingly sophisticated price-tracking tools on their smartphones and other devices, consumers have become bolder, and they know that they often have the upper hand during a tough season for retailers. Recognizing the new reality, some retailers, desperate for sales and customer loyalty, have begun training their employees in the art of bargaining with customers."

The New York Times

According to Alison Kenny Paul, vice chairwoman and leader of the retail and distribution practice at Deloitte (www.deloitte.com), some retailers are training employees on the rules of bargaining. While it is mainly department or floor managers who are given the authority to make deals, other employees are now being coached to recognize when a consumer needs to negotiate and to spot the consumer getting ready to walk out the door.

"Retailers panicked a few years ago when they realized that some consumers were using bricks-and-mortar stores to view products, only to walk out and order them at a lower price online. Now they are trying to 'turn lemons into lemonade' by using that model as an opportunity to work with customers and even cement their loyalty."

Alison Kenny Paul
U.S. Retail & Distribution Leader
Deloitte

37.4 Personalized Pricing

Using customers' buying profiles, either from their online purchase history or loyalty program in-store purchases, retailers are able to make intelligent guesses about what customers will want to buy next, when they will want it, and how much they will be willing to pay. Retailers, particularly in the supermarket sector, are using customers' buying history logged with their loyalty program purchases to customize coupon promotions for individuals. Promotions are then tailored to the customer profiles.

"For the past decade, e-commerce sites have altered prices based on your Web habits and personal attributes. What is your geography and your past buying history? How did you arrive at the e-commerce site? What time of day are you visiting? An entire literature has emerged on the ethics, legality and economic promise of pricing optimization."

Scientific American

Supermarkets offer personalized prices via smartphone apps and loyalty card swipes. A mobile app identifies shoppers when they scan products through their frequent shopper number or phone number and creates special e-coupons on the spot. The apps also use a shopper's location in store aisles to personalize offers.

"As more supermarkets experiment with personalized pricing, the more likely it becomes that you and the shopper standing next to you will pay two different prices for the same quart of milk. Same store, same milk, different prices."

ABC News

A survey by RetailWire (www.retailwire.com) found that marketers rank personalized pricing/promotion as the #1 pricing strategy in combating problems caused by pricing transparency.

37.5 Pricing Market Research

Market research companies offer two general types of pricing studies: those which determine acceptance of a product or service sold at a specified price, and those which determine the possible effect on demand of different price levels (i.e., elasticity).

A directory of companies that provide pricing consulting studies is available online at www.greenbook.org/market-research-firms/price-research.

37.6 Pricing Research Centers

Columbia University, Center for Pricing and Revenue Management, Uris Hall, Room 408, New York, NY 10027. (212) 851-5815. (http://www7.gsb.columbia.edu/cprm/)

Fordham University, Pricing Center, Graduate School of Business, 113 West 60th Street, New York, NY 10023. (212) 636-6296. (www.fordham.edu/info/24395/fordham_university_pricing_center)

Rochester University, Center for Pricing, Simon Business School, Schlegel Hall, Rochester, NY 14627. (585) 276-3381. (www.simon.rochester.edu/about-simon/centers-for-excellence/the-center-for-pricing/index.aspx)

University of California Berkeley, Pricing Program, Haas School of Business, 2000 Center Street, Berkeley, CA 94704. (http://executive.berkeley.edu/programs/pricing-profitability-information-age)

38

PRIVACY ISSUES

38.1 Overview

Consumers are increasingly reacting to the continuous invasion of privacy in their lives. They feel, rightfully, that marketers are watching virtually every aspect of their lives, even while they are in their own homes.

> **"A surveillance society is taking root. Video cameras peer constantly from lamp poles and storefronts. Smartphones relay a dizzying barrage of information about their owners to sentinel towers dotting cities and punctuating pasture-land. Meanwhile, on the information superhighway, every stop by every traveler is noted and stored by Internet service providers like Google, Verizon, and Comcast. Retailers scan, remember, and analyze each purchase by every consumer. Smart TVs know what we're watching – soon they will have eyes to watch us watching them – and smart meters know if we've turned out the lights."**
>
> *Time*

General surveys indicate that consumers have concerns about their privacy, both online and offline. However, it is difficult to ascertain their concerns about specific actions by marketers because few people really understand what these activities are. And there is a general misconception that the government is protecting their privacy.

"My national phone surveys going back to 1999 show that the majority of Americans know companies follow them, but they have little understanding of data mining or targeting. They also think the government protects them more than it does regarding the misuse of their information and against price discrimination."

Prof. Joseph Turow, Ph.D., Associate Dean
Annenberg School For Communication
University of Pennsylvania

Consumers' concerns about privacy are also sometimes difficult to gauge because they are self-contradictory about marketer's use of their information.

"People may claim to worry about privacy issues but look at what they actually do online ... willingly surrendering personal information for a coupon or in a Facebook discussion. The disconnect between what people say and do shows that policymakers and academics misjudge the extent to which the public really cares about the use of data about them by marketers."

Mark Dolliver, Analyst
The Digital Privacy Dilemma

38.2 Identity Fraud and Theft

According to the *2016 Identity Fraud Study*, by Javelin Strategy & Research (www.javelinstrategy.com), 13.1 million consumers were identity fraud victims in 2015, a 3% increase over the prior year. The amount stolen decreased by 6% to $15 billion.

The Bureau of Justice Statistics (www.bjs.gov) classifies Identity theft as follows:

- Misuse of an existing account such as a credit card or online account: 86% of incidents
- Unauthorized use of personal information to open a new account: 4% of incidents
- Misuse of personal information for fraudulent purposes such as getting medical care, housing, a job, or other benefits: 3% of incidents
- Multiple types of theft: 7% of incidents

In 2015, the U.S. switched to EMV, an open-standard set of specifications for smart card payments and acceptance devices which is designed to reduce in-person fraud and the profitability of counterfeit card operations. Fraudsters have reacted by moving away from existing card fraud to focus on new account fraud. This drove a 113% increase in incidence of new account fraud, which now accounts for 20% of all fraud losses.

38.3 Attitudes About Privacy

Americans' Attitudes About Privacy, Security, And Surveillance, a 2015 report by Pew Research Center (www.pewinternet.org) reported the following attitudes among U.S. adults:

- Ninety-three percent (93%) of adults say that being in control of who can get information about them is important.
- Ninety percent (90%) say that controlling what information is collected about them is important.
- Americans say they do not wish to be observed without their approval; 88% say it is important that they not have someone watch or listen to them without their permission.
- Eighty-five percent (85%) of adults say that not being disturbed at home is important.
- The following percentages of adults say they are not confident that records of their activity maintained by various online entities will remain private and secure:
    - Online advertisers who place ads on the websites they visit: 75%
    - Social media sites they use: 69%
    - Search engine providers: 66%
    - Online video sites they use: 66%
- Adult Internet users think that various online entities should not save records or archives of their activity:
    - Online advertisers who place ads on the websites they visit: 50%
    - Social media sites they use: 40%
    - Search engine providers: 40%
    - Online video sites they use: 44%
- Just 6% of adults say they are 'very confident' that government agencies can keep their records private and secure, while another 25% say they are 'somewhat confident.'

"The majority of Americans believe it is important that they be able to maintain privacy and confidentiality in commonplace activities of their lives. Most strikingly, these views are especially pronounced when it comes to knowing what information about them is being collected and who is doing the collecting. These feelings also extend to their wishes that they be able to maintain privacy in their homes, at work, during social gatherings, at times when they want to be alone and when they are moving around in public."

Pew Research Center, 5/20/15

38.4 Online Privacy

Since 2010, TRUSTe (www.truste.com) has published a Consumer Privacy Index study. The following are findings from the 2015 report:

- Ninety-two percent (92%) of U.S. Internet users worry about their privacy online. Forty-two percent (42%) are more worried than they were one year ago.
- Fifty-five percent (55%) of U.S. Internet users trust businesses with their personal information; 45% do not have this trust. This is a three-year low for this metric.
- Twenty-two percent (22%) of U.S. Internet users do not trust anyone to protect their online privacy.
- Top causes of concern among U.S. Internet users about their online privacy are as follows:
  - Companies collecting and sharing personal information with other companies: 36%
  - Security threats to online data: 36%
  - Government online surveillance: 28%
  - Companies tracking web-surfing behavior: 22%
  - Social media sites sharing details with advertisers: 19%
- Ninety-one percent (91%) of U.S. Internet users avoid doing business with companies they do not believe protect their online privacy.
- Seventy-seven percent (77%) of U.S. Internet users have moderated their online activity in the past year due to privacy concerns. The following are actions taken:

- Have not clicked on an online ad: 57%
- Withheld personal information: 51%
- Have not downloaded an app product: 35%
- Stopped an online transaction: 25%
- Deleted an online account: 9%

- Seventy-eight percent (78%) of U.S. Internet users believe they are primarily responsible for protecting their privacy online. The following are steps taken to protect privacy in the past year:
  - Deleted cookies: 63%
  - Changed privacy settings: 44%
  - Turned off location tracking: 25%
  - Read privacy policies: 23%
  - Opted out of behavioral ads: 10%
- U.S. Internet users want the following actions implemented as measures to lower concerns about online privacy:
  - Companies being more transparent about how they are collecting and using data: 37%
  - More active enforcement of measures to protect privacy online: 37%
  - Identify clearer ways to hold companies accountable for protecting privacy online: 34%
  - Passing legislation: 27%
  - Governments being more transparent about how they are collecting and using data: 22%
  - Online privacy best practices taught in schools: 20%
- U.S. Internet users say the following actions by Internet companies would increase trust related to use of their personal information:
  - Give clear procedures for removing personal information: 47%
  - Ask for permission before using cookies: 31%
  - Offer notice and ways to opt out of targeted ads: 31%
  - Give information on how personal information is used: 30%
  - Easy opportunities to stop being contacted by third parties: 30%
  - Privacy policies in easy to understand language: 21%

38.5 Mobile Privacy

The *2015 U.S. Mobile App Report*, by comScore (www.comscore.com) reported smartphone user who are comfortable with apps accessing their location as follows:

- Very comfortable: 13%
- Somewhat comfortable: 29%
- Neither comfortable nor uncomfortable: 28%

- Somewhat uncomfortable: 19%
- Very uncomfortable: 12%

In a November 2015 survey by Skyhook Wireless (www.skyhookwireless.com), adult app users said they have turned on location services for the following app categories:

- Weather: 65%
- Social networks: 38%
- Travel: 23%
- Photo and video: 18%
- News: 16%

"Privacy and security are critical to mobile users, most of whom have some understanding of how revealing their mobile data – including location – can be to advertisers, publishers, governments and other Internet users. And for many, that means not using location services at all, potentially diminishing their mobile experiences."

eMarketer, 11/25/15

38.6 Whom Do Consumers Trust?

The Harris Poll (www.theharrispoll.com) asked adults how much trust they have in various entities handling their personally identified information (such as credit card information, contact information, and so forth) in a properly confidential and secure manner. Responses were as follows:

	Trust	Don't Trust
• Health providers (e.g. doctors and hospitals):	79%	21%
• Major online retailers (e.g. Amazon, eBay):	74%	26%
• Banks and brokerage companies:	68%	32%
• Small and/or independent online retailers:	55%	45%
• State and local governments:	52%	48%
• Search and portal sites (e.g. Google, Yahoo!):	49%	51%
• Federal government:	48%	52%
• Social networking sites (like Facebook or MySpace):	28%	72%

By age, adults trust the following entities handling their personal identification:

	18-to-34	35-to-44	45-to-54	55+
• Health providers (e.g. doctors and hospitals):	78%	78%	76%	82%
• Major online retailers (e.g. Amazon, eBay):	74%	72%	74%	76%
• Banks and brokerage companies:	70%	65%	63%	71%
• Small and/or independent online retailers:	55%	58%	58%	53%
• State and local governments:	61%	52%	49%	46%
• Search and portal sites (e.g. Google, Yahoo!):	55%	54%	50%	41%
• Federal government:	58%	51%	48%	39%
• Social networking sites (like Facebook or MySpace):	42%	34%	27%	14%

Adults said they view the following as a threat to their privacy:

- Cyber-criminals: 88%
- Social networking sites (e.g. Facebook, Google+): 70%
- People with wearable, camera-equipped devices: 63%
- The federal government: 60%
- People with camera-equipped phones: 59%
- State and local governments: 56%
- Search and portal sites (e.g. Google, Yahoo!): 53%
- Banks and brokerage companies: 43%
- Small and/or independent online retailers: 42%
- Major online retailers (e.g. Amazon, eBay): 35%
- Health providers (e.g. doctors and hospitals): 31%

39

PURCHASE DECISION MAKING

39.1 Top Priorities

A study by Duke University's Fuqua School of Business, commissioned by the American Marketing Association (www.ama.org), reported customers' leading priorities as follows:

- Quality: 31.0%
- Trust: 18.7%
- Service: 17.9%
- Low price: 16.8%
- Innovation: 9.1%
- Brand: 6.6%

39.2 Deciding Where To Shop

A 2015 survey by TimeTrade (www.timetrade.com) asked adults the main reason they decided to purchase a product at a specific store when choosing between four retailers regarding an item with the same price. Responses were as follows (percentage of respondents):

- The overall in-store experience: 64%
- Quick service: 30%
- Staff knowledge about merchandise: 6%

In a survey by The NPD Group (www.npd.com), consumers said the following were extremely important factors in deciding where to shop (percentage of respondents):

- Price: 85%
- Sales and special deals: 75%
- Convenience of location: 60%
- Ease of shopping: 60%
- Customer service: 56%

"Price trumps sales and special deals, customer service, and convenience as a factor in deciding where to shop for the majority of U.S. consumers."

The NPD Group

According to a by Society For New Communications Research (www.sncr.org), important factors influencing how consumers form impressions of companies are as follows (percentage of respondents):

	Very Important	Mildly Important
• Quality of products/services:	80%	17%
• Cost of products/services:	55%	37%
• Customer care program:	37%	41%
• Friend, family, other trusted people:	34%	42%
• Customer reviews/ratings on social media:	30%	43%
• Social conscience:	19%	38%
• Rewards program:	18%	42%
• Years company in business:	15%	39%
• Media reports:	13%	43%
• Company ads:	10%	33%
• Social media presence:	7%	21%

39.3 Trust in Shopping Recommendations

The *2015 Consumer Trust Survey*, by Citrix (www.citrix.com), reported the most trusted sources of information among U.S. adults when making purchase decisions as follows (percentage of respondents):

- Friends and family: 81%
- Online reviews: 76%
- Third-party experts: 70%
- Websites: 67%
- Articles and news: 63%
- Videos: 63%
- Marketing materials: 55%
- Bloggers: 55%
- Social media: 49%
- Advertising: 47%

According to a survey by Edelman (www.edelman.com), credible sources of information about companies or products are as follows (percentage of respondents):

- An academic or expert: 70%
- Technical expert with the company: 64%
- Financial or industry expert: 53%
- CEO: 50%
- Non-government organization representative: 47%
- Governmental official: 43%
- Person like yourself: 43%
- Regular employee: 34%

In the *Global Online Consumer Survey*, by The Nielsen Company (www.nielsen.com), 90% of respondents said they trust recommendations from people they know. The following are percentages that trust various other sources:

- Consumer opinions posted online: 70%
- Brand websites: 70%
- Editorial content (e.g. newspaper): 69%
- Brand sponsorships: 64%
- TV: 62%
- Newspaper: 61%
- Magazines: 59%
- Billboards/outdoor advertising: 55%
- Radio: 55%
- Emails signed up for: 54%
- Ads before movies: 52%
- Search engine results ads: 41%
- Online video ads: 37%
- Online banner ads: 33%
- Text ads on mobile phones: 24%

According to a survey by Bridge Ratings (www.bridgeratings.com), consumers rate trusted sources of information as follows (rated on a scale of 1-to-10):

- Friends, family, and acquaintances: 8.6
- Strangers with expertise: 7.9
- Teachers: 7.3
- Religious leaders: 6.9
- Newspapers and magazines: 6.1
- Favorite radio personality: 5.5
- TV news reporters: 5.2
- Bloggers: 2.8
- Advertising: 2.2
- Telemarketers: 1.4

39.4 Influence Of Social Media

A recent Harris Poll (www.theharrispoll.com) survey asked consumers the likelihood that they would make a purchase based on a friend's post on a social media site. Responses by age were as follows:

	Very Likely	Fairly Likely	Somewhat Likely	Not Likely
• 18-to-34:	9%	19%	40%	33%
• 35-to-44:	9%	13%	31%	47%
• 45-to-54:	4%	8%	28%	60%
• 55-to-64:	1%	7%	24%	67%
• 65 and older:	2%	5%	17%	78%

39.5 Shopper Decision Priorities

The *Brand Landscape Report*, by The NPD Group (www.npd.com), explored the factors that go into purchase decisions made by shoppers. The assessment found that priorities vary by product category and the gender of the shopper.

For various product categories, consumers consider a product for purchase as follows:

Apparel

Female

1. Is a brand I've had success with
2. Has the features/benefits I want
3. Is my style
4. Offers real solutions for me
5. Fits well
6. Is comfortable
7. Has a lot of sales or special deals
8. Offers good value for the money
9. Is a brand friends wear
10. Is affordable

Male

1. Is a brand I've had success with
2. Is my style
3. Has the features/benefits I want
4. Offers good value for the money
5. Offers real solutions for me
6. Is comfortable
7. Is affordable
8. Has a lot of sales or special deals
9. Is a brand I can trust
10. Fits well

Athletic Footwear

Female

1. Is my style
2. Fits me
3. Offers real solutions for me
4. Offers real solutions for my activities
5. Is comfortable
6. Is fun to wear
7. Is growing in popularity
8. Is a brand I can trust
9. Has a fashionable look
10. Has a broad selection

Male

1. Is my style
2. Offers real solutions for me
3. Offers real solutions for my activities
4. Fits me
5. Is fun to wear
6. Is growing in popularity
7. Is comfortable
8. Offers good value for the money
9. Has a fashionable look
10. Has a broad selection

Consumer Electronics

	Female		Male
1.	Is a brand currently owned	1.	Is a brand currently owned
2.	Works well with what I own already	2.	Is growing in popularity
3.	Has the features & benefits I want	3.	Offers real solutions for me
4.	Is growing in popularity	4.	Has the features & benefits I want
5.	Offers real solutions for me	5.	Offers product bundles or packages
6.	Offers good value for the money	6.	Works well with what I already own
7.	Has a fashionable look	7.	Has a lot of sales or special deals
8.	Is socially responsible	8.	Offers good value for the money
9.	Is a brand I can trust	9.	Has the latest trend
10.	Has a broad selection	10.	Is socially responsible

Toys

	Female		Male
1.	I/my child is a fan of the character	1.	I collect this brand
2.	Is growing in popularity	2.	I/my child is a fan of the character
3.	I collect this brand	3.	Is growing in popularity
4.	Has the features/benefits I want	4.	Is trendy or is "in" right now
5.	Is trendy or is "in" right now	5.	Has a broad selection
6.	Has a broad selection	6.	Has the features/benefits I want
7.	Has the latest trend	7.	Has the latest trend
8.	Has a lot of sales or special deals	8.	Has the latest technology
9.	Offers good value for the money	9.	Has a lot of sales or special deals
10.	A good gift idea	10.	A good gift idea

39.6 Deals and Bargains

According to *Time*, 40% of items purchased by consumers are at some discount, an increase from 10% of sales in 1990 that were discounted.

"There's not a weekend where an average specialty retailer in the mall is not offering some kind of 30% to 40% off deal. It certainly feels like the consumer is not shopping unless there's some kind of deal attached to it. And it's very hard to pull back when the consumer gets used to buying things on sale."

Bloomberg Businessweek

In a survey of Millennials by IRI (www.iriworldwide.com), item price ranked as the #1 influencer of brand selection, ahead of previous usage and trust of brands, shopper loyalty cards, and advertising. Eighty-seven percent (87%) of survey respondents said price was among the two top influencers.

39.7 Impulse Buying

Shapiro+Raj (www.shapiroraj.com) report that every week nearly one-third of all consumers are involved in an impulse purchase. The urge to take advantage of discounts or price promotions accounts for approximately 50% of impulse purchases. Unity Marketing (www.unitymarketingonline.com) found buying on impulse is an important factor in discretionary purchases for approximately 40% of consumers.

> **"If shoppers bought only what they needed, few retailers would remain in business. Fortunately, impulse buying is a way of life for many consumers."**
>
> *Chain Store Age*

A survey by Gallup (www.gallup.com) reported the following percentages of consumers had made impulse purchases in the prior month:

- Millennials: 42%
- Generation Xers: 40%
- Baby Boomers: 39%

In a 2015 survey by Chase (www.chase.com), 83% of Millennials said they had made an impulse purchase. This was especially likely on payday or when they were cruising shopping websites online. In those instances, their urge to purchase items on impulse alone exceeded that of other age groups.

Male Millennial shoppers make slightly fewer impulse purchases than females. When they shop impulsively, 50% of men said they were likely to spend on electronics, compared with only 27% of female shoppers. For female shoppers, 61% said their impulse buys were mostly clothing, while only 43% of men said clothing lured them to impulse shopping. Twenty percent (20%) of female shoppers cited "retail therapy" – the comfort and relief that comes from purchasing something new after a particularly trying day or event – as a primary reason for impulsive shopping, compared with 9% of males. Seven in 10 women have made impulse purchases after seeing price promotions; 60% of men have done so.

"Just because Millennials make impulse purchases doesn't mean they feel good about it. Chase found that Millennials were more likely to express regret or dissatisfaction after an impulse purchase. Others more attuned to their impulsive spending habits tried to stay away from shopping altogether when they were emotional to avoid the risk of buying."

eMarketer, 1/19/16

39.8 Checkout

According to a 2015 survey by CFI Group (www.cfigroup.com), the checkout process is the No. 1 driver of customer satisfaction with retailers, at 28%, ahead of price, at 26%. Sixty-five percent (65%) of adults report having used self-checkout registers at the front of a retail store.

In a 2015 Harris Poll, 29% of adults cited slow checkout as a major source of frustration when shopping at retail establishments; 21% find long lines problematic.

"Even when shoppers decide on a store, the checkout process may make or break their experience."

eMarketer, 8/6/15

39.9 Brand Engagement

Brands face a major challenge when trying to increase customer engagement: Consumers are busy and spend little time 'engaging' with brands while shopping. According to a 2015 study by the Ehrenberg-Bass Institute of Marketing Science (www.marketingscience.info), the average consumer spends 13 seconds purchasing a brand in-store. Online, the average consumer spends 19 seconds purchasing, and the majority spend less than 10 seconds.

"The idea that consumers 'engage' with brands is no doubt true for a small set of consumers and a small set of high involvement categories and brands, but for the vast majority of brands, consumers are not engaged to or with brands. They're just buying them. The simple truth is this: For most categories, consumers have a small repertoire of brands that are acceptable, and they spend little time thinking about purchase decisions. Their lives are already full of spouses, kids, events and other activities, and most people simply don't have the time or energy to engage with brands in any meaningful way."

Randall Beard, President
Nielsen North America

39.10 Buying Direct From Brands

The *2015 Consumer Preferences Survey*, by BrandShop (www.brandshop.com), found that 82% of online shoppers would prefer to have the option of buying direct from brands or an online retailer. Given the option, 88% would buy direct from the brand.

"While most purchases take place over third party channels, it is now understood that consumers prefer to buy directly from a brand if given the option. The confidence and authenticity a consumer experiences from transacting directly with a brand is not easily replicated by third parties."

Center for Media Research, 10/14/15

40

RESPONSE TO ADVERTISING

40.1 Preferred Media For Ads

A Harris Poll (www.theharrispoll.com) found that consumers, by age, find the following most useful in deciding what products and services to purchase:

	18-to-34	35-to-44	45-to-55	55 & older	Total
• Television commercials:	50%	38%	35%	23%	37%
• Newspaper ads:	6%	13%	14%	31%	17%
• Internet search engine ads:	10%	15%	16%	16%	14%
• Radio ads:	3%	4%	3%	2%	3%
• Internet banner ads:	4%	1%	1%	<1%	1%
• All media viewed equally:	27%	29%	31%	27%	28%

Harris also found that consumers, by age, find the following most helpful when shopping for bargains:

	18-to-34	35-to-44	45-to-55	55 & older	Total
• Newspaper/magazine ads:	15%	16%	24%	33%	23%
• Online ads:	22%	26%	17%	12%	18%
• Direct mail/catalogs:	15%	13%	14%	10%	12%
• TV commercials:	17%	12%	8%	7%	11%
• Radio ads:	2%	3%	<1%	1%	2%
• All media viewed equally:	31%	31%	36%	36%	34%

CrossView (www.crossview.com) found shoppers' preference for delivery of retail promotions as follows:

- Email: 37%
- Mailer: 23%
- Text message: 18%
- In-store: 11%
- Social media: 9%
- Other: 3%

40.2 Positive Response To Ads

A survey by Truth Central, the thought leadership unit of McCann (http://truthcentral.mccann.com/), found that 71% of consumers feel positive about the advertising sector, 67% of consumers feel positive about the advertising they see around them, 57% of consumers say advertising gives them something to talk about, and 39% of consumers say they love advertising. When asked how advertising benefits them, survey participants responded as follows:

- Helps me keep informed about the latest offers: 87%
- Helps me know what the latest trends are: 83%
- Entertains me and makes me laugh: 77%

Microsoft Advertising (www.advertising.microsoft.com) found attitudes toward advertising through four specific platforms as follows:

	Computer	TV	Smartphone	Gaming Console
• Fun to watch:	32%	54%	28%	30%
• Generally like the ads:	29%	46%	25%	26%
• Regularly notice ads:	54%	64%	39%	31%
• More meaningful and relevant:	35%	48%	29%	27%
• Helpful if targeted to preferences:	50%	54%	40%	33%
• Rarely notice ads:	36%	29%	43%	38%
• Very annoying:	58%	43%	62%	43%

40.3 Negative Response To Ads

In a recent Harris Poll, consumers, by age, said they chose not to purchase a certain brand for the following reasons:

	18-to-34	35-to-44	45-to-55	55 & older	Total
• Found the ads distasteful:	37%	34%	32%	37%	35%
• Didn't like the spokesperson:	29%	24%	27%	30%	28%
• Didn't like program or event sponsored by the brand:	26%	26%	26%	30%	27%

A separate Harris Poll found that 91% of consumers ignore at least some types of ads. The following are the types of ads that consumers, by age, tend to ignore or disregard the most:

	18-to-34	35-to-44	45-to-55	55 & older	Total
• Internet banner ads:	43%	50%	48%	45%	46%
• Internet search engine ads:	20%	14%	17%	15%	17%
• Television commercials:	7%	10%	15%	20%	13%
• Radio ads:	11%	10%	9%	7%	9%
• Newspaper ads:	7%	7%	5%	5%	6%
• None of these:	14%	9%	6%	8%	9%

40.4 Response to Irrelevant Ads

Almost every online consumer has received information while visiting a website that has nothing to do with their personal interests or demographics. *Online*

Personal Experience, a survey conducted for Janrain (www.janrain.com) by the Harris Poll, found that people are running out of patience with irrelevant ads.

When asked about their response to irrelevant online ads, responses were as follows:

- I get frustrated with websites when content, offers, ads, promotions, etc. appear that have nothing to do with my interests: 74%
- I would leave the site if asked for donations from a political party that I dislike the most: 67%
- I would leave the site if shown ads for a dating service (response from married survey participants only): 57%
- I would leave the site if shown a recommendation to purchase underwear that is for the opposite gender: 50%

40.5 Ignoring Ads

A recent Harris Poll assessing various types of media found that 92% of adults typically ignore at least one type of ad. Survey participants identified the ads they most ignore as follows (multiple responses allowed):

- Online banner ads: 73%
- Online social media ads: 62%
- Online search engine ads: 59%
- TV ads: 37%
- Radio ads: 36%
- Newspaper ads: 35%

40.6 Ad Influence On Millennials

A survey by Adroit Digital (www.adroitdigital.com) asked Millennials (ages 18-to-33) which advertising media is most influential in how they perceive brands. Responses were as follows (multiple responses allowed):

- Television: 70%
- Magazines: 60%
- Online display: 42%
- Online video: 39%
- Freestanding kiosks: 31%
- Mobile: 33%
- Radio: 21%
- Billboards: 21%

41

RESPONSE TO CUSTOMER SERVICE

41.1 Impact of Good Customer Service

New Rules of Customer Engagement, an October 2015 report by Verint Systems (www.verint.com), reported that 89% of consumers say good service definitely makes them feel more positive about brands.

According to the *Customer Service Barometer*, by American Express (www.amex.com), consumers are willing to spend, on average, 13% more with companies that deliver great customer service.

41.2 Impact of Poor Customer Service

According to *Customer Experience Survey*, a November 2015 report by Aspect (www.aspect.com), consumers say they have stopped doing business with a company because of poor customer service, as follows:

- General retail: 52%
- Telecommunications: 23%
- Travel: 12%
- Financial: 11%
- Big-box electronics: 10%

By generation, consumers have stopped doing business with a general retail company because of poor customer service as follows:

- Millennials: 54%
- Generation X: 50%
- Baby Boomers: 52%

In a 2016 survey by Onestop (www.onestop.com), adults assessed the likelihood of making another purchase from a store after a good vs. bad customer service experience as follows (percentage of respondents):

	Good Experience	Bad Experience
Very Likely:	63.3%	2.0%
Likely:	31.7%	3.4%
Neutral:	4.3%	18.8%
Unlikely:	0.8%	47.8%
Highly Unlikely:	0.7%	27.7%

eMaketer (www.emarketer.com) reported that 53% of men and 52% of women had quit shopping at a retailer they previously shopped at because of a bad experience with a sales associate.

> **"A good or bad customer service experience can affect whether consumers will buy from a store again."**
>
> eMarketer, 3/18/16

The third annual *Customer Service Report*, published in 2015 by Corvisa (www.corvisa.com) reported that 48% of U.S. consumers had stopped doing business with a company because of negative customer service in the prior 12 months. Among Millennials, 25% said they wold stop doing business after one negative interaction.

American Express' *Customer Service Barometer* reported that 55% of U.S. adults had walked away from an intended purchase in the prior 12 months because of a poor customer service experience. Adults estimate that they tell about 24 people about bad customer service experiences during the course of a year.

41.3 Impact By Segment

A March 2016 survey by Temkin Group (www.temkingroup.com) scored customer service experience by sector on a 1-to-7 scale (1 = poor; 5 = ok; 7 = excellent) as follows:

- Hotels: 4.4
- Auto insurers: 4.2
- Banks: 4.1
- Credit card issuers: 3.8
- Appliance manufacturers: 3.7
- Computer manufacturers: 3.5
- Auto dealers: 3.4
- Airlines: 3.2
- Wireless carriers: 3.0
- Health plans: 1.1
- TV/Internet service providers: 0.6

While customer service is important across all consumer sectors, the influence varies by segment. The following are some industry-specific influences:

Airlines

An assessment by *Forbes* found airline quality ratings (i.e., on-time arrivals, denied boardings, mishandled baggage, and customer complaints) do not seem to influence revenue.

> **"Rude flight attendants, delayed arrivals, stale meals. Frequent flyers have plenty to gripe about. But does better customer service actually sell more tickets? Apparent correlation: zero."**
>
> *Forbes*

Drugstores and Pharmacies

The *National Pharmacy Study*, conducted by J.D. Power and Associates (www.jdpower.com), found customer service, not price, was most important among consumers with respect to store loyalty at drugstores and pharmacies.

E-Commerce

Customer service ranks low among attributes most important to online shoppers. In a survey by A.T. Kearney (www.atkearney.com), the ability to find specific products, free shipping, finding favorite brands, best prices, ease of navigation, site security, special promotions, free samples, peer reviews, and the availability of new products all ranked above customer service.

Still, many online shoppers do expect some level of customer service. In a survey by OneUpWeb (www.oneupweb.com), 32% of Internet users said they expect live chat. A survey by comScore (www.comscore.com) found 35% of online shoppers would like online retailers to improve the availability of live customer service.

Restaurants

Emphatica (www.empathica.com) found that 20% of consumers value good service over good food at fine- and casual-dining establishments.

A Gallup Poll (www.gallup.com) found that the biggest driver of engagement in a fast-food restaurant is being treated as a valued customer. Warmth of the greeting ranked second in the survey; taste of food ranked third. Gallup found that a fully engaged customer will spend $33.90 on fast food per month, 16% more than the $29.24 spent by a non-engaged consumer.

41.4 Factors Contributing To Good Customer Service

A survey by Dimensional Research (www.dimensionalresearch.com) asked consumers about recent interactions with customer service departments of mid-sized companies. Responses were as follows:

Good Customer Service

- The problem was resolved quickly: 69%
- The person who helped me was nice: 65%
- The problem was resolved in one interaction: 63%
- The outcome was what I was originally hoping for: 47%

Bad Customer Service

- I had to explain my problem to multiple people: 72%
- The person I dealt with was unpleasant: 67%
- My problem took too long to resolve: 65%
- The problem was not resolved: 51%

> **"Interestingly, [Dimensional Research] found that among those who said they had had a positive customer service experience, more said it was because they received a quick resolution to their problem, rather than a desirable outcome."**
>
> *eMarketer*

42

RESPONSE TO REVIEWS

42.1 Online Consumer Reviews

Ratings sites – like epinions.com to rate consumer products, yelp.com to rate restaurants, ratemds.com to rate doctors, tripadvisor.com to rate hotels and destinations – have become recognized sources consumers rely on for reviews about products and services.

A survey by ChannelAdvisor (www.channeladvisor.com) found that 92% of Internet users read product reviews. Among these people, 89% have been influenced to make a purchase or deterred from purchasing a specific product as the result of reviews. Only 3% of those who have read reviews say their decisions have been unaffected by reviews.

Among those who use reviews, about a quarter also post their own opinions. According to eMarketer (www.emarketer.com), 34.4 million consumers, or 20% of the U.S. population, share advice online about products or services.

Consumers are increasingly accessing reviews while shopping. Compete (www.compete.com) reports that 45% of smartphone users have looked at third-party or consumer reviews of a product while in a store.

In a survey by The Society For New Communications Research (www.sncr.org), 73% of Internet users said customer reviews were important in helping form their impression of companies.

When asked in a 2015 survey by SheSpeaks (www.shespeaks.com) about the sources of product information they find credible and trustworthy, responses by female adult Internet users were as follows:

- Online product reviews or blogs by peer consumers: 43%
- Online product reviews on shopping websites: 38%
- Online product reviews by journalists or analysts: 7%
- Information on product packaging: 6%
- Posts by brands/companies on social media: 2%
- Product advertising or infomercials: 1%

Women are most likely to search for product reviews online if they are shopping for electronics (77%), appliances (72%) or cosmetics (63%), according to the survey.

"Online product reviews written by regular people – whether they know them personally or not – are what's most likely to get women to hit the 'buy' button, according to SheSpeaks. Asked about the most credible source for information about products, U.S. female Internet users overwhelmingly said 'only product reviews.' "

eMarketer, 6/30/15

BrightLocal (www.brightlocal.com) reported consumers' response to online customer reviews in 2015 and, for comparison in 2010, as follows:

	2010	2015
• Positive customer reviews make me trust a business more:	55%	68%
• I read reviews but they don't influence my decision on which businesses to use:	19%	21%
• I don't take notice of online customer reviews:	26%	11%

"Customer reviews have gotten more important for businesses over the years. And that means positive reviews appear to be having a bigger effect."

eMarketer, 9/1/15

42.2 Online Research

According to Opinion Research Corp. (www.opinionresearch.com), the most researched product and service categories are as follows (percentage of consumers that have researched prior to purchase):

- Travel/recreation/leisure: 82%
- Electronic goods: 80%

- Household products/services: 66%
- Clothing: 55%
- Automotive: 55%
- Personal care: 40%
- Food: 24%

A study by YouGov (www.yougov.com) found that 79% of Internet users check online reviews at least some of the time before making a purchase; only 7% say they never check reviews. YouGov classified reviews as follows:

- Mixed reviews: 57%
- Good reviews: 54%
- Bad reviews: 21%
- Neutral reviews: 12%

42.3 Posting Reviews

A survey by YouGov asked Internet users who posted online consumer reviews their reasons for doing so. Responses were as follows:

- Help others make better purchase decisions: 62%
- Polite to leave feedback: 35%
- Share positive good experience: 27%
- Make sure good vendors get business: 25%
- Warn about bad experience: 13%
- Expose bad vendors: 12%
- Improve ranking as customer: 7%
- Become well known reviewer: 5%

By age, reasons for posting reviews were as follows:

	18-34	35-54	55+
• Help others make better purchase decisions:	56%	62%	67%
• Polite to leave feedback:	36%	38%	33%
• Share positive good experience:	19%	27%	34%
• Make sure good vendors get business:	18%	25%	30%
• Warn about bad experience:	10%	11%	17%
• Expose bad vendors:	8%	10%	16%
• Improve ranking as customer:	6%	10%	3%
• Become well known reviewer:	7%	6%	3%

"According to a study by YouGov, consumers don't write online reviews to release anger. Instead, among U.S. Internet users who posted online customer reviews, the top reason for doing so was to help others make better purchasing decisions."

Center for Media Research, 11/5/15

42.4 Travel Reviews

Among all product and service categories, travel reviews are the most used by consumers.

According to Forrester Research (www.forrester.com), approximately one-third of travelers who research trips via the Internet read reviews. Of those who book hotels online, a third have changed plans based on other travelers' comments.

Expedia-owned TripAdvisor (www.tripadvisor.com), the largest online travel review site, had posted more than 320 million consumer reviews of hotels, attractions, and restaurants across the globe as of April 2016. The site has 350 million unique monthly visitors, according to comScore (www.comscore.com).

42.5 Consumer Electronics Reviews

Among all product and service categories, consumer electronics (CE) reviews are the second most used by consumers.

A survey by Weber Shandwick (www.webershandwick.com) found that consumers seek out opinions about consumer electronics products they are considering as follows:

- Search for reviews online: 74%
- Ask someone their opinion: 66%
- Read 'likes' or recommendations on a social networking site: 47%
- Watch an online video with someone's experiences: 37%
- Ask their social network friends or followers: 28%

Seventy-two percent (72%) conduct at least two of these activities.

Among those who use online reviews, 65% have been inspired enough by a favorable consumer review to buy a CE product they weren't considering, and 59% have been similarly inspired by a professional review.

Among those using consumer reviews, 95% report gaining confidence in a purchase decision; 86% have gained confidence because of professional reviews.

Comparing consumer and professional reviews, 77% of consumers say they pay more attention to professional reviews; 23% give preference to professional reviews.

Eighty percent (80%) of those who use reviews say they have had concerns about authenticity. Specific concerns are as follows (percentage of respondents):

- A positive review may be posted by the manufacturer's employee or agent, not an actual consumer: 51%
- A negative review may be posted by the manufacturer's employee or agent, not an actual consumer: 39%
- A review reads more like an advertisement than an objective assessment of the product's benefits and drawbacks: 39%
- A review appears to be entirely negative or entirely positive: 37%

43

RESPONSE TO VISUALS

43.1 Overview

Visual content can have a major influence on consumer behavior. From studying brain scans and tracking eye movements, researchers have discovered that visual content is simply processed differently than text. Visuals communicate more information, more effectively.

> **"Processing print isn't something the human brain was built for. The printed word is a human artifact. It's very convenient and it's worked very well for us for 5,000 years, but it's an invention of human beings. By contrast Mother Nature has built into our brain our ability to see the visual world and interpret it. Even the spoken language is much more a given biologically than reading written language."**
>
> Prof. Marcel Just, Ph.D., Director
> Center for Cognitive Brain Imaging
> Carnegie Mellon University
> Center for Media Research, 1/28/16

43.2 Response to Visuals

A study by Nate Birt, a researcher at University of Missouri-Columbia, published in *Content Marketing* in June 2015, reported the following findings:

- Ninety percent (90%) of the information transmitted to the brain is visual.
- Visual content generates 94% more views.

- Tweets with images get 150% more retweets, 18% more clicks, and 89% more favorites.
- People retain 80% of what they see, 20% of what they read, and 10% of what they hear.
- Visuals are processed 60,000 times faster than text.
- Eighty percent (80%) of the text on most pages does not get read.

43.3 Eye Tracking

A January 2016 report by Eye Faster (www.eyefaster.com) provides the following finding of eye-tracking research:

- The human eye constantly scans the scene, moving abruptly in "saccades" lasting 20 to 40 microseconds, with in between 'fixations,' (still periods) of 100 to 400 microseconds. Since the brain processes visual information after the eyes fixate for 200 microseconds, over a half-hour shopping trip, says the report, a customer's eyes fixate 1,800 times. That provides marketing messages between 200 microseconds and one second to communicate.
- The eyes focus on a small window, so everything in one's peripheral vision is a blur. As a result, products that are near eye level in a retail store are much more likely to be seen than those placed on high or low shelves. The ideal product placement is from 30° below eye level to 10° above.
- Being used to reading left to right and up to down, message that are not displayed in that order feel confusing and off-putting. Consumers have trouble with vertical lettering and text in unusual places. The rule of design for visuals is that they should not get so fancy with the design that the message disappears.
- Shoppers give some products more visual consideration than others. One example is packaged salads. In one study, people picked up and considered three bags of package salad for every one bag purchased. But salad dressing hardly merits any consideration at all. In another study, the average shopper spent 62 seconds looking at salad dressing and only noticed 7% of the available products.
- When shoppers look for known brands, products that look similar to the categories' leading brand are more likely to catch a customers' eye than those that look completely different. If a product doesn't match the category look and feel, it is unlikely to register as an option.
- A brand may be of higher quality or be less expensive than the competition, but if it doesn't give consumers a positive feeling, they won't buy it. Since the majority of purchase decisions are made on the subconscious level where feelings rule, emotional factors like shape, color, and the memories a package provokes are of the utmost importance.

"Most consumers cannot readily explain why they sample a new product or regularly purchase one particular brand, but the truth can be discovered in their eyes. From numerous eye-tracking studies surprising insights emerge into why customers buy some products while walking right past others."

Kirk Hendrickson, CEO
Eye Faster
Center for Media Research, 1/28/16

43.4 Response to Color

Color psychology studies emotions and reactions of people to colors. Research in the field has found that people react differently to certain colors and that these colors elicit different emotional states, behaviors, and moods. Using colors that are appropriate in marketing can be important in eliciting a desired consumer behavior.

The following are emotions and meanings that have been found to correspond with certain colors among consumers in the North American culture (source: MyeVideo [www.myevideo.com]):

- Black: sophistication, elegance, mystery
- Blue: trust, belonging, freshness
- Gold: prestige, luxury
- Green: nature, freshness, growth, abundance
- Orange: playfulness, warmth, liveliness
- Pink: gentleness, kindness, safeness
- Purple: classiness, spirituality, dignity
- Red: excitement, strength, passion, speed, danger
- Silver: prestige, coldness
- White: moral purity, holiness, innocence, youth, gentleness
- Yellow: warmth, happiness, joy, cowardice

"Did you ever walk into a store only to discover that it wasn't a store but actually a restaurant? We tend to associate colors to certain things. If you're going to a pharmacy, you expect it to be white. A kindergarten not so much. If you know that red encourages action, you might want use it on your retail website because red encourages shoppers to take advantage of your offers. If you are creating a video about all-natural herbal remedies, it would make sense that you use a lot of green. It would be a complete miss if you used, let's say, purple, since purple is such a rare color in nature. Have you noticed that fast food restaurants are mostly yellow, red, or orange? It's no wonder that these particular colors are so dominant in these places. They encourage visitors to eat faster and then leave, which is the real reason why these kinds of restaurants exist. Have you noticed that toys, books, or websites for kids are usually adorned with pastel and primary colors? The reason is that small children love these colors and they react to them more positively than to other combinations of stronger colors."

Mia Styles, CMO
MyeVideo, 8/19/15

44

SHOPPING RESEARCH

44.1 Product Research

The *2015 Connected Shopper Report*, by the Harris Poll (www.harrispoll.com), reported that 79% of adults compare prices and product attributes online prior to making purchases. Resources used for online research are as follows (percentage of respondents):

• Online-only retailer sites:	56%
• Bricks-and-mortar retailer sites:	51%
• Brand sites:	35%
• Comparison shopping websites:	16%
• Social media:	10%
• Digital fliers:	10%

44.2 Cross-Channel Research

"Showrooming" is the practice where customers go to a bricks-and-mortar retail location, make a decision on what item to buy and, instead of heading to the check-out aisle, use a mobile device to find a better price online where they ultimately make their purchase. "Webrooming" occurs when consumers buy in a store after researching a purchase online.

GfK (www.gfk.com) reported that 28% of consumers engage in showrooming; 41% practice webrooming.

By age, those who showroom or webroom are as follows:

	Showrooming	Webrooming
• 18-to-24:	39%	34%
• 25-to-34:	32%	46%
• 35-to-49:	29%	43%
• 50-to-68:	18%	30%

44.3 Comparison Shopping Websites

Comparison shopping websites, or sites that aggregate product listings from various retailers but do not directly sell products themselves, have become popular among consumers.

The most visited comparison shopping sites in 2015, ranked by number of monthly unique visitors, were as follows (source: eBizMBA [www.ebizmba.com]):

- Google Shopping (www.google.com/shopping): 20.50 million
- Coupons (www.coupons.com): 20.25 million
- Biz Rate (www.bizrate.com): 19.00 million
- Shop At Home (www.shopathome.com): 18.00 million
- Slick Deals (www.slickdeals.com): 17.50 million
- NexTag (www.nextag.com): 8.00 million
- Woot (www.woot.com): 7.00 million
- Shopping (www.shopping.com): 6.70 million
- Shopzilla (www.shopzilla.com): 6.50 million
- Shop (www.shop.com): 6.00 million
- Fat Wallet (www.fatwallet.com): 5.50 million
- Pronto (www.pronto.com): 4.20 million
- Price Grabber (www.pricegrabber.com): 4.00 million
- Shop Local (www.shoplocal.com): 3.50 million
- Deal News (www.dealnews.com): 2.00 million

44.4 Research Via Mobile Devices

The New Digital Divide, a report by Deloitte (www.deloitte.com), found that the use of mobile devices before or during in-store shopping trips influences approximately $593 billion of in-store retail sales, or 19% of total bricks-and-mortar sales.

According to a December 2015 study by Y&R (www.yr.com), 51% of adults primarily research products via smartphone. The demographics of those who do so are as follows:

Gender

- Female: 54%
- Male: 47%

Age

- 18-to-29: 32%
- 30-to-44: 36%
- 45-to-59: 19%
- 60 and older: 13%

The Consumer Technology Association (CTA; www.cta.tech) reported that 58% of shoppers prefer to look up information on their mobile devices while shopping in stores, rather than talk to a salesperson. Shoppers ages 25-to-44 and men are most likely to prefer to access their device for product information. Nearly two-thirds feel that the information they gather on their mobile devices is more helpful than in-store information from product displays or sales literature.

“Mobile has become an important channel for shoppers as they research products. These shoppers skew younger as well as female.”

eMarketer, 1/7/16

45

SPENDING FOR GOODS VS. EXPERIENCES

45.1 A Shift From Goods To Experiences

As some consumers are beginning to realize they have all the material things they need, many are shifting their interests toward seeking new experiences. This is especially true for older consumers who have been accumulating all their lives.

> **"With the attitude of 'been there, done that' in buying more things, Boomers will turn away from a focus on consuming things, to a hunger for experiences and personal development. Service industries that satisfy the mature Boomers' craving for personal enhancement will fare well. These include travel providers, especially adventure travel modified for aging Boomers' health and fitness levels; health and beauty spas; and colleges and adult-education experiences, including training such as cooking or language schools."**
>
> Pamela N. Danziger, CEO
> Unity Marketing

Favoring experiences over goods extends across generations. When asked "which is more important for you personally" in a survey by Zipcar (www.zipcar.com), 61% of 18-to-34 year-olds picked "experiences" over "possessions." A nearly identical proportion of older respondents responded similarly.

"A familiar refrain is that Millennials would rather spend on experiences than on acquiring "stuff." A related theme states that they care more about access to goods than ownership of them. A report by The Intelligence Group called young people "the first generations of NOwners, or those who prize access over ownership."

eMarketer

45.2 Purchase Satisfaction

In their book *Happy Money: The Science of Smarter Spending* (Simon & Schuster), authors Elizabeth Dunn and Michael Norton draw on years of quantitative and qualitative research to present five principles that can make spending a rewarding experience for consumers. The principle Buy Experiences shows material purchases being less satisfying than experiences such as vacations or concerts.

"One of the most common things people do with their money is get stuff. But we have shown ... in research that stuff isn't good for you. It doesn't make you unhappy, but it doesn't make you happy. But one thing that does make us happy is an experience."

Michael Norton, Ph.D.
Associate Professor of Marketing
Harvard Business School

45.3 Research Findings

Studies at Cornell University and Harvard University have found favorable consumer response to purchases of experiences over material goods. Research by Thomas D. Gilovich, Ph.D., a professor of psychology at Cornell University, and his colleagues suggests that when people spend for an experience such as a trip, they are likely to feel better about that purchase in the long run versus spending the same amount on clothes.

In one study, Dr. Gilovich examined the uniqueness of objects and experiences. He found that a major reason why people regret buying objects is that after they own the object, they can continue to compare it to other objects that are available. When they buy a computer, for instance, they may regret the purchase when they find another one that is faster, smaller, and cheaper. When they go on a vacation, though, that experience is relatively unique. It is hard to compare a particular trip with other trips they might have taken, so they spend less time comparing the experience to other things they might have done.

Research by Daniel Gilbert, Ph.D., a professor of psychology at Harvard University, has also found that spending on experiences is more rewarding than spending on goods. One of the reasons is that experiences can be shared.

> **"Happiness, for most people not named Sartre, is other people; and experiences are usually shared – first when they happen and then again and again when we tell our friends."**
>
> Prof. Daniel Gilbert, Ph.D.
> Harvard University

While the memories of experiences can endure, objects generally wear out their welcome, according to Dr. Gilbert, who provides the following example: "If you really love a rug, you might buy it. The first few times you see, you might admire it, and feel happy. But over time, it will probably reveal itself to be just a rug." Psychologists call this habituation, economists call it declining marginal utility.

46

THEME APPEAL

46.1 Overview

Content providers and advertisers generally try to match genre themes with their audience.

A September 2015 survey by Nielsen (www.nielsen.com) identified the themes that resonate most with consumers.

> **"Successful marketing campaigns require more than identifying the right channel for reaching consumers. It's also about delivering the right message. How can marketers ensure their ads stand out? A key element is knowing how to connect their audience with messages that resonate most."**
>
> Nielsen, 9/15

46.2 Themes That Resonate Most

Nielsen reported the following themes resonate most with adults in North America (percentage of respondents):

- Humorous: 50%
- Value-oriented: 38%
- Real-life situations: 35%
- Family-oriented: 33%
- Pets/animals-centered: 27%
- Health-related: 24%
- High-Energy action: 17%
- Sentimental: 15%
- Aspirational: 13%

- Kids-centered: 13%
- Sports-themed: 12%
- Sexual: 11%
- Competitive: 10%
- Celebrity endorsements: 8%
- Car-themed: 6%
- Athlete endorsements: 5%

46.3 Theme Preferences by Generation

By generation, themes that resonate are as follows (percentage of respondents):

	Gen Z	Millennials	Gen X	Boomers	Seniors
• Real-life situations:	40%	44%	43%	45%	44%
• Humorous:	37%	37%	38%	46%	46%
• Health-themed:	31%	37%	38%	42%	40%
• Value-oriented:	31%	32%	33%	37%	39%
• High-energy action:	28%	28%	21%	16%	8%
• Aspirational:	25%	25%	20%	16%	13%
• Family-oriented:	24%	35%	42%	39%	32%
• Sentimental:	17%	18%	17%	15%	8%
• Celebrity endorsements:	16%	14%	8%	7%	2%
• Sports-themed:	16%	14%	14%	12%	10%
• Competitive:	13%	14%	11%	10%	9%
• Pets/animals-centered:	13%	14%	16%	23%	24%
• Sexual:	13%	12%	9%	7%	3%
• Kids-centered:	9%	19%	23%	16%	12%
• Athlete endorsements:	8%	8%	6%	6%	4%
• Car-themed:	8%	12%	11%	9%	9%

"Trying to connect with consumers emotionally? Start by considering whom you're trying to reach. Some messages resonate well across every generation. Other messages, however, have niche appeal."

Nielsen, 9/15

PART VI: AFFLUENT CONSUMERS

47

AFFLUENCE PROFILE

47.1 Overview

Consumers that comprise the luxury marketplace are typically categorized as follows:

- Upper-class: Top 20% of U.S. households
- Affluent: Top 10% of U.S. households
- Wealthy: Top 1% of U.S. households
- Rich: Top 0.1% of U.S. households
- Ultra-rich: Top 0.01% of U.S. households

47.2 Upper-Class Consumers

The upper-class is typically defined as the highest quintile of households, or the top 20% of U.S. households.

A 2015 study by Edward N. Wolff, Ph.D., an economist at New York University, reported the highest quintile control 88% of wealth in the United States.

The Census Bureau reported the median net worth of the highest quintile is $630,754. The median wealth of the highest quintile of households by age of householder is as follows:

- Under 35: $153,616
- 35-to-44: $448,824
- 45-to-54: $654,229
- 55-to-64: $889,867
- 65 and older: $899,608

47.3 Affluent Consumers

The wealthiest 10% of U.S. households are typically dubbed 'affluent.' The September 2014 *Federal Reserve Bulletin* put the total number of those millionaire households at 11.53 million. That makes virtually everyone in the top 10% of U.S. households a millionaire.

The top 10% of households hold 76% of wealth and the top 5% hold 62%, according to Dr. Wolff.

The top 10% of households, excluding the top 1%, controlled 34.6% of U.S.

wealth in 2013.

Affluent consumers saw their wealth increase in the aftermath of the Great Recession. The *Federal Reserve Bulletin* reported that the share of total income of the top 3% of Americans grew to 30.5% in 2013 from 27.7% in 2010. The top 3% saw their share of wealth rise from 44.8% in 1989 to 54.4% in 2013. The next 7%, who are wealthier than 90% of the rest of the nation, had a minimum net worth of $941,700 in 2013.

Excluding the high-net-worth households, or the upper 1%, the affluent market is comprised primarily of people who are careful spenders and aggressive savers. They are generally not conspicuous or ostentatious consumers.

47.4 Wealthy Consumers

The top 1% of U.S. households are typically characterized as wealthy. There are 1.1 million households in this category.

These consumers have the following profile (source: American Affluence Research Center [www.affluenceresearch.org]):

- With an average annual income of $982,000, they earn about 14% of the total income earned by all American households.
- They account for about 20% of all consumer spending.
- They have a minimum net worth of $6 million.
- With an average net worth of $15.3 million, they control 39.8% of the total wealth among U.S. households.

Dr. Wolff reports that the top 1% control 35% of wealth in the U.S.

47.5 Rich and Ultra-rich Consumers

The top 0.1% of households, excluding the top 0.01%, control 10.4% of U.S. wealth; there are 100,000 households in this category. The threshold for being in the top 0.1% is wealth of about $20 million.

The top 0.01% of households control 11.1% of U.S. wealth. The 16,000 families in this category, often dubbed the 'ultra-rich,' possess $6 trillion in assets, equal to the total wealth of the bottom two-thirds of American families. The threshold for being in the top 0.01% is wealth of about $100 million.

47.6 Spending By High-Net-Worth Households

The *Affluent Barometer* by Ipsos (www.ipsos-na.com) assessed annual spending by affluent consumers as follows:

- Automotive: $398 billion (20% of total)
- Personal insurance: $227 billion (11% of total)
- Home and garden: $208 billion (10% of total)

- Education: $201 billion (10% of total)
- Groceries: $193 billion (9% of total)
- Travel: $170 billion (8% of total)
- Apparel, accessories, eyewear: $133 billion (7% of total)
- Computers, electronics, home entertainment: $115 billion (6% of total)
- Charitable donations: $ 96 billion (5% of total)
- Leisure, entertainment & dining: $ 91 billion (4% of total)
- Personal care & wellness: $ 55 billion (3% of total)
- Weddings: $ 25 billion (1% of total)
- Alcoholic beverages: $ 25 billion (1% of total)
- Watches, jewelry, fine writing instruments: $ 22 billion (1% of total)
- Skin care, cosmetics & fragrance: $ 21 billion (1% of total)
- Other: $ 57 billion (3% or total)

Luxury brand companies must take an entirely different approach when selling to the high-net-worth spender because they are a different breed from the general affluent consumer. They spend freely, and they spend frequently and extravagantly. They not only have the interest and the resources to purchase exclusive, expensive items, but their wealth – and often fame – adds a level of distinction to the luxury brands they are buying. It is becoming harder for the super-rich to differentiate themselves, and many of them go to greater lengths to make the statement that they are successful. Further, the 'massification' of luxury drives them to consume and splurge even more.

The New Jet Set, a report by *Elite Traveler*, included a survey of 661 high-net-worth individuals who own private jets. Participants in the survey, which was conducted by Prince & Associates (www.russalanprince.com), had an average income of $9.2 million and a net worth of $89.3 million. The following was average annual spending by this group for luxury goods:

- Fine art: $1.75 million
- Home improvement: $ 542,000
- Yacht rentals: $ 404,000
- Jewelry: $ 248,000
- Luxury cars: $ 226,000
- Events at hotels/resorts: $ 224,000
- Villa/chalet rentals: $ 168,000
- Hotels/resorts: $ 157,000
- Watches: $ 147,000
- Cruises: $ 138,000
- Fashion & accessories: $ 117,000
- Spas: $ 107,000
- Experiential travel: $ 98,000
- Wine and spirits: $ 29,000

"The thing that surprises me about the survey is the depth of their pockets. These folks don't make financial decisions when making a luxury purchase. For them, it's like me going to Starbucks."

Doug Gollan, Editor-in-Chief
Elite Traveler

The New Jet Set reported holiday season spending by survey participants – either for themselves or gifts – as follows:

- Yacht charters: $367,000
- Jewelry: $ 74,600
- Gifts to charity: $ 62,100
- Villa and ski house rental: $ 61,700
- Hotel or resort stay: $ 54,600
- Watches: $ 44,900
- Holiday entertaining: $ 29,800
- Fashion accessories: $ 29,100
- Wines and spirits for entertaining: $ 14,200

The survey also found that 51% of the super-rich were planning to host an event or reception at a hotel, spending on average $36,300, and 75% were planning to send gifts to the tune of, on average, $29,200.

48

POPULATION CENTERS OF U.S. AFFLUENCE

48.1 Most Affluent ZIP Codes

Based on data from the Internal Revenue Service (www.irs.gov), *The Washington Post* (May 2015) reported the highest income per tax return in the following ZIP codes (source: Internal Revenue Service [www.irs.gov]):

	# Returns	Income Per Return
• New York, NY 10104:	14	$2,976,929
• New York, NY 10112:	294	$2,239,881
• Miami Beach, FL 33109:	191	$2,180,105
• New York, NY 10004:	1,336	$2,118,766
• New York, NY 10153:	84	$1,567,452
• New York, NY 10167:	97	$1,412,072
• New York, NY 10158:	44	$1,399,205
• Wilmington, DE 19898:	22	$1,356,182
• New York, NY 10111:	505	$1,234,972
• New York, NY 10151:	25	$ 995,480
• Fresno, CA 93778:	29	$ 955,345
• Universal City, CA 91608:	55	$ 908,418
• Chattanooga, TN 37450:	19	$ 865,579
• Dayton, OH 45423:	43	$ 841,674
• Jersey City, NJ 07399:	82	$ 809,817
• Corpus Christi, TX 78471:	31	$ 782,419
• New York, NY 10271:	45	$ 779,333
• New York, NY 10154:	124	$ 765,202
• Memphis, TN 38157:	20	$ 758,000
• Tallahassee, FL 32306:	53	$ 749,566
• Northbrook, IL 60065:	132	$ 725,371
• New York, NY 10152:	165	$ 712,818
• Houston, TX 77010:	247	$ 670,198
• Henderson, NV 89011:	68	$ 665,559
• Foster City, CA 94400:	15	$ 659,333
• Pittsburgh, PA 15259:	11	$ 589,273
• New York, NY 10106:	108	$ 578,259
• Fort Lauderdale, FL 33394:	35	$ 565,314
• Tulsa, OK 74121:	27	$ 560,259
• New Hyde Park, NY 11042:	176	$ 556,392

- Dallas, TX 75247: 264 $ 548,640
- Medina, WA 98039: 1,514 $ 546,770
- Los Angeles, CA 90067: 3,141 $ 546,672
- New York, NY 10155: 40 $ 545,500
- Mill Neck, NY 11765: 360 $ 544,244
- New York, NY 10020: 870 $ 543,366
- Atherton, CA 94027: 3,738 $ 537,684
- New York, NY 10105: 67 $ 533,687
- New York, NY 10110: 573 $ 533,480
- Incline Village, NV 89451: 1,362 $ 529,403
- Minneapolis, MN 55440: 292 $ 523,034
- Glenbrook, NV 89413: 261 $ 507,318
- New York, NY 10165: 381 $ 499,273
- New Vernon, NJ 07976: 761 $ 497,928
- Chicago, IL 60604: 409 $ 479,396
- Morristown, NJ 07962: 267 $ 465,648
- Ross, CA 94957: 1,215 $ 461,347
- Palm Beach, FL 33480: 6,564 $ 457,517
- Memphis, TN 38124: 140 $ 454,929
- Chicago, IL 60606: 1,064 $ 452,781
- Oldwick, NJ 08858: 471 $ 452,749
- Gibson Island, MD 21056: 173 $ 450,012
- Lexington, KY 40580: 16 $ 424,750
- Pensacola, FL 32581: 25 $ 421,040
- Hunt Valley, MD 21031: 44 $ 420,909
- Acton, ME 04000: 16 $ 418,188
- New York, NY 10055: 127 $ 417,795
- Greenwich, CT 06831: 7,465 $ 414,686
- Kentfield, CA 94914: 195 $ 410,995
- Greens Farms, CT 06436: 181 $ 410,950
- San Francisco, CA 94111: 2,459 $ 408,623
- Far Hills, NJ 07931: 1,564 $ 401,311
- Weston, MA 02193: 3,316 $ 400,922
- Old Westbury, NY 11568: 1,785 $ 398,473
- New York, NY 10169: 232 $ 395,897
- Boston, MA 02110: 2,111 $ 395,215
- Roanoke, VA 24005: 10 $ 394,400
- Wilson, WY 83014: 997 $ 392,598
- New York, NY 10286: 38 $ 388,447
- Dallas, TX 75270: 27 $ 382,037
- Salt Lake City, UT 84133: 10 $ 378,200
- New York, NY 10166: 190 $ 375,511
- Boston, MA 02205: 221 $ 374,597
- Jackson, MS 39272: 51 $ 374,216

• Salt Lake City, UT 84145:	16	$ 374,188
• Springfield, MO 65800:	17	$ 372,353
• Minneapolis, MN 55415:	438	$ 372,311
• Dallas, TX 75201:	2,364	$ 372,255
• Rancho Santa Fe, CA 92067:	4,912	$ 372,108
• Dumont, TX 79232:	18	$ 368,611
• Charlottesville, VA 22905:	327	$ 367,875
• Glenview, KY 40025:	90	$ 367,022
• Portola Valley, CA 94028:	3,572	$ 365,873
• Beaverton, OR 97076:	29	$ 364,034
• Springfield, MA 01115:	50	$ 362,480
• Minneapolis, MN 55402:	842	$ 359,827
• Hartford, CT 06156:	20	$ 358,050
• Purchase, NY 10577:	1,620	$ 354,473
• Sea Island, GA 31561:	241	$ 351,178
• Kenilworth, IL 60043:	1,315	$ 348,016
• Lexington, KY 40583:	178	$ 346,640
• Earth City, MO 63045:	15	$ 345,800
• New York, NY 10175:	74	$ 344,419
• Montchanin, DE 19710:	217	$ 343,710
• Fort Wayne, IN 46866:	57	$ 342,860
• Portland, OR 97291:	97	$ 341,660
• Jacksonville, FL 32232:	62	$ 339,145
• Boca Grande, FL 33921:	653	$ 336,328
• New York, NY 10100:	35	$ 334,200
• Indianapolis, IN 46282:	12	$ 332,833

48.2 Most Expensive ZIP Codes

Forbes has assessed the zip codes with the highest median home values annually since 2005. The 2015 list is as follows:

• Atherton (near Palo Alto), CA 94027:	$10,564,038
• Sagaponack (the Hamptons), NY 11962:	$ 7,416,538
• New York, NY 10012:	$ 7,302,117
• Woody Creek, CO 81656:	$ 7,020,893
• New York (Tribeca), NY 10013:	$ 6,076,018
• Fisher Island Miami Beach), FL 33109:	$ 5,560,077
• Woodside, CA 94062:	$ 5,533,534
• Hidden Hills, CA 91302:	$ 5,074,231
• Aspen, CO 81611:	$ 5,003,783
• Hillsborough, CA 94010:	$ 4,951,458
• Los Altos Hills, CA 94022:	$ 4,927,038
• Alpine, NJ 07620:	$ 4,867,731
• Belvedere, CA 94920:	$ 4,626,731

- Beverly Hills, CA 90210: $ 4,553,181
- New York, NY 10065: $ 4,406,262
- Glenbrook, NV 89413: $ 4,267,371
- Santa Monica, CA 90402: $ 4,228,951
- Water Mill, NY 11976: $ 4,221,615
- Cherry Hills Village, CO 80111: $ 4,199,808
- Ross, CA 94957: $ 4,178,846

48.3 Millionaire Households By State

According to Phoenix Marketing International (www.phoenixmi.com), 6,504,201 households, or 5.37% of all U.S. households, had assets of $1 million or more in 2015. The number of millionaire households in each state in 2015 and ratio of millionaire to total households was as follows:

	Total HH	$1 million +	Ratio
• Alabama:	1,919,962	84,802	4.42%
• Alaska:	273,225	18,726	6.85%
• Arizona:	2,510,996	120,315	4.79%
• Arkansas:	1,171,886	48,457	4.13%
• California:	13,097,549	772,555	5.90%
• Colorado:	2,127,178	124,514	5.85%
• Connecticut:	1,383,854	100,996	7.30%
• Delaware:	357,328	22,782	6.38%
• District of Columbia:	299,672	18,861	6.29%
• Florida:	7,839,517	383,290	4.89%
• Georgia:	3,755,662	175,557	4.67%
• Hawaii:	478,317	34,678	7.25%
• Idaho:	606,752	26,555	4.38%
• Illinois:	4,894,599	280,266	5.73%
• Indiana:	2,556,127	118,094	4.62%
• Iowa:	1,253,520	66,285	5.29%
• Kansas:	1,137,134	57,676	5.07%
• Kentucky:	1,756,596	74,389	4.23%
• Louisiana:	1,796,638	82,473	4.59%
• Maine:	562,629	27,881	4.96%
• Maryland:	2,237,507	172,249	7.70%
• Massachusetts:	2,638,781	179,657	6.81%
• Michigan:	3,915,936	188,705	4.82%
• Minnesota:	2,172,362	130,330	6.00%
• Mississippi:	1,133,798	44,626	3.94%
• Missouri:	2,418,499	111,483	4.61%
• Montana:	431,683	20,899	4.84%
• Nebraska:	748,590	39,007	5.21%
• Nevada:	1,054,251	48,230	4.57%

New Hampshire:	527,269	35,846	6.80%
New Jersey:	3,273,605	237,064	7.24%
New Mexico:	811,365	39,321	4.85%
New York:	7,502,148	437,889	5.84%
North Carolina:	3,936,705	177,291	4.50%
North Dakota:	318,190	18,492	5.81%
Ohio:	4,651,051	221,667	4.77%
Oklahoma:	1,520,327	69,158	4.55%
Oregon:	1,585,295	78,099	4.93%
Pennsylvania:	5,078,566	275,792	5.43%
Rhode Island:	416,126	24,162	5.81%
South Carolina:	1,899,618	85,731	4.51%
South Dakota:	344,608	17,487	5.07%
Tennessee:	2,580,393	114,295	4.43%
Texas:	9,600,635	490,634	5.11%
Utah:	945,290	50,903	5.38%
Vermont:	260,540	15,435	5.92%
Virginia:	3,201,996	215,451	6.73%
Washington:	2,770,334	161,220	5.82%
West Virginia:	767,361	33,259	4.33%
Wisconsin:	2,336,787	116,648	4.99%
Wyoming:	240,400	14,016	5.83%

48.4 Millionaires By Metropolitan Area

According to the *2015 United States Wealth Report*, published by Capgemini (www.capgemini.com), the following metropolitan areas have the greatest number of individuals with assets of $1 million and more:

- New York, NY: 963,000
- Los Angeles, CA: 364,000
- Chicago, IL: 282,000
- Washington, DC: 236,000
- San Francisco, CA: 222,000
- Boston, MA: 162,000
- Houston, TX: 150,000
- Philadelphia, PA: 146,000
- San Jose, CA: 136,000
- Dallas, TX: 126,000
- Detroit, MI: 116,000
- Seattle, WA: 98,000

48.5 Market Resources

Capgemini, 623 Fifth Avenue, 33rd Floor, New York, NY 10022. (212) 314-8000. (www.capgemini.com)

Phoenix Marketing International, 6423 Montgomery Street, Suite 12, Rhinebeck, NY 12572. (845) 876-8228. (www.phoenixmi.com)

49

AFFLUENT E-COMMERCE

49.1 Shopping Channels of the Affluent

According to the Shullman Research Center (www.shullman.net), 51% of affluent consumers purchase luxury items online. For comparison, 87% make such purchases in retail stores. Among those who make high-end purchases online, most do so using laptop or desktop computers; use of smartphones and tablets is cited by only 10% and 7%, respectively.

Approximately half of affluent consumers say they do not always feel comfortable shopping via the Internet. Forty percent (40%) say they do not like using smartphones to buy, 21% say they feel the same way about tablets, and 8% don't feel comfortable shopping by computer. For comparison, 25% do not like shopping by phone or by mail order, and 10% are uncomfortable buying in stores.

Among affluents who shop online, 40% say convenience is the primary reason they do so; 19% cite price as the primary reason.

Forty-three percent (43%) of adults with household incomes of $500,000 or above say they do not buy online at all.

The *Affluent Barometer*, by Ipsos (www.ipsos-na.com), reported that when they shop online, luxury shoppers primarily use the following types of e-commerce sites:

- Sites of specific brands: 39%
- Multi-brand sites not solely focused on luxury goods: 36%
- Luxury sites that contain inventory from various brands: 22%

WealthSurvey, by the Luxury Institute (www.luxuryinstitute.com) assessed shopping channels used by affluent consumers to make recent purchases. Responses by age were as follows:

	<50	50+
• Retail stores:	78%	78%
• Websites using a computer:	78%	76%
• Websites using a tablet:	26%	16%
• Catalogs/mailers:	13%	20%
• Telephone customer service rep:	15%	16%
• Websites using a mobile device:	25%	8%
• Mobile app:	20%	7%
• Tablet app:	15%	8%

49.2 Market Assessment

Global Luxury E-tailing Market 2015-2019, a February 2016 report by Technavio (www.technavio.com), assessed the global luxury e-commerce market as follows:

- 2014: $21.4 billion
- 2015: $24.5 billion
- 2016: $28.0 billion
- 2017: $32.0 billion
- 2018: $36.5 billion
- 2019: $41.8 billion

The 2014-2019 compound growth rate is 14.3%.

With a 11.67% marketshare, Nordstrom is the marketshare leader. Neiman Marcus and Saks Fifth Avenue rank #2 and #3, with 5.36% and 4.20% marketshares, respectively. Net-A-Porter and Ralph Lauren rank #4 and #5, respectively, in the luxury e-commerce market.

49.3 M-Commerce

The Luxury Institute (www.luxuryinstitute.com) reports the mobile-commerce (m-commerce) activities of affluent smartphone and tablet users as follows:

	Smartphone	Tablet
• Search for store information:	49%	41%
• Look up product details while on-the-go:	33%	18%
• Compare prices while shopping in-store:	29%	13%
• View product images:	28%	42%
• Receive special deals or discounts:	28%	22%
• Compare prices while on-the-go:	27%	15%
• Look up product details while shopping in-store:	27%	11%
• Read user reviews and recommendations:	26%	42%
• Check status of an order:	23%	36%
• Check availability at other retailers:	20%	24%
• Opt-in to receive marketing messages:	11%	10%
• Watch product videos:	10%	21%

50

AFFLUENCE MARKET RESEARCH

50.1 Overview

Several organizations publish data and analyses of affluent consumers and strategies for marketing to this segment. This chapter lists the primary sources:

50.2 Research Organizations and Publications

American Affluence Research Center

- Since 2002, the American Affluence Research Center (www.affluenceresearch.org) has published the semiannual *Affluent Market Tracking Study*. The study tracks the 12-month outlook of the wealthiest 10% of U.S. households. The economy; the stock market; personal earnings, savings and investment objectives; and spending plans for 17 product categories and eight major expenditures are assessed.

Boston Consulting Group

- Boston Consulting Group (www.bcg.com) publishes *Global Wealth*, which includes an assessment of millionaire households globally; 63 markets are assessed.

Forbes

- *Forbes* publishes annual lists of the wealthiest people in the United States and worldwide.

Ipsos

- Ipsos (www.ipsos-na.com) has conducted the annual *Affluent Survey* since 1977 and conducts monthly *Affluent Barometer* surveys assessing the lifestyles, media habits, and spending of 68.5 million Affluent Americans with at least $100,000 in annual household income.

Knight Frank

- Since 2005, Knight Frank (www.knightfrank.com) has published the Wealth Report, a global perspective on wealth and investment opportunities and strategies.

Luxury Daily

- *Luxury Daily* is an online newsletter on luxury marketing.

Luxury Institute

- Luxury Institute (www.luxuryinstitute.com) developed the Luxcelerate System to help retailers improve client data collection, conversion, and retention rates.

Luxury Society

- Luxury Society (www.luxurysociety.com) is a membership-based business resource for the luxury industry, connecting more than 31,000 executives in 150 countries to brands, insights, service providers, and networking opportunities.

Martini Media

- Martini Media (www.martinimediainc.com) publishes *The Martini Report*, quarterly reports that quantify the role of digital media in the lifestyles and spending habits of affluent consumers.

RBC Wealth Management

- RBC Wealth Management (www.rbcwealthmanagement.com) publishes *Wealth Through The Prism of Culture and Mobility*, an annual assessment of internationally mobile wealthy individuals (IMWIs), those who live, work, or spend more than half their time outside their home country and have investable assets of at least $1 million.

Shullman Research Center

- The Shullman Research Center (www.shullman.net) publishes the results of surveys of affluent consumers in its *Luxury and Affluence Monthly Pulse*. Shullman surveys four groups of consumers: those making over $75,000, those making $250,000 or more, those making upward of $500,000, and, for comparison, the general population.

Unity Marketing

- Unity Marketing (www.unitymarketingonline.com) publishes *Luxury Trend Report*, providing an assessment of various aspects of spending by affluent households.
- Unity Marketing also publishes the *Luxury Tracking Study*, a quarterly report about what products and brands luxury consumers are buying and how much they spend on luxuries.
- In 2014, Unity Marketing launched *Millionaire Market Monitor* in conjunction with the American Affluence Research Center.

Wealth-X

- Wealth-X (www.wealthx.com) publishes *World Ultra Wealth Report*, an annual global assessment of Ultra High Net Worth (UHNW) individuals. UHNW individuals have been described variously as those with at least $30 million in investable assets, or with a disposable income of more than $20 million, or as those with more than $50 million in wealth.

50.3 Market Resources

American Affluence Research Center, 2426 Loxford Lane, Alpharetta, GA 30009. (770) 740-2200. (www.affluenceresearch.org)

Boston Consulting Group (BCC), 1 Exchange Place, Boston MA 02109. (617) 973-1200. (www.bcg.com)

Capgemini, 623 Fifth Avenue, 33rd Floor, New York, NY 10022. (212) 314-8000. (www.capgemini.com)

Ipsos, 1271 Avenue of the Americas, 15th Floor, New York, NY 10020. (212) 265-3200. (www.ipsos-na.com)

Knight Frank, 55 Baker Street, London W1U 8AN, United Kingdom Tel.: +44 (0) 20 7629 8171. (www.knightfrank.com)

Luxury Daily, 401 Broadway, Suite 1408, New York, NY 10013. (212) 334-6366. (www.luxurydaily.com)

Luxury Institute, 115 East 57th Street, 11th Floor, New York, NY 10022. (646) 792-2669. (www.luxuryinstitute.com)

Luxury Society, 7 Avenue Krieg, 1208 Geneva, Switzerland. (www.luxurysociety.com)

Martini Media, 415 Brannan Street, San Francisco, CA 94107. (415) 913-7446. (www.martinimediainc.com)

RBC Wealth Management, 60 S. 6th Street, Minneapolis, MN 55402. (612) 371-7750. (www.rbcwealthmanagement.com)

The Affluence Collaborative. (212) 225-9339. (www.affluencecollaborative.com)

The Shullman Research Center, 8 Quintard Avenue, Old Greenwich, CT 06830. (203) 990-0541. (www.shullman.net)

Unity Marketing, 206 E. Church Street, Stevens, PA 17578. (717) 336-1600. (www.unitymarketingonline.com)

Wealth Engine, 4330 East West Highway, Bethesda, MD 20814. (877) 928-3544. (www.wealthengine.com)

Wealth-X, 8 Marina Boulevard, #05-02, Marina Bay Financial Centre, Singapore 018981. Tel.: +1 877 887 8454. (www.wealthx.com)

PART VII: MIDDLE-CLASS CONSUMERS

51

DEFINING THE MIDDLE CLASS

51.1 Income-Based Definitions

The middle class is typically defined as households in the middle three quintiles (i.e., incomes in the 20th percentile to 80th percentile range). In 2014, this included households with incomes between $21,432 and $112,262. With this definition, the middle class is always the middle 60% of households ranked by income.

Pew Research Center (www.pewresearch.org) defines middle-income adults as those that live in households with incomes two-thirds to double the national median size-adjusted household income, about $42,000 to $125,000 annually in 2014 for a three-person household. Lower-income households have incomes less than two-thirds of the median, and upper-income households have incomes that are more than double the median. Household incomes are adjusted for the cost of living in metropolitan areas. With this definition, the middle class varies as the income distribution in the U.S. shifts. As discussed in Chapter 52 of this handbook, the size of the middle class in the U.S. has been dropping for several years and continues to decline.

"Today's economy has been called rigged against the middle class. During the recovery from the 2008 recession, income increased 31% for the top 1% buy just 0.4% for 99% of Americans."

Time, 5/30/16

51.2 Self-Identification As Middle Class

A study by the Congressional Research Service (CRS, www.loc.gov/crsinfo/) recognizes that the middle class can be defined as a psychological perception, or the self assessment of one's financial situation compared with those around them. Other studies have found a strong link between relative income and self-reported happiness.

Pew Research Center found in 2015 that nearly 90% of adults considered themselves middle class, regardless of whether their incomes languished near the poverty line or skimmed the top stratum of earners.

"Middle income is not necessarily the same thing as middle class. Even as the proportion of households in the middle-income brackets has narrowed, people's identification with the middle class remains broad. It's not only what you have, but how you feel. The middle-class label is as much about aspirations among Americans as it is about economics."

The New York Times, 4/11/15

The traditional bedrocks of a middle-class life are adequate housing and health care, college for the children plus retirement savings, generally with a personal vehicle, and a regular summer vacation. And even though consumption was once a useful shorthand guide to a middle-class lifestyle, it is no longer as reliable in a world where smartphones and flat-screen TVs are staples in a majority of households below the poverty line and retirement savings, even among top earners, are often treated as a luxury.

Ultimately, what people need to feel part of the middle class is a sense of economic security, according to Thomas Hirschl, Ph.D., a sociologist at Cornell University and co-author of *Chasing the American Dream*.

52

MIDDLE CLASS FALLING BEHIND

52.1 Trend Assessment

A May 2016 study by Pew Research Center (www.pewresearch.org) assessed the current economic profiles of major metropolitan areas (see Chapter 88 of this handbook) and compared this data with economic profiles of 2000. Findings were as follows:

- Decrease in share of households that are middle income: 89% of metros
- Increase in share of households that are upper income: 75% of metros
- Increase in share of households that are lower income: 70% of metros

---

"The American middle class is losing ground in metropolitan areas across the country, affecting communities from Boston to Seattle and from Dallas to Milwaukee."

Pew Research Center, 5/11/16

52.2 Decline Of Middle-Income Households

"Middle-income" households are defined by Pew Research Center as those with an income that is two-thirds to double that of the U.S. median household income, after incomes have been adjusted for household size. For a three-person household, the middle-income range was about $42,000 to $125,000 annually in 2014. Lower-income households have incomes less than two-thirds of the median, and upper-income households have incomes that are more than double the median.

In 1970, 61% of U.S. households were middle-income. By 2015, the share of households in the middle-income tier dropped to 50%.

"After more than four decades of serving as the nation's economic majority, the American middle class is now matched in number by those in the economic tiers above and below it."

Pew Research Center, 12/9/15

Forty-nine percent (49%) of U.S. aggregate income went to upper-income households in 2014, up from 29% in 1970. The share accruing to middle-income households was 43% in 2014, down substantially from 62% in 1970.

Middle-income Americans have fallen further behind financially in the 21st century. In 2014, the median income of these households was 4% less than in 2000. Moreover, because of the housing market crisis and the Great Recession, their median wealth (assets minus debts) fell by 28% from 2001 to 2013.

52.3 Decline In Wealth

Pew Research Center assesses that the wealth (assets minus debts) of upper-income households more than doubled over the span of 30 years from 1983 to 2013 while the wealth of middle-income households dropped.

Before the onset of the Great Recession, the median wealth of middle-income families increased from $95,879 in 1983 to $161,050 in 2007, a gain of 68%. But the economic downturn eliminated that gain almost entirely.

By 2010, the median wealth of middle-income families had fallen to about $98,000, where it still stood in 2013. Upper-income families more than doubled their wealth from 1983 to 2007 as it climbed from $323,402 to $729,980. Despite losses during the recession, these families recovered somewhat since 2010 and had a median wealth of $650,074 in 2013, more than double their wealth in 1983.

52.4 Demographic Shifts

The less-educated, younger, married-with-children, and Caucasian households have lost the largest share of middle-income households.

The following is a comparison of demographics of middle-income adults in 2015 with all U.S. households and 30-year (1971-2015) change in share by each demographic (source: Pew Research Center):

Age	Pct. of All Households	Pct. of Middle-Income	30-Year Change
• 18-to-29:	21%	22%	-9%
• 30-to-44:	25%	26%	-2%
• 45-to-64:	34%	34%	2%
• 65 and older:	19%	18%	9%
Race/Ethnicity			
• Caucasian:	65%	67%	-13%
• Hispanic:	15%	15%	3%
• African-American:	12%	11%	4%
• Asian-American:	6%	6%	3%
Education			
• Less than high school graduate:	12%	9%	-25%
• High school graduate:	30%	31%	-10%
• Some college/two-year degree:	28%	32%	18%
• Bachelor's degree or more:	30%	28%	18%
Family Status			
• Married, no children at home:	24%	24%	2%
• Married, with children at home:	28%	30%	-21%
• Unmarried:	49%	46%	20%
Nativity			
• U.S. born:	84%	85%	-2%
• Foreign born:	16%	15%	2%

"As a group, middle-income adults look much like U.S. adults overall, in terms of their demographic and socioeconomic characteristics. By some measures, middle-income adults are more similar to all adults today than was true in 1971."

Pew Research Center, 12/9/15

53

INCOME & WEALTH INEQUALITY

53.1 Overview

In a speech on economic mobility, President Barack Obama called income inequality and lack of upward mobility the defining challenge of our times.

The Great Recession widened the gap between the wealthy and the rest of the U.S. population.

An ongoing assessment of income distribution at the University of California, Berkeley found that the richest 1% in America secured 19% of national income in 2012, their biggest share since 1928. The top 10% of earners held a record 48.2%. During the recovery between 2009 and 2012, real-family incomes rose by an average of 4.6%, though this was skewed by a 31.4% increase for the top 1%. For the other 99% incomes rose by just 0.4%.

According to Robert Reich, Ph.D., an economics professor at University of California, Berkeley and author of *Inequality For All* (2013, 72 Productions), the average male U.S. worker in 1978 earned $48,000, adjusted for inflation, while the average member of the Upper One Percent earned $390,000, or eight times as much. By 2010, the middle-class male's wages had declined to $33,000, while the One Percenter was making $1.1 million, or 33 times more. Prof. Reich says that the wealthiest 400 people in the U.S. today have more money than the bottom 150 million Americans combined.

53.2 Economic Inequality Assessment

A 2015 study by the Organization for Economic Cooperation and Development (OECD, www.oecd.org) reported that the richest 10% of American households earns about 28% of the overall income pie, roughly consistent with what you see among the rich in other countries. The wealthiest 10% of U.S. households have garnered 76% of wealth in the U.S., significantly higher than in most other affluent countries.

"When we think about and discuss economic inequality in this country, we usually focus on income inequality. But there's another type of inequality that gets a lot less attention. It arguably contributes far more to the divide between the haves and have-nots in this country: wealth inequality."

The Washington Post, 5/21/15

The OECD, a group of 34 mostly developed economies, calculates Gini coefficients for most of its member countries, both before and after taxes and transfer payments, to assess economic inequalities. Before accounting for taxes and transfers, the U.S. ranks 10th in income inequality; among the countries with more unequal income distributions are France, the U.K., and Ireland. But after taking taxes and transfers into account, the U.S. had the second-highest level of inequality, behind only Chile.

53.3 Analysis For Major U.S. Cities

A study by the Brookings Institution (www.brookings.edu) assessed inequality in the 50 largest U.S. cities using the "95/20 ratio." This figure represents the income at which a household earns more than 95% of all other households, divided by the income at which a household earns more than only 20% of all other households. Using Census Bureau data, Brookings found across the 50 largest U.S. cities the 95/20 ratio was 10.8, compared to 9.1 for the country as a whole. The 95/20 ratio ranged from 18.8 to 6.0 among the largest cities. Cities with the highest income gap were Atlanta, San Francisco, and Miami.

The 95/20 ratios for the 50 largest cities are as follows:

	20th Percentile	95th Percentile	95/20 Ratio
• Atlanta, GA:	$14,850	$279,827	18.8
• San Francisco, CA:	$21,313	$353,576	16.6
• Miami, FL:	$10,438	$164,013	15.7
• Boston, MA:	$14,604	$223,838	15.3
• Washington, DC:	$21,782	$290,637	13.3
• New York, NY:	$17,119	$226,675	13.2
• Oakland, CA:	$17,646	$223,965	12.7
• Chicago, IL:	$16,078	$201,460	12.5
• Los Angeles, CA:	$17,657	$217,770	12.3

- Baltimore, MD: $13,522 $164,995 12.2
- Houston, TX: $17,344 $205,490 11.8
- Philadelphia, PA: $12,850 $151,026 11.8
- Dallas, TX: $17,811 $200,367 11.2
- Detroit, MI: $ 9,083 $101,620 11.2
- Minneapolis, MN: $17,753 $193,777 10.9
- Memphis, TN: $13,520 $145,015 10.7
- Cleveland, OH: $ 9,432 $100,903 10.7
- Tulsa, OK: $17,359 $183,407 10.6
- Denver, CO: $19,770 $208,810 10.6
- Fresno, CA: $15,665 $160,360 10.2
- Charlotte, NC: $21,998 $219,126 10.0
- Kansas City, MO: $16,353 $161,488 9.9
- Long Beach, CA: $19,255 $185,543 9.6
- Austin, TX: $21,738 $207,594 9.5
- Portland, OR: $20,152 $191,492 9.5
- Tucson, AZ: $13,798 $130,327 9.4
- Sacramento, CA: $17,901 $168,858 9.4
- Milwaukee, WI: $13,328 $125,363 9.4
- El Paso, TX: $16,206 $151,745 9.4
- Indianapolis, IN: $16,230 $150,346 9.3
- Seattle, WA: $26,156 $239,549 9.2
- Louisville, KY: $16,924 $152,792 9.0
- Albuquerque, NM: $18,646 $168,121 9.0
- Nashville, TN: $18,539 $166,032 9.0
- San Diego, CA: $25,126 $224,814 8.9
- San Jose, CA: $31,047 $273,766 8.8
- Jacksonville, FL: $17,411 $152,329 8.7
- Phoenix, AZ: $19,186 $167,503 8.7
- San Antonio, TX: $18,518 $158,566 8.6
- Columbus, OH: $17,238 $147,496 8.6
- Oklahoma City, OK: $18,835 $160,125 8.5
- Raleigh, NC: $24,113 $199,911 8.3
- Omaha, NE: $19,649 $161,910 8.2
- Fort Worth, TX: $20,992 $168,989 8.1
- Colorado Springs, CO: $22,213 $175,034 7.9
- Wichita, KS: $19,516 $151,068 7.7
- Las Vegas, NV: $21,380 $164,344 7.7
- Mesa, AZ: $21,007 $157,190 7.5
- Arlington, TX: $24,169 $175,759 7.3
- Virginia Beach, VA: $31,051 $187,652 6.0

"A city where the rich are very rich, and the poor very poor, is likely to face many difficulties. It may struggle to maintain mixed-income school environments that produce better outcomes for low-income kids. It may have too narrow a tax base from which to sustainably raise the revenues necessary for essential city services. And it may fail to produce housing and neighborhoods accessible to middle-class workers and families, so that those who move up or down the income ladder ultimately have no choice but to move out."

Alan Berbe, Senior Fellow
Brookings Institution

PART VIII: BRAND PREFERENCE SURVEYS

54

BRAND EQUITY

54.1 Overview

The Harris Poll (www.theharrispoll.com) has assessed brand equity for consumer product and retail brands through EquiTrend® surveys since 1989.

The 2016 EquiTrend assessment surveyed over 40,000 U.S. consumers.

54.2 Top Brands Among Adults

The following brands ranked highest among adults in the 2016 EquiTrend study:

Airlines

Full Service Airlines

1. Delta Air Lines
2. Alaska/Horizon Airlines
3. American Airlines
4. Hawaiian Airlines
5. United Airlines

Brands ranked below category average: Air Canada, US Airways

Value Airlines

1. Southwest Airlines
2. JetBlue Airways

Brands ranked below category average: Frontier Airlines, Spirit Airlines, Virgin America Airlines

Appliances

Major Appliances

1. KitchenAid
2. Kenmore
3. Whirlpool
4. Samsung
5. LG
6. GE
7. Maytag
8. Wolf

Brands ranked below category average: Amana, Bosch, Electrolux, Frigidaire, Haier, Jenn-Air, Sub-Zero, Thermador, Viking

Single Serve Coffee Makers

1. Keurig
2. Tassimo

Brands ranked below category average: Black & Decker, Breville, Bunn, Cuisinart, Hamilton Beach, Mr. Coffee, Nespresso, Starbucks Verisimo

Small Kitchen Appliances

1. KitchenAid
2. Cuisinart
3. Crock-Pot
4. GE
5. Calphalon
6. Black & Decker

Brands ranked below category average: Hamilton Beach, Oster, Proctor Silex, Rival, Sunbeam, Waring

Automotive

Auto Service Centers

1. Discount Tire
2. Valvoline Instant Oil Change
3. Napa AutoCare Center
4. Goodyear Tire and Service Network
5. WalMart Tire & Lube Express
6. Mobil 1 Lube Express
7. Pennzoil 10 Minute Oil Change Center

Brands ranked below category average: AAMCO Transmission, Firestone Complete Auto Care, Grease Monkey Automotive Service Centers, Havoline xpress lube, Jiffy Lube Oil Change Centers, Meineke Car Care Center, Midas Auto Service Express, National Tire and Battery (NTB), PepBoys Automotive Service Centers, Precision Tune Auto Care, Sears Automotive Centers

Full Line Automotive

1. Toyota
2. Honda
3. Ford
4. GMC
5. Chevrolet
6. Nissan
7. Subaru

Brands ranked below category average: Buick, Chrysler, Dodge, Fiat, Hyundai, Jeep, Kia, Mazda, MINI Cooper, Mitsubishi, Ram, Scion, Volkswagen

Luxury Automotive

1. Lexus
2. Porsche
3. Acura
4. Mercedes-Benz

5. BMW
6. Tesla
7. Cadillac

Brands ranked below category average: Audi, Infiniti, Jaguar, Land Rover, Lincoln, Volvo

Motor Oil
1. Pennzoil
2. Valvoline
3. Rotella
4. Mobil
5. Shell

Brands ranked below category average: Castrol, Havoline, Mobil 1, Quaker State

Motorcycles
1. Harley-Davidson
2. Ducati

Brands ranked below category average: BMW, Honda, Kawasaki, Suzuki, Yamaha

OEM Branded Infotainment
1. Chevy MyLink
2. Cadillac CUE
3. BMW iDrive
4. Audi MMI
5. Hyundai Bluelink
6. Toyota Entune

Brands ranked below category average: Buick IntelliLink/GMC IntelliLink, HondaLink/AcuraLink, Infiniti InTouch, Kia UVO, Mercedes COMAND, Nissan Connect, Sync/MyFord Touch/MyLincoln Touch

Tires
1. Michelin
2. Goodyear
3. Bridgestone
4. BFGoodrich
5. Pirelli

Brands ranked below category average: Continental, Cooper, Dunlop, Firestone, General, Hankook, Kelly, Kumho, Uniroyal, Yokohama

Computers

Computer Manufacturer
1. Apple Computers
2. Apple iMac
3. Hewlett-Packard (HP) Computers
4. Apple Macbook Series Computers
5. Dell Computers
6. Samsung Computers

7. Microsoft Surface Pro Series Computer

Brands ranked below category average: Acer Computers, ASUS Computers, Fujitsu Computers, Gateway Computers, Google Chromebook Computers, Lenovo Computers, Microsoft Surfacebook, Panasonic Computers, Toshiba Computers

Operating System

1. Apple OS X
2. Google Chrome OS
3. Windows 7
4. Windows 10

Brands ranked below category average: Linux, Windows 8

Printing & Imaging

1. HP Printing & Imaging
2. Kodak Printing & Imaging
3. Canon Printing & Imaging
4. Samsung Printing & Imaging

Brands ranked below category average: Brother Printing and Imaging, Dell Printing & Imaging, Epson Printing & Imaging, Konica Minolta Printing & Imaging, Kyocera Mita Printing & Imaging, Lexmark Printing & Imaging, Panasonic Printing & Imaging, Ricoh Printing & Imaging, Sharp Printing & Imaging, Toshiba Printing & Imaging, Xerox Printing & Imaging

Tablet Computers

1. Apple iPad
2. Samsung Galaxy
3. Kindle Fire

Brands ranked below category average: ASUS Transformer Pad, Google Nexus, Microsoft Surface Tablets, Sony Xperia

Consumer Electronics

Car Audio

1. Bose In-Vehicle Audio
2. Boston Acoustics In-Vehicle Audio
3. Pioneer In-Vehicle Audio
4. Sony In-Vehicle Audio
5. Alpine In-Vehicle Audio
6. harman/kardon In-Vehicle Audio

Brands ranked below category average: Beats In-Vehicle Audio, Clarion In-Vehicle Audio, Infinity In-Vehicle Audio, JBL In-Vehicle Audio, Panasonic In-Vehicle Audio

Digital Cameras

1. Canon Digital Cameras
2. Sony Digital Cameras
3. Nikon Digital Cameras
4. Samsung Digital Cameras
5. GoPro Digital Cameras

Brands ranked below category average: Casio Digital Cameras, FujiFilm Digital Cameras, Kodak Digital Cameras, Olympus Digital Cameras, Panasonic Digital Cameras, PENTAX Digital Cameras, RICOH Digital Cameras

Gaming Console

1. Nintendo 3DS/3DS XL
2. Sony PlayStation 4 (PS4)
3. Sony PlayStation 3 (PS3)
4. Sony PSP/PSP Vita
5. Nintendo Wii
6. Microsoft Xbox 360

Brands ranked below category average: Microsoft Xbox One, Nintendo Wii U, NVIDIA SHIELD Gaming Console

Home Electronics

1. Sony
2. Samsung Home Electronics
3. LG Home Electronics
4. Sonos Home Electronics
5. Panasonic Home Electronics
6. VIZIO Home Electronics

Brands ranked below category average: Dynex Home Electronics, Hitachi Home Electronics, iHome Home Electronics, Insignia Home Electronics, JVC Home Electronics, Mitsubishi Home Electronics, Philips Home Electronics, Sanyo Home Electronics, Sharp Home Electronics, Toshiba Home Electronics

Media Streaming Devices

1. Google Chromecast
2. Apple TV

Brands ranked below category average: Amazon Fire TV, Roku

Smartwatchs

1. Samsung Galaxy Gear Smartwatch
2. Apple iWatch
3. Android Wear Watch

Brands ranked below category average: Sony Smartwatch

Wearable Fitness

1. Fitbit Fitness Trackers

Brands ranked below category average: Adidas miCoach Fitness Watch, Jawbone Up Fitness Trackers, Nike Fuelband Fitness Trackers

Financial Services

Discount Brokerage

1. Fidelity Investments Financial Services
2. Scottrade
3. TD Ameritrade

Brands ranked below category average: Charles Schwab Financial Services, E*TRADE

Investment

1. The Vanguard Group
2. Franklin Templeton Investments
3. T. Rowe Price Financial Services
4. ShareBuilder
5. UBS
6. Principal Financial

Brands ranked below category average: Ameriprise Financial, Edward Jones, Merrill Lynch, Morgan Stanley, Prudential Investments, Raymond James, TIAA-CREF, Wells Fargo Advisors

Mobile Payment

1. PayPal
2. Checkout by Amazon
3. Amazon Payments
4. PayPal Here
5. Pay With Amazon
6. Visa Checkout

Brands ranked below category average: American Express Serve, Apple Passbook, Apple Pay, Google Wallet, MasterCard MasterPass, Square

National Banks

1. Chase

Brands ranked below category average: Bank of America, Citibank, Wells Fargo

Payment Card

1. Visa
2. MasterCard

Brands ranked below category average: American Express, Discover Card

Real Estate Agencies

1. Real Living Real Estate
2. Sotheby's International Realty
3. Keller Williams
4. Better Homes and Gardens Real Estate
5. RE/MAX

Brands ranked below category average: Berkshire Hathaway HomeServices Real Estate, Century 21 Real Estate, Coldwell Banker, ERA Real Estate, Prudential Real Estate

Super Regional Banks

1. Capital One
2. Ally Bank
3. Regions Bank
4. PNC Bank
5. BB&T Bank

Brands ranked below category average: Citizens Bank, Fifth Third Bank, HSBC Bank, KeyBank, M&T Bank, Santander Bank, SunTrust Bank, U.S. Bank

Tax Preparation

1. TurboTax
2. TaxACT

Brands ranked below category average: H&R Block, Jackson Hewitt

Hotels

Economy

1. Microtel Inn & Suites
2. Days Inn
3. Red Roof Inn

Brands ranked below category average: Americas Best Value Inn, EconoLodge, Motel 6, Rodeway Inn, Super 8

Extended Stay

1. Homewood Suites by Hilton
2. Candlewood Suites

Brands ranked below category average: Extended Stay America, MainStay Suites, Residence Inn

Full Service

1. Hilton Hotels & Resorts
2. Marriott Hotels
3. Courtyard Marriott
4. Hilton Garden Inn
5. Hyatt Hotels and Resorts
6. Embassy Suites

Brands ranked below category average: Crowne Plaza Hotels & Resorts, Doubletree by Hilton, Hyatt Place Hotels, Kimpton Hotels, Radisson Hotels & Resorts, Renaissance Hotels, Sheraton Hotels & Resorts, SpringHill Suites, Westin Hotels & Resorts, Wyndham Hotels and Resorts

Luxury Hotel

1. W Hotels and Resorts
2. Four Seasons Hotels and Resorts
3. Grand Hyatt
4. The Ritz Carlton

Brands ranked below category average: Conrad Hotels & Resorts, InterContinental Hotels & Resorts, Omni Hotels & Resorts, Park Hyatt, Waldorf Astoria Hotels & Resorts

Mid-Market Hotel

1. Hampton Inn & Suites
2. Holiday Inn Express Hotels & Resorts
3. Holiday Inn Hotels & Resorts
4. Country Inns & Suites by Carlson
5. Fairfield Inns and Suites
6. Best Western Hotels
7. Comfort Suites

Brands ranked below category average: Clarion Hotels, Comfort Inn, Howard Johnson Hotels, LaQuinta Inns & Suites, Quality Inn & Suites, Ramada Hotels, Sleep Inn Hotels

Household Products

Cookware

1. KitchenAid
2. Calphalon
3. LeCreuset
4. All-Clad
5. Farberware

Brands ranked below category average: Anolon, Circulon, Emerilware, Paula Deen Cookware, Rachael Ray Cookware, Teflon Cookware, T-fal, Wolfgang Puck Cookware

Delivered Gifts

1. Edible Arrangements
2. Harry & David

Brands ranked below category average: 1-800-Flowers, FTD Inc., Giftbaskets.com, Wine Country Gift Baskets

Greeting Cards

1. Hallmark
2. Hallmark Signature
3. American Greetings
4. Papyrus
5. Hallmark Ink & Main
6. Shoebox

Brands ranked below category average: Carlton, DaySpring, Hallmark Mahogany, Hallmark Studio Ink, Hallmark Vida, Just For You from American Greetings Cards, Recycled Paper Greetings Cards

Paint

1. KILZ
2. Behr
3. Sherwin-Williams
4. Benjamin Moore

Brands ranked below category average: Dutch Boy, Glidden Paint, Martha Stewart Living Paint, Olympic Paint, Pittsburgh Paints, Pratt & Lambert, Sears Easy Living Paint, Valspar

Power Tools

1. Craftsman Tools
2. DeWALT Tools
3. Black & Decker Tools

Brands ranked below category average: Bosch Tools, Campbell Hausfeld Tools, Hilti Tools, Hitachi Tools, Makita Tools, Milwaukee Tools, PORTER-CABLE Tools, RIDGID Tools, Ryobi Tools, SKIL Tools

Vacuum Cleaners

1. Dyson
2. Hoover
3. Kenmore

4. Shark
5. Black & Decker
6. Bissell

Brands ranked below category average: Dirt Devil, Electrolux, Eureka, LG, Oreck, Panasonic

Window Coverings

1. Hunter Douglas
2. Levolor

Brands ranked below category average: Kirsch

Insurance

Auto Insurance

1. AAA Auto Insurance
2. State Farm Auto Insurance
3. USAA Auto Insurance
4. American Family Auto Insurance
5. Nationwide Auto Insurance
6. Farmers Auto Insurance

Brands ranked below category average: Allstate Auto Insurance, Esurance Auto Insurance, GEICO Auto Insurance, Liberty Mutual Auto Insurance, MetLife Auto Insurance, Progressive Auto Insurance, The General Auto Insurance, The Hartford Auto Insurance, Travelers Auto Insurance

Health Insurance

1. Blue Cross and Blue Shield
2. UnitedHealthcare
3. Kaiser Permanente
4. WellPoint

Brands ranked below category average: Aetna, Amerigroup, Cigna, Coventry Health Care, Health Net, Humana

Home Insurance

1. State Farm Home Insurance
2. AAA Home Insurance
3. USAA Home Insurance

Brands ranked below category average: Allstate Home Insurance, American Family Home Insurance, Farmers Home Insurance, GEICO Home Insurance, Liberty Mutual Home Insurance, MetLife Home Insurance, Nationwide Home Insurance, Progressive Home Insurance, The Hartford Home Insurance, Travelers Home Insurance

Life Insurance

1. State Farm Life Insurance
2. American Family Life Insurance
3. AAA Life Insurance
4. Transamerica Life Insurance Company

Brands ranked below category average: AIG Direct Life Insurance, Allstate Life Insurance, Guardian Life Insurance, MassMutual Insurance, MetLife Life Insurance, New York Life Insurance Company,

Northwestern Mutual Life Insurance, Pacific Life Insurance, Prudential Life Insurance, USAA Life Insurance

Media

Factual Entertainment TV

1. History Channel
2. Discovery Channel
3. Food Network
4. National Geographic Channel
5. ID (Investigation Discovery)
6. HGTV (Home & Garden Television)
7. Travel Channel
8. Discovery Life Channel
9. Nat Geo WILD

Brands ranked below category average: American Heroes Channel, Animal Planet, Crime & Investigation, Destination America, Discovery (en Espanol), Discovery Fit & Health, H2, Military History Channel, Science, TLC, truTV, Velocity

General Entertainment TV

- AMC (American Movie Classics)
- FX
- A&E
- TBS
- ABC Family
- TNT (Turner Network Television)
- USA
- BBC America
- Comedy Central
- Hallmark Channel
- Syfy
- TV Land
- LMN (Lifetime Movie Network)
- Lifetime
- IFC (Independent Film Channel)

Brands ranked below category average: BET (Black Entertainment Television), Bravo, E! Entertainment, FYI, G4, Logo, Nick at Nite, Oprah Winfrey Network (OWN), Oxygen, Spike, Sundance Channel, Univision, WE (Women's Entertainment)

Internet Radio Service

1. Pandora Internet Radio
2. iTunes
3. SiriusXM Satellite Radio
4. Amazon Music with Prime Music

Brands ranked below category average: Apple Music, iHeartRadio, NPR Music, Slacker Radio, Spotify Radio, TuneIn

Kids' TV
1. Discovery Family Channel
2. PBS KIDS
3. Disney XD
4. Disney Channel
5. Sprout Network (formerly PBS Kids Sprout)
6. Cartoon Network

Brands ranked below category average: Boomerang, Disney Junior, Nick Jr., Nickelodeon, Nicktoons, TeenNick

Music TV
1. Great American Country (GAC)
2. Fuse
3. CMT Network (Country Music Television)
4. VH1

Brands ranked below category average: MTV

News Services
1. Google News
2. National Public Radio (NPR)
3. Yahoo! News
4. BBC News
5. Reuters
6. Associated Press (AP)
7. CNN Online
8. United Press International (UPI)

Brands ranked below category average: Al Jazeera America, Bloomberg Businessweek, Fox News Online, Los Angeles Times, MSNBC Online, New York Times, The Huffington Post, The Wall Street Journal, The Washington Post, USA Today

Pay Cable TV Networks
1. HBO

Brands ranked below category average: Cinemax, Showtime, Starz

Social Networking
1. YouTube
2. Pinterest
3. OpenTable.com
4. Facebook
5. Google+
6. Groupon
7. Instagram

Brands ranked below category average: Flickr, Foursquare, GrubHub, KIK Messenger, LinkedIn, LivingSocial, Reddit, Snapchat, Tumblr, Twitter, Vine, yp.com (Yellow Pages)

Sports TV
1. ESPN
2. NBC Sports
3. Fox Sports News Channel
4. NFL
5. CBS Sports
6. Fox Sports 1
7. Yes
8. NFL Red Zone

Brands ranked below category average: FUEL, MLB, NBA, NHL, Tennis, The Golf Channel

TV Networks
1. (tie) ABC
1. (tie) CBS
3. PBS (Public Broadcasting Service)

Brands ranked below category average: Fox, NBC, The CW

TV News
1. The Weather Channel

Brands ranked below category average: CNBC, CNN, Fox News Channel, MSNBC News Channel, POP (formerly TV Guide Network)

TV Service Providers
1. Google Fiber
2. Advanced TV
3. Verizon FiOS
4. XFINITY by Comcast
5. Optimum
6. AT&T U-verse
7. Charter Spectrum

Brands ranked below category average: Cox Communications, DirecTV, Dish, Time Warner Cable

Video Streaming Subscriptions
1. Netflix
2. Amazon Prime Instant Video
3. Twitch.tv
4. HBO GO
5. Hulu Plus
6. Vevo

Brands ranked below category average: CBS All Access, Crackle, Funny or Die, HBO NOW, MLB.TV, NFL Game Pass, Playstation Vue, Redbox Instant, Showtime (Subscription Streaming TV Service), Sling TV, The Blaze, WWE Network, You Tube Red

Non-Profit Organizations

Animal Welfare

1. Best Friends Animal Society
2. American Society for the Prevention of Cruelty to Animals (ASPCA)
3. The Humane Society of the United States
4. PetSmart Charities
5. PETCO Foundation

Brands ranked below category average: People for the Ethical Treatment of Animals (PETA)

Disability

1. Special Olympics
2. Goodwill
3. Autism Speaks
4. National Autism Association
5. March of Dimes

Brands ranked below category average: Autism Society of America, Easter Seals, National Down Syndrome Congress, National Down Syndrome Society, The American Association of People with Disabilities (AAPD), United Cerebral Palsy (UCP)

Disabled Veterans Association

1. Wounded Warrior Project

Brands ranked below category average: Disabled American Veterans (DAV), Paralyzed Veterans of America

Environmental

1. Wildlife Conservation Society
2. The Nature Conservancy
3. World Wildlife Fund (WWF)
4. National Wildlife Federation
5. Natural Resources Defense Council (NRDC)

Brands ranked below category average: Audubon, Environmental Defense Fund (EDF), Greenpeace USA, Sierra Club

Health

1. St. Jude Children's Research Hospital
2. Shriners Hospitals for Children
3. Make-A-Wish
4. The Jimmy Fund
5. American Cancer Society
6. American Heart Association/American Stroke Association
7. American Heart Association
8. Stand Up To Cancer (SU2C)
9. Children's Miracle Network
10. Susan G Komen for the Cure
11. American Diabetes Association

12. The Breast Cancer Research Foundation
13. Juvenile Diabetes Research Foundation International (JDRF)

Brands ranked below category average: Alzheimer's Association, American Lung Association, American Stroke Association, Arthritis Foundation, Asthma and Allergy Foundation of America (AAFA), Avon Foundation for Women, Cystic Fibrosis Foundation, Leukemia & Lymphoma Society (LLS), LIVESTRONG, Michael J. Fox Foundation, Muscular Dystrophy Association (MDA), National Kidney Foundation, National Multiple Sclerosis Society, National Stroke Association, Planned Parenthood, World Health Organization (WHO)

International Aid

1. Food For The Poor
2. ChildFund International
3. Bill and Melinda Gates Foundation
4. Doctors Without Borders/Medecins Sans Frontieres (MSF)
5. Partners in Health
6. Heifer International
7. Save the Children
8. Catholic Relief Services
9. Free the Children
10. Oxfam America

Brands ranked below category average: Amnesty International, CARE, Clinton Foundation/Clinton Health Access Initiative, Ford Foundation, The Rockefeller Foundation, The World Bank, UNICEF, USAID, World Vision

Social Services Non-Profit

1. Habitat for Humanity
2. Ronald McDonald House Charities
3. American Red Cross
4. The Salvation Army
5. Feeding America

Brands ranked below category average: AARP Foundation, Catholic Charities USA, Children's Defense Fund (CDF), Dave Thomas Foundation, Feed The Children, United Way, USO (United Services Organization), VFW - Veterans Of Foreign Wars, Volunteers of America

Youth

1. Girl Scouts of the USA
2. The Y-YMCA
3. Boys & Girls Clubs of America
4. Reading Is Fundamental (RIF)

Brands ranked below category average: 4-H, Big Brothers Big Sisters, Boy Scouts of America, Junior Achievement

Online Organizations

Health Information Website

1. WebMD
2. MayoClinic.org

Brands ranked below category average: CNN Health, Drugs.com, Lifescript.com, MSN Health, NIH.gov (National Institute of Health), Yahoo! Health

Online Auto Shopping
1. Kelley Blue Book (KBB.com)
2. Edmunds.com

Brands ranked below category average: AutoTrader.com, Cars.com, eBay Motors, TRUECar.com

Online Computer Retailers
1. Apple.com
2. BestBuy.com
3. Microsoft.com
4. Newegg.com

Brands ranked below category average: CDW.com, Dell.com, HP.com, PCMall.com, Sony.com, TigerDirect.com

Online Department Stores
1. Kohls.com
2. Macys.com
3. JCP.com (JC Penney)

Brands ranked below category average: NeimanMarcus.com, Nordstrom.com, Sears.com

Online Home Search
1. Zillow.com

Brands ranked below category average: HomeFinder.com, Homes.com, Realtor.com, Trulia.com

Online Job Search
1. Indeed.com
2. USAJobs.com
3. Snagajob.com

Brands ranked below category average: CareerBuilder.com, Glassdoor, Monster.com, SimplyHired.com

Online Travel Services
1. Expedia.com
2. Orbitz.com
3. priceline.com
4. KAYAK.com
5. Hotels.com

Brands ranked below category average: Travelocity.com, Trivago

Restaurants

Burgers
1. In-N-Out Burger
2. Five Guys Burgers and Fries
3. Culver's

4. Wendy's
5. Sonic America's Drive-In
6. Whataburger
7. Steak 'n Shake

Brands ranked below category average: Burger King, Carl's Jr., Checkers/Rally's, DQ Grill & Chill, Hardee's, Jack in the Box, McDonald's, White Castle

Casual Dining

1. IHOP (International House of Pancakes)
2. Outback Steakhouse
3. LongHorn Steakhouse
4. Red Lobster Seafood Restaurants
5. Bonefish Grill
6. Applebee's
7. Chili's Grill & Bar
8. Buffalo Wild Wings

Brands ranked below category average: Bahama Breeze, Denny's, Ruby Tuesday, Shoney's, TGI Fridays

Chicken

1. Chick-fil-A
2. Zaxby's
3. Popeyes

Brands ranked below category average: Bojangles', Boston Market, Church's Chicken, El Pollo Loco, KFC Restaurants (Kentucky Fried Chicken)

Coffee & Snacks

1. Dunkin' Donuts Stores
2. Krispy Kreme
3. Starbucks Coffee Shops
4. Einstein Bros Bagels

Brands ranked below category average: Bruegger's Bagels, Caribou Coffee Shops, McCafe, Seattle's Best Coffee Shops, Tim Hortons

Fast Casual Mexican

1. Moe's Southwest Grill
2. Taco Bell
3. Qdoba Mexican Grill
4. Baja Fresh Mexican Grill

Brands ranked below category average: Chipotle Mexican Grill, Del Taco

Italian

1. Olive Garden
2. Maggiano's Little Italy

Brands ranked below category average: Carrabba's Italian Grill, Romano's Macaroni Grill

Pizza
1. Pizza Hut
2. Papa John's Pizza
3. Domino's Pizza

Brands ranked below category average: CiCi's Pizza, Little Caesars Pizza

Sandwich Shops
1. Subway
2. Panera Bread

Brands ranked below category average: Arby's, Blimpie, Jimmy John's, Quiznos

Retail

Department Stores
1. Macy's
2. Kohl's
3. JCPenney

Brands ranked below category average: Belk, Dillard's, Sears

Discount Shoes Stores
1. DSW Shoes
2. Famous Footwear

Brands ranked below category average: Payless ShoeSource

Electronics
1. Best Buy Stores
2. Apple Store

Brands ranked below category average: B&H Photo Video, Brookstone Retail Stores, Game Stop Retail Store, h.h. gregg appliances & electronics, Microsoft Store, Radio Shack

Hardware & Home Stores
1. The Home Depot
2. Lowe's

Brands ranked below category average: Ace Hardware, Menards, True Value

Luxury Department Stores
1. Nordstrom

Brands ranked below category average: Bloomingdale's, Lord & Taylor, Neiman Marcus, Saks 5th Avenue

Off-Price Retailer
1. TJ Maxx
2. Marshalls

Brands ranked below category average: Burlington Coat Factory, Ross Dress For Less

Sporting Goods Store
1. Cabela's

2. Dick's Sporting Goods
3. Finish Line Sporting Goods
4. REI
5. Sports Authority
6. Bass Pro Shops

Brands ranked below category average: Champs Sports, Dunham's Sports, Eastern Mountain Sports, Foot Locker, Gander Mountain, Lady Foot Locker, MC Sports, Modell's Sporting Goods

Sports League

1. NFL (National Football League)
2. NCAA Football (college football)
3. MLB (Major League Baseball)
4. NBA (National Basketball Association)
5. Premier League Soccer

Brands ranked below category average: Formula 1 Racing, MLS (Major League Soccer), NASCAR (auto racing), NCAA Basketball (college basketball), NHL (National Hockey League), PGA TOUR (Professional Golfers Association), UFC (Ultimate Fighting Championship), WWE (World Wrestling Entertainment)

Telecommunications

Mobile Networks

1. Verizon
2. AT&T

Brands ranked below category average: Cricket Wireless, Sprint, T-Mobile, Virgin

Mobile Operating Systems

1. Apple iOS
2. Android

Brands ranked below category average: Blackberry, Windows 10 Mobile

Smartphones

1. Apple iPhone Series Smartphones
2. Samsung Galaxy Series Smartphones
3. LG Smartphones

Brands ranked below category average: Blackberry Smartphones, Google Nexus Series Smartphones, HTC Smartphones, Microsoft Lumia Series Smartphones, Motorola Moto Series Smartphones, Nokia Lumia Series Smartphones, Sony Xperia Series Smartphones

Other

Cruise Lines

1. Disney Cruise Line
2. Royal Caribbean International
3. Norwegian Cruise Line
4. Holland America Cruise Line

Brands ranked below category average: Carnival Cruise Lines, Celebrity Cruises, Princess Cruises

Movie Theaters
1. Regal Cinemas
2. AMC Theatres
3. Carmike Cinemas

Brands ranked below category average: Cinemark Theatres, Showcase Cinemas

Moving Trucks
1. U-Haul Moving Truck Rental

Brands ranked below category average: Budget Moving Truck Rental, Penske Moving Truck Rental, Ryder Moving Truck Rental

Package Delivery
1. UPS (United Parcel Service)

Brands ranked below category average: FedEx, United States Postal Service (USPS)

54.3 Market Resources

The Harris Poll, 60 Corporate Woods, Rochester, NY 14623. (585) 272-8400. (http://www.theharrispoll.com/equitrend-rankings/2016)

55

BRAND INDEX

55.1 Overview

YouGov (www.yougov.com), an Internet-based market research firm, developed BrandIndex (www.brandindex.com), a measure of brand perception among the public. The measurement assesses 15 categories, as follows:

- Ad awareness
- Attention
- Brand awareness
- Buzz
- Current customer
- Customer satisfaction
- Former customer
- General impression
- Purchase consideration
- Purchase intent
- Quality
- Recommendation
- Reputation
- Value
- Word of mouth exposure

BrandIndex assesses nine consumer sectors, as follows:

- Automotive
- Consumer goods
- Financial services
- Food & drink
- Media & entertainment
- Retail
- Technology & telecoms
- Travel & leisure
- Utilities & services

55.2 Buzz Ranking

The 2015 BrandIndex survey included 1.5 million interviews with U.S. adults.

The 2015 ranking for the Buzz category, which assesses how much people have heard about each brand in the media or through word of mouth was as follows:

Airlines

1. Southwest
2. Delta Air Lines
4. JetBlue
4. Alaska Air
5. American Airlines

Appliances

1. LG
2. Whirlpool
3. Kenmore
4. Maytag
5. GE

Apparel & Footwear Manufacturers

1. Nike
2. Skechers
3. New Balance
4. Levi's
5. Under Armour

Automobiles

1. Ford
2. Toyota
3. Chevrolet
4. Honda
5. Subaru

Auto Fuel

1. Shell
2. Chevron
3. Sunoco
4. Valero
5. Arco

Auto Insurance

1. Geico
2. State Farm
3. Aflac
4. Allstate
5. Nationwide

Banks
1. Capital One
2. Chase
3. TD Bank
4. Wells Fargo
5. PNC Bank

Beer
1. Samuel Adams
2. Budweiser
3. Redd's Apple Ale
4. Dos Equis
5. Corona

Beverages
1. V8
2. Coca Cola
3. Ocean Spray
4. Gatorade
5. Pepsi

Car Rental
1. Enterprise
2. Hertz
3. Budget
4. National
5. Avis

Cruises
1. Royal Caribbean
2. Norwegian Cruse Lines
3. Princess Cruises
4. Holland America Line
5. Celebrity Cruises

Hair & Skin Care
1. Dove
2. Olay
3. Neutrogena
4. Aveeno
5. Cover Girl

Health Insurance
1. Blue Cross/Blue Shield
2. Humana
3. United Healthcare
4. Kaiser Permanente
5. Aetna

Hospitals
1. Cancer Treatment Centers of America
2. Mayo Clinic
3. Johns Hopkins
4. Cleveland Clinic
5. University of Texas MD Anderson Cancer Center

Hotels
1. Marriott
2. Holiday Inn Express
3. Holiday Inn
4. Hilton
5. Best Western

Internet Search
1. Google
2. Yahoo!
3. Bing
4. Yahoo! Answers
5. MSN

Internet Social Media
1. YouTube
2. Google
3. Pinterest
4. Facebook
5. Google+

Investment
1. Fidelity
2. E-Trade
3. TD Ameritrade
4. Charles Schwab
5. Edward Jones

Restaurant - Casual Dining

1. Olive Garden
2. Panera Bread
3. Outback Steakhouse
4. Applebee's
5. Red Lobster

Restaurants - Quick-Service

1. Subway
2. Wendy's
3. Chick-Fil-A
4. Pizza Hut
5. Sonic

Restaurants - Lighter Fare

1. Dunkin' Donuts
2. Dairy Queen
3. Krispy Kreme
4. Starbucks
5. Baskin Robbins

Retail - Apparel

1. Old Navy
2. Victoria's Secret
3. Kohl's
4. JCPenney
5. Macy's

Retail - Discount

1. Amazon.com
2. Costco
3. Target
4. eBay
5. Dollar Tree

Snacks

1. M&M
2. Cherrios
3. Reese's
4. Doritos
5. Snickers

Spirits

1. Jack Daniel's
2. Grey Goose
3. Bailey's
4. Captain Morgan
5. Crown Royal

Streaming Video & Music

1. Netflix
2. YouTube
3. Pandora
4. Amazon Instant Video/Amazon Prime Video
5. Hulu

Tools & Hardware

1. John Deere
2. Craftsman
3. Black & Decker
4. DeWalt
5. Andersen Windows

Travel Agents

1. Trivago
2. Priceline.com
3. Hotwire.com
4. Travelocity
5. Expedia

TV Networks

1. History Channel
2. Discovery Channel
3. PBS
4. Food Network
5. HBO

55.3 Market Resources

YouGov, 38 West 21st Street, 5th Floor, New York, NY 10010. (646) 537-9818. (www.yougov.com)

56

CUSTOMER EXPERIENCE

56.1 Overview

Temkin Group (www.temkingroup.com), a customer experience research and consulting company, publishes annual Temkin Ratings (www.temkinratings.com) in three components of customer experience, as follows:

- Effort
- Emotion
- Success

Temkin ranks over 100 companies in each category. This chapter presents a list of the top 20 in each category.

56.2 Temkin Ratings

The following are the 2016 Temkin Ratings:

Overall Experience

	Company	Segment
1.	Publix	Supermarkets
2.	H-E-B	Supermarkets
3. (tie)	Chick-fil-A	Fast food
3. (tie)	Kroger	Supermarkets
3. (tie)	Save-a-Lot	Supermarkets
3. (tie)	True Value	Retailers
9. (tie)	Aldi	Supermarkets
9. (tie)	Amazon.com	Retailers
7. (tie)	Credit unions	Banks
7. (tie)	O'Reilly Auto Parts	Retailers
7. (tie)	Wegmans	Supermarkets
12. (tie)	Dollar Tree	Retailers
12. (tie)	Food Lion	Supermarkets
12. (tie)	Giant Eagle	Supermarkets
12. (tie)	QVC	Retailers
12. (tie)	Regions	Banks
12. (tie)	ShopRite	Supermarkets
12. (tie)	Subway	Fast food
12. (tie)	USAA	Banks

20. (tie)	Dollar General	Retailers
20. (tie)	Hy-Vee	Supermarkets
20. (tie)	IHOP	Fast food
20. (tie)	Little Caesar's	Fast food
20. (tie)	Sam's Club	Retailers
20. (tie)	Trader Joe's	Supermarkets
20. (tie)	Wawa Food Markets	Supermarkets
20. (tie)	Winn-Dixie	Supermarkets

Effort

1. (tie)	O'Reilly Auto Parts	Retailers
1. (tie)	Publix	Supermarkets
1. (tie)	Save-a-Lot	Supermarkets
1. (tie)	True Value	Retailers
5. (tie)	Aldi	Supermarkets
5. (tie)	Credit unions	Banks
5. (tie)	H-E-B	Supermarkets
5. (tie)	Kohl's	Retailers
5. (tie)	Regions	Banks
10. (tie)	Chick-fil-A	Fast food
10. (tie)	Giant Eagle	Supermarkets
10. (tie)	Kroger	Supermarkets
10. (tie)	Little Caesar's	Fast food
10. (tie)	PetSmart	Retailers
10. (tie)	Subway	Fast food
10. (tie)	Wegmans	Supermarkets
17. (tie)	Ace Hardware	Retailers
17. (tie)	Hardees	Fast food
17. (tie)	QVC	Retailers
17. (tie)	Michaels	Retailers

Emotion

1.	Publix	Supermarkets
2. (tie)	Chick-fil-A	Fast food
2. (tie)	Residence Inn	Hotels
4. (tie)	H-E-B	Supermarkets
4. (tie)	Kroger	Supermarkets
4. (tie)	Save-a-Lot	Supermarkets
4. (tie)	True Value	Retailers
8. (tie)	Amazon	Computers/tablets
8. (tie)	Amazon.com	Retailers
8. (tie)	QVC	Retailers
8. (tie)	Wawa Food Markets	Supermarkets
12. (tie)	Food Lion	Supermarkets

12. (tie)	Piggly Wiggly	Supermarkets
12. (tie)	Wegmans	Supermarkets
15. (tie)	Aldi	Supermarkets
18. (tie)	Credit unions	Banks
15. (tie)	IHOP	Fast food
18. (tie)	Sam's Club	Retailers
15. (tie)	ShopRite	Supermarkets
18. (tie)	Subway	Fast food

Success

1.	Publix	Supermarkets
2.	H-E-B	Supermarkets
3.	Wegmans	Supermarkets
4. (tie)	Chick-fil-A	Fast food
7. (tie)	Credit unions	Banks
4. (tie)	Dollar Tree	Retailers
4. (tie)	Kroger	Supermarkets
7. (tie)	Aldi	Supermarkets
7. (tie)	Amazon.com	Retailers
7. (tie)	True Value	Retailers
7. (tie)	USAA	Banks
12. (tie)	Regions	Banks
12. (tie)	Save-a-Lot	Supermarkets
12. (tie)	ShopRite	Supermarkets
12. (tie)	So. California Gas Co.	Utilities
12. (tie)	The Hartford	Insurance carriers
12. (tie)	Trader Joe's	Supermarkets
18. (tie)	PNC	Banks
18. (tie)	Subway	Fast food
18. (tie)	USAA	Banks

56.3 Top Rated by Sector

By sector, the following companies had the highest ratings in the 2016 Temkin Ratings:

- Airlines: Southwest Airlines
- Auto dealers: Toyota
- Banks: Credit unions
- Computer/tablet makers: Amazon
- Credit card issuers: USAA
- Fast food chains: Chick-fil-A
- Health plans: Kaiser Permanente
- Hotel chains (tie): Holiday Inn Express

- Hotel chains (tie): Residence Inn
- Insurance carriers: USAA
- Internet services: Google
- Investment firms (tie): Edward Jones
- Investment firms (tie): Fidelity Investments
- Major appliances: Whirlpool
- Parcel delivery services: UPS
- Rental car agencies (tie): Enterprise
- Rental car agencies (tie): National
- Retailers: True Value
- Supermarket chains: Publix
- TV service providers: DirecTV
- Utilities (tie): Florida Power & Light Co.
- Utilities (tie): Southern California Gas Company
- Wireless carriers (tie): MetroPCS
- Wireless carriers (tie): TracFone
- Wireless carriers (tie): Virgin Mobile

56.4 Market Resources

Temkin Group, 48 White Oak Road, Waban, MA 02468. (617) 916-2075. (www.temkingroup.com)

57

CUSTOMER LOYALTY ENGAGEMENT

57.1 Overview

Brand Keys (www.brandkeys.com) produces an annual assessment of brand leaders in customer loyalty engagement. Initiated in 1997, the Brand Keys Customer Loyalty Engagement Index ranks brands based on their ability to engage consumers and create loyal customers.

The Brand Keys data paints a detailed picture of the category drivers that engage customers, engender loyalty, and drive real profits. The comparison is aimed to define how the consumer will view the category, compare offerings and, ultimately, buy.

57.2 Customer Loyalty Engagement Rankings

The 2016 assessment by Brand Keys examines customers' relationships with 635 brands in 72 categories.

By category, the top brands in the 2016 Customer Loyalty Engagement Index are as follows:

- Airline: JetBlue
- Allergy medications, OTC: Zyrtec
- App-based rideshare: Lyft
- Athletic footwear (tie): New Balance
- Athletic footwear (tie): Nike
- Automotive (tie): Ford
- Automotive (tie): Hyundai
- Banks: Wells Fargo
- Beer, light: Samuel Adams Light
- Beer, regular: Samuel Adams
- Bottled water: Dasani
- Breakfast bars (tie): Kellogg's Nutri-Grain
- Breakfast bars (tie): Kind
- Car rental: Avia
- Casual/fast casual dining (tie): Panera
- Casual/fast casual dining (tie): Shake Shack
- Coffee, out-of-home (tie): Dunkin' Donuts
- Coffee, out-of-home (tie): Starbucks
- Coffee, packaged: Dunkin' Donuts

- Cosmetics, luxury: Chanel
- Cosmetics, mass: Neutrogena
- Credit cards: Discover
- Deodorants: Degree
- E-readers: Kindle
- File hosting: Dropbox
- Flat-screen TV: Samsung
- Gasoline: Shell
- Headphones: Beats by Dr. Dre
- Hotel, economy: Microtel by Wyndham
- Hotel, midscale: Hampton Inn
- Hotel, luxury: Ritz-Carlton
- Hotel, upscale: Omni
- Ice cream: Häagen-Dazs
- Instant messaging apps: WhatsApp
- Insurance, auto (tie): Geico
- Insurance, auto (tie): Progressive
- Insurance, home: Met Life
- Insurance, life: New York Life
- Laptop computers: Apple
- Lip balm: ChapStick
- Major league sports: National Football League
- News, evening: CBS
- News, morning: Good Morning America (ABC)
- Office copiers (tie): Konica
- Office copiers (tie): Minolta
- Mutual funds: Vanguard
- Natural food stores: The Fresh Market
- Online brokerage: Options House
- Online music: Pandora
- Online payment services: PayPal
- Online retailers: Amazon.com
- Online travel site: Travel Advisor
- Online video streaming: Netflix
- Pain relievers, OTC: Advil
- Parcel delivery: UPS
- Pet food, cats: Iams
- Pet food, dogs: Purina One
- Pizza: Domino's
- Printers: HP
- Quick-serve restaurants: Subway
- Retail, apparel: Victoria's Secret
- Retail, department store: Marshall's
- Retail, discount: Target

- Retail, home improvement: Home Depot
- Retail, sporting goods: REI
- Search engine: Google
- Smartphone: Apple
- Social networking sites: Facebook
- Soft drinks, diet: Diet Coke
- Soft drinks, regular: Pepsi
- Tablets: Apple
- Tequila: Jose Cuervo
- Ticketing sites: Ticketmaster
- Toothpaste: Colgate
- Video games: Call of Duty
- Vodka: Svedka
- Warehouse clubs: Costco
- Whiskey: Jack Daniels
- Wireless phone service: AT&T

57.3 Market Resources

Brand Keys, 115 East 57th Street, 11th Floor, New York, NY 10022. (212) 532-6028. (www.brandkeys.com)

58

CUSTOMER SATISFACTION

58.1 Overview

The American Customer Satisfaction Index (ACSI, www.theacsi.org) is a national economic indicator of satisfaction with the quality of products and services available to U.S. household consumers. Established in 1994, the ACSI produces indices of customer satisfaction on a 0-100 scale.

The ACSI is based on about 65,000 interviews conducted annually, with 250 to 260 interviews completed per company/agency. Industry sample sizes vary from 750 to 10,000, depending on the number of measured companies in each industry.

The ACSI is produced by the Stephen M. Ross Business School at the University of Michigan (www.bus.umich.edu) in partnership with the American Society for Quality (www.asq.org) and CFI Group (www.cfigroup.com), a consulting firm. ForeSee Results (www.foreseeresults.com) sponsors the e-commerce and e-business measurements.

This chapter presents 2015 ACSI scores for consumer brands in 46 categories.

58.2 ACSI Scores

ACSI scores from 2015 surveys and change from 2014 scores are as follows:

Airlines

- JetBlue: 81 (2.5%)
- Southwest: 78 (no change)
- Alaska Air: 75 (n/a)
- Delta: 71 (no change)
- American: 66 (no change)
- Allegiant: 65 (n/a)
- United: 60 (no change)
- Frontier: 58 (n/a)
- Spirit: 54 (n/a)
- All others: 73 (4.3%)
- Sector average: 71 (2.9%)

Apparel

- Levi Strauss: 78 (-2.5%)
- Nine West: 77 (-4.9%)
- VF: 76 (-9.5%)

- Hanesbrands: 74 (-5.1%)
- All others: 72 (-6.5%)
- Sector average: 76 (-2.6%)

Athletic Shoes

- Nike: 78 (no change)
- adidas: 77 (no change)
- All others: 81 (-2.5%)
- Sector average: 80 (-2.5%)

Automobiles and Light Vehicles

- Lexus (Toyota): 84 (no change)
- Acura (Honda): 83 (7.8%)
- Lincoln (Ford): 83 (n/a)
- Mercedes-Benz: 83 (-3.5%)
- Subaru: 82 (-3.5%)
- Toyota: 82 (-1.2%)
- BMW: 82 (2.5%)
- Hyundai: 81 (no change)
- Mazda: 80 (no change)
- Volkswagen: 80 (-4.8%)
- Honda: 80 (-3.6%)
- Buick (GM): 80 (-3.6%)
- Cadillac (GM): 80 (no change)
- Volvo: 79 (n/a)
- Ford: 79 (-2.5%)
- Chevrolet (GM): 79 (-3.7%)
- GMC (GM): 78 (-4.9%)
- Audi (Volkswagen): 78 (-1.3%)
- Kia: 78 (-4.9%)
- Nissan: 77 (-4.9%)
- Mitsubishi: 77 (n/a)
- Infiniti (Nissan): 77 (n/a)
- Dodge (Fiat Chrysler): 76 (-2.6%)
- Mini (BMW): 76 (n/a)
- Jeep (Fiat Chrysler): 75 (-5.1%)
- Chrysler (Fiat Chrysler): 74 (-8.6%)
- Fiat (Fiat Chrysler): 73 (n/a)
- All others: 75 (-7.4%)
- Sector average: 79 (-3.7%)

Banks

- Regions Bank: 79 (n/a)
- PNC Bank: 78 (n/a)

- BB&T: 77 (n/a)
- Capital One: 77 (n/a)
- U.S. Bank: 76 (n/a)
- Fifth Third Bank: 75 (n/a)
- TD Bank: 75 (n/a)
- Wells Fargo Bank: 75 (4.2%)
- SunTrust Bank: 74 (n/a)
- Citibank: 73 (-1.4%)
- Chase: 71 (-4.1%)
- Citizens Bank: 70 (n/a)
- Bank of America: 68 (-1.4%)
- All others: 80 (no change)
- Sector average: 76 (no change)

Breweries

- MillerCoors: 78 (-3.7%)
- Anheuser-Busch InBev: 74 (-3.9%)
- All others: 76 (-7.3%)
- Sector average: 76 (-3.8%)

Cellular Phones/Smartphones

- Apple: 80 (1.3%)
- Samsung Electronics: 80 (-1.2%)
- Motorola Mobility (Google): 79 (2.6%)
- Blackberry: 78 (5.4%)
- HTC: 77 (2.7%)
- Nokia: 75 (-2.6%)
- LG Electronics: 74 (1.4%)
- All others: 71 (no change)
- Sector average: 78 (no change)

Computer Software

- Microsoft: 75 (no change)
- All others: 74 (-3.9%)
- Sector average: 74 (-2.6%)

Department and Discount Stores

- Nordstrom: 82 (-4.7%)
- Dillard's: 80 (-1.2%)
- Fred Meyer: 79 (n/a)
- Belk: 77 (n/a)
- Kohl's: 77 (-3.8%)
- Dollar Tree: 76 (-3.8%)
- Meijer: 76 (-2.6%)

- Target: 75 (-6.3%)
- Dollar General: 74 (-1.3%)
- JCPenney: 74 (-3.9%)
- Macy's: 73 (-7.6%)
- Ross: 74 (n/a)
- Sears: 71 (-2.7%)
- Walmart: 66 (-2.9%)
- All others: 77 (-4.9%)
- Sector average: 74 (-3.9%)

Drug Stores

- Kroger: 81 (no change)
- Target: 80 (2.6%)
- Kmart: 76 (n/a)
- Walgreens: 76 (-3.9%)
- CVS: 71 (-7.3%)
- Rite Aid: 69 (-11.5%)
- Safeway: 69 (n/a)
- Walmart: 68 (no change)
- All others: 75 (-7.4%)
- Sector average: 73 (-5.2%)

Fixed Line Telephone Service

- Vonage: 73 (n/a)
- Bright House Networks: 73 (n/a)
- CenturyLink: 70 (-1.4%)
- Charter Communications: 69 (no change)
- Cox Communications: 68 (-2.9%)
- Verizon Communications: 68 (-6.8%)
- Cablevision Systems: 67 (n/a)
- AT&T: 65 (-9.7%)
- Comcast: 64 (-4.5%)
- Time Warner Cable: 63 (-3.1%)
- Windstream Communications: 61 (n/a)
- Frontier Communications: 59 (n/a)
- All others: 76 (-2.6%)
- Sector average: 69 (-5.5%)

Food Products

- Dole: 81 (-2.4%)
- H.J. Heinz: 81 (-6.9%)
- ConAgra: 80 (-2.4%)
- Kellogg: 80 (-1.2%)
- Mars: 80 (-5.9%)

- Quaker: 80 (-5.9%)
- Campbell Soup: 79 (-4.8%)
- Hershey: 79 (-8.1%)
- Kraft: 79 (-6.0%)
- General Mills: 78 (-8.2%)
- Néstle: 78 (-8.2%)
- Tyson Foods: 78 (-1.3%)
- All others: 69 (-10.4%)
- Sector average: 76 (-3.8%)

Health Insurance

- Humana: 71 (n/a)
- Kaiser Permanente: 71 (n/a)
- Blue Cross/Blue Shield: 70 (1.4%)
- Anthem: 69 (4.5%)
- Aetna: 68 (4.6%)
- UnitedHealth: 66 (-8.3%)
- Cigna: 60 (n/a)
- All others: 71 (-2.7%)
- Sector average: 69 (-1.4%)

Hotels

- Marriott: 80 (-1.2%)
- Hilton: 80 (2.6%)
- Hyatt: 80 (2.6%)
- La Quinta: 76 (n/a)
- Starwood: 76 (no change)
- InterContinental: 76 (-2.6%)
- Best Western: 74 (no change)
- Choice: 73 (-1.4%)
- Wyndham: 68 (-5.6%)
- Motel 6: 63 (n/a)
- All others: 73 (-3.9%)
- Sector average: 75 (-2.6%)

Household Appliances

- General Electric: 82 (6.5%)
- LG: 82 (n/a)
- Electrolux: 81 (2.5%)
- Samsung: 81 (n/a)
- Whirlpool: 80 (-1.2%)
- Bosch: 79 (n/a)
- All others: 81 (no change)
- Sector average: 81 (no change)

Internet Brokerage

- Vanguard: 80 (n/a)
- Scottrade: 79 (n/a)
- Charles Schwab: 78 (-2.5%)
- Edward Jones: 78 (n/a)
- Fidelity: 77 (1.3%)
- E*Trade: 74 (-2.6%)
- TD Ameritrade: 73 (-1.4%)
- Merrill Edge (Bank of America): 73 (n/a)
- All others: 76 (-7.3%)
- Sector average: 76 (-10.6%)

Internet News and Information

- FOXNews.com: 76 (no change)
- USAToday.com: 74 (-2.6%)
- ABCNews.com: 74 (no change)
- MSNBC.com: 75 (2.7%)
- NYTimes.com: 76 (4.1%)
- CNN.com (Time Warner): 73 (4.3%)
- TheHuffingtonPost.com: 71 (-1.4%)
- All others: 72 (-6.5%)
- Sector average: 73 (-1.4%)

Internet Portals and Search Engines

- Google: 78 (-6.0%)
- Bing.com (Microsoft): 72 (-1.4%)
- MSN (Microsoft): 74 (1.4%)
- Yahoo!: 75 (1.6%)
- AOL: 74 (5.7%)
- About.com: 71 (n/a)
- Answers.com: 67 (n/a)
- All others: 75 (-2.6%)
- Sector average: 76 (-5.0%)

Internet Retail

- Amazon.com: 83 (-3.5%)
- Newegg: 79 (-2.5%)
- eBay: 75 (-5.1%)
- Overstock.com: 73 (-5.2%)
- Netflix: 76 (-6.2%)
- All others: 80 (-1.2%)
- Sector average: 80 (-2.4%)

Internet Service Providers

- AT&T (U-verse): 69 (6.2%)
- Verizon Communications (FiOS): 68 (-4.2%)
- Bright House Networks: 63 (n/a)
- Frontier Communications: 61 (n/a)
- Cablevision Systems: 61 (n/a)
- CenturyLink: 60 (-7.7%)
- Time Warner Cable: 58 (7.4%)
- Cox Communications: 58 (-9.4%)
- Charter Communications: 57 (-6.6%)
- Mediacom Communications: 57 (n/a)
- Comcast: 56 (-1.8%)
- All others: 65 (no change)
- Sector average: 63 (no change)

Internet Social Media

- Pinterest: 78 (2.6%)
- Wikipedia: 77 (4.1%)
- Instagram (Facebook): 76 (n/a)
- YouTube (Google): 76 (4.1%)
- Facebook: 75 (11.9%)
- Google+: 75 (5.6%)
- Twitter: 71 (2.9%)
- Tumblr (Yahoo!): 69 (n/a)
- LinkedIn: 67 (1.5%)
- All others: 71 (-2.7%)
- Sector average: 74 (4.2%)

Internet Travel

- Expedia: 77 (1.3%)
- Orbitz: 75 (-2.6%)
- Priceline: 75 (no change)
- Travelocity.com: 75 (1.4%)
- All others: 78 (no change)
- Sector average: 78 (1.3%)

Personal Care and Cleaning Products

- Clorox: 82 (-3.5%)
- Unilever: 80 (no change)
- Colgate-Palmolive: 79 (-4.8%)
- Dial: 79 (-2.5%)
- Procter & Gamble: 75 (-8.5%)
- All others: 75 (-8.5%)
- Sector average: 77 (-6.1%)

Personal Computers

- Apple: 84 (no change)
- Amazon: 78 (n/a)
- Dell: 78 (2.6%)
- Samsung: 78 (n/a)
- ASUS: 77 (n/a)
- Levano: 74 (n/a)
- Toshiba: 73 (-2.7%)
- Hewlett-Packard: 73 (-1.4%)
- Acer: 70 (-7.9%)
- All others: 76 (-7.3%)
- Sector average: 77 (-1.3%)

Property & Casualty Insurance

- Farm Bureau: 80 (n/a)
- Property and Casualty Insurance: 79 (no change)
- State Farm: 78 (-3.7%)
- GEICO: 77 (no change)
- Nationwide: 75 (n/a)
- AAA: 75 (n/a)
- Progressive: 74 (-2.6%)
- Allstate: 73 (-5.2%)
- American Family: 73 (n/a)
- Liberty Mutual: 73 (n/a)
- Travelers: 73 (n/a)
- Farmers: 71 (-7.8%)
- All others: 83 (5.1%)
- Sector average: 79 (no change)

Restaurants - Full-Service

- Texas Roadhouse: 83 (n/a)
- LongHorn Steakhouse (Darden): 81 (n/a)
- Cracker Barrel: 80 (n/a)
- Olive Garden (Darden): 79 (-1.3%)
- Applebee's: 78 (no change)
- Outback Steakhouse: 78 (-2.5%)
- Red Lobster: 77 (-1.3%)
- Red Robin: 77 (n/a)
- TGI Fridays: 76 (n/a)
- Denny's: 75 (n/a)
- Chili's: 74 (no change)
- Ruby Tuesday: 73 (n/a)
- All others: 83 (no change)
- Sector average: 82 (no change)

Restaurants - Limited-Service

- Chick-fil-A: 86 (n/a)
- Chipotle Mexican Grill: 83 (n/a)
- Panera Bread: 80 (n/a)
- Dunkin' Donuts: 78 (4.0%)
- Pizza Hut (Yum! Brands): 78 (-4.9%)
- Papa John's: 78 (-4.9%)
- Subway: 77 (-1.3%)
- Domino's: 75 (-6.3%)
- Little Caesars: 74 (-7.5%)
- Starbucks: 74 (-2.6%)
- Arby's: 74 (n/a)
- KFC (Yum! Brands): 73 (-1.4%)
- Wendy's: 73 (-6.4%)
- Taco Bell (Yum! Brands): 72 (no change)
- Burger King: 72 (-5.3%)
- Jack in the Box: 72 (n/a)
- McDonald's: 67 (-5.6%)
- All others: 84 (2.4%)
- Sector average: 80 (no change)

Soft Drinks

- Coca-Cola: 79 (-4.8%)
- Dr. Pepper Snapple: 79 (-3.7%)
- PepsiCo: 78 (-6.0%)
- All others: 74 (-7.5%)
- Sector average: 79 (-4.8%)

Specialty Retail Stores

- Costco: 81 (-3.6%)
- L Brands (-Victoria's Secret, Bath & Body Works): 81 (-2.4%)
- Barnes & Noble: 79 (-2.5%)
- TJX: 78 (no change)
- GameStop: 78 (1.3%)
- Menards: 78 (no change)
- PetSmart: 77 (-3.8%)
- Petco: 76 (n/a)
- Burlington Coat Factory: 76 (n/a)
- BJ's Wholesale Club: 76 (-6.2%)
- Sam's Club: 76 (-5.0%)
- Staples: 75 (-5.1%)
- Toys “R” Us: 75 (n/a)
- Gap: 75 (no change)

- AutoZone: 75 (n/a)
- Bed Bath & Beyond: 75 (-7.4%)
- Big Lots: 74 (-3.9%)
- Best Buy: 74 (-3.9%)
- Lowe's: 74 (-8.6%)
- Home Depot: 73 (-3.9%)
- Advance Auto Parts: 72 (n/a)
- Abercrombie & Fitch: 65 (n/a)
- All others: 78 (-1.3%)
- Sector average: 77 (-2.5%)

Subscription Television Services

- Verizon Communications (FiOS): 71 (4.4%)
- AT&T (U-verse): 69 (no change)
- DirecTV: 68 (-1.4%)
- Cablevision Systems: 67 (n/a)
- DISH Network: 67 (no change)
- Bright House Networks: 65 (n/a)
- Charter Communications: 63 (5.0%)
- Cox Communications: 62 (-1.6%)
- Suddenlink Communications: 57 (n/a)
- Comcast: 54 (-10.0%)
- Time Warner Cable: 51 (-8.9%)
- Mediacom Communications: 51 (n/a)
- All others: 66 (no change)
- Sector average: 63 (-3.1%)

Supermarkets

- Wegmans: 86 (1.2%)
- Trader Joe's: 83 (-2.4%)
- H-E-B: 82 (no change)
- Publix: 82 (no change)
- Aldi: 81 (no change)
- Hy-Vee: 78 (n/a)
- Kroger: 76 (-2.6%)
- Delhaize America (Food Lion, Hannaford): 76 (-1.3%)
- ShopRite: 75 (-2.6%)
- Meijer: 74 (n/a)
- BI-LO: 74 (-6.3%)
- Whole Foods: 73 (-9.9%)
- Supervalu: 71 (-5.3%)
- Target: 71 (-12.3%)
- A&P: 70 (n/a)

- Ahold USA (Stop & Shop, Giant): 70 (-2.8%)
- Albertsons: 68 (-8.1%)
- Giant Eagle: 67 (-6.9%)
- Wal-Mart: 67 (-5.6%)
- All others: 77 (no change)
- Sector average: 73 (-3.9%)

Wireless Telephone Services

- TracFone Wireless: 77 (n/a)
- Verizon Wireless: 71 (-2.8%)
- AT&T Mobility: 70 (2.9%)
- T-Mobile: 70 (1.4%)
- Sprint Nextel: 65 (-4.4%)
- All others: 73 (1.3%)
- Sector average: 70 (-2.8%)

58.3 Market Resources

American Customer Satisfaction Index (ACSI), 625 Avis Drive, Ann Arbor, MI 48108. (734) 913-0788. (www.theacsi.org)

ForeSee Results, 2500 Green Road, Suite 400, Ann Arbor, MI 48105. (800) 621-2850. (www.foreseeresults.com)

59

REPUTATION RANKING

59.1 Overview

Since 1999, The Harris Poll (www.theharrispoll.com) has surveyed consumers to determine corporate reputation ratings for the 100 most visible companies in the U.S., as perceived by the general public.

In the reputation survey, consumers rate perceptions across 20 attributes, classified into six dimensions of corporate reputation, as follows:

Emotional Appeal

- Admire & respect
- Feel good about
- Trust

Financial performance

- Growth prospects
- Low risk investment
- Outperforms competitors
- Record of profitability

Products & Services

- High quality
- Innovative
- Stands behind
- Value for money

Responsibility

- Community responsibility workplace environment
- Good employees
- Good place to work
- Rewards employees fairly

Social Responsibility

- Environmental
- Supports good causes

Vision & Leadership

- Clear vision for the future
- Excellent leadership
- Market opportunities

Ratings for the 20 attributes are compiled into a Reputation Quotient® (RQ®) to establish the reputation ranking.

59.2 Rankings 2016

The reputations of the 100 most visible companies in the U.S. among the general public are ranked as follows:

1. Amazon.com: 83.96
2. Apple: 83.03
3. Google: 82.97
4. USAA: 81.27
5. The Walt Disney Company: 81.18
6. Publix Super Markets: 80.94
7. Samsung: 80.44
8. Berkshire Hathaway: 80.37
9. Johnson & Johnson: 80.23
10. Kellogg Company: 79.92
11. The Vanguard Group: 79.76
12. FedEx Corporation: 79.60
13. Costco: 79.53
14. The Clorox Company: 79.40
15. Procter & Gamble Co.: 79.39
16. General Mills: 79.18
17. Honda Motor Company: 79.16
18. The Coca-Cola Company: 78.96
19. Nestle: 78.83
20. Microsoft: 78.57
21. Meijer: 78.50
22. UPS: 78.22
23. Chick-fil-A: 78.18
24. Netflix: 77.98
25. The Kraft Heinz Company: 77.94
26. Lowe's: 77.65
27. Sony: 77.58
28. Nike: 77.50
29. Aldi: 77.49
30. Whirlpool Corporation: 77.23
31. eBay: 76.51

32. Best Buy: 76.46
33. BMW: 76.37
34. Fidelity Investments: 76.26
35. The Kroger Company: 75.68
36. Southwest Airlines: 75.64
37. Nordstrom: 75.58
38. The Home Depot: 75.55
39. American Express: 75.53
40. IBM: 75.43
41. LG Corporation: 75.32
42. Kohl's: 75.04
43. Yum! Brands: 75.00
44. Whole Foods Market: 75.00
45. CVS (CVS Health): 74.88
46. Kaiser Permanente: 74.83
47. Unilever: 74.82
48. Walgreens: 74.69
49. Target: 74.24
50. Ford Motor Company: 74.10
51. Tyson Foods: 74.09
52. General Electric: 73.97
53. Hobby Lobby: 73.37
54. Hewlett-Packard Company: 72.93
55. The Allstate Corporation: 72.80
56. Dell: 72.76
57. State Farm Insurance: 72.73
58. Macy's: 72.40
59. PepsiCo: 72.22
60. Facebook: 72.09
61. Discover Financial Services: 71.67
62. Starbucks Corporation: 71.67
63. Toyota Motor Corporation: 71.50
64. Chipotle: 71.00
65. Safeway: 70.88
66. United States Postal Service: 70.86
67. Verizon Communications: 70.30
68. 21st Century Fox: 70.28
69. AT&T: 69.74
70. Wells Fargo & Company: 69.73
71. Chevron: 69.20
72. Walmart: 69.09
73. T-Mobile: 68.46
74. Royal Dutch Shell: 68.24
75. Delta Air Lines: 68.13

76.	JPMorgan Chase & Co.:	67.93
77.	JCPenney:	67.64
78.	Capital One Financial Corp.:	67.47
79.	Burger King:	67.16
80.	Cox Enterprises:	67.02
81.	General Motors:	66.27
82.	Fiat Chrysler Automobiles:	66.07
83.	United Airlines:	65.99
84.	McDonald's:	65.78
85.	ExxonMobil:	65.42
86.	Koch Industries:	65.32
87.	Sprint Corporation:	65.18
88.	Time Warner Cable:	64.85
89.	Citigroup:	64.80
90.	Charter Communications:	64.78
91.	Sears Holdings Corporation:	64.69
92.	Bank of America:	64.26
93.	Dish Network:	62.22
94.	AIG:	61.15
95.	Goldman Sachs:	60.44
96.	Monsanto:	60.43
97.	Comcast:	60.21
98.	BP:	59.13
99.	Halliburton:	56.26
100.	Volkswagen Group:	54.75

59.3 Market Resources

Harris Poll, a Nielsen Company, 60 Corporate Woods, Rochester, NY 14623. (585) 272-8400. (www.theharrispoll.com)

PART IX: ETHNIC FOCUS

60

AFRICAN-AMERICAN CONSUMERS

60.1 Overview

African Americans, also referred to as Black Americans, are Americans who have total or partial ancestry from any of the native populations of Sub-Saharan Africa, according to the U.S. Census Bureau (www.census.gov). Black Hispanics are generally not classified as African Americans.

African Americans constitute the third largest racial and ethnic group in the U.S., trailing Caucasians and Hispanic Americans.

When asked in a survey by Nielsen (www.nielsen.com) which term is preferable, 44% said they preferred Black, 43% preferred African American, and 11% did not have a preference.

60.2 Profile

Census 2010 counted 38.9 million people, or 12.6% of the total U.S. population, of Black- or African-American-only ancestry. An additional 1.0 million people reported Black as well as one or more other races in that census. Combined, there were 42.0 million African Americans, representing 13.6% of the population.

Since 2000, the Black population increased by 17.9%, a rate that is 1.6 times greater than overall growth. For comparison, the total U.S. population has increased by only 11.3% since 2000.

The Black population at mid-year 2016 was 42.9 million, or 13.2% of the total U.S. population.

The African-American population in the U.S. is distributed by age as follows (source: Nielsen):

- 0-to-17: 28%
- 18-to-34: 25%
- 35-to-44: 14%
- 45-to-64: 24%
- 65 and older: 9%

A majority of African Americans (55%) reside in the South; 72% live in the central areas of cities. A quarter (25%) of African-American households live in suburban areas.

According to Nielsen, African Americans live in the following housing locales:

- Big city urban: 29.4%
- Metropolitan suburban: 24.9%
- Mid-size cities/satellites: 21.8%
- Small towns and rural: 24.0%

According to a 2015 study by Pew Research Center (www.pewresearch.org), 8.7% of the U.S. black population is foreign-born, an increase from 6.7% in 2000, 4.9% in 1990, and 3.1% in 1980. Approximately 3.8 million black immigrants live in the U.S., more than four times as many as in 1980.

"A wave of immigration from the Caribbean, Africa, and Latin America is reshaping the U.S. Black population."

USA Today, 4/10/15

60.3 Households, Income, and Expenditures

The *Consumer Expenditure Survey 2014*, published by the Census Bureau in September 2015, reported on Black households (HH), and all U.S. households for comparison, as follows:

	Black HH	All HH
• Number of households:	16,297	127,006
• Age of head of household (HH):	48	50
• Head of HH (female/male):	61%/39%	52%/48%
• People per HH:	2.5	2.5
• Children under 18 per HH:	0.7	0.6
• Adults 65+ per HH:	0.2	0.4
• Housing (homeowner/renter):	44%/56%	63%/37%

The median income of African-American households was $44,769; the median for all U.S. households was $66,877.

Distribution of expenditures is as follows:

- Housing: 37.1%
- Transportation: 17.4%
- Food at home: 8.9%
- Healthcare: 5.4%
- Food away from home: 5.1%
- Apparel: 4.3%

- Entertainment: 3.6%
- Personal care: 1.4%
- Other: 16.8%

60.4 Buying Power

The Selig Center for Economic Growth at the University of Georgia (www.selig.uga.edu) estimates African-American buying power as follows:

	Buying Power	Pct. of Consumer Spending
• 1990:	$ 318 billion	7.4%
• 2000:	$ 590 billion	8.2%
• 2009:	$ 910 billion	8.5%
• 2014:	$1.14 trillion	8.7%
• 2015:	$1.20 trillion	8.8%

African Americans controlled more disposable personal income than any other U.S. minority group until 2006, when it was equaled by Hispanic-American buying power in the United States. Hispanics actually surpassed Blacks as the nation's largest minority group seven years before, based on population counts. But in terms of spending power, 2007 marked the first year that Hispanics' buying power led that of Blacks.

The following are the largest African-American consumer markets:

- New York: $91 billion
- Texas: $72 billion
- Georgia: $66 billion
- California: $64 billion
- Florida: $63 billion
- Maryland: $57 billion
- Illinois: $46 billion
- North Carolina: $44 billion
- Virginia: $42 billion
- New Jersey: $36 billion

This ranking is largely based on overall populations, not on ethnic concentration. Only Maryland, North Carolina, and Virginia do not rank among the top 10 markets for all consumers.

The largest percentage of buying power marketshare is as follows:

- District of Columbia: 29%
- Mississippi: 24%
- Maryland: 22%
- Georgia: 21%
- Louisiana: 20%
- South Carolina: 18%
- Alabama: 18%

- Delaware: 15%
- North Carolina: 14%
- Virginia: 13%

According to the Selig Center, African Americans spend more than non-Black households on electricity, phone services, children's clothing, and footwear. They also spend a significantly higher proportion on groceries, housing, natural gas, women's and girls clothing, and gasoline. Blacks and non-Blacks spend about the same proportion for housekeeping supplies, furniture, floor coverings, appliances, men's and boys' clothing, medical supplies, TVs, reading materials, education, tobacco products, and life insurance. Compared to non-Blacks, Blacks spend much less of their money on eating out, alcoholic beverages, household operations, vehicle purchases, health care, entertainment, and pensions.

60.5 Population Centers

According to the 2010 Census, the following metropolitan areas have the highest African-American population:

- New York, NY: 3.36 million
- Atlanta, GA: 1.71 million
- Chicago, IL: 1.65 million
- Washington, DC: 1.44 million
- Philadelphia, PA: 1.24 million
- Miami, FL: 1.17 million
- Houston/Galveston, TX: 1.03 million
- Detroit, MI: 980,451
- Dallas/Ft. Worth, TX: 961,871
- Los Angeles, CA: 907,618
- Baltimore, MD: 778,879
- Memphis, TN: 601,043
- Virginia Beach, VA: 522,409
- St. Louis, MO: 516,446
- Charlotte, NC: 421,105
- Cleveland, OH: 416,528
- New Orleans, LA: 397,095
- Richmond, VA: 375,427
- San Francisco, CA: 363,905
- Orlando, FL: 344,820
- Boston, MA: 331,292
- Tampa, FL: 329,334
- Riverside, CA: 322,405
- Birmingham, AL: 318,373
- Jacksonville, FL: 292,881

60.6 Use Of Media

A 2015 study by Nielsen and *Essence* reported time spent with media among African-Americans and the general population as follows:

	African-Americans	General Population
• Television:	201.7 hours/month	141.3 hours/month
• Magazines:	52%	22%
• Radio:	12 hours/week	6 hours/week

> **"According to a survey by Nielsen and *Essence*, African-Americans consume more content than other groups on all fronts, through various mainstream and niche media outlets and platforms. In a consumer marketplace cluttered with options, African-Americans choose the best-fit media outlets for news gathering and entertainment purposes, reporting above-average consumption across each platform."**
>
> Center for Media Research, 2/23/15

According to the Internet & American Life Project by Pew Research Center (www.pewinternet.org), 78% of African-American adults used the Internet in 2015.

Use of social networks in 2015 was as follows (sources: Pew Research Center and *Advertising Age*):

	African-Americans	General Population
• Facebook:	67%	71%
• Instagram:	38%	26%
• LinkedIn:	28%	28%
• Twitter:	27%	23%
• Pinterest:	12%	28%

60.7 Market Resources

Black Consumers and Brand Loyalty - U.S., Mintel, December 2015. (http://store.mintel.com/black-consumers-and-brand-loyalty-us-december-2015)

Black Consumers' Lifestyles and Entertainment - U.S., Mintel, April 2015. (http://store.mintel.com/black-consumers-lifestyles-and-entertainment-us-april-2015)

Black Millennials - U.S., Mintel, February 2015. (http://store.mintel.com/black-millennials-us-february-2015)

The Multicultural Economy, The Selig Center for Economic Growth at the University of Georgia. (www.terry.uga.edu/selig/buying_power.html)

The State of the News Media: African American, Pew Project for Excellence in Journalism, 2015. (www.journalism.org/2015/04/29/african-american-media-fact-sheet/)

61

ARAB-AMERICAN CONSUMERS

61.1 Overview

Arab Americans constitute an ethnicity made up of several waves of immigrants from the Arabic-speaking countries of southwestern Asia and North Africa that have settled in the United States since the 1880s. Their Arab heritage reflects a culture that is thousands of years old and includes 23 Arab countries as diverse as Egypt, Lebanon, Morocco, Yemen, Tunisia, and Palestine.

The U.S. Census Bureau (www.census.gov) considers anyone who reported being Algerian, Bahraini, Egyptian, Emirati, Iraqi, Jordanian, Kuwaiti, Lebanese, Libyan, Moroccan, Omani, Palestinian, Qatari, Saudi Arabian, Syrian, Tunisian, and Yemeni to be of Arab ancestry.

While the majority of the population of the Arab World is composed of people of the Muslim faith, 63% of Arab Americans are Christian. Twenty-four percent (24%) of Arab Americans are Muslim; 13% are of other faiths or claim no religious affiliation.

According to the Arab American Institute (www.aaiusa.org), 89% of Arab Americans over age 25 have obtained at least a high school diploma. More than 45% have a bachelor's degree or higher, compared to 28% of Americans at large, and 18% of Arab Americans have a post-graduate degree, which is nearly twice the average (10%) of non-Arab Americans.

Similar to the national average, about 60% of Arab-American adults are in the labor force; 5% are unemployed. Seventy-three percent (73%) percent of working Arab Americans are employed in managerial, professional, sales, or administrative fields. Twelve percent (12%) are government employees.

61.2 Profile

Census 2010 reported 1.52 million Arab Americans, a 27% increase from Census 2000. Between 1990 and 2000, the Arab-American population grew 38%, according to the Census Bureau.

By Arab ancestry, Census 2010 reported populations and number of households as follows:

	Population	Households
• Lebanese:	485,917	181,127
• Egyptian:	179,853	60,137
• Syrian:	147,426	56,040
• Palestinian:	83,241	25,679

• Moroccan:	74,908	23,365
• Iraqi:	73,896	22,979
• Jordanian:	60,056	18,134
• Yemeni:	29,358	6,812

Zogby Poll International (www.zogby.com) reported that there are 3.5 million Americans of ancestry belonging to one of the 23 United Nations member countries of the Arab World, although they don't necessarily self-report as Arabs.

Between 2005 and year-end 2015, 131,010 immigrant refugees from Iraq and Syria were accepted into the U.S., according to the United States Citizenship and Immigration Services (www.uscis.gov).

61.3 Buying Power

The Census Bureau reported the median household income for Arab households in 2010 at $56,433, about $4,500 higher than the median household income of $52,029 for all households in the United States. Lebanese households had the highest median income ($67,264), while Iraqi and Yemeni households had lower median incomes ($32,075 and $34,667, respectively).

61.4 Population Centers

The following states have the highest Arab-American populations:

- California: 272,485
- Michigan: 191,607
- New York: 149,627
- Florida: 100,627
- Texas: 91,568
- New Jersey: 85,956
- Illinois: 85,465
- Ohio: 65,813
- Massachusetts: 65,150
- Pennsylvania: 60,870

Ninety-four percent (94%) of Arab Americans live in metropolitan areas. Los Angeles, Detroit, New York City, Chicago, and Washington, DC, are the top five metropolitan areas of Arab-American concentration.

Among cities with 100,000 or more in population, the following have the highest percentages of Arabs:

- Sterling Heights, MI: 3.69%
- Jersey City, NJ: 2.81%
- Warren, MI: 2.51%
- Allentown, PA: 2.45%

- Burbank, CA: 2.39%
- Glendale, CA: 2.07%
- Livonia, MI: 1.94%
- Arlington, VA: 1.77%
- Paterson, NJ: 1.77%
- Daly City, CA: 1.69%

The 2010 Census reported an Arab-American population of 5.0% in Bayonne, New Jersey, a city of 63,000.

61.5 Market Resources

Arab American Institute, 1600 K Street NW, Suite 601, Washington, DC 20006. (202) 429-9210. (www.aaiusa.org)

Arab Households in the United States: 2006-2010, American Community Survey Briefs, U.S. Census Bureau, May 2013. (www.census.gov/prod/2013pubs/acsbr10-20.pdf)

62

ASIAN-AMERICAN CONSUMERS

62.1 Overview

The U.S. Census Bureau (www.census.gov) refers to Asian Americans as persons having ancestry from any of the original peoples of the Far East, Southeast Asia, or the Indian subcontinent. This includes people who indicate their race(s) as Asian or report entries such as Chinese, Filipino, Indian, Vietnamese, Korean, Japanese, and other Asian.

62.2 Profile

Census 2010 counted 14.7 million people, or 4.8% of the total U.S. population, of Asian-only ancestry. An additional 2.6 million people reported their ethnicity as Asian as well as one or more other ethnicity. Combined, 17.3 million Asian Americans were counted, representing 5.6% of the population.

The Asian-American population at mid-year 2016 was 17.5 million, or 5.4% of the total U.S. population.

The relative youth and affluence of the Asian-American community is attractive to marketers. With a median age of 32, the Asian-American population is five years younger than the overall U.S. median age.

The Asian population includes many groups, who differ in language, culture, and length of residence in the United States. Some of the Asian groups, such as the Chinese and Japanese, have been in the U.S. for several generations. Other groups, such as the Hmong, Vietnamese, Laotians, and Cambodians, are comparatively recent immigrants. The following were the largest Asian groups counted in the 2010 U.S. census (including those with one or more other race):

- Chinese: 4.0 million
- Asian Indian: 3.8 million
- Filipino: 3.4 million
- Vietnamese: 1.7 million
- Korean: 1.7 million
- Japanese: 1.3 million
- Pakistani: 409,000
- Cambodian: 277,000
- Hmong: 260,000
- Thai: 238,000

- Laotian: 232,000
- Bangladeshi: 147,000

The Asian population in the U.S. is distributed by age as follows (source: U.S. Census Bureau):

- Under 15 years: 19.2%
- Under 21 years: 27.0%
- Over 21 years: 73.0%
- 55 years and over: 17.6%
- 65 years and over: 8.9%

"On October 3, 1965, Pres. Lyndon Johnson signed the Immigration and Nationality Act into law, sweeping away a system that favored white Europeans over other races. One of its main consequences was the beginning of mass immigration to America from Asia. By most indicators, these incomers have done better than any other ethnic minority group. Indeed, they have long been described as the model minority: prosperous, well-educated and quiescent."

The Economist, 10/3/15

62.3 Households, Income, and Expenditures

The *Consumer Expenditure Survey 2014*, published by the Census Bureau in September 2015, reported on Asian-American households (HH), and all U.S. households for comparison, as follows:

	Asian-Am. HH	All HH
• Number of households:	5,627	127,006
• Age of head of household (HH):	44	50
• Head of HH (female/male):	48%/52%	52%/48%
• People per HH:	2.8	2.5
• Children under 18 per HH:	0.7	0.6
• Adults 65+ per HH:	0.3	0.4
• Housing (homeowner/renter):	48%/52%	63%/37%

The median income of Asian-American households in 2014 was $88,517; the median for all U.S. households was $66,877.

Distribution of expenditures was as follows:

• Food at home:	7.3%
• Food away from home:	6.1%
• Housing:	34.8%
• Apparel:	3.4%
• Transportation:	15.2%
• Entertainment:	3.9%
• Personal care:	1.1%
• Healthcare:	5.4%
• Other:	22.8%

62.4 Buying Power

The Selig Center for Economic Growth at the University of Georgia (www.selig.uga.edu) estimates Asian-American buying power as follows:

	Buying Power	Pct. of Consumer Spending
• 1990:	$116 billion	2.7%
• 2000:	$269 billion	3.7%
• 2009:	$509 billion	4.7%
• 2014:	$696 billion	5.3%
• 2015:	$775 billion	5.6%

The following are the largest Asian-American consumer markets:

• California:	$172 billion
• New York:	$ 54 billion
• Texas:	$ 34 billion
• New Jersey:	$ 34 billion
• Illinois:	$ 24 billion
• Hawaii:	$ 23 billion
• Washington:	$ 18 billion
• Florida:	$ 17 billion
• Virginia:	$ 17 billion
• Massachusetts:	$ 14 billion

Compared to the overall consumer market, Asian-American spending is much more focused geographically. The five and the 10 states with the largest Asian consumer markets account for 59% and 75% of Asian buying power, respectively. By contrast, the five and the 10 largest total consumer markets account for 39% and 56% of U.S. buying power, respectively.

The 10 states with the largest shares of total Asian buying power are as follows:

• Hawaii:	46.5%
• California:	11.8%

- New Jersey: 8.3%
- Washington: 6.6%
- Nevada: 6.5%
- New York: 6.4%
- Maryland: 5.1%
- Virginia: 5.1%
- Illinois: 4.8%
- Massachusetts: 4.5%

According to the Selig Center, Asian-American households spend nearly 22% more than the average U.S. household on homes, furniture, clothing, footwear, vehicle purchases, public transportation, education, cash contributions, and pensions and Social Security. They also spend more on food (groceries and dining out) and insurance. Asian households spend less than average on utilities, healthcare, tobacco products, entertainment, floor coverings, major appliances, personal care products and services, housekeeping supplies, and alcoholic beverages.

62.5 Educational Attainment

Forty-nine percent (49%) of Asian-Americans have a bachelor's degree, compared with 28% of the general population. Whereas Asian-Americans make up 5.6% of the population of the United States, they make up more than 30% of the recent American maths and physics Olympiad teams and Presidential Scholars, and 25% to 30% of National Merit Scholarships. Among those offered admission to New York's most selective public high schools, Stuyvesant High School and Bronx High School of Science, 75% and 60%, respectively, are Asian. (The Asian population of New York City is 13%.)

Current immigration is increasing the educational disparity between Asians and other groups because recent immigrants are even more highly qualified than earlier cohorts: 61% of recent immigrants from Asia have a bachelor's degree, compared with 30% of recent non-Asian migrants.

"It is their educational outperformance that is most remarkable."

The Economist, 10/3/15

62.6 Population Centers

The following are the states with the highest Asian populations (including those of mixed race) and their percentages of the total population within these areas:

	Population	Percentage
• California:	4.15 million	10.9%
• New York:	1.17 million	6.2%
• Hawaii:	703,000	58.0%
• Texas:	644,000	3.1%
• New Jersey:	524,000	6.2%
• Illinois:	474,000	3.8%
• Washington:	396,000	6.7%
• Florida:	333,000	2.1%
• Virginia:	305,000	4.3%
• Massachusetts:	265,000	4.2%

The following are the cities with the highest Asian populations (including those of mixed race) and the percentages of the total population within these states:

	Population	Percentage
• New York, NY:	873,000	10.9%
• Los Angeles, CA:	407,000	11.0%
• San Jose, CA:	258,000	28.8%
• San Francisco, CA:	253,000	32.6%
• Honolulu, HI:	252,000	67.7%
• San Diego, CA:	189,000	15.5%
• Chicago, IL:	141,000	4.9%
• Houston, TX:	114,000	5.8%
• Seattle, WA:	85,000	15.0%
• Fremont, CA:	81,000	39.8%

The following cities have the highest concentration of Asian Americans:

- Honolulu, HI: 67.7%
- Daly City, CA: 53.6%
- Fremont, CA: 39.8%
- Sunnyvale, CA: 34.2%
- San Francisco, CA: 32.6%
- Irvine, CA: 32.3%
- Garden Grove, CA: 32.2%
- Santa Clara, CA: 31.4%
- Torrance, CA: 31.1%
- San Jose, CA: 28.8%

The following counties have the most Asian American-owned businesses:

- Los Angeles, CA: 140,411
- Queens, NY: 48,241

- Orange, CA: 46,015
- Honolulu, HI: 35,376
- Santa Clara, CA: 30,007
- New York, NY: 29,020
- Cook, IL: 27,779
- Kings, NY: 25,989
- Harris, TX: 24,922
- Alameda, CA: 24,908

62.7 Recent Population Growth

In its study *State of the Asian American Consumer*, Nielsen reported on the dramatic growth among Asian Americans compared to other ethnic populations in the U.S. Based on 2012 figures by Nielsen, the Asian-American population tops 18.2 million and has increased over 51.0% since 2000, making this the highest growth rate of any multicultural segment in the U.S. For comparison, the Hispanic growth rate was 50.6% for the same period, 2000-2012.

According to Pew Research Center, Indian Americans have been the fastest-growing immigrant population among Asian Americans, with 87.2% of Indian Americans in 2010 being foreign-born. Also ranking high among this group is level of education, according to the center, with more than 70% of Indian Americans ages 25 and older having a college degree. And the median annual income is higher for Indian Americans compared with all Asian Americans, $88,000 vs. $66,000, respectively. For comparison, this figure is $49,800 for all U.S. households.

62.8 Market Resources

Asian-American Studies Center at the University of California, Los Angeles. (www.aasc.ucla.edu)

Demographics Of Asian Americans, Pew Research Social & Demographic Trends. (www.pewsocialtrends.org/2013/04/04/asian-groups-in-the-u-s/)

63

HISPANIC- & LATINO-AMERICAN CONSUMERS

63.1 Overview

Hispanic Americans and Latino Americans are residents of the United States with origins in the countries of Latin America or the Iberian peninsula.

The terms Hispanic American and Latino American are typically used interchangeably. Technically, however, Hispanic is a narrower term which mostly refers to persons of Spanish-speaking origin or ancestry. Latino is more frequently used to refer more generally to anyone of Latin American origin or ancestry, including Brazilians.

Hispanics are not a race but an ethnic group, which is extremely difficult to define. There are no physical qualities that define Hispanics, not even language – 15% of California's Hispanics do not speak Spanish. Among Hispanics that participated in the 2010 Census, 41% identified themselves as "some other race" on the census race question or did not respond to the race question at all.

> **"Hispanic is an ethnic origin and not a race. Demographers have been trying to explain that one for decades. No one struggles with the distinction between race and ethnicity more than Hispanics themselves."**
>
> *Demo Memo*

63.2 Profile

According to Census 2010, 308.7 million people resided in the United States in April 2010, of which 50.5 million (or 16%) claimed Hispanic or Latino origin. The Hispanic population increased from 35.3 million in 2000, when this group made up 13% of the total population. The Hispanic population increased 43.0% between Census 2000 and Census 2010, while the non-Hispanic population increased 4.9% during that period.

The Hispanic- and Latino-American population at mid-year 2016 was 56.7 million, or 17.5% of the total U.S. population.

According to the Pew Research Hispanic Trends Project (www.pewhispanic.org), Hispanic Americans are distributed by nationality as follows:

	Population	Pct. of Total
• Mexican:	33.54 million	64.6%
• Puerto Rican:	4.92 million	9.5%
• Salvadoran:	1.95 million	3.8%
• Cuban:	1.89 million	3.6%
• Dominican:	1.53 million	2.9%
• Guatemalan:	1.22 million	2.3%
• Columbian:	989,000	1.9%
• Spaniard:	707,000	1.4%
• Honduran:	702,000	1.4%
• Equadorian:	645,000	1.2%
• Peruvian:	556,000	1.1%
• Nicaraguan:	395,000	0.8%
• Venezuelan:	259,000	0.5%
• Argentinean:	242,000	0.5%

The Census Bureau projects that by 2050 there will be 102.6 million Hispanics living in the U.S., constituting 24% of the population. The percentage is projected to rise to 28.6% by 2060.

63.3 Households, Income, and Expenditures

The *Consumer Expenditure Survey 2014*, published by the Census Bureau in September 2015, reported on Hispanic and Latino households (HH), and all U.S. households for comparison, as follows:

	Hispanic HH	All HH
• Number of households:	16,283	127,006
• Age of head of household (HH):	43	50
• Head of HH (female/male):	56%/44%	52%/48%
• People per HH:	3.2	2.5
• Children under 18 per HH:	1.0	0.6
• Adults 65+ per HH:	0.2	0.4
• Housing (homeowner/renter):	44%/56%	63%/37%

The median income of Hispanic- and Latino-American households was $53,054; the median for all U.S. households was $66,877.

Distribution of expenditures is as follows:

• Food at home:	9.6%
• Food away from home:	6.5%
• Housing:	36.6%

- Apparel: 4.6%
- Transportation: 18.2%
- Entertainment: 3.9%
- Personal care: 1.2%
- Healthcare: 4.6%
- Other: 14.8%

The *Consumer Expenditure Survey* indicates that Hispanic households spend is about 82% as much as the average non-Hispanic household. Hispanic households spend more on telephone services, men's and boys' clothing, children's clothing, and footwear. Also, Hispanics spend a higher proportion of their money on food (groceries and restaurants), housing, utilities, and transportation. Hispanics spend about the same as non-Hispanics on housekeeping supplies, furniture, appliances, women's and girls clothing, and personal care products and services. Compared to non-Hispanics, they spend substantially less on alcoholic beverages, healthcare, entertainment, reading materials, education, tobacco products, cash contributions, and personal insurance and pensions.

63.4 Buying Power

The Selig Center for Economic Growth at the University of Georgia (www.selig.uga.edu) estimates Hispanic-American buying power and percentage of total U.S. consumer spending as follows:

	Buying Power	Pct. of Spending
• 1990:	$ 212 billion	5.0%
• 2000:	$ 489 billion	6.8%
• 2009:	$ 978 billion	9.1%
• 2014:	$1.33 trillion	10.2%
• 2015:	$1.50 trillion	11.0%

The following are the largest Hispanic consumer markets:

- California: $265 billion
- Texas: $176 billion
- Florida: $107 billion
- New York: $ 81 billion
- Illinois: $ 44 billion
- New Jersey: $ 39 billion
- Arizona: $ 34 billion
- Colorado: $ 22 billion
- New Mexico: $ 20 billion
- Georgia: $ 17 billion

Hispanics and their buying power are much more geographically concentrated than non-Hispanics. California alone accounts for 26% of Hispanic buying power. The five states and the 10 states with the largest Hispanic markets account for 66% and 80% of Hispanic buying power, respectively. In contrast, the five states with the largest non-Hispanic markets account for only 39% of total buying power, and the 10 largest non-Hispanic markets account for only 54% of total buying power.

The 10 states with the largest share of Hispanic buying power are as follows:

- New Mexico: 30.9%
- Texas: 20.4%
- California: 18.4%
- Arizona: 16.2%
- Florida: 15.8%
- Nevada: 15.3%
- Colorado: 11.5%
- New York: 9.6%
- New Jersey: 9.6%
- Illinois: 8.9%

63.5 Population Centers

Census 2010 reported Hispanic or Latino populations by state, percentages of total state populations, and population changes from Census 2000 as follows:

	Population	Pct.	Change
• Alabama:	185,000	3.9%	144.8%
• Alaska:	39,000	5.5%	51.8%
• Arizona:	1.89 million	29.6%	46.3%
• Arkansas:	186,000	6.4%	114.2%
• California:	14.01 million	37.6%	27.8%
• Colorado:	1.04 million	20.7%	41.2%
• Connecticut:	479,000	13.4%	41.6%
• Delaware:	73,000	8.2%	96.4%
• District of Columbia:	54,000	9.1%	21.8%
• Florida:	4.22 million	22.5%	57.4%
• Georgia:	854,000	8.8%	96.1%
• Hawaii:	120,000	8.9%	37.8%
• Idaho:	176,000	11.2%	73.0%
• Illinois:	2.03 million	15.8%	32.5%
• Indiana:	390,000	6.0%	81.7%
• Iowa:	151,000	5.0%	83.7%
• Kansas:	300,000	10.5%	59.4%
• Kentucky:	132,000	3.1%	121.6%
• Louisiana:	193,000	4.2%	78.7%
• Maine:	17,000	1.3%	80.9%
• Maryland:	471,000	8.2%	106.5%
• Massachusetts:	628,000	9.6%	46.4%
• Michigan:	436,000	4.4%	34.7%

• Minnesota:	250,000	4.7%	74.5%
• Mississippi:	81,000	2.7%	105.9%
• Missouri:	212,000	3.5%	79.2%
• Montana:	28,000	2.9%	58.0%
• Nebraska:	167,000	9.2%	77.3%
• Nevada:	716,000	26.5%	81.9%
• New Hampshire:	36,000	2.8%	79.1%
• New Jersey:	1.56 million	17.7%	39.2%
• New Mexico:	953,000	46.3%	24.6%
• New York:	3.42 million	17.6%	19.2%
• North Carolina:	800,000	8.4%	111.1%
• North Dakota:	13,000	2.0%	73.0%
• Ohio:	355,000	3.1%	63.4%
• Oklahoma:	332,000	8.9%	85.2%
• Oregon:	450,000	11.7%	63.5%
• Pennsylvania:	719,000	5.7%	82.6%
• Rhode Island:	131,000	12.4%	43.9%
• South Carolina:	236,000	5.1%	147.9%
• South Dakota:	22,000	2.7%	102.9%
• Tennessee:	290,000	4.6%	134.2%
• Texas:	9.46 million	37.6%	41.8%
• Utah:	358,000	13.0%	77.8%
• Vermont:	9,000	1.5%	67.3%
• Virginia:	632,000	7.9%	91.7%
• Washington:	756,000	11.2%	71.2%
• West Virginia:	22,000	1.2%	81.4%
• Wisconsin:	336,000	5.9%	74.2%
• Wyoming:	50,000	8.9%	58.6%

According to a 2012 report by the Pew Research Hispanic Trends Project, the largest metropolitan areas by Hispanic or Latino population are as follows:

		Hispanic Population	**Pct. of Total**
1.	Los Angeles-Long Beach, CA:	5,724,000	44.5%
2.	New York-Northeastern, NJ:	4,243,000	23.9%
3.	Houston-Brazoria, TX:	2,044,000	36.3%
4.	Riverside-San Bernardino, CA:	2,012,000	47.4%
5.	Chicago, IL:	1,934,000	21.1%
6.	Dallas-Fort Worth, TX:	1,746,000	27.9%
7.	Miami-Hialeah, FL:	1,610,000	65.7%
8.	Phoenix, AZ:	1,136,000	29.7%
9.	San Antonio, TX:	1,090,000	55.5%
10.	San Francisco-Oakland-Vallejo, CA:	1,088,000	22.2%
11.	San Diego, CA:	1,000,000	32.2%
12.	Washington, DC/MD/VA:	774,000	14.0%

13. McAllen-Edinburg-Pharr-Mission, TX:	707,000	90.7%
14. El Paso, TX:	662,000	82.3%
15. Denver-Boulder, CO:	596,000	23.1%
16. Las Vegas, NV:	571,000	29.2%
17. Fresno, CA:	552,000	50.9%
18. Orlando, FL:	543,000	25.4%
19. Atlanta, GA:	530,000	10.8%
20. Austin, TX:	502,000	31.0%
21. San Jose, CA:	482,000	27.0%
22. Tampa-St. Petersburg-Clearwater, FL:	456,000	16.4%
23. Fort Lauderdale-Hollywood-Pompano Beach, FL:	442,000	25.2%
24. Philadelphia, PA/NJ/NJ:	420,000	7.9%
25. Bakersfield, CA:	416,000	49.4%
26. Albuquerque, NM:	411,000	47.0%
27. Boston, MA-NH:	403,000	9.9%
28. Sacramento, CA:	375,000	19.2%
29. Brownsville-Harlingen-San Benito, TX:	359,000	88.1%
30. Tucson, AZ:	341,000	34.7%
31. Ventura-Oxnard-Simi Valley, CA:	333,712	40.4%
32. Visalia-Tulare-Porterville, CA:	269,611	60.8%
33. Stockton, CA:	268,103	39.0%
34. West Palm Beach-Boca Raton-Delray Beach, FL:	253,108	19.1%
35. Salt Lake City-Ogden, UT:	242,681	15.4%
36. Laredo, TX:	240,864	95.7%
37. Seattle-Everett, WA:	238,560	9.0%
38. Portland, OR-WA:	226,356	10.9%
39. Modesto, CA:	216,473	42.0%
40. Charlotte-Gastonia-Rock Hill, NC-SC:	189,279	9.7%
41. Santa Barbara-Santa Maria-Lompoc, CA:	182,941	43.1%
42. Minneapolis-St. Paul, MN:	175,426	5.6%
43. Raleigh-Durham, NC:	171,551	10.7%
44. Detroit, MI:	167,569	3.9%
45. Kansas City, MO-KS:	161,062	8.6%
46. Corpus Christi, TX:	157,275	54.1%
47. Milwaukee, WI:	147,510	9.5%
48. Merced, CA:	141,097	55.1%
49. Salinas-Sea Side-Monterey, CA:	139,394	51.5%
50. Las Cruces, NM:	138,829	65.9%
51. Providence-Fall River-Pawtucket, MA/RI:	134,815	13.0%
52. Oklahoma City, OK:	130,397	12.8%
53. Hartford-Bristol-Middleton-New Britain, CT:	127,897	17.3%
54. Greensboro-Winston Salem-High Point, NC:	126,593	8.9%
55. Odessa, TX:	124,633	45.5%
56. Baltimore, MD:	123,029	4.6%

57.	Santa Rosa-Petaluma, CA:	121,330	25.0%
58.	Yuma, AZ:	117,471	59.8%
59.	Fort Myers-Cape Coral, FL:	113,839	18.4%
60.	Indianapolis, IN:	112,857	6.1%

Census 2010 reported the places with the highest percentage of Hispanics or Latinos as follows:

- East Los Angeles, CA: 97.1%
- Laredo, TX: 95.6%
- Hialeah, FL: 94.7%
- Brownsville, TX: 93.2%
- McAllen, TX: 84.6%
- El Paso, TX: 80.7%
- Santa Ana, CA: 78.2%
- Salinas, CA: 75.0%
- Oxnard, CA: 73.5%
- Downey, CA: 70.7%

63.6 Hispanic Use Of Media

Weekly media consumption among Hispanic Americans and, for comparison, non-Hispanics is as follows (source: comScore [www.comscore.com]):

	Hispanic	Non-Hispanic
• Internet (all screens):	8.7 hours	11.6 hours
• TV:	8.3 hours	10.9 hours
• Mobile phone:	4.1 hours	3.6 hours
• Radio (including in-car):	3.5 hours	3.9 hours
• Newspaper:	1.9 hours	2.0 hours
• Magazine:	1.7 hours	1.6 hours

According to the Internet & American Life Project by Pew Research Center (www.pewinternet.org), 81% of Hispanic-American adults used the Internet in 2015.

A survey by Pew Research Internet Project (www.pewinternet.org) found that 60% of Hispanic mobile Internet users go online mostly using their smartphone; 34% of the overall U.S. population do so.

Use of social networks in 2015 was as follows (sources: Pew Research Center and *Advertising Age*):

	Hispanic-Americans	General Population
• Facebook:	73%	71%
• Instagram:	34%	26%
• Twitter:	25%	23%
• Pinterest:	21%	28%
• LinkedIn:	18%	28%

A survey by comScore (www.comscore.com) found that Hispanics are more receptive to online advertising than are non-Hispanics. Responses of each group are as follows:

	Hispanic	Non-Hispanic
• I am more likely to remember the brands I see advertised on my tablet than on offline media:	46%	37%
• I am more likely to remember the brands I see advertised on my smartphone than on offline media:	38%	27%
• Digital customer reviews and posts from friends or fans have compelled me to further inquire about the product being discussed:	38%	24%
• If online advertising speaks to me, I am inclined to visit the website of the advertised brand:	38%	24%
• Internet ads have motivated me to visit a retail store for the product or service being advertised:	38%	22%

63.7 Bicultural Hispanics

Findings in *FOCUS: Latino*, by Horowitz Research (www.horowitzresearch.com), show that bicultural Latinos, defined as Hispanics who feel strong cultural ties to both their U.S. and Hispanic identities, represent 53% of U.S. Hispanics. The study further found this group to be more educated, higher earners compared to other Hispanics, and younger overall.

"We typically define bicultural Hispanics as first- or second-generation U.S. citizens who grew up here. This group has parents who immigrated to the U.S. and were raised in either a purely Spanish-speaking or bilingual household and spent the majority of their life going to U.S. public schools. They've grown up around American customs and the English language since an early age, but they've maintained their Hispanic heritage and culture from their home life."

Aleena Roeschley, Research Director
Communicus
eMarketer, 12/24/15

According to a 2015 study by the Pew Research Hispanic Trends Project, 68% percent of Hispanics ages 5 or older speak English very well, an increase from 59% who spoke English proficiently in 2000.

The following is the language status of Hispanic-Americans ages 5 and older:

- Speak Spanish or another language at home and speak English very well: 41%
- Speak only English at home: 26%
- Speak Spanish or another language at home and speak English less than very well: 26%
- Speak Spanish or another language at home and do not speak English: 7%

"Although most of the nation's Hispanics speak Spanish at home, a growing share speak English proficiently."

Demo Memo, 5/18/15

Think Now Research (www.thinknowresearch.com) reported that Hispanic Millennials consume media as follows:

- Both English and Spanish equally: 40%
- Mostly English: 20%
- English only: 16%
- Mostly Spanish: 16%
- Spanish only: 9%

63.8 Market Resources

Hispanic Fact Pack - 2016 Edition, *Advertising Age*, August 2016. (http://adage.com/trend-reports/report.php?id=101)

FOCUS: Latino, Horowitz Associates, annual since 2001. (www.horowitzresearch.com/services/studies/focus-latino)

Pew Research Center Hispanic Trends Project. (www.pewhispanic.org)

Statistical Portrait Of Hispanics In The United States, Pew Research Center Hispanic Trends Project, April 2016. (www.pewhispanic.org/2016/04/19/statistical-portrait-of-hispanics-in-the-united-states-key-charts/)

The Multicultural Economy, The Selig Center for Economic Growth at the University of Georgia. (www.terry.uga.edu/selig/buying_power.html)

64

JEWISH-AMERICAN CONSUMERS

64.1 Overview

Jewish Americans, also called American Jews, include both those of Jewish faith and people of Jewish ethnicity.

The American-Jewish population is composed predominantly of Ashkenazi Jews and their U.S.-born descendants, comprising about 90% of the American Jewish population.

> **"Secularism has a long tradition in Jewish life in America, and most U.S. Jews seem to recognize this: 62% say being Jewish is mainly a matter of ancestry and culture, while just 15% say it is mainly a matter of religion. Even among Jews by religion, more than half (55%) say being Jewish is mainly a matter of ancestry and culture, and two-thirds say it is not necessary to believe in God to be Jewish."**
>
> *A Portrait Of Jewish Americans*
> Pew Research

64.2 Profile

American Jewish Year Book 2016, 116th Edition, by Sergio DellaPergola (2016, Springer Publishing) puts the core American Jewish population at 5,425,000.

The community self-identifying as Jewish by birth, irrespective of halakhic (unbroken maternal line of Jewish descent or formal Jewish conversion) status, numbers about 7 million, or 2.5% of the U.S. population.

The nature of Jewish identity is changing in America. According to *A Portrait Of Jewish Americans*, a report by the Religion & Public Life Project at Pew Research Center (www.pewresearch.org), the percentage of U.S. adults who say they are Jewish when asked about their religion has declined by about half since the late 1950s and currently is a little less than 2%. Meanwhile, the number of Americans with direct Jewish ancestry or upbringing who consider themselves Jewish, yet describe themselves as atheist, agnostic or having no particular religion, appears to be rising and is now about 0.5% of the U.S. adult population. Twenty-two percent (22%) of American Jews now describe themselves as having no religion.

The changing nature of Jewish identity stands out sharply among generations. Among Jewish Americans who are seniors, 93% identify as Jewish on the basis of religion; only 7% describe themselves as having no religion. Among Jewish Americans who are Millennials, 68% identify as Jews by religion, while 32% describe themselves as having no religion as well as identify as Jewish on the basis of ancestry, ethnicity or culture.

Within the community, intermarriage rates seem to have risen substantially. Among Jewish Americans who have gotten married since 2000, 58% have a non-Jewish spouse. Among those who got married in the 1980s, that figure was 42%.

Despite the changes in Jewish identity, 94% of American Jews say they are proud to be Jewish.

64.3 Buying Power

According to the Pew Project on Religion and Public Life, 25% of Jewish Americans report household incomes of over $150,000, compared to 8% of all U.S. households. The higher incomes are, in part, because Jewish Americans are generally better educated. While 27% of Americans have had college or postgraduate education, 59% of American Jews and 66% of Reform Jews have. Twenty-five percent (25%) of American Jews hold a graduate degree, compared with 6% of the general American population.

64.4 Population Centers

According to the Glenmary Research Center (www.glenmary.org), the following are the metropolitan areas with the highest Jewish populations:

- New York, NY: 3,750,000
- Miami, FL: 535,000
- Los Angeles, CA: 490,000
- Philadelphia, PA: 285,000
- Chicago, IL: 265,000
- San Francisco, CA: 210,000
- Boston, MA: 208,000
- Washington, DC-Baltimore, MD: 165,000

The counties with the largest Jewish population are as follows (Jewish as a percentage of total population also given):

	Total	Percentage
• Los Angeles County, CA:	564,700	5.9%
• Kings County, NY:	379,000	15.4%
• New York County, NY:	314,500	20.5%
• Queens County, NY:	238,000	10.7%
• Cook County, IL:	234,400	4.4%
• Broward County, FL:	213,000	13.1%
• Nassau County, NY:	207,000	15.5%
• Palm Beach County, FL:	167,000	14.8%
• Miami-Dade County, FL:	124,000	5.5%
• Middlesex County, MA:	113,700	7.8%
• Suffolk County, NY:	100,000	7.0%
• Baltimore/Baltimore County, MD:	94,500	7.7%
• Westchester County, NY:	94,000	10.2%
• Rockland County, NY:	90,000	31.4%
• Philadelphia County, PA:	86,600	5.7%
• Montgomery County, MD:	83,800	9.1%
• Bergen County, NJ:	83,700	9.5%
• Bronx County, NY:	83,700	6.3%
• Cuyahoga County, OH:	79,000	5.7%
• Oakland County, MI:	77,200	6.5%
• Essex County, NJ:	76,200	9.6%
• Clark County, NV:	75,000	5.5%
• San Diego County, CA:	70,000	2.5%
• Fulton County, GA:	65,900	8.1%
• Monmouth County, NJ:	65,000	10.6%
• Montgomery County, PA:	59,550	7.9%
• Santa Clara County, CA:	54,000	3.2%
• San Francisco County, CA:	49,500	6.4%
• St. Louis County, MO:	47,100	4.6%
• Middlesex County, NJ:	45,000	6.0%
• Norfolk County, MA:	38,300	5.9%
• Denver County, CO:	38,100	6.6%
• Camden County, NJ:	38,000	7.1%
• Bucks County, PA:	34,800	5.8%
• Allegheny County, PA:	34,600	2.7%
• Richmond County, NY:	33,700	7.6%
• Morris County, NJ:	33,500	7.1%
• Alameda County, CA:	32,500	2.3%
• Hennepin County, MN:	31,600	2.8%
• Union County, NJ:	30,100	5.8%
• Hartford County, CT:	30,000	3.5%
• New Haven County, CT:	28,900	3.5%

64.5 Market Resources

A Portrait Of Jewish Americans, Pew Research Religion & Public Life Project. (www.pewforum.org/2013/10/01/jewish-american-beliefs-attitudes-culture-survey/)

American Jewish Year Book 2016, Springer Publishing, 2016. (http://www.springer.com/us/book/9783319245034)

The Jewish Center, 131 West 86th Street, New York, NY 10024. (212) 724-2700. (www.jewishcenter.org)

65

MUSLIM-AMERICAN CONSUMERS

65.1 Overview

Because the United States does not track population by religion in its Census, there is no recognized source of data on the U.S. Muslim population.

According to the Gallup Organization (www.gallup.com), American Muslims are one of the most racially diverse religious groups in the United States.

Twenty-four percent (24%) of Arab Americans are Muslim. Census 2010 reported 1.52 million Arab Americans.

Native-born American Muslims are mainly African Americans who make up about a quarter of the total Muslim population. Many have converted to Islam during the last seventy years.

65.2 Profile

Self-Described Religious Identification of Adult Population, published by the Census Bureau in 2012, listed 2.6 million Americans of Muslim faith in 2008 (most recent data available).

A 2011 assessment by Pew Research Center (www.pewresearch.org) placed the number at 2.8 million.

According to the study *Muslim Americans: Middle Class and Mostly Mainstream*, by Pew Research Center, of all Muslim Americans, 65% are foreign-born, with about 34% of Pakistani or South Asian origin and 26% of Arab origin. Of U.S.-born Muslims, 25% are African American. Of all U.S.-born Muslims, 21% converted to Islam, 14% were raised Muslim.

The percentage of foreign-born U.S. Muslims by country of origin is as follows:

- Iran: 12%
- Pakistan: 12%
- India: 7%
- Lebanon: 6%
- Bangladesh: 5%
- Afghanistan: 4%
- Bosnia & Herzegovina: 4%
- Iraq: 4%
- Jordan: 3%
- Palestinian territories: 3%
- Morocco: 3%

- Africa (unspecified): 2%
- Egypt: 2%
- Israel: 2%
- Saudi Arabia: 2%
- Somalia: 2%
- Sudan: 2%
- Other: 19%

The makeup of the Muslim-American population is as follows:

Gender

- Male: 54%
- Female: 46%

Age

- 18-to-29: 29%
- 30-to-49: 48%
- 50-to-64: 18%
- 65 and older: 5%

Muslim Americans, a 2011 report by Pew Research Center, provides the following profile of Muslim Americans:

- A majority of Muslim Americans (56%) say that most Muslims who come to the U.S. want to adopt American customs and ways of life; just 20% say that Muslims in this country want to be distinct from the larger American society.

"When it comes to many aspects of American life, Muslim Americans look similar to the rest of the public. Comparable percentages say they watch entertainment television, follow professional or college sports, recycle household materials, and play video games."

Pew Research Center

- U.S. Muslims are about as likely as other Americans to report household incomes of $100,000 or more (14% of Muslims, compared with 16% of all adults).
- Overall, 46% say they are in excellent or good shape financially; among the general public, 38% say this.

- Muslim Americans are as likely as the public overall to have graduated from college (26% of Muslims vs. 28% among the general public).
- Because as a group Muslim Americans are younger than the general public, twice as many report being currently enrolled in a college or university class (26% vs. 13%). Similar numbers of Muslim Americans and members of the general public report being self-employed or owning a small business (20% for Muslim Americans, 17% for the general public).

65.3 Buying Power

The buying power of Muslim Americans is more than $170 billion a year, according to JWT (www.jwt.com).

65.4 Population Centers

According to Pew Research Center, the following are the most populous U.S. regions with Muslim-Americans residents:

- South: 32%
- Northeast: 29%
- Midwest: 22%
- West: 18%

According to the *2010 U.S. Religious Census*, by the Association of Statisticians of American Religious Bodies (www.asarb.org), the counties with the largest Muslim populations are as follows:

- Cook (Illinois): 201,152
- Harris (Texas): 117,148
- Kings (New York): 95,126
- Dallas (Texas): 84,256
- Queens (New York): 81,456
- Los Angeles (California): 69,080
- Warren (Michigan): 67,775
- DuPage (Illinois): 59,821
- Fairfax (Virginia): 50,108
- New York (New York): 42,545

65.5 Market Resources

American Muslim Consumer Conference. (www.americanmuslimconsumer.com)

Muslim American Outreach, Allied Media Corporation. (www.allied-media.com/muslim_americans/Public_Relations_Muslim_American_Community_Outreach.html)

The Muslim Journal (www.muslimjournal.com)

66

NATIVE-AMERICAN CONSUMERS

66.1 Overview

According to the Office of Management and Budget (www.omb.gov), American Indian or Alaska Native refers to a person as having ethnic origin from any of the original peoples of North and South America (including Central America) and who maintains tribal affiliation or community attachment.

Native Americans are the indigenous peoples within the boundaries of the present-day United States, including those in Alaska and Hawaii. They are composed of numerous distinct tribes and ethnic groups, many of which survive as intact political communities.

According to interviews conducted by the Census Bureau, most with an expressed preference refer to themselves as 'American Indians' or simply 'Indians'; this term has been adopted by major media and some academic groups, but does not traditionally include Native Hawaiians or certain Alaska Natives, such as Aleut, Yup'ik, or Inuit peoples.

66.2 Profile

Census 2010 counted 2.9 million people, or 0.9% of the total U.S. population, of American-Indian- or Alaska-Native-only ancestry. An additional 2.3 million people reported their ethnicity as American Indian or Alaska Native as well as one or more other races. Combined, 5.3 million American Indians or Alaska Natives were counted, representing 1.7% of the population.

The 2014 American Community Survey, published in November 2015 by the Census Bureau, reported the nation's population of American Indians and Alaska Natives, including those of more than one race, at 5.4 million. They made up about 2% percent of the total population. Of this total, about 48% were American Indian and Alaska Native only, and about 52% were American Indian and Alaska Native in combination with one or more other races.

The Census Bureau projects the population of American Indians and Alaska Natives, alone or in combination, in 2060 at 10.2 million. This will constitute 2.4% of the total U.S. population.

According to the *American Community Survey*, there are 1,122,043 American Indian and Alaska Native family households. Of these, 54.7% were married-couple families, including those with children.

The median age of the American Indian and Alaska Native population is 31.0 years; 437,339 are age 65 and over. This compares with a median age of 37.4 for the U.S. population as a whole.

Seventy-eight percent (78%) of single-race American Indians and Alaska Natives 25 and older have at least a high school diploma, GED certificate, or alternative credential; 14% have obtained a bachelor's degree or higher. For the overall U.S. population, these figures are 86% and 29%, respectively.

The Bureau of Indian Affairs (www.bia.gov) recognized 566 Indian tribes at year-end 2015. The Cherokee is the largest tribe, with 819,000 individuals; it has 284,000 full-blood individuals. The Navajo, with 286,000 full-blood individuals, is the largest tribe if only full-blood individuals are counted; the Navajo are the tribe with the highest proportion of full-blood individuals, 86.3%.

Twenty-nine percent (29%) of single-race American Indians and Alaska Natives live in poverty. For the nation as a whole, the poverty rate is 16%.

According to the U.S. Department of Health and Human Services, 14% of Native Americans are in poor or fair health, compared with 10% of the overall population. Twenty-seven percent (27%) of Native Americans lack health insurance, compared with 17% of the overall population.

66.3 Buying Power

In 2014, the median household income of single-race American Indian and Alaska Native households was $45,968. This compares with $66,877 for all U.S. households.

The Selig Center for Economic Growth at the University of Georgia (www.selig.uga.edu) estimates Native-American buying power as follows:

	Spending	Pct. of Consumer Spending
• 1990:	$20 billion	0.5%
• 2000:	$39 billion	0.5%
• 2009:	$65 billion	0.6%
• 2014:	$83 billion	0.6%

The Selig Center notes that the growth in Native American buying power is supported by rapid population growth and growth in the number of Native-American-owned businesses.

The following states have the largest marketshare of Native-American buying power:

- California: $9.4 billion
- Oklahoma: $6.5 billion
- Texas: $4.9 billion
- Arizona: $3.9 billion
- New Mexico: $2.6 billion
- Washington: $2.5 billion
- Florida: $2.5 billion

- Alaska: $2.4 billion
- North Carolina: $2.3 billion
- New York: $2.3 billion

The states with the largest Native-American shares of total buying power are as follows:

- Alaska: 8.6%
- Oklahoma: 5.3%
- New Mexico: 4.5%
- Montana: 3.4%
- South Dakota: 3.3%
- North Dakota: 2.7%
- Arizona: 2.0%
- Wyoming: 1.3%
- Nevada: 1.0%
- Washington: 1.0%

66.4 Population Centers

By state, Census 2010 reported the proportion of residents citing American Indian or Alaska Native ancestry and total Native-American population as follows:

	Pct.	Population
• California:	1.0%	362,801
• Oklahoma:	8.6%	321,687
• Arizona:	4.6%	296,529
• New Mexico:	9.4%	193,222
• Texas:	0.7%	170,972
• North Carolina:	1.3%	122,110
• New York:	0.6%	106,906
• Alaska:	14.8%	104,871
• Washington:	1.5%	103,869
• South Dakota:	8.8%	71,817
• Florida:	0.4%	71,458
• Montana:	6.3%	62,555
• Michigan:	0.6%	62,007
• Minnesota:	1.1%	60,916
• Colorado:	1.1%	56,010
• Wisconsin:	1.0%	54,526
• Oregon:	1.4%	53,203
• Illinois:	0.3%	43,963
• North Dakota:	5.4%	36,591
• Utah:	1.2%	32,927
• Georgia:	0.3%	32,151
• Nevada:	1.2%	32,062

- Louisiana: 0.7% 30,579
- Virginia: 0.4% 29,225
- New Jersey: 0.3% 29,026
- Alabama: 0.6% 28,218
- Kansas: 1.0% 28,150
- Missouri: 0.5% 27,376
- Pennsylvania: 0.2% 26,843
- Ohio: 0.2% 25,292
- Arkansas: 0.8% 22,248
- Idaho: 1.4% 21,441
- Maryland: 0.4% 20,420
- Tennessee: 0.3% 19,994
- South Carolina: 0.4% 19,524
- Massachusetts: 0.3% 18,850
- Indiana: 0.3% 18,462
- Nebraska: 1.2% 18,427
- Mississippi: 0.5% 15,030
- Wyoming: 2.4% 13,336
- Connecticut: 0.3% 11,256
- Iowa: 0.4% 11,084
- Kentucky: 0.2% 10,120
- Maine: 0.6% 8,568
- Rhode Island: 0.6% 6,058
- Delaware: 0.5% 4,181
- Hawaii: 0.3% 4,164
- West Virginia: 0.2% 3,787
- New Hampshire: 0.2% 3,150
- Vermont: 0.4% 2,207
- District of Columbia: 0.3% 2,079

Seventy percent (70%) of Native Americans lived in urban areas 2012, an increase from 45% in 1970. Metropolitan areas with significant Native-American populations include Minneapolis, Denver, Phoenix, Tucson, Chicago, Oklahoma City, Houston, New York City, and Rapid City.

There were 326 federally recognized American Indian reservations in 2015. There were 630 American Indian and Alaska Native legal and statistical areas for which the Census Bureau provides statistics.

Census 2010 reported that 22% of American Indians and Alaska Natives, alone or in combination, lived in American Indian areas or Alaska Native Village Statistical Areas. These American Indian areas include federal American Indian reservations or off-reservation trust lands, Oklahoma tribal statistical areas, tribal designated statistical areas, state American Indian reservations, and state designated American Indian statistical areas.

66.5 Market Resources

Facts for Features: American Indian and Alaska Native Heritage, U.S. Census Bureau, November 2015. (www.census.gov/newsroom/facts-for-features/2015/cb15-ff22.html)

National Congress of American Indians (www.ncai.org)

The Multicultural Economy, The Selig Center for Economic Growth at the University of Georgia. (www.terry.uga.edu/selig/buying_power.html)

U.S. Department of Interior, Bureau of Indian Affairs (www.bia.gov)

PART X: GENDER FOCUS

67

FEMALE CONSUMERS

67.1 Profile

According to the Census Bureau (www.census.gov), the U.S. female population at year-end 2015 was 163.2 million, which represents 50.8% of the population. Distribution by age is as follows:

- Under 18: 37.3 million
- 18-to-64: 100.4 million
- 65 and older: 25.6 million

The median age for females is 39.1.

Census 2010 counted 157.0 million females.

Educational Attainment in the United States, a report from the U.S. Census Bureau, counted 31.4 million women ages 25 and older with a bachelor's degree or more education, higher than the corresponding number for men (30.0 million). Women have a larger share of high school diplomas as well as associate's, bachelor's, and master's degrees. Fewer women than men have a professional or doctoral degree. Educational attainment is an important consumer metric because adults with higher education typically have higher incomes and spend more.

According to *School Enrollment in the United States*, by the U.S. Census Bureau, 56.9% of college students were women during the 2015-2016 academic year. Thirty-four percent (34%) more women graduated than men in 2015, and by 2023, the U.S. Department of Education expects female grads to outnumber males by 47%.

67.2 Working Women

According to the U.S. Bureau of Labor Statistics (www.bls.gov), 59% of adult women work or are actively seeking employment.

Among women who don't work, 27% do not because of family responsibilities; 14% don't because their family doesn't want them to work. Only 6% of men do not work because of either of these reasons.

Women are found to have higher career aspirations than men. According to a study by Pew Research Center (www.pewresearch.org), 66% of women ages 18-to-34 say that being successful in a high-paying career or profession is very important in their lives; 59% of men in that age group feel the same way.

Women now hold the majority of professional positions in several occupations, including journalism, law, marketing, and communications. These are, in general, among the highest paying occupations. In 47 of the 50 largest U.S. metro areas, single women in their 20s and without children earn more money than their male peers.

> **"Women ages 25-to-34 are the first generation to start their careers near parity with men, earning 93% of men's wages. Single women now buy homes at greater rates than single men, a big step in independent wealth-building."**
>
> *The Economist*, 4/16/16

Overall career outlooks appear bright for women. Of the 15.3 million new jobs projected for the next decade, the vast majority will be in fields that currently attract more women than men. Of the 12 job titles projected by the Bureau of Labor Statistics to grow the most through 2018, women dominate 10 categories.

According to *Profile America*, from the Census Bureau, women own 29% of all non-farm businesses; women are also equal partners with men in the ownership of another 17% of businesses. Women own 52% of all businesses operating in the healthcare and social assistance sector.

67.3 Mothers

According to the National Center for Health Statistics (www.cdc.gov/nchs/), the general fertility rate in 2015 was 62.5 births per 1,000 women ages 15-to-44, down less than 1% from 2014 and the lowest since World War II. The United States registered 3,977,745 births in 2015.

Profile America provides the following assessment of mothers:

Overall

- Estimated number of mothers in the United States: 85.4 million
- Percentage of 15-to-44-year-old women who are mothers: 54%
- Percentage of women 40-to-44 who have given birth: 82%
- Total fertility rate, or number of births per woman: 2.0
- Average age of women when they give birth for the first time: 25.1

Moms Who Have Recently Given Birth

- Number of births registered in the United States in 2010 (most recent data available): 4.01 million

- Births to teens ages 15-to-19: 409,840
- Births to mothers ages 45-to-54: 7,934
- Rate of twin births per 1,000 total births: 32.6

Stay-at-Home and Working Mothers

- Number of stay-at-home moms: 5.0 million
- Proportion of married-couple family groups with children under 15 with a stay-at-home mother: 23%
- Proportion of mothers with a recent birth who were in the labor force: 61%

Single Moms

- Number of single mothers living with children younger than 18: 9.9 million

The following are other facts provided by *Profile America*:

- Among the 37.8 million mothers with children younger than 18 living at home, 94% live with their biological children only; 3% live with stepchildren, 2% with adopted children, and less than 1% with foster children.
- Of the four million women ages 15-to-44 who had a birth in the last year, 1.5 million, or 38%, were to women who were not married, who were separated, or married but with an absent spouse. Of those 1.5 million mothers, 425,000, or 28%, were living with a cohabiting partner.

67.4 Working Mothers

Sixty-six percent (66%) of women with children ages 17 or younger are working women. Among those working mothers, 74% work full time and 26% work part time.

According to Pew Research Center's Social & Demographic Trends Project (www.pewsocialtrends.org), 62% of working mothers would prefer to work part time.

According to Scarborough Research (www.scarborough.com), working mothers comprise the highest percentage of the adult population in the following cities:

- Des Moines, IA: 12%
- Honolulu, HI: 12%
- New Orleans, LA: 12%
- Kansas City, MO: 11%
- San Antonio, TX: 11%

The cities with the lowest percentage of working moms are as follows:

- Pittsburgh, PA: 6%
- Greenville, SC: 7%
- Knoxville, TN: 7%

According to another study by Pew Research Center, 40% of all households with children under the age of 18 include mothers who are either the sole or primary source of income for the family. The share was just 11% in 1960.

Of these breadwinner moms, 5.1 million (37%) are married mothers who earn more than their husbands; 8.6 million (63%) are single mothers. In households where women out-earn their spouses, median family income is $80,000 – compared to the national median of $57,100.

67.5 Engaging Moms

With significant influence over $2.4 trillion in annual household spending, mothers are an important market for brands. Determining the preferences of moms and keeping this cohort engaged is critical for businesses.

A recent study by PunchTab (www.punchtab.com) found that 81% of moms will engage more with a brand when offered some type of reward. The following is an assessment of engagement motivators:

- Would like free products and services from the brand: 83%
- Moms will engage more with a brand when some type of reward is in place: 81%
- Would be interested in a loyalty program for a parent company: 73%
- Would be interested in receiving perks associated with elite status (e.g. free shipping or branded merchandise) as reward: 67%
- Would sign up for regular mail updates when reward is offered: 59%
- Would share content on Facebook when offered reward: 50%
- Would share personal details and purchase behavior if offered incentive: 41%

A study by Babycenter (www.babycenter.com) found that moms are great at engaging other moms, with 59% of moms saying they've responded to a recommendation from other moms on parenting sites.

A survey by Burst Media (www.burstmedia.com) found the following are digital channels where mothers post about products/services:

	18-34	35-54	55+
• Social network and sharing sites:	69.6%	55.4%	61.6%
• Shopping/retail and e-commerce sites:	56.8%	51.7%	48.2%
• Independent sites and blogs:	36.1%	29.8%	40.1%
• Portals and news sites:	23.3%	10.5%	9.0%
• Other:	22.9%	22.0%	20.5%

67.6 Affluent Women

According to *Affluent Working Women*, a report by International Demographics (www.themediaaudit.com), affluent working women with family incomes of $75,000 or more comprise 10.1% of the 80 largest metropolitan areas. The following are the markets with the highest percentages of affluent working women:

- Washington, DC: 14.7%
- Southern New Hampshire: 13.0%
- San Jose, CA: 12.5%
- Hartford, CT: 12.3%
- Minneapolis-Saint Paul, MN: 11.9%
- Little Rock, AR: 11.7%
- Omaha-Council Bluffs, NE: 11.7%
- San Francisco, CA: 11.6%
- Baltimore, MD: 11.4%
- Madison, WI: 11.3%

According to Ipsos (www.ipsos.com), there are 15.6 million affluent (annual household incomes of $100,000 or more) female heads of household ages 18-to-54.

According to the Luxury Institute (www.luxuryinstitute.com), 72% of women in households with incomes of $150,000 or higher work; 54% work full time.

Affluent women are most likely to control the food and clothing purchase decisions for their household. In households above this income level, women make the decisions about the following:

- Home appliance purchases: 68%
- Family vacations: 61%
- Electronics purchases: 40%
- Vehicle purchases: 40%
- Real estate purchases: 31%

Overall, these women make approximately 68% of the purchases on behalf of their household. When purchasing, these women have a decided preference for products that are made by established and well-known brands.

67.7 Purchase Decision Making

Eighty-five percent (85%) of purchasing decisions are made or influenced by women, according to The 85% Niche (www.85percentniche.com). Frank About Women (www.frankaboutwomen.com) puts the figure at 80%.

Findings of a study by Fleishman-Hillard (www.fleishman.com) reveal that women consider themselves the primary decision-maker in their home. Seventy-nine percent (79%) say their opinion determines family financial decisions, 74% are primarily responsible for buying groceries and basic supplies, and 55% are primarily responsible for paying the bills.

Fleishman-Hillard estimates that women will control two-thirds of the consumer wealth in the U.S. over the next decade.

68

MALE CONSUMERS

68.1 Profile

According to the Census Bureau (www.census.gov), the U.S. male population at year-end 2015 was 158.2 million, which represents 49.2% of the population. Distribution by age is as follows:

- Under 18: 39.7 million
- 18-to-64: 99.0 million
- 65 and older: 19.5 million

The median age for men is 36.2 years.

Census 2010 counted 151.8 million males. The median age for men is 35.8 years.

Educational Attainment in the United States, a report from the Census Bureau, counted 30.0 million men ages 25 and older with a bachelor's degree or more education, lower than the corresponding number for women (31.4 million). More men than women have a professional or doctoral degree but they have a lower share of high school diplomas as well as associate's, bachelor's, and master's degrees.

According to *School Enrollment in the United States*, by the U.S. Census Bureau, 43.1% of college students were male during the 2015-2016 academic year.

68.2 Fathers

Profile America, a report from the Census Bureau, estimated there are 70.1 million fathers in the United States. Among these, 25.3 million fathers are part of married-couple families with children younger than 18. Twenty-two percent (22%) are raising three or more children younger than 18.

There are 1.8 million single fathers; 15% of single parents are men. Forty-six percent (46%) of single fathers are divorced, 30% have never been married, 19% are separated, and 6% are widowed. Nine percent (9%) of single fathers are raising three or more children younger than 18.

According to data by Pew Research Center (www.pewsocialtrends.org), roughly 2.0 million fathers are stay-at-home dads. At peak, 2.2 million men reported being stay-at-home dads in 2010 – just after the official end of the recession.

The primary reason for staying at home with the children among men was illness or disability, cited by 35% of stay-at-home dads. Caring for the family and the inability to find work, the reason for 21% and 23% of fathers, respectively, increased sharply in recent years. In 1989 these figures were 5% and 15%, respectively. Those in school, retired or other comprised 22% of stay-at-home dads.

The annual joint report by the Census Bureau and the Bureau of Labor Statistics, with differing metrics than Pew for assessing stay-at-home dads, estimates there are 214,000 stay-at-home dads. This study primarily considers married fathers with children younger than 15 and who have remained out of the labor force for at least one year primarily so they can care for the family while their wives work outside the home.

A Tale Of Two Fathers, by Pew Research Center (www.pewresearch.org), reported that an increasing number of fathers live apart from their children. But, those living with their children are more involved in their lives than in the past.

"The role of fathers in the modern American family is changing in important and countervailing ways. Fathers who live with their children have become more intensely involved in their lives, spending more time with them and taking part in a greater variety of activities. However, the share of fathers who are residing with their children has fallen significantly in the past half century."

Pew Research Center

In 1960, only 11% of children in the U.S. lived apart from their fathers. That share has risen to 27%. The share of minor children living apart from their mothers increased only modestly, from 4% in 1960 to 8%.

More than one-in-four fathers with children ages 18 or younger now live apart from their children – with 11% living apart from some of their children and 16% living apart from all of their children. One-in-five absent fathers say they visit their children more than once a week, but an even greater share (27%) say they have not seen their children at all in the past year.

Almost all fathers who live with their children take an active role in their children's day-to-day lives through activities such as sharing meals, helping with homework, and playing.

In 1965, married fathers with children younger than age 18 living in their household spent an average of 2.6 hours per week caring for those children. Fathers' time spent caring for their children rose gradually over the past two decades, to 2.7 hours per week in 1975 and 3 hours per week in 1985. From 1985 to 2000, the amount of time married fathers spent with their children more than doubled, to 6.5 hours.

68.3 Blurring Gender Roles

While women still do the majority of work in the home, studies have found that men are more involved domestically than in past decades.

According to Prof. Scott Coltrane, Ph.D., a sociologist and dean of the College of Arts & Sciences at University of Oregon, compared with the 1960s, the portion of housework done by men in couple households has doubled, with men now doing 30% of housework compared with only 15% in the past. Men have also tripled the amount of childcare they give.

According to *Meet The Modern Dad*, a study by The Parenting Group (www.parenting.com), fathers say the following tasks are mostly their responsibility:

- Grocery shopping: 49%
- Cooking: 43%
- Driving kids to/from school, activities and appointments: 39%
- Getting kids ready for school or daycare: 36%

A survey by Yahoo! (www.yahoo.com) found that 51% of men are primarily responsible in their household for grocery shopping. For laundry and cooking the percentages are 41% and 39%, respectively.

"Men have long been discouraged from playing an equal role at home. That is, at last, starting to change."

The Economist, 6/16/16

Despite the increase in their roles in the household, the vast majority of men still take a secondary role in household chores and childcare. Less than 3% of men are stay-at-home dads.

68.4 Activities Among Young Men

College Enrollment and Work Activity of 2015 High School Graduates, published in May 2016 by the Bureau of Labor Statistics (www.bls.gov), the status of men ages 16-to-24 in October 2015 was as follows (percentage of all 16-to-24 year-old men in parenthesis):

- Not in school, had a job or were looking for work: 7.3 million (38%)
- In college: 5.8 million (30%)
- In high school: 4.9 million (25%)
- Not in school, did not have a job, and were not looking for work: 1.4 million (7%)

"Among the nation's 19 million men ages 16-to-24, more than 1 million were not doing much of anything when the Bureau of Labor Statistics took a look at their activities in October 2015."

Demo Memo, 5/13/16

68.5 Purchasing Decision Making

Marketing to Men, a study by Jacobs Media (www.jacobsmedia.com), reported that men and women share purchase decision-making for big ticket items as follows:

	Male	Female
• Sole decision maker:	24.4%	27.9%
• Play a key role but share in decision:	34.7%	27.8%
• Share decision equally:	36.7%	37.6%
• Have some, but not primary, influence:	2.8%	4.8%
• No role in decision:	0.5%	0.6%

A January 2016 survey by Crosstap (www.crosstap.com) asked Millennial men who is the primary decision maker for family-related purchases in their household. Responses were as follows:

- We try to share the decision making evenly: 53%
- I definitely am the decision maker: 25%
- My spouse is the decision maker: 23%

In a survey by Yahoo!, men reported that they had become more involved in decision-making related to the following household purchases (percentage of respondents):

- Consumer packaged goods: 60%
- Apparel: 54%
- Housewares and household goods: 54%
- Personal care products: 53%
- Baby and child care products: 50%
- Toys: 50%

“As patterns of motherhood in the U.S. have shifted, so have patterns of fatherhood – with hyper-involved new dads getting much attention even as fathers who do not live with their kids at all have become common. Some aspects of father behavior get disproportionate attention, while others are neglected.”

eMarketer, 4/6/16

PART XI: GENERATIONAL FOCUS

69

GENERATIONAL COMPARISONS

69.1 Overview

Market researchers typically categorize adult consumers into four generations, as follows:

	Year of Birth	Age (in 2016)
• Seniors (Silent Generation):	1945 and before	71 and older
• Baby Boomers:	1946-1964	52-to-70
• Generation X:	1965-1979	37-to-51
• Millennials (Gen Y):	1980-2000	16-to-36

Youth, born 2001-present and ages 15 and younger in 2016, are categorized as Generation Z.

69.2 Unique Characteristics

Pew Research Center (www.pewresearch.org) asked people of all ages what makes their generation unique. Responses were as follows (percentage of respondents):

Seniors

- Experienced World War II: 14%
- Experienced the Great Depression: 14%
- Smarter: 13%
- Honest: 12%
- Work ethic: 10%
- Values/morals: 10%

Baby Boomers

- Work ethic: 17%
- Respectful: 14%
- Values/morals: 8%
- Largest generation: 6%
- Smarter: 5%

Generation X

- Technology: 12%
- Work ethic: 11%
- Conservative/traditional: 7%
- Smarter: 6%
- Respectful: 5%

Millennials

- Technology: 24%
- Music and pop culture: 11%
- Liberal/tolerant: 7%
- Smarter: 6%
- Clothes: 5%

69.3 Generational Self-Identification

A 2015 survey by Pew Research Group asked adults what descriptions applied to their generation. Responses were as follows:

	Millennial	Gen X	Boomers	Seniors
• Compassionate:	27%	33%	47%	60%
• Cynical:	31%	24%	16%	7%
• Entrepreneurial:	35%	33%	35%	32%
• Environmentally-conscious:	40%	37%	41%	40%
• Greedy:	43%	24%	19%	8%
• Hard-working:	36%	54%	77%	83%
• Idealistic:	39%	28%	31%	26%
• Moral:	17%	27%	46%	64%
• Patriotic:	12%	26%	52%	77%
• Politically active:	17%	20%	37%	42%
• Religious:	12%	21%	42%	63%
• Responsible:	24%	43%	66%	78%
• Self-reliant:	27%	37%	51%	65%
• Self absorbed:	59%	30%	20%	7%
• Tolerant:	33%	33%	38%	36%
• Wasteful:	49%	29%	20%	10%
• Willing to sacrifice:	15%	27%	45%	61%

70

SENIOR CONSUMERS

70.1 Profile

Those born before 1946 have been tagged with various monikers, the most common being simply 'Seniors.' The youngest Seniors turned 71 in 2016.

The Senior generation is also frequently dubbed the 'Silent Generation,' a name coined by *Time* magazine in 1951, which described the generation as "working fairly hard and saying almost nothing."

Census 2010 counted 40.27 million Americans ages 65 or older, representing 13.0% of the population. The Senior population increased 15.1% from Census 2000, when 34.99 million people in that age demographic represented 12.4% of the population.

The U.S. Census Bureau (www.census.gov) estimated the year-end 2015 Senior population at 29.19 million.

70.2 Daily Activities

According to Pew Research Center's Social & Demographic Trends Project (www.pewsocialtrends.org), daily activities among those ages 65 or older are as follows (percentage of respondents):

- Talk with family or friends: 90%
- Read a book, magazine, or newspaper: 83%
- Take a prescription medication: 83%
- Watch one hour or more of television: 77%
- Pray: 76%
- Drive a car: 65%
- Spend time on a hobby: 43%
- Take a nap: 40%
- Go shopping: 39%
- Use the Internet: 28%
- Get some type of vigorous exercise: 22%

Seniors say the benefits of growing older include the following:

- More time with family: 70%
- Not working: 66%
- More times for hobbies/interests: 65%

- More financial security: 64%
- Less stress: 59%
- More respect: 59%
- More travel: 52%
- Volunteer work: 52%
- Second career: 14%

70.3 Living Arrangements

Seniors' living arrangements are as follows:

	65-74	75-84	85+	All
• Own home or apartment:	95%	90%	80%	92%
• Child's/family member's home:	2%	4%	5%	3%
• Assisted living facility:	2%	4%	15%	4%

Characteristics among those living independently are as follows:

	65-74	75-84	85+	All
• Live in age-restricted community:	6%	11%	20%	10%
• Live alone:	30%	47%	66%	41%

Aging in America, by Prince Market Research (www.pmresearch.com), reports that 89% of Seniors feel that the ability to live independently and remain in their home is very important. More than half (53%), however, are concerned with their ability to do so. Seniors cited three primary concerns that could jeopardize their ability to live independently: health problems (53%), memory problems (26%), and the inability to drive/get around (23%).

The majority of Seniors (55%) view themselves as very independent in that they receive no assistance from their children – and seem content with that fact; 75% said their children are involved enough in their life. Seniors who do require help from others receive assistance with household maintenance (20%), transportation (13%), and healthcare (8%). Only 1% reported receiving any financial support.

According to Pew Research Center's Social & Demographic Trends Project, 63% of those ages 65 or older feel they are in excellent or good health. For those living in the west, that figure rises to 72%.

By region, those that say they don't feel old are as follows:

- West: 79%
- Northeast: 72%
- South: 71%
- Midwest: 66%

"If a latter-day Ponce de Leon were to search for a modern fountain of youth, he'd do well to explore America's West. There he'd find the highest concentration of older adults in the United States who don't think of themselves as old."

Pew Research Center

70.4 Working Seniors

The *2015 Current Population Survey*, by the Census Bureau, reported 11% of females and 15% of males over age 65 work full time. By education, those that do so are as follows:

- No high school diploma: 8%
- High school graduate: 13%
- Some college: 15%
- Associate's degree: 14%
- Bachelor's degree: 21%
- Master's degree: 17%
- Doctoral degree: 28%
- Professional degree: 33%

70.5 Buying Power

Recent data by the Federal Reserve show elderly Americans to be among the wealthiest, with people 75 and older showing a median family net worth of almost $195,000 in constant 2013 dollars, up from $131,000 from 1989. This group's prosperity today comes from prime years of working – plus investing and saving – during a period when the economy consistently grew an average 3.5% a year – the period between 1962 and 1991. More than anything, however, this group benefitted from ownership of homes and investments that have soared in value.

Based on spending patterns, researchers for the Bureau of Labor Statistics (www.bls.gov) segment Seniors as follows:

- Basic Need-Meeters (26.9%): The largest and poorest cluster, this segment had an average income of $33,147 and spent just $23,679. Because of their limited resources, Basic Need-Meeters must devote the largest share of their spending to essentials – 43%.

- Housing Burdened (25.9%): 78% of households in this cluster are still making mortgage payments, compared with only 23% to 34% of households in other clusters. Consequently, the Housing Burdened devote the largest share of their budget to mortgage (rent) – 42% of their spending vs only 5% to 17% among other clusters.
- Healthcare Burdened (21.1%): The second-poorest cluster, this group is defined by its outsized out-of-pocket healthcare spending – or 27% of its $29,818 overall spending. Other groups devote only 10% to 12% of their spending to healthcare.
- Transportation Burdened (12.1%): Although this group spent an average $44,245, it had to devote a hefty 33% of that spending to transportation. Fully, 60% of this group live in smaller cities of the South and Midwest.
- Happy Retirees (6.3%): This is the richest group, with average annual spending of $54,813. They devote 31% of their budget to "expendables" like entertainment, travel and household operations.
- Balanced Budgeters (5.4%): This group is almost as affluent as Happy Retirees, but it spends less ($47,920 vs $54,813). An average amount of their spending is devoted to various budget items, which is why they are considered "balanced."

70.6 Financial Challenges

Twelve percent (12%) of seniors run out of money before they die. *A Look At The End-of-Life Financial Situation in America*, by the Employee Benefit Research Institute (www.ebri.org), reports the percentages of seniors, by age, that run out of money as follows:

	Households With Non-Housing Assets = Zero Before Death	Households With Total Assets = Zero Before Death
• 65 to 74:	25.3%	15.8%
• 75 to 84:	18.5%	10.5%
• 85 and older:	20.6%	12.2%

"How many of the oldest Americans run out of money before they die? One in eight, according to a study by the EBRI."

Demo Memo, 5/5/15

70.7 Media Activities

According to the Pew Internet & American Life Project (www.pewinternet.org),

53% of Seniors use the Internet. Once online, the Internet becomes a part of daily life for the majority of Seniors.

Overall, 82% of all adult Internet users go online on an average day. Among adults age 65 and older, 70% use the Internet on a typical day.

Focalyst (www.focalyst.com) provides the following assessment of online Seniors and, for comparison, those that do not go online:

	Internet Users	Not Online
• Annual household income:	$55,000	$27,000
• Average monthly household expenditures:	$ 1,754	$ 1,059
• Married/partnered:	70%	48%
• Employed:	26%	13%
• Attended college:	75%	42%

Pew Research Center found similar usage among Seniors based on income, reporting that Internet usage among Seniors with an annual household income of $75,000 or more tops 90%, with 82% using broadband at home. For Seniors earning less than $30,000 annually, 39% go online and 25% have broadband at home.

The Cable & Telecommunications Association for Marketing (www.ctam.org) reports the following activities among online Seniors:

- Use email: 94%
- Shop online: 77%
- Access health and medical information: 71%
- Read news: 70%
- Manage finances and banking: 59%
- Play free online games: 47%

According to Pew Research Center, Senior ownership of media and technology devices is as follows:

- Cellphone: 69%
- Desktop: 48%
- Laptop: 32%
- eReader: 11%
- Tablet: 8%

70.8 Trends

Although Seniors haven't adopted technology as rapidly as other demographics, several new innovations are being tailored specifically for this group. One such is Lively, a monitoring system enabled with sensors to detect unusual patterns, like skipped medication or missed meals. Oscar Tech has designed a pair of apps that are Senior-user-friendly and designed to keep a Senior connected remotely to another party. True Link Financial is a company offering a debit card that a caregiver can monitor for unusual activity.

The sector is buoyed by various startups and groups like Aging2.0 (www.aging2.com), a global organization on a mission to accelerate innovation to improve the lives of older adults around the world.

In addition to the growth in products and services designed to help Seniors stay in their homes, developers are designing and planning modern communities specifically for Seniors. These new Senior-centric concepts will blend housing, social and networking in one community.

71

BABY BOOMER CONSUMERS

71.1 Profile

The oldest of the Baby Boomers – born in 1946 and 2.8 million in number – turned 70 in 2016; the youngest Boomers – born in 1964 – turned 52.

Census 2010 counted 76.94 million Americans born between 1946 and 1964, representing 24.9% of the population.

The U.S. Census Bureau (www.census.gov) estimated the year-end 2015 Baby Boomer population at 72.88 million.

71.2 Generational Characteristics

AARP (www.aarp.org) provides the following insight into Baby Boomer households:

- Thirty-seven percent (37%) of Baby Boomers have a child age 18 or younger living in the household.
- Over five million Baby Boomer parents have recently had an adult child move back into the home, partially due to the rise of "adultolescents" who've boomeranged back into the parental household.
- Four million Baby Boomers have a parent living with them.
- Eighty-two percent (82%) of Boomers use the Internet, engaging in activities such as instant messaging, downloading music or movies, financial transactions, and online gaming.
- Contrary to popular perception, few Baby Boomers are downsizing. Only 6% expect to be living in a smaller home within five years.
- Just 11% of Baby Boomers plan to stop working altogether when they reach retirement age.

According to Pew Research Center's Social & Demographic Trends Project (www.pewsocialtrends.org), 52% of Baby Boomers say they are considering delaying retirement because of the financial setbacks of the Great Recession.

The Nielsen Company (www.nielsen.com) provides the following facts about Baby Boomers:

- They dominate 1,023 out of 1,083 consumer packaged goods categories.
- They watch the most video among demographic groups: 9:34 hours per day.
- They comprise ⅓ of all TV viewers, online users, and social media users.
- They watch time-shift TV more than 18-to-24 year olds (2:32 vs. 1:32).

According to Nielsen, while Baby Boomers account for 38.5% of spending on consumer packaged goods; less than 5% of advertising spending targets them.

"You'll find that people over age 50 drive today's economy, whether up or down. Ninety million people with full wallets and low-balance credit cards are a lot of consumers to ignore. The 50+ cohort controls 75% of the wealth in this country, earns $2.3 trillion annually compared to $1 trillion for the 18-to-34 group, and they stand to inherit between $14 trillion and $20 trillion over the next 20 years."

Brandweek

71.3 Media Activities

According to the Pew Internet & American Life Project (www.pewinternet.org), 81% of younger Baby Boomers and 76% of older Baby Boomers use the Internet. Top online activities are as follows:

	Younger Boomers (45-54)	Older Boomers (55-64)
• Email:	91%	93%
• Search engines:	86%	87%
• News:	84%	85%
• Buy products:	73%	75%
• Book travel:	70%	67%
• Watch videos:	62%	55%
• Bank online:	58%	56%
• Social networks:	50%	43%

Social networks use by Baby Boomers is as follows:

	Younger Boomers (45-54)	Older Boomers (55-64)
• Facebook:	32%	9%
• LinkedIn:	31%	12%
• Twitter:	24%	6%
• Pinterest:	25%	8%
• Google+:	5%	6%

A recent study by Ipsos (www.ipsos.com) found Boomers rely heavily on the Internet to gain access to information. Among those who use the Internet at home, 14.8 hours weekly is spent; 4.8 hours are spent online away from home.

71.4 Trends

Baby Boomers & Their Homes: On Their Own Terms, a survey by The Demand Institute (www.thedemandinstitute.org), found that one-third of Boomers plan to move when they retire. Of those ages 50-to-69, 37% said they intend to move.

Before the Great Recession, much had been made about the incomes of Baby Boomers and the wealth they stood to inherit from their Senior parents. Not only has this cohort seen its inheritance dwindle in the wake of the Great Recession, many lost much of their own personal wealth as their home values plummeted. The worse off among them are those who, today, owe more on their home than what it is worth.

This harsh reality has stymied the plans of Boomers who not only had hopes of retiring, but who also were planning to cash in on their current home and move after doing so. For those who own their home, the dream of selling the suburban homestead – where the kids grew up, and in some cases have returned – and downsizing to a cozy condo in a lively urban center has also been dashed.

For the first time in 90 years, American cities are growing faster than their suburbs. This is because city centers are where almost everyone wants to live, and few want a home in the 'burbs. So, of the 20.1 million Senior households that will attempt to sell their homes between 2015 and 2030, an estimated 7.4 million won't be able to find people to buy them, according to research from University of Utah.

An unexpected trend in housing among Boomers is that of renting versus ownership. Between 2002 and 2012, the number of renters ages 55-to-64 increased by 80%. For partial comparison, the rate of home ownership dropped by 2.5% among those ages 60-to-64.

72

GENERATION X CONSUMERS

72.1 Profile

Most analysts classify those born 1965 thru 1979, a span of 15 years, as Generation X. With no major event providing a marker for the boundaries of this generation – as the end of World War II did for the Baby Boom Generation – some analysts classify only those born 1965 thru 1975 as Gen X. Whatever definition is used, analysts agree that consumers now in their 30s and 40s differ in many ways from Baby Boomers that proceeded them and Millennials that followed.

Census 2010 counted 61.03 million Americans born between 1965 and 1979, representing 19.8% of the population.

The ethnic makeup of Generation X is as follows (source: U.S. Census Bureau):

- Caucasian: 72.8%
- Hispanic: 16.8%
- African American: 13.2%
- Asian: 1.6%
- Other: 5.6%

Generation X is significantly smaller in number than either the Baby Boomer or the Millennial generations – and, it seems, often overshadowed by these generations.

"It's so annoying. First, it was always the Baby Boomers overshadowing everything. Then there was this brief period in the mid-'90s when Gen X was cool. Now it's, 'What are the new kids doing?'"

Lisa Chamberlain, Author
Slackonomics: Generation X in the Age of Creative Destruction

---

The U.S. Census Bureau (www.census.gov) estimated the year-end 2015 Generation X population at 61.82 million.

72.2 Generational Characteristics

What Generation X is, perhaps foremost in importance, is the best-educated generation in U.S. history. Almost half of Gen Xers have a 2- or 4-year college degree, and more than 10% have a graduate degree. Gen X households typically include two income-earning spouses; 68% have dual incomes.

Several recent surveys have shown that younger workers, especially those in Generation X, hold a work/life balance, opportunities for growth, and good work relationships higher in importance than generations before them. Gen X employees view work as secondary to their lives outside the office, which may mean more time with their children or time to pursue a hobby.

According to Ann A. Fishman, president of Generational-Targeted Marketing Corp. (www.annfishman.com), Gen Xers have different values from Boomers, especially related to their careers. They want to enjoy their jobs as well as have time for their own lives. So Gen Xers are often willing to trade off less money for more freedom.

72.3 Affluent Gen Xers

The *2015 Affluent Survey* by Ipsos (www.ipsos.com) reported Generation X households comprise 37% of households with at $100,000 or more in annual income; 44% of affluent households are Baby Boomer households.

"For the first time ever, the affluent population of the United States has more Generation Xers than Baby Boomers."

Center for Media Research, 9/29/15

72.4 Spending Behaviors

Generation X has often been characterized as being non-materialistic, shunning fashion, brand names, and technological advancements. These values, to some extent, were the generation's effort to distinguish itself from the Baby Boomer's preppy era of the early 1980s. However, while they may not yet have the affluence of Baby

Boomers, Gen Xers have plenty of style and a desire to show it off. This segment initially affected fashion and style, then music and movies, and now is influencing the marketing of furniture and housewares.

For all its individuality and the promise that might have been for marketers as Generation X approached its peak earning years, Gen X reached the height of its earnings power during the Great Recession. Now holding mortgages on homes worth less than when they bought, saddled with tens of thousands of dollars in student loans, on average, and raising children under age 18 who are dependent upon them, the timing of the Great Recession could not have been worse for this generation. This generation has earned more than their parents, but their net worth is significantly less as a result of debt.

72.5 Media Activities

According to recent estimates by eMarketer (www.emarketer.com), nearly 95% of Gen Xers use mobile phones; 60% of that group use smartphones. Among Gen Xers, 72.2% use the mobile Internet at least monthly.

Gen X Internet users also are avid consumers of online content. They typically use social networking sites on at least a monthly basis (74.5% of Gen X web users), and 65.6% use Facebook in particular. Growth in these areas, as in Internet usage as a whole, is relatively flat due to market saturation. Twitter, however, reaches only 14.7% of Gen X Internet users, eMarketer estimates, and usage is growing quickly and expected to reach 19.5% of this audience in 2017.

Digital video is even more popular among Gen X Internet users than social networking, with 78.7% downloading or streaming video online at least once per month.

Generation X bridges traditional and digital media usage and its members are virtually always connected, thanks to mobile devices. Born before the digital revolution, Gen X is the first generation to come of age with PCs and the Internet. Its members are fully comfortable using both traditional and digital media channels.

72.6 Trends

A recent ShullmanPulse survey found the following characteristics among the Gen X cohort (www.shullman.net):

Personal Financial Goals

- Have enough money for daily living expenses: 51%
- Have enough money for unexpected emergency expenses: 44%
- Have enough income for retirement: 42%
- Reduced debts: 37%
- Remain financially independent: 36%
- Improve standard of living: 31%
- Provide protection for family in case of death: 27%
- Keep up with inflation: 27%

- Become financially independent: 26%
- Have personal control over assets: 23%
- Have fun/a challenge: 21%
- Provide for children's college expenses: 19%
- Save/invest for some future "big ticket" expenditure: 19%
- Buy a home: 16%
- Avoid or minimize taxes: 14%
- Provide an estate for spouse or children: 12%
- Become rich: 12%
- Have guaranteed, fixed-return investments: 10%
- Start a business: 8%
- Make quick profits: 7%
- Provide for grandchildren's college expenses: 5%

Current Concerns

- Own health: 35%
- The price of gasoline: 34%
- Having enough money saved to retire comfortably: 29%
- Family's health: 28%
- Impact of Obamacare: 28%
- Economy going into recession: 24%
- Out of work and finding a job: 19%
- Inflation: 19%
- Political gridlock in D.C.: 18%
- Resolving U.S. debt limit issue: 18%
- Moral decline: 18%
- Terrorism: 17%
- Crime: 15%
- Political corruption and financial scandals: 14%
- Poverty and social inequity: 14%
- Effective gun control: 13%
- The value of the U.S. dollar: 13%
- Taking care of parents: 13%
- Threats against the environment: 11%
- Arranging a good education for children or grandchildren: 11%
- Climate change: 11%
- Able to afford to send children or grandchildren to college: 10%

72.7 Looking Ahead

A 2015 survey by Allianz Life (www.allianzlife.com) found that 68% of Gen Xers believe they will never have enough money saved to quit working; 67% feel the general financial targets considered necessary for retirement are not realistic.

Eighty-four percent (84%) of Gen Xers say that stopping work at age 65 and retreating to a life of leisure is a bygone fantasy.

"Gen Xers, many of whom are saddled with student loan debt and whose prime working years fell during the Great Recession, are doubtful about their financial future."

USA Today

Despite the financial challenges, 53% of Gen Xers believe "everything is going to work out," 46% say they will "just figure it out when I get there."

73

MILLENNIAL CONSUMERS

73.1 Profile

Most analysts classify those born from 1980 thru 2000, a span of 20 years, as the Millennial generation (also known as Generation Y or Echo Boomers). In 2016, Millennials spanned ages 16 through 36.

Census 2010 counted 93.40 million Americans born between 1980 and 2000, representing 30.3% of the population.

The U.S. Census Bureau (www.census.gov) estimated the year-end 2015 Millennial population at 92.21 million.

Already the largest generation in the U.S., immigration will further boost the number of Millennials by 2020, according to the Census Bureau.

The ethnic makeup of the Millennials is as follows (source: U.S. Census Bureau):

- Caucasian: 61.0%
- Hispanic: 17.0%
- African American: 15.0%
- Asian: 3.4%
- Other: 3.6%

"Today's teens and young adults are quite the multi-cultural bunch. The 16-to-19, 20-to-26 and 27-to-36 groups are almost identically multi-cultural, as 42% of each comprises Hispanics, African Americans, and Asian Americans. This is only the tip of the iceberg – U.S. Census data shows that African Americans, Asian Americans, and Hispanics will generate the vast majority of the U.S. population growth over the next few decades."

Nielsen

The buying power of Millennials is estimated at $600 billion. Pew Research Center (www.pewresearch.org) estimated Millennial buying power at $2.45 trillion in 2015. In 2017, their buying power is projected to eclipse that of Baby Boomers.

In addition to the assessment of Millennials in this chapter, an assessment of college students is presented in Chapter 75.

According to a study by the Urban Land Institute (www.uli.org), Millennial residency is as follows:

- City neighborhood outside downtown: 34%
- Small city/town (population under 50,000): 19%
- Downtown/near downtown: 14%
- Dense, older suburb: 13%
- Newer, outlying suburb: 11%
- Rural community: 10%

73.2 Generational Characteristics

Analysts agree that Millennials differ in many ways from the Baby Boomers and Generation X that proceeded them: They were raised with the Internet and digital technologies and they multitask well. Millennials don't just embrace technology, for them it's a way of life.

Advertising Age provides the following characteristics of Millennials:

- Millennials spend almost 15 hours a day interacting with various media and communications technologies.
- More than one-half of Millennials talk on the phone regularly while watching television.
- Twenty percent (20%) of adult Millennials (ages 18-to-31) have at least 25 friends in their social network.
- Fifty-nine percent (59%) of Millennials spend at least an hour a day talking on their cellphones.
- Console gaming is, by far, the leading leisure activity for Millennial males. Watching television and talking on cellphones are most popular with Millennial females.
- Approximately 11 million Millennials are married – two-thirds of those who are married have children.
- Forty-five percent (45%) of Millennials refer to themselves as non-white.
- Eighty-four percent (84%) of Millennials believe that getting a college degree is important.
- Fifty-one percent (51%) of Millennials say it's important to volunteer for community service, and 48% have done so.

In its study *Millennials in Adulthood*, Pew Research Social & Demographic Trends found the following traits most common among the demographic:

- A full 50% of Millennials describe themselves as political independents, and 29% say they are not affiliated with any religion. These figures are the highest levels of political and religious disaffiliation recorded for any generation since Pew began its polling on the topics.

- Millennials have emerged into adulthood with low levels of social trust. Just 19% of Millennials surveyed said most people can be trusted. This compares with 31% of Gen Xers, 37% of Seniors, and 40% of Boomers.
- In spite of overwhelming financial burdens like under- and unemployment and substantial college debt, Millennials show the most optimism about their finances. Thirty-two percent (32%) say they have enough money to lead the lives they want and 52% expect to in the future. No other demographic group showed such optimism. Interestingly, 51% don't believe Social Security benefits will be available to them when they retire.

73.3 Impact Of The Great Recession

Many of the young adult Millennials who expected to be in the early stage of a career saw their plans derailed by the Great Recession.

Financial recovery was a slow process for many Millennials, but the majority were back on track by 2015.

The *General Social Survey*, published in November 2015 by the Census Bureau, reported that 54% of Millennials said their financial situation was getting better. This was an increase from 39% and 34% who said this in 2012 and 2010, respectively.

The national unemployment rate for adults ages 18-to-34 declined to 7.7% in the first third of 2015, a significant recovery from the 12.4% who were unemployed in 2010.

> **"Five years into the economic recovery, things are looking up for young adults in the U.S. labor market. Unemployment is down, full-time work is up and wages have modestly rebounded."**
>
> Pew Research Center, 7/29/15

73.4 Millennial Households

The term Boomerang Generation has been coined to reflect those young adults who have returned to their parents' home, many overburdened with student loan debt as well as unemployment. According to Pew Research Center, 24% of Millennials have moved back home at least once during or shortly after the Great Recession.

About 35% of Millennials head up their own household, according to Pew

Research Center. This rate is relatively unchanged since 2012 and even lower than the level observed in the depths of the Great Recession.

The number of young adults heading their own households is no higher in 2015 (25 million) than it was before the recession began in 2007 (25.2 million). In 2010, 69% of 18-to-34-year-olds lived independently. As of May 2015, only 67% of Millennials were living independently. Over the same time period, the share of young adults living in their parents' homes increased from 24% to 26%.

"In spite of these positive economic trends and the growth in the 18- to 34-year-old population, there has been no uptick in the number of young adults establishing their own households. This may have important consequences for the nation's housing market recovery, as the growing young adult population has not fueled demand for housing units and the furnishings, telecom and cable installations, and other ancillary purchases that accompany newly formed households."

Pew Research Center, 7/29/15

According to the Clark University *Poll Of Emerging Adults*, more people ages 18-to-29 live with their parents than with a spouse.

73.5 Affluent Millennials

While many Millennials are struggling with their careers and personal finances, others are achieving financial success.

In its report *The Rising Cost of Not Going to College*, Pew found incomes highest among college-educated Millennials. A comparison of those ages 25-to-32 with and without a bachelor's degree shows median household incomes of $89,079 and $39,942, respectively. With each passing generation, the difference in income grows, the variance is 20% between Millennials today.

International Demographics (www.themediaaudit.com) reported that 7.3 million households headed by an 18-to-34 year-old in the 81 largest metropolitan areas had an annual income in excess of $100,000.

Merrill Edge (www.merrilledge.com) reported that young adults (ages 18-to-34) in households with investable assets of between $50,000 and $250,000 began their retirement savings at an average age of 22. For comparison, Baby Boomers began saving, on average, at age 35. These Millennials say they plan to save an average of $2.5 million by retirement, considerably more ambitious than affluents ages 51-to-64, who anticipate saving $260,000. Among all adults in affluent households, the average retirement savings goal is $860,000.

The Merrill Edge survey found that 47% of affluent Millennial households with children are willing to cut back on family vacations in order to contribute to a college fund for their kids; 45% would forego purchasing a new car.

73.6 Shopping Attitudes

In a survey by the Urban Land Institute (www.uli.org), Millennials expressed their attitude toward shopping as follows:

	Female	Male
• Love to shop:	44%	29%
• Shop when necessary and enjoy it:	45%	51%
• Shopping is a necessary chore; I can deal with it:	9%	15%
• Hate shopping:	3%	5%

Still, shopping at bricks-and-mortar stores dominates among Millennials. The following are percentages based on retail formats they visit at least once a month (source: Urban Land Institute):

- Discount department stores: 91%
- Neighborhood and community shopping centers: 74%
- Enclosed malls: 64%
- Full-line department stores: 64%
- Big-box power centers: 63%
- Chain apparel stores: 58%
- Neighborhood business districts: 54%

In a survey by DDB Worldwide (www.ddb.com), adults ages 18-to-24 profiled their e-commerce activities as follows:

	Female	Male
• Ideally would buy everything online:	33%	40%
• Typically shop on auction sites:	31%	43%
• Typically use shopping apps on mobile phone:	28%	30%
• Typically use retail store apps:	24%	27%
• An extreme couponer:	23%	22%
• Have requested a price match using mobile phone:	21%	25%
• Typically use mobile phone to scan and find the best price in town for a specific item:	20%	25%
• Typically shop for and buy items on mobile phone:	19%	24%

73.7 Use Of Digital Media

According to eMarketer (www.emarketer.com), 96% of Millennials used the Internet at year-end 2015; 74% had home broadband; 82% owned a smartphone.

At year-end 2015, Millennials had social media accounts as follows (source: Harvard University Institute for Politics):

- Facebook: 81%
- Instagram: 46%
- Twitter: 38%
- Snapchat: 36%
- Pinterest: 34%
- Tumblr: 14%

By demographic, Millennial social media users were as follows:

	Facebook	Instagram	Twitter	Snapchat	Pinterest	Tumblr
Gender						
• Female:	83%	56%	40%	42%	55%	19%
• Male:	79%	35%	37%	31%	12%	9%
Age						
• 18-to-24:	82%	50%	42%	46%	34%	19%
• 25-to-35:	81%	39%	34%	24%	33%	8%
Race/Ethnicity						
• Caucasian:	83%	41%	38%	40%	38%	14%
• African-American:	78%	55%	45%	25%	27%	11%
• Hispanic:	77%	49%	32%	34%	28%	15%

74

GENERATION Z CONSUMERS

74.1 Profile

The generation born in or after 2001 has been dubbed 'Generation Z.' They are also simply called 'youth.' Youth ages 10-to-12 are often referred to as tweens; teens are ages 13-to-17.

The U.S. Census Bureau (www.census.gov) estimated the year-end 2015 Generation Z population at 65.26 million.

The ethnic distribution of Generation Z is as follows (source: Census Bureau):

- Caucasian/White: 52.4%
- Hispanic/Latino: 24.1%
- African American/Black: 13.8%
- Asian American: 4.6%
- Multiracial: 4.0%
- American Indian/Alaskan Native: 0.9%
- Native Hawaiian/Pacific Islander: 0.2%

"Society is starting to obsess over the next generation that will define American culture. Marketers and academics are turning attention to this group, which has billions in buying power and is already shaping the culture."

Time, 1/4/16

74.2 Activities

The National Center for Education Statistics (http://nces.ed.gov) reported that 50.1 million students attended public elementary and secondary schools in the 2015-2016 academic year. Of these, 35.2 million were in pre-kindergarten through grade 8, and 14.9 million were in grades 9 through 12. Roughly 4.9 million students attended private schools.

According to *Beyond The Classroom*, by the Census Bureau, 57% of children ages 6-to-17 years old participate in at least one after-school extracurricular activity. Children are most likely to participate in sports (35%), clubs (29%), and lessons like music, dance and language (29%).

According to the *National Youth Fitness Survey*, by the National Center for Health Statistics (NCHS, www.cdc.gov/nchs), just 24.8% of youths ages 12-to-15 engage in moderate to vigorous physical activity at least 20 minutes a day, both inside and outside of school.

74.3 Spending Behaviors

Youth buying power is challenging to assess because personal spending by teens and tweens, by parents on their behalf, and spending for general costs of raising a family are intertwined.

Mintel (www.mintel.com) estimates that 8-to-12 year olds are spending an estimated $30 billion of their own money and $150 billion of their parents' money annually.

Packaged Facts (www.packagedfacts.com) estimates annual spending by U.S. teens at $250 billion. Other estimates of teen spending are up to $400 billion.

Piper Jaffrey (www.piperjaffrey.com) conducts semi-annual surveys of teens about their spending. According to their report *Taking Stock With Teens*, annual spending by teens for fashion goods is about $1,100.

Taking Stock With Teens reported the spending mix by category as follows:

- Clothing: 20%
- Food: 22%
- Accessories/personal care: 10%
- Car: 7%
- Shoes: 9%
- Electronics: 8%
- Video games: 7%
- Music/movies: 6%
- Concerts/movies/events: 6%
- Books/magazines: 2%
- Furniture: 1%
- Other: 3%

The following are other findings of *Taking Stock With Teens - Spring 2016*:

- Restaurants represented 22% of overall spending for upper-income teens; overall teens are choosing limited-service concepts at a 50% greater rate than full-service concepts.
- Teens are spending more time on Netflix and YouTube compared with traditional TV. The amount of time they spend on these websites combined equates to 66%

versus traditional TV at 26%.

- The only two categories that exceed male teen spending on video games (13%) are food (20%) and clothing (15%).
- The beauty category's wallet share among upper-income females reached 10%, the highest value in 10 years.

"The rise of Generation Z is good news for retailers."

Rascher Press, 4/18/16

The majority of teens report that they are saving money for a specific purpose. Fifty-seven percent (57%) say they are saving for clothes, 51% are saving for college, and 36% are saving for a car.

74.4 Use Of Media

According to Nielsen (www.nielsen.com), the monthly time youth, by age, spend using media is as follows (hours:minutes):

	2-11	12-17
• Traditional TV:	102:54	86:39
• Time-shifted TV:	10:40	8:21
• DVD/Blu-Ray:	8:12	4:33
• Game console:	12:31	17:52
• Multimedia device:	1:57	1:22
• Internet on a computer:	4:49	6:47
• Video on the Internet:	6:16	6:20
• AM/FM radio:	n/a	36:05

According to a 2015 report by Pew Research Center (www.pewinternet.org), 87% of teenagers have access to a desktop or laptop computer, 81% to a gaming console, and 58% to a tablet computer. Sixty-eight percent (68%) of teens ages 13 and 14 have a smartphone; 76% of those ages 15-to-17 own one.

In 2015, teens used social media platforms as follows (percentage of all teens ages 13-to-17):

- Facebook: 71%
- Instagram: 52%
- Snapchat: 41%
- Twitter: 33%

- Google+: 33%
- Vine: 21%
- Tumblr: 14%
- Other: 11%

74.5 Market Resources

KidSay, 804 N. Meadowbrook Drive, Suite 116, Olathe, KS 66062. (913) 390-8110. (www.kidsay.com)

KidzEyes and *TeenEyes*, C+R Research Services, 500 North Michigan Avenue, Chicago, IL 60611. (312) 828-9200. (www.crresearch.com)

Taking Stock With Teens, Piper Jaffrey, 800 Nicollet Mall, Suite 1000, Minneapolis, MN 55402. (800) 333-6000. (www.piperjaffrey.com/teens)

PART XII: SEGMENTATION

75

COLLEGE STUDENTS

75.1 Student Population

According to the National Center for Education Statistics (NCES, www.nces.ed.gov), 20.2 million students attended U.S. colleges and universities for the 2015-2016 academic year, constituting an increase of about 4.9 million since fall 2000. College enrollment peaked at 20.4 million with the 2011-2012 academic year. The following is the distribution of students:

Gender
- Female: 11.5 million
- Male: 8.7 million

Age
- Under 25 years: 12.2 million
- 25 years and older: 8.2 million

Curriculum
- Full-time: 12.6 million
- Part-time: 7.6 million

Institutions
- Two-year institutions: 7.0 million
- Four-year institutions: 13.2 million

Program
- Undergraduate: 17.3 million
- Postbaccalaureate: 3.0 million

Increases in the traditional college-age population and rising enrollment rates have contributed to the increase in college enrollment. Between 2000 and 2013, the 18- to 24-year-old population rose from approximately 27.3 million to approximately 31.5 million. The percentage of 18- to 24-year-olds enrolled in college also was higher in 2013 (39.9%) than in 2000 (35.5%).

NCES projects enrollment to increase to 22.6 million by the 2023-2024 academic year.

During the 2015-2016 academic year, colleges and universities awarded 952,000 associate's degrees, 1.8 million bachelor's degrees, 802,000 master's degrees, and 179,000 doctor's degrees.

College students' residency for the 2015-2016 school year was as follows (source: Prosper Business Development [www.goprosper.com]):

- At home: 47.7%
- Off campus apartment or housing: 24.0%
- Dorm room or college housing: 22.5%
- Fraternity or sorority house: 4.0%

The Institute of International Education (www.iie.org) reports that about 260,000 U.S. students study abroad.

Enrollments of foreign students at U.S. institutions is approximately 690,000. An estimated $20 billion is pumped into the U.S. economy as a result.

75.2 Spending

The *2015 College Explorer Study*, conducted by Crux Research (www.cruxresearch.com) for re:fuel (www.refuelnow.com), estimated that the 21.6 million students that began classes in Fall 2015 had $523 billion in total spending power. This spending included $203 billion in discretionary spending and $320 billion in non-discretionary spending (on items such as tuition, room & board and books & supplies).

Discretionary spending was distributed as follows:

- Food: $51.8 billion
- Automotive: $28.3 billion
- Clothing and shoes: $21.2 billion
- Desktop/laptop: $20.0 billion
- Cellphone/smartphone: $16.7 billion
- Other technology: $14.7 billion
- Video games: $12.5 billion
- Entertainment: $12.5 billion
- Personal care products: $12.1 billion
- Cosmetics: $ 7.4 billion
- Printers: $ 5.5 billion

Food expenditures were distributed as follows:

- Grocery stores: 50%
- Restaurants: 32%
- Convenience stores: 18%

During a typical month in the 2015-2016 academic year, college students visited retail and leisure destinations as follows (average number of visits per month):

- Grocery store: 5.9
- Quick-service restaurant: 5.7
- Gym/fitness center: 5.4
- Large retail store: 5.2

- Off-campus convenience store: 4.1
- Sit-down restaurant: 3.6
- Drug store: 3.4
- Apparel/clothing store: 2.9
- Campus bookstore: 2.6
- Electronics store: 1.5
- Video game store: 1.5
- Home improvement/DIY store: 1.3
- Health/nutrition store: 1.0

75.3 Financial Management

In a March 2016 survey by Sallie Mae (www.salliemae.com), college students assessed their ability to manage their personal finances as follows:

- Excellent: 24%
- Good: 41%
- Average: 29%
- Poor: 6%

Debt among students is as follows:

- Student loan: 52%
- Credit card debt: 23%
- Vehicle loan: 13%
- Mortgage: 9%
- Medical debt: 7%

To pay for purchases, 86% of students generally rely on cash, 85% carry a debit card, and 56% have a credit card.

75.4 Use Of Technology

On average, college students own 6.9 devices, with laptop computers topping ownership at 85%. Ownership of tech devices by college students is as follows (source: re:Fuel):

- Laptop computer: 85%
- Smartphone: 69%
- Videogame console: 68%
- MP3 player: 67%
- Printer: 62%
- Digital camera: 61%
- Flat screen TV: 60%
- Desktop computer: 48%
- Tablet computer: 36%

- Handheld gaming system: 35%
- Feature phone: 33%
- Camcorder/video recorder: 25%
- E-Reader: 21%
- TiVo/DVR: 18%

These wired students mostly use their devices for in-class note-taking and studying, but with 14.4 daily hours of multitasking across devices, entertainment runs a close second in usage. From downloading content to playing games to interacting on social networks, usage of a second screen is also popular with this demographic.

Nearly half (49%) of college students report daily usage of a second screen while watching television, with 63% using Facebook or Twitter, 58% surfing other online sites, 50% playing games, and 37% doing school work.

2015 College Explorer Study reported that students spend 141.6 hours per week with tech devices, a figure which includes multitaksing and use for studying, work, and leisure. Time spend by device is as follows:

- Cellphone/smartphone: 45.8 hours
- Computer: 40.1 hours
- Television: 22.5 hours
- Video game console: 11.3 hours
- Tablet: 10.5 hours
- Handheld gaming device: 6.9 hours
- eReader: 4.5 hours

75.5 Marketing To College Students

In a survey by Student Monitor (www.studentmonitor.com), students said they prefer the following methods to get information about products/services (percentage of respondents):

- Word-of-mouth: 48%
- Ad on the Internet: 39%
- Ad of TV: 31%
- Free samples in store: 29%
- Information on the Internet: 21%
- Email with information: 21%
- Online product reviews: 18%
- Ad on the radio: 17%
- Free gift with purchase: 16%
- Free samples distributed on campus: 16%
- Ad in magazine: 16%

Concentric Marketing (www.getconcentric.com) recently queried college students' views on various marketing topics. The following are some findings of the study:

- Nearly half of the 96% of college students with a Facebook account said they don't believe brands should be on social media. Seventy percent (70%) report following three or fewer brands across all social media channels.
- Forty-nine percent (49%) of college students said they stick with brands that they know and trust. Over 40% of those surveyed buy brands that are recommended by friends and family. Only 30% said that brands mean little and their purchase decisions are price driven. In terms of brand categories, survey participants reported feeling the most connections with clothing/apparel brands, followed closely by technology.
- Although college students are digitally adept and show a bias for convenience, they still prefer a traditional bricks-and-mortar shopping experience over e-commerce for the majority of their regular purchases.

75.6 Market Resources

2015 College Explorer Study, 15th Edition, re:fuel and Crux Research, June 2015.

National Center for Education Statistics, 1990 K Street NW, Washington, DC 20006. (202) 502-7300. (www.nces.ed.gov)

76

CONSUMERS WITH DISABILITIES

76.1 Profile

According to *Profile America*, from the U.S. Census Bureau (www.census.gov), 36 million people, or 12% of the U.S. population, have disabilities. By demographic, those with disabilities are as follows:

Gender

- Females: 12.3%
- Males: 11.6%

Age

- 5-to-17: 5.0%
- 18-to-64: 10.0%
- 65 and older: 37.0%

The percentage of people with various types of disabilities is as follows:

- Difficulty walking or climbing stairs: 19.4%
- Difficulty concentrating, remembering or making decisions: 13.5%
- Hearing: 10.2%
- Vision: 6.5%

Among those ages 16 and older with a disability, 72% are not in the workforce; 27% of the overall adult population is not in the workforce.

The National Data Program for the Sciences (www.norc.org) at the University of Chicago puts the number of people with a disability higher, estimating that 29% of adult Americans suffer from some disability; 8% have three or more conditions that restrict their ability to function. The most common limitation among the disabled is not being able to carry out basic physical activities like walking, lifting, or carrying things, which affects 16% of adults. This is followed by not being able to participate fully in regular daily activities and other physical disabilities (both 10%), difficulty remembering things (9%), a serious hearing loss (6%), a serious vision problem (5%), and a mental-health disability (5%).

WE Media (www.wemedia.com) estimates that 23 million parents in the U.S. have at least one child between the ages of 5 and 16 with special needs.

The Social Security Administration (www.ssa.gov) reported 4.6 million people under age 65 were receiving Supplemental Security Income because of disabilities as of May 2016.

76.2 Market Assessment

The special needs community has nearly $200 billion in discretionary spending, according to the U.S. Department of Labor, two times the spending power of teens and more than 17 times the spending power of tweens. Other estimates are even higher.

Americans with physical disabilities have combined discretionary income of more than $250 billion annually, and the 20 million families with at least one member with a disability represent additional annual disposable income of approximately $258 billion, according to W.C. Duke Associates (www.wcduke.com).

Fortune estimated that people with disabilities command approximately $1 trillion in household purchasing power.

> **"Handicapitalism. It's a term that describes what's behind a dawning realization in business: People with disabilities shouldn't be viewed as charity cases or regulatory burdens, but rather as profitable marketing targets. Now, mainstream companies, from financial services to cellphone makers, are going beyond what's mandated by law and rapidly tailoring products to attract them."**
>
> *The Wall Street Journal*

According to Open Doors Organization (ODO, www.opendoorsnfp.org) and the U.S. Travel Association (www.ustravel.org), people with disabilities spend $13.6 billion on 31.7 million trips annually. The airline industry sees $3.3 billion in annual spending by travelers with disabilities; spending in the lodging sector is $4.2 billion.

Seventy-one percent (71%) of adults with disabilities dine out at least once a week.

76.3 Marketing To People With Disabilities

Many large companies are raising their profile among people with disabilities. MetLife, for example, is reaching out to this community with a division dedicated to assisting families with special needs in planning for their futures. The company's integrated program includes a comprehensive website, strategic alliances with national non-profit organizations, and TV ads aired during prime-time that feature individuals with special needs. The program has won awards from the National Business & Disability Council (www.nbdc.com).

Still, while some 100 companies have aired commercials featuring people with disabilities, such ads are relatively rare.

The most recent Paralympic Games offered a marketing opportunity for companies. Official Sponsors and Partners included Adidas, Budweiser, Coca-Cola, Haier, Johnson & Johnson, McDonald's, Samsung, UPS, Visa, and Volkswagen.

Disability Matters, an annual conference hosted by Springboard Consulting (www.consultspringboard.com), brings together marketers that focus on marketing to people with disabilities. The 2016 Disability Matters conference was held April 19-21 in Durham, North Carolina.

76.4 Market Resources

Open Doors Organization, 8623 W. Bryn Mawr Avenue, Suite 508, Chicago, IL, 60631. (773) 388-8839. (www.opendoorsnfp.org)

Springboard Consulting, 14 Glenbrook Drive, Mendham, NJ 07945. (973) 813-7260. (www.consultspringboard.com)

77

FAMILIES WITH CHILDREN

77.1 Profile

According to the U.S. Census Bureau (www.census.gov), the are 34.7 million families (44%) with children under 18 living at home. At peak, 57% of families had children under 18 living at home – in 1953.

"The consequences of the ongoing 'Baby Bust' are readily apparent in the *2015 Current Population Survey*. The number of households with children under age 18 fell by 965,000 between 2014 and 2015 – a substantial 2.4% decline."

Demo Memo

Families And Living Arrangements, by the Census Bureau, reported households with children by ethnicity/race of householder as follows:

- Hispanic: 43%
- Asian-American: 36%
- African-American: 31%
- Caucasian: 25%

By generation of householder, *Families And Living Arrangements* reported households with children under age 18 as follows:

- Millennials: 47%
- Generation X: 56%
- Baby Boomers: 12%
- Older Americans: 1%

By income, the distribution of the nation's 74 million child-dwelling families is as follows (source: *Families And Living Arrangements*):

- In a family with an income below $25,000: 21%
- In a family with an income between $25,000 and $49,999: 21%
- In a family with an income between $50,000 and $99,999: 28%
- In a family with an income of $100,000 or more: 30%

The average number of people under age 18 per U.S. household has been as follows (source: Census Bureau):

- 1964: 1.24
- 1970: 1.09
- 1980: 0.79
- 1990: 0.69
- 2000: 0.69
- 2010: 0.64
- 2015: 0.60

Among families with children under 18 at home, there are 5.0 million stay-at-home moms and 154,000 stay-at-home dads.

Analysts estimate that more than 18 million young adults ages 20-to-34 live with their parents, representing about one-third of that age group.

Some five million American grandparents live with one of their grandchildren, according to the Census Bureau. Dubbed 'grandfamilies,' these households represent nearly 7% of American families.

For a great number of families now, the economy may be a factor in deciding family size, including whether to have children at all. The U.S. recorded 4.25 million live births in 2008 – the first full year of the recession – down about 68,000 from the prior year and the first annual decline in births since the start of the decade, according to the National Center for Health Statistics (NCHS, www.cdc.gov/nchs). The number of births declined further in 2009 to 4.13 million and to 3.95 million in 2012.

For comparison, the following number of U.S. women are projected to remain child free:

- 1 in 8 with high income
- 1 in 14 with middle income
- 1 in 20 with low income

In 1976, one in 10 women had no children; in 2014 that figure was one in five.

77.2 Working Parents

For most families with children under age 18, all parents in the household are employed. According to *Employment Characteristics of Families*, published in 2015 by the Bureau of Labor Statistics (www.bls.gov), employment status of parents with children living at home has been as follows:

Married couple families, both mother and father employed

- Total with children under age 18: 60.2%
- With children ages 6-to-17 only: 70.4%
- With children under age 6: 55.3%

Female-headed single-parent families, mother employed

- Total with children under age 18: 69.4%
- With children ages 6-to-17 only: 74.3%
- With children under age 6: 62.1%

Male-headed single-parent families, father employed

- Total with children under age 18: 81.9%
- With children ages 6-to-17 only: 81.3%
- With children under age 6: 82.7%

> **"Among the nation's children under age 15, only 20% live the *Leave it to Beaver* lifestyle – two parents, married, and a mother who does not work because she is caring for the family."**
>
> Demo Memo, 3/6/16

77.3 Cost Of Raising Children

The U.S. Department of Agriculture (www.usda.gov) has calculated estimates of expenditures for raising children. According to the most recent report, it will cost an estimated $304,480 for a middle-income couple to raise a child for 18 years, not including the cost of college.

Spending is distributed as follows:

- Housing: 30%
- Child care and education: 18%
- Food: 16%
- Transportation: 14%
- Healthcare: 8%
- Clothing: 6%
- Miscellaneous: 8%

Child-rearing expenses vary considerably by household income level. For a child in a two-child, two-spouse family, annual expenses ranged from $9,130 to $10,400, on average, (depending on age of the child) for households with before-tax income less than $61,530, from $12,800 to $14,970 for households with before-tax income between $61,530 and $106,540, and from $21,330 to $25,700 for households with before-tax income more than $106,540.

On average, households in the lowest income group spend 25% of their before-tax income on a child; those in the middle-income group spend 16%; and those in the highest group spend 12%.

Compared with expenditures on each child in a two-child, two-spouse family, expenditures by two-spouse households with one child average 25% more on the single child. Expenditures by households with three or more children average 22% less on each child.

Child-rearing expense patterns of single-parent households with a before-tax income less than $61,530 were 7% lower than those of two-spouse households in the same income group. Most single-parent households were in this income group (compared with about one-third of two-spouse families).

Annual expenditures for raising one, two, or three children, by age of the youngest child, are as follows:

	Married Family	Single-Parent Family
One-child Household		
• Age 2:	$16,180	$10,440
• Age 5:	$16,210	$11,620
• Age 8:	$16,000	$11,350
• Age 11:	$17,110	$12,150
• Age 14:	$18,030	$12,690
• Age 17:	$18,710	$12,330
Two-child Household*		
• Age 2:	$27,910	$17,360
• Age 5:	$27,940	$18,280
• Age 8:	$27,770	$18,070
• Age 11:	$28,650	$18,690
• Age 14:	$29,390	$19,110
• Age 15:	$29,940	$18,830

* Age of older child: 16

	Married Family	Single-Parent Family
Three-child Household*		
• Age 2:	$33,020	$20,720
• Age 5:	$33,040	$21,430
• Age 8:	$32,910	$21,270
• Age 11:	$33,590	$21,740
• Age 12:	$34,170	$22,070

* Age of older children: 13, 16

77.4 Shopping And Spending Characteristics

A survey by The Nielsen Company (www.nielsen.com) found that children accompany parents on about 13% of food shopping trips; their presence makes adult shoppers 150% more likely to buy seasonal items, like pumpkins and turkey.

According to *Parental Attitudes Toward Family-Friendly Establishments*, 75% of parents with young children deliberately seek out establishments that have child-accommodating amenities. Such amenities might include the availability of high chairs, child-friendly restrooms, or child activity centers.

77.5 Inter-Generational Households

According to *The Return of the Multi-Generational Family Household*, a report by the Social & Demographic Trends Project at Pew Research Center (www.pewsocialtrends.com), U.S. family households are distributed by generational category as follows:

- Two generations (parent and minor child/children): 47%
- One generation: 34%
- Multi-generational: 16%
- Other: 1%

According to the U.S. Census Bureau, the number of households with family and relatives other than children living in the household, and the increase since 2000, is as follows:

	Households	Increase
• Parents living in adult children's household:	3.6 million	62.7%
• Live-in brothers or sisters:	3.5 million	24.0%
• Other relatives in household:	3.3 million	65.0%
• Grandchildren in household:	5.8 million	10.6%

According to Amy Gover, a multi-generational issues expert at AARP (www.aarp.org), the most common multi-generational household is one with a grandparent as head of household with adult children that have moved in with their children, an arrangement usually spurred by the needs of one or both to combine resources and save money. The second most popular arrangement is a grandparent moving in with an adult child's family, usually for caregiving reasons.

Census 2010 counted 3.1 million children in the U.S. living without a parent in the household; 59% were living with grandparents.

Pew Research Center found that grandparents who are primary caregivers of grandchildren are relatively young: 67% are under age 60 and 13% are under 45.

There were also 6.2 million households in 2010 with non-relatives, including unmarried partners and roommates, an 8% increase from 2000.

According to Stephanie Coontz, Ph.D., a family history professor at Evergreen State College, a host of factors – among them higher housing costs and the struggling economy – is prompting families to combine expenses. Also, inter-generational households are common among the country's growing number of immigrants.

77.6 Stepfamilies

According to *A Portrait Of Stepfamilies*, a report by Pew Social & Demographic Trends Project, 42% of American adults have at least one step-relative in their family. Three-in-10 have a step- or half-sibling, 18% have a stepparent, and 13% have at least one stepchild.

> **"Several sweeping changes in the demography of American family life in the past half century – including increases in divorce and in the share of babies born out of wedlock – have contributed to the prevalence of step-relatives."**
>
> Pew Research Center

Seventy percent (70%) of adults who have at least one step-relative say they are very satisfied with their family life. Those who don't have any step-relatives register slightly higher levels of family satisfaction (78% very satisfied).

People with step-relatives are just as likely as others to say that family is the most important element of their life. However, they typically feel a stronger sense of obligation to their biological family members (be it a parent, a child or a sibling) than to their step-relatives, according to Pew surveys.

77.7 Market Trends: Adult Children At Home

According to an analysis of Census Bureau data by Pew Research Center, a record 21.6 million Millennial adults (those ages 18-to-34) live in their parents' home, an increase from 18.5 million for youth of the same age in 2007. It should be noted that between one-third and half of this group are college students, and some students reside in dormitories during the academic year. Nonetheless, this is the highest share in at least four decades for this age group.

Among young adults ages 25-to-34, 10.7 million lived at home in 2014. This represents 25.2% of all in this age demographic. For comparison, 18.7% and 11.0% of 25-to-34 year olds lived at home in 2007 and 1980, respectively. In 2014 alone, 1.8 million young adults moved back home.

77.8 Centers For Family Research

Center for Economic Research On The Family, Clemson University, Sirrine Hall, Clemson, SC 29634. (www.clemson.edu/economics/cerf/index.html)

Center for Family & Demographic Research, Bowling Green State University, Five Williams Hall, Bowling Green, OH 43403. (419) 372-7279. (www.bgsu.edu/organizations/cfdr/)

Center for Family Research, University of Georgia, 1095 College Station Road, Athens, GA 30602. (706) 425-2992. (www.cfr.uga.edu)

Center for Family Studies, University of California Riverside, Olmstead Hall, 3rd Floor, Riverside CA, 92521. (http://familystudies.ucr.edu/)

Center for Marital and Family Studies, University of Denver, 2155 S. Race Street, Denver, CO 80208. (303) 871-3062. (www.du.edu/psychology/marriage/)

Center for Research on Families, University of Massachusetts, 135 Hicks Way, 622 Tobin Hall, Amherst, MA 01003. (413) 545-4631. (www.umass.edu/family/)

Family Research Center, University of North Carolina Greensboro, 536 Highland Avenue, Greensboro, NC 27402. (336) 334-3601. (www.uncg.edu/frc/)

78

FAMILY CAREGIVERS

78.1 Profile

According to the Pew Internet & American Life Project (www.pewinternet.org), 39% of U.S. adults provide care for a child or adult with significant health issues, an increase from 30% who did so in 2010.

According to Gallup (www.gallup.com), 35% of caregivers say the person receiving care lives with them. The ailments of the person receiving care are as follows:

- Non-specific age-related: 19%
- Alzheimer's disease/dementia: 15%
- Heart disease: 8%
- Type 2 diabetes: 7%
- Cancer: 7%
- Stroke/aneurysm: 5%
- Arthritis: 4%
- Memory decline: 3%
- COPD: 2%
- Eye disease: 2%
- Parkinson's disease: 2%
- Other: 17%

"More than one in six Americans who work a full- or part-time job also report assisting with care for an elderly or disabled family member, relative, or friend."

Gallup

The Alzheimer's Association (www.alz.org) estimates that over 10 million family members, friends, and neighbors provide unpaid care for a person with Alzheimer's disease or other dementia. Combined, they provide 8.4 billion hours of unpaid care annually, a contribution estimated at $89 billion.

A survey by the Health Resources and Services Administration (www.hrsa.gov), part of the U.S. Department of Health and Human Services, found that more than one-fifth of U.S. households with children have at least one child with special needs. For many of these families, much of the care the children receive is at-home family care.

78.2 Eldercare

According to *Unpaid Eldercare In The United States*, published in September 2015 by the Bureau of Labor Statistics, 16% of the U.S. population ages 15 and over, or 40.4 million people, provide unpaid eldercare. Among these people, 61% are employed, 47% are employed full-time, and 57% are female.

The following is a summary of the report:

- Individuals ages 45-to-64 are the most likely to provide eldercare (23%), followed by those ages 65 and over (17%).
- Nearly one-half of eldercare providers have provided care for two years or less, while 15% have provided care for 10 years or more.
- Seventy percent (70%) of eldercare providers care for only one person. Twenty-two percent (22%) of eldercare providers care for two people, and 7% care for three or more.
- Eighty-three percent (83%) of eldercare providers care only for people with whom they did not live.
- Twenty-two percent (22%) of all eldercare providers are parents with children under age 18 living with them.
- Over half of eldercare providers ages 15-to-34 care for a grandparent, while the majority of providers ages 35-to-64 care for a parent. Providers ages 65 and over are more likely than those in other age groups to care for a friend or neighbor.
- On a given day, 24% of providers engage in eldercare. Eldercare providers who are ages 65 and older are the most likely to provide care on a given day.
- There are 6.3 million eldercare providers who care solely for someone with whom they live. On average over all days – including days they did and did not provide care – these providers spend 2.8 hours per day providing care.
- Eldercare providers who care for a spouse or unmarried partner spend an average of 4.0 hours per day providing care (includes days they do and do not provide care).
- On days they provide eldercare, they spend an average of 3.2 hours in caregiving activities. Providers ages 65 and over spend the most time providing eldercare (4.4 hours), and providers ages 15-to-24 spend the least amount of time (1.1 hours).
- On weekend days of providing care, eldercare providers spend an average of 3.6 hours doing so. This compares to an average of 3.0 hours for those who provide care on weekdays.
- On days they provide eldercare, women spend more time providing this care than do men (3.5 hours compared with 2.7 hours).
- On days they provide care, 39% of eldercare providers engage in caregiving associated with household activities, spending on average 40 minutes per day in these activities. This includes 28% of providers who engage in eldercare associated

with food preparation and cleanup and 12% who provide eldercare associated with housework.

- Thirty-two percent (32%) of eldercare providers engage in caregiving associated with leisure and sports on days they provide care, spending 1.1 hours per day in these activities. This includes 20% of eldercare providers who engage in eldercare associated with socializing and communicating and 13% who provide care while watching TV.
- Women are more likely than men to provide eldercare associated with household activities on days they provide care (41% compared with 35%), whereas women and men are about equally likely to provide eldercare associated with leisure and sports (33% and 30%, respectively).
- There are 8.7 million eldercare providers whose children live with them. Of these parents, nearly one-third (32%) have a child under age 6, and the remainder (69%) are parents whose youngest child is between ages 6-to-17.
- Fifty percent (50%) of eldercare providers who are parents of children under the age of 18 provide care for their own parent.
- Most (78%) eldercare providers who are parents are employed, and 63% are employed full time. Eighty-five percent (85%) of caregiving fathers are employed full time, compared with 45% of mothers.
- Sixteen percent (16%) of eldercare providers who are parents have no spouse or unmarried partner present in the household.
- Eldercare providers who are parents are less likely to provide daily care than the overall population of eldercare providers (12% compared with 21%).

78.3 Demographics Of Caregivers

Caring for a loved one is an activity that cuts across most demographic groups, but is especially prevalent among adults ages 30-to-64, a group traditionally still in the workforce. By demographic, the percentages of adults who are caregivers are as follows (source:
Pew Internet & American Life Project):

Gender

- Female: 40%
- Male: 37%

Age

- 18-to-29: 36%
- 30-to-49: 42%
- 50-to-64: 44%
- 65 and older: 30%

Race/Ethnicity

- Black: 40%

- Caucasian: 39%
- Hispanic: 32%

Annual Household Income
- Less than $30,000: 36%
- $30,000 to $49,999: 38%
- $50,000 to $74,999: 46%
- $75,000 and higher: 43%

The percentages of adults who provide eldercare are as follows (source: Bureau of Labor Statistics):

Gender
- Female: 18%
- Male: 16%

Age
- 18-to-24: 12%
- 25-to-34: 10%
- 35-to-44: 13%
- 45-to-54: 23%
- 55-to-64: 22%
- 65 and older: 16%

Race/Ethnicity
- Black: 16%
- Caucasian: 17%
- Hispanic: 10%

Employment Status
- Full-time worker: 16%
- Part-time worker: 18%
- Not employed: 15%

78.4 The Cost Of Caregiving

According to Gallup, caregiving costs the U.S. economy about $25.2 billion per year in lost productivity. Caregivers report missing an average of 6.6 workdays per year because of caregiving responsibilities.

Caregiving In The U.S. - Needs, Issues and Insights, by the AARP Caregiving Advisory Panel (www.aarp.org/home-family/caregiving/caregiving-advisory-panel/), reported that 96% of caregivers influence decisions regarding the purchase of caregiving health products; 79% of caregivers purchase nearly all of those products.

AARP estimates that unpaid caregivers provide the equivalent of $350 billion worth of eldercare annually, more than total annual Medicare spending.

78.5 Support For Caregivers

There is evidence that caregivers experience considerable health issues as a result of their focus on caring for others. In the National Caregiver Survey by AARP and the National Alliance for Caregiving (www.caregiving.org), 31% of adult caregivers reported stress, anxiety, or depression.

A four-year study at University of Pittsburgh found caregiver mortality rates are 63% above those of non-caregivers. According to Prof. David W. Coon, Ph.D., at Arizona State University, the depression rate among caregivers is 23%.

Researchers at New York University School of Medicine reported that even a short period of counseling can have a long-term beneficial impact on the emotional well-being of caregivers.

Some employers are now offering eldercare programs aimed at the health and well-being of workers who also are caregivers. Raytheon, for example, offers employee caregiver seminars on self-care and emotional support. At Nike and Intel, Powerful Tools for Caregivers, a program developed by Legacy Health Systems (www.legacyhealth.org), is offered. IBM, Exxon Mobil, and Texas Instruments have funded development of an online version of Powerful Tools. Similarly, companies like PepsiCo, KPMG, and Northrop Grumman are offering services to caregivers that range from parent networks to Web seminars to financial planning. By encouraging workers who also have eldercare duties to take better care of themselves, employers hope not only to raise productivity, but also to scale down healthcare costs.

Retailers are also beginning to provide support. Kmart, for example, offers The Caregivers Marketplace, a cash-back program for the purchase of brand-name healthcare products commonly purchased by caregivers. It is the first program to assist family caregivers in managing everyday healthcare product expenses.

Some assisted-living facilities are also offering services for eldercare-giving families through "respite stay" programs, where the senior family member is signed up for a short-term stay. This allows caregivers time off for, say, vacation, or even for caring for their own major personal needs, like surgery, for example. Costs typically range from $150 to $200 daily and include meals, snacks, housekeeping, laundry, personal care assistance, and basic clinical care.

A specialized media sector also has evolved to serve this demographic – from publications like *Today's Caregiver*, with approximately 50,000 subscribers who pay $18 a year for the periodical, to *Exceptional Parents*, a publication for parents of special needs children, to a host of online resources.

78.6 Market Resources

AARP Caregiving Advisory Panel. (www.aarp.org/home-family/caregiving/caregiving-advisory-panel/)

Family Caregiver Alliance, 785 Market Street, Suite 750, San Francisco, CA 94103. (415) 434.3388. (www.caregiver.org)

National Alliance for Caregiving, 4720 Montgomery Lane, 2nd Floor, Bethesda, MD 20814. (www.caregiving.org)

Unpaid Eldercare In The United States, Bureau of Labor Statistics, September 2015. (www.bls.gov/news.release/pdf/elcare.pdf)

79

IMMIGRANT CONSUMERS

79.1 Profile

Statistical Portrait of the Foreign-Born Population in the United States, published in April 2016 by Pew Research Center (www.pewresearch.org), provides the following assessment:

- Foreign-born population: 42,235,749
- U.S. citizenship: 47.3%
- Speaking English at least very well (ages 5 and older): 50.4%
- Median age: 43 years
- Female: 51.3%
- Male: 48.7%
- Married (ages 18 and older): 7.5%
- Women ages 15-to-44 giving birth in past year: 52.4%
- High school graduate or less: 28.6%
- Bachelor's degree or more: 66.3%
- In labor force: $26,000
- Median annual earnings (among those with earnings): $49,071
- Median annual household income: 86.4%
- In family households: 17.7%
- Living in poverty:

Census 2010, by the U.S. Census Bureau (www.census.gov), reported that 12.5% of the population (38.52 million people) was foreign-born. This count does not include undocumented immigrants, of which there is an estimated 12 million living in the United States.

The immigrant population in the U.S. peaked in 2007, when 12.7% of the total population was foreign-born. Prior to 2007, the foreign-born population of the United States had continuously increased in size and as a percentage of the total population for almost five decades: from 9.6 million, or 4.7%, in 1970 to 14.1 million, or 6.2%, in 1980, 19.8 million, or 7.9%, in 1990, and 31.1 million, or 11.1%, in 2000.

The nativity region of the U.S. foreign-born population is distributed as follows:

- Latin America: 53.1%
- Asia: 27.7%
- Europe: 12.7%
- Africa: 3.9%
- Other regions: 2.7%

The foreign-born population is distributed by country of birth as follows:

- Mexico: 29.8%
- China: 5.2%
- Phillippines: 4.5%
- India: 4.3%
- El Salvador: 3.0%
- Vietnam: 3.0%
- Korea: 2.6%
- Cuba: 2.6%
- Canada: 2.1%
- Guatemala: 2.1%
- Dominican Republic: 2.1%
- All other countries: 38.8%

Residency of the foreign-born population in 2010, by state, was as follows:

- Alabama: 147,000
- Alaska: 49,000
- Arizona: 925,000
- Arkansas: 120,000
- California: 9.95 million
- Colorado: 487,000
- Connecticut: 460,000
- Delaware: 74,000
- District of Columbia: 72,000
- Florida: 3.48 million
- Georgia: 920,000
- Hawaii: 224,000
- Idaho: 98,000
- Illinois: 1.74 million
- Indiana: 281,000
- Iowa: 116,000
- Kansas: 171,000
- Kentucky: 128,000
- Louisiana: 152,000
- Maine: 44,000
- Maryland: 730,000
- Massachusetts: 943,000
- Michigan: 614,000
- Minnesota: 358,000
- Mississippi: 60,000
- Missouri: 213,000
- Montana: 19,000
- Nebraska: 106,000
- Nevada: 507,000

- New Hampshire: 68,000
- New Jersey: 1.76 million
- New Mexico: 196,000
- New York: 4.18 million
- North Carolina: 665,000
- North Dakota: 15,000
- Ohio: 433,000
- Oklahoma: 190,000
- Oregon: 367,000
- Pennsylvania: 691,000
- Rhode Island: 133,000
- South Carolina: 205,000
- South Dakota: 22,000
- Tennessee: 266,000
- Texas: 3.98 million
- Utah: 218,000
- Vermont: 21,000
- Virginia: 806,000
- Washington: 811,000
- West Virginia: 23,000
- Wisconsin: 256,000
- Wyoming: 17,000

In 2010, the following states had the highest percentages of foreign-born population:

- California: 25.8%
- New York: 10.8%
- Texas: 10.3%
- Florida: 9.0%
- New Jersey: 4.6%
- Illinois: 4.5%
- Massachusetts: 2.4%
- Arizona: 2.4%
- Georgia: 2.4%
- Washington: 2.1%
- Virginia: 2.1%
- All other states: 23.4%

The annual number of naturalizations generally has risen over the past few decades. In 2015, 729,995 foreign-born residents of the United States became naturalized citizens. Asia was the leading region of birth for naturalized citizens, with 35% of the total. Mexico was the leading country of birth (13% of all naturalizations), followed by India, Philippines, Dominican Republic, and China. The median age of newly naturalized citizens was 40.

79.2 Second-Generation Americans

According to *Second-Generation Americans: A Portrait of the Adult Children of Immigrants*, a report by the Pew Research Social & Demographic Trends Project (www.pewsocialtrends.org), there are 20 million adults born in the U.S. who have at least one immigrant parent. The adult second generation is young (median age 38, compared with 46 for U.S. adults overall) and has no racial or ethnic majority group.

Among the key measures on which the second generation U.S.-born adults are better off than immigrant adults: Their median adjusted annual household income and home ownership rates are higher. They are more likely to hold a college degree. The share in poverty is lower. On all these measures, second generation adults are at least as well off as the overall adult population

79.3 U.S.-Born Children

The 14th Amendment to the U.S. Constitution grants an automatic right to citizenship to anyone born in the U.S.

The Pew Research Hispanic Trends Project (www.pewhispanic.org) estimated 340,000 of the four million babies born each year in the United States are the offspring of unauthorized immigrants.

Unauthorized immigrants comprise slightly more than 4% of the adult population of the U.S., but because they are relatively young and have high birthrates, their children make up a much larger share of both the newborn population (8%) and the child population (7% of those younger than age 18) in the U.S.

Of the 5.1 million children (younger than age 18) of unauthorized immigrants, 79% were born in this country and therefore are U.S. citizens. In total, four million U.S.-born children of unauthorized immigrant parents reside in the U.S.; there are 1.1 million foreign-born children of unauthorized immigrant parents.

79.4 Life In The U.S.

A Place to Call Home: What Immigrants Say Now About Life in America, a study by Public Agenda (www.publicagenda.org), asked immigrants their feelings about their lives in the United States. Responses were as follows:

- Somewhat happy: 53%
- Extremely happy: 34%
- Generally disappointed: 10%

When asked if they could do it over again, or what would be their choice, responses were as follows:

- Come to the United States: 71%
- Stay in birth country: 19%
- Pick a different country: 6%
- Don't know: 3%

There are an estimated 1.5 million immigrant-owned U.S. businesses, according to a study for the Small Business Association (www.sba.gov). In all, immigrants own 12.5% of U.S. businesses and account for 11.6% of all small business income.

79.5 Assimilation

Measuring assimilation is challenging because it is difficult to define. For some, it's the ability to speak English or the willingness to become a U.S. citizen. With others, it may be as superficial as appearance or style of dress. Others, still, maintain aspects of their native culture in private while displaying traits of American culture in public.

According to the Census Bureau, English proficiency among the 41 million foreign-born population living in the United States is as follows:

- Very proficient in English: 49.9%
- Speak a language other than English at home but speak English very well: 34.5%
- Speak English but not well: 19.3%
- Speak only English at home: 15.4%
- Do not speak English at all: 9.6%

More than 80% of immigrants say they have tried to learn English. Among Spanish-speaking immigrants residing in the U.S. for more than 15 years, 75% speak English regularly; 91% of their children and 97% of their grandchildren can speak English well, according to the Anti-Defamation League (www.adl.org).

A study by the Manhattan Institute for Policy Research (MIRP, www.manhattan-institute.org) assessed how well immigrants fit in with native-born Americans in three areas: economic, cultural, and civic. The assessment, which was directed by Prof. Jacob L. Vigdor, Ph.D., Public Policy Studies and Economics at Duke University, found that the nation's immigrants are adopting American ways just as quickly as they were in 1990, despite a doubling in their numbers. This contrasts with the historical trend that the level of assimilation typically drops during times of high immigration because there are more newcomers who are different from native-born Americans. This happened, for example, between 1900 and 1920, when the immigrant population grew by 40% and assimilation occurred more slowly. The MIRP study found, however, that Mexicans, the largest immigrant group, are making slower progress at assimilating than others. While assimilating well culturally, Mexicans have a low civic assimilation.

79.6 Future Growth

According to Pew Research Center, if current trends continue, the population of the United States will rise to 438 million in 2050, from 296 million in 2005, with 82% of the increase from new immigrants and their U.S.-born descendants. Of the 117 million people added to the population during this period, 67 million will be first-generation immigrants, and 50 million will be their U.S.-born children or grandchildren.

The following are other projections:

- Nearly one in five Americans (19%) will be an immigrant in 2050, compared with one in eight (12%) in 2005. By 2025, the immigrant, or foreign-born, share of the population will surpass the peak of the last great wave of immigration a century before.
- The major role of immigration in national growth builds on the pattern of recent decades, during which immigrants and their U.S.-born children and grandchildren accounted for most of the population increase.
- The Latino population, already the nation's largest minority group, will triple in size and will account for most of the nation's population growth from 2005 through 2050. Hispanics will make up 29% of the U.S. population in 2050, compared with 14% in 2005.
- Births in the United States will play a growing role in Hispanic and Asian population growth; as a result, a smaller proportion of both groups will be foreign-born in 2050 than now.

79.7 Market Resources

Center for Immigration Studies, 1522 K Street NW, Suite 820, Washington, DC 20005. (202) 466-8185. (www.cis.org)

Pew Research Hispanic Trends Project, 1615 L Street NW, Suite 700, Washington, DC 20036. (202) 419-3600. (www.pewhispanic.org)

Migration Policy Institute, 1400 16th Street NW, Suite 300, Washington, DC 20036. (202) 266-1940. (www.migrationpolicy.org)

80

LGBT CONSUMERS

80.1 Profile

Between 6% and 7% of the adult U.S. population self-identifies as lesbian, gay, bisexual, and transgender (LGBT), suggesting that there is a LGBT adult population of 15 million to 16 million in the U.S. Some estimates, however, place the number of LGBT people at up to 30 million, or roughly 10% of adults. Unlike estimates of other populations, the LGBT population generally includes adults over the age of 18 – the age when a person is more likely to be fully aware and able to define sexual orientation or gender identity.

A study directed by Prof. Amy Falkner, an associate dean at the S.I. Newhouse School of Public Communications at Syracuse University, provides the following facts about LGBT households:

- Twenty-one percent (21%) of females and nearly 5% of males have a child under age 18 living at home.
- Eleven percent (11%) of males and 8% of females have a child or children ages 18 and older.
- Four percent (4%) of males and 8% of females are grandparents.
- Seventy-seven percent (77%) of males and 73% of females are employed full-time.
- Twelve percent (12%) of males and 15% of females work for a government entity.
- Thirty-seven percent (37%) are employed at a company providing domestic-partner health benefits.
- Twelve percent (12%) of male and 9% of female households own a second home.
- Ninety-seven percent (97%) of gay Americans are out to their families, friends, or at work; 85% are out to family, 95% to friends, and 74% at the workplace.
- Fifty-three percent (53%) of females are partnered, as are 42% of males, with the largest percentage together four to seven years.
- Thirty-two percent (32%) of males and 66% of females plan on adding children to their family in the next three years.
- Fifty-seven percent (57%) of males and 45% of females live in cities.

A study by Gary J. Gates, Ph.D., of the Williams Institute at the University of California at Los Angeles (www.law.ucla.edu/williamsinstitute/), based on the Census Bureau's *American Community Survey*, found that 31% of same-sex households who identify themselves as spouses are raising children, compared with 43% of hetrosexual households.

Transgender people – those who identify with a gender other than that which they were assigned at birth – number about 1.5 million, or 0.5% of the U.S. population.

80.2 Coming Out Survey

According to a survey by The Harris Poll (www.theharrispoll.com) in conjunction with Witeck Communications (www.witeck.com), a large majority of gay and lesbian adults are "out" and honest with others about their sexual orientation. The survey showed that four out of five (80%) gay and lesbian adults consider themselves "out" as a gay or lesbian person.

In terms of their relationships, 95% of gay and lesbian adults consider themselves open about their sexual orientation to their close friends. Seventy-nine percent (79%) of gay and lesbian adults consider themselves open about their sexual orientation with their acquaintances/casual friends. When it comes to the workplace, a significant majority (67%) of gay and lesbian adults reported being open about their sexual orientation with their co-workers/colleagues.

Among heterosexuals, 87% said that if someone were to come out to them as gay, lesbian, bisexual, or transgender, it would have a positive impact or no impact on how they would view gay, lesbian, bisexual, or transgender people. Also, 67% agree that if someone they knew was gay or lesbian, they'd want that individual to be open and honest with them about it, rather than feel the need to hide who he or she really is.

A 2015 survey by Pew Research Center (www.pewresearch.org) found that 52% of adults have close friends or family members that are gay or lesbian.

80.3 Same-Sex Marriage

Anyone who had reported being married to someone of the same gender in the 2000 Census was reclassified as an "unmarried partner." The Bureau changed its survey and Census 2010 reported 131,729 married same-sex couples. Of the 646,454 reporting same-sex households, 514,735 consider themselves partnered rather than married.

In June 2015, the Supreme Court expanded same-sex marriage rights across the U.S. At the time of the ruling, 35 states had already enacted legislation allowing same-sex marriage.

Public opinion polls about gay marriage skew toward increased support for legalization of gay marriage. A May 2016 poll by Gallup found support for gay marriage at 68%, a record high, and more than double the support of 27% Gallup first measured when the question was asked in 1996.

80.4 Buying Power

Witeck Communications estimated adult LGBT buying power at $884 billion in 2015.

Although past studies have portrayed the LGBT community as an affluent subgroup, more recent findings suggest they are probably no better off than heterosexual consumers. Research at the University of Maryland found that, on average, partnered gay males earn $10,000 less annually than straight married men. Partnered lesbians, however, generally earn $7,000 a year more than straight married women. But one key difference influencing disposable income is that gays and lesbians, collectively, have fewer children.

"Buying power is not the same as wealth. There is no evidence that same-sex households are more affluent or, on average, earn more than others, which is little more than a stereotype. We recognize economic research that strongly suggests that gay men appear likely to earn slightly less than their heterosexual counterparts, for instance and that LGBT populations of color particularly face many job and earnings barriers."

Bob Witeck, CEO
Witeck Communications

A recent survey conducted by The Nielsen Company (www.nielsen.com) found that spending power aside, U.S. same-sex partnered households make 16% more shopping trips than the average U.S. household (173 average shopping trips vs. 149 average shopping trips for total U.S. households).

These additional trips result in CPG spending of $8,651 vs. $6,898, with m/m households making 182 shopping trips compared to f/f households making 163 trips.

Buy rates for same-sex households for select CPG products are as follows:

Female/Female Purchase Index

- Pet care: 132
- Butter and margarine: 128
- Coffee: 125
- Cat food: 125
- Frozen novelties: 123
- Gum: 123
- Yogurt: 122
- Paper products: 121
- Frozen baked goods: 121

- Fresh produce: 121
- Vitamins: 119
- Flour: 119
- Salad dressing: 119
- Nuts: 119

Male/Male Purchase Index
- Liquor/beer/wine: 222
- Men's toiletries: 190
- Refrigerated meal starters: 173
- Coffee: 173
- Fresheners and deodorizers: 164
- Dog food: 163
- Oral Hygiene: 156
- Medications and remedies: 152
- Pet Care: 150
- Yogurt: 149
- Shaving needs: 147
- Nuts: 146
- Vitamins: 145
- Frozen novelties: 144
- Dairy snacks and spreads: 141

80.5 Population Centers

According to real-estate site Trulia (www.trulia.com), the following are the ZIP codes with the most gay residents:

Same-sex Female Couples
- 02657 (Provincetown, Cape Cod, MA)
- 01062 (Northhampton, MA)
- 01060 (Northhampton, MA)
- 02160 (Jamaica Plain, Boston, MA)
- 19971 (Rehoboth Beach, DE)
- 95446 (Guernville, north of San Francisco, CA)
- 02667 (Wellfleet, Cape Cod, MA)
- 94619 (Redwood Heights/Skyline, Oakland, CA)
- 30002 (Avondale Estates, suburban Atlanta, GA)
- 94114 (Castro, San Francisco, CA)

Same-sex Male Couples
- 94114 (Castro, San Francisco, CA)
- 92264 (Palm Springs, CA)
- 02657 (Provincetown, Cape Cod, MA)

- 92262 (Palm Springs, CA)
- 33305 (Wilton Manors, Fort Lauderdale, FL)
- 90069 (West Hollywood, Los Angeles, CA)
- 75219 (Oak Lawn, Dallas, TX)
- 19971 (Rehoboth Beach, DE)
- 48069 (Pleasant Ridge, suburban Detroit, MI)

"The best available Census data on same-sex couples supports the understanding that LGBT households skew into major metro and suburban areas."

Bob Witeck, CEO
Witeck Communications

Of all same-sex households, 51% are female couples and 49% are male couples, which means that of all U.S. households 0.3% are male couples and 0.3% of are female couples.

Some neighborhoods are found to have a concentration of same-sex couples more than 10 times that national average.

Conceived of by Bonnie McGowan in 1999, Birds of a Feather, in Pecos, New Mexico, which opened in 2004, is the first retirement community to open that was specifically developed for LGBT older adults. There are also communities in Portland, Oregon, and Fort Myers, Florida, and similar projects are underway in Philadelphia, Chicago, San Francisco, and Minneapolis.

According to Services & Advocacy for GLBT Elders (SAGE, www.sageusa.org), there are currently between 1.75 million and 4 million gays and lesbians over age 65, numbers that are expected to double by 2030. Today, living in an LGBT-retirement community is an option for this group.

About 49% of Americans older than 65 considered poor or low-income, and this includes LGBT seniors. As such, the issue of affordable housing is critical to this demographic.

At the other end of the economic spectrum are wealthy gay couples. Catering to this market is Fountaingrove Lodge in Santa Rosa, California, with high-end amenities and luxury residences priced up to $1 million. There is an upscale restaurant on site.

80.6 Activities

According to Community Marketing, Inc. (CMI, www.communitymarketing.com), the following are percentages of gay and lesbian consumers who regularly engage in various activities:

	Lesbians	Gay Men
• Dine out with friends:	90%	88%
• Attend a concert:	32%	24%
• Go to a club or bar:	31%	50%
• Go to the movies:	28%	40%
• Attend live theater:	26%	39%
• Visit a museum:	18%	24%

One major area recognized as an outlet for the discretionary income spent by the LGBT community is travel. According to the *20th Annual LGBT Tourism Study*, published in December 2015 by Community Marketing, the annual economic impact of LGBT travelers is over $100 billion, about 10% of the U.S. travel market.

Approximately 85% of the LGBT community take annual vacations, compared with a national average of 64%. More than one-third take three or more trips. Almost 50% travel abroad, compared with the national average of 9%.

Similar to all travelers, location and price are key factors when LGBT travelers select a hotel, but an "LGBT friendly" reputation is also an important motivator.

Further, the CMI survey estimates that 79% of LGBTs in the United States hold a valid passport, which translates into a significant amount of potential international travel, and compares to about 39% of the U.S. population overall holding a passport, according to the U.S. State Department.

80.7 Internet Usage

According to eMarketer (www.emarketer.com), the following are the leading media activities of U.S. gay and lesbian Internet users:

	Gay males	Lesbians
• LGBT sites/blogs:	67%	58%
• Network/cable TV:	68%	57%
• Mainstream sites/blogs:	57%	46%
• Mainstream general newspapers:	55%	46%
• LGBT email newsletters:	41%	45%
• LGBT pubs for my city or region:	50%	42%
• Mainstream radio:	41%	39%
• Mainstream magazines:	43%	34%
• LGBT national magazines(s):	38%	30%
• Streaming video on computer:	38%	30%
• Alternative newspapers:	29%	26%
• Mainstream email newsletters:	24%	21%
• Satellite radio:	23%	17%

• LGBT-dedicated TV shows:	23%	16%
• Podcasts:	14%	13%
• LGBT radio:	11%	8%
• LGBT mobile apps:	25%	6%

A Harris Poll found that gay and lesbian Internet users are more likely than heterosexuals to use social networks and blogs. The following is a comparison of use by each group:

	Gays & Lesbians	Heterosexuals
Social Networks		
• Facebook:	73%	65%
• MySpace:	32%	22%
• LinkedIn:	22%	16%
Blogs		
• Any type:	54%	40%
• News/current issues blogs:	36%	25%
• Personal blogs:	28%	19%
• Entertainment blogs:	25%	16%
• Political blogs:	22%	14%
• Travel blogs:	16%	8%
• Music blogs:	16%	6%
• Gay and lesbian blogs:	35%	n/a

A survey by Community Marketing found that 88% of U.S. lesbian and bisexual female and 79% of gay and bisexual male Internet users use Facebook.

80.8 Market Resources

Community Marketing Inc., 584 Castro Street, Suite 834, San Francisco, CA 94114. (415) 437-3800. (www.communitymarketing.com)

Services & Advocacy for GLBT Elders (SAGE), 305 Seventh Avenue, 15th Floor, New York, NY 10001. (212) 741-2247. (www.sageusa.org).

Witeck Communications, 2120 L Street NW, Suite 850, Washington, DC 20037. (202) 887-0500. (www.witeck.com)

81

MARRIED COUPLES

81.1 Profile

Among the total U.S. population age 18 and older, the share of men and women who are married fell from 57% in 2000 to 51% in 2010, the lowest percentage since the government began collecting marital status data more than 100 years ago.

The median age of their first marriage is 29.34 for men and 27.0 for women. In 1970, the ages were 22.5 and 20.6, respectively, according to the *Families and Living Arrangements*, published in 2015 by the U.S. Census Bureau (www.census.gov).

"The age at first marriage is continuing to rise. Cohabitation is continuing to rise in popularity. Marriage is something that is more optional now and it's also something increasingly people do later in the life course."

Susan Brown, Ph.D., Co-Director
Center for Family & Demographic Research
Bowling Green State University

Ironically, although only one-half of adults are married, 71% said in a Harris Poll (www.theharrispoll.com) that they believe marriage is important to Americans in general, and 75% said it is important personally. Responses by gender and age were as follows:

Gender	**Important to Americans**	**Important Personally**
• Female:	70%	79%
• Male:	72%	72%
Age		
• 18-to-36:	68%	73%
• 37-to-48:	69%	77%

- 49-to-67: 70% 75%
- 68 and older: 84% 81%

The *National Longitudinal Survey of Youth Born In 1997*, published in April 2016 by the Bureau of Labor Statistics (www.bls.gov), reported the marital status of people on their 29th birthday as follows:

Female
- Single: 35%
- Cohabiting: 20%
- Married: 45%

Male
- Single: 44%
- Cohabiting: 20%
- Married: 36%

"Young adults have been postponing marriage. The latest results from the NLSY 1997 are more evidence of this trend."

Demo Memo, 4/13/16

According to *Remarriage In The United States*, published in March 2015 by the Census Bureau, 52% of adults have been married only once, 13% have been married twice, and 4% have been married three or more times.

81.2 Buying Power

According to the Census Bureau, the median income for married-couple households was $68,426 in 2014. This was 28% above the overall median household income of $53,657.

There were 60.2 million married-couple households in 2014, or 48% of all U.S. households. Their combined income was over $4 trillion.

81.3 Trends

A study by the Urban Institute (www.urban.org) assessed that among women, the percentage who had married by age 40 was 91% for older Boomers, 87% for younger Boomers, and 82% for Generation X. Among younger Millennial women, even if marriage rates return to pre-recession levels, only 77% will have married by age 40. If marriage rates do not rebound, only 69% will have married by age 40. For Millennial men, the projections are 73% with a rebound and 65% without.

"The economic shock of the recession put marriage on hold for many young adults and marriage rates are returning slowly (if at all) to pre-recession levels. With respect to marriage at least, our projections indicate that many of these Millennials will not recover in the future from the opportunities they have missed as young adults. Not only will Millennials be the biggest 'singles' generation in history, but marital status will split the generation into haves and have-nots. That's because marriage rates are higher for college graduates, who earn more and tend to marry one another."

Urban Institute

If there is an upside to the lower marriage rate among Millennials, it is a lower divorce rate. Sheela Kennedy, Ph.D., and Steven Ruggles, Ph.D., researchers at the Minnesota Population Center, University of Minnesota (www.pop.umn.edu/), found that while the overall divorce rate in the U.S. continues to climb, divorce has been declining among adults under age 35. This is largely because fewer are marrying and those who do marry are the most compatible.

Among adults ages 35 and older, about half have experienced divorce or separation by their late fifties.

"The Baby Boom generation was responsible for the extraordinary rise in marital instability after 1970. They are now middle-aged, but their pattern of high marital instability continues."

Sheela Kennedy, Ph.D., and
Steven Ruggles, Ph.D.
University of Minnesota

As divorce rates hit all-time highs, so too are the number of remarriages. According to Pew Research Social & Demographic Trends (www.pewsocialtrends.org), almost 42 million adults in the U.S. have been married more than once, up from 22 million in 1980. The number of remarried adults has tripled since 1960, when there were 14 million. Among adults who are presently married, roughly a quarter (23%) have been married before, compared with 13% in 1960.

"Fully four-in-ten new marriages included at least one partner who had been married before, and two-in-ten new marriages were between people who had both previously stepped down the aisle. This snapshot is only the latest manifestation of a decades-long rise in the number of Americans who have ever remarried."

Pew Research Center

Research by Jeffrey Dew, Ph.D., a professor of family studies at Utah State University, indicates that financial conflict is a top predictor of divorce. Couples who report disagreeing over finances once a week are over 30% more likely to divorce than couples who disagree about finances a few times per month. Prof. Dew also found that couples who had no assets were 70% more likely to divorce than couples with at least $10,000 in assets.

According to *Women, Men and the New Economics of Marriage*, a report by Pew Research Center's Social & Demographic Trends Project, 28% of married women have more education than their husbands, while 19% of married men are more educated that their wives; couples are equally educated in 53% of marriages. This is a reversal of this statistic in 1970, when 28% of husbands were more educated and 20% of wives had a higher level of education.

Since men, particularly working class and poor men, have absorbed 75% of job losses since 2007, researchers foresee that economic conditions will ultimately undercut marriage in working class communities, furthering a "divorce divide" that has been growing since the 1980s between couples with college degrees and those with less education.

Research at the National Marriage Project (http://nationalmarriageproject.org/) at the University of Virginia found that men are 61% less likely to be happy in a marriage if they work fewer hours than their wives.

81.4 Research Centers

Center for Marital and Family Studies, University of Denver, 2155 S. Race Street, Denver, CO 80208. (303) 871-3062. (www.du.edu/psychology/marriage/)

National Center for Marriage & Research, Bowling Green State University, 005 Williams Hall, Bowling Green, OH 43403. (419) 372-4910. (http://ncfmr.bgsu.edu)

National Marriage Project, University of Virginia, P.O. Box 400766, Charlottesville, VA 22904. (434) 982-4509. (www.virginia.edu/marriageproject/)

Pew Research Social & Demographic Trends, 1615 L Street NW, Suite 700, Washington, DC 20036. (202) 419-4300. (www.pewsocialtrends.org)

Population Center, University of Minnesota, 50 Willey Hall 225, 19th Avenue South, Minneapolis, MN 55455. (612) 624-5818. (www.pop.umn.edu/)

Urban Institute, 2100 M Street NW, Washington, DC 20037. (202) 833-7200. (www.urban.org)

82

MILITARY CONSUMERS

82.1 Active Personnel

The United States Armed Forces consists of the Army, Navy, Marine Corps, Air Force, and Coast Guard.

In FY2016, there were 1.51 million active personnel in the U.S. Armed Forces, distributed as follows:

- United States Army: 460,000
- United States Air Force: 491,700
- United States Navy: 380,900
- United States Marine Corps: 182,000
- United States Coast Guard: 36,000

Eighty-five percent (85%) of active personnel are male; 15% are female.

There are 850,000 men and women serving in reserve components of the U.S. Armed Forces, distributed as follows:

- United States National Guard: 358,000
- United States Army Reserve: 205,000
- United States Air National Guard: 106,000
- United States Air Force Reserve: 71,000
- United States Navy Reserve: 62,000
- United States Marine Corps Reserve: 40,000
- United States Coast Guard Reserve: 7,000

There are 681,000 civilians employed by the U.S. Armed Forces, distributed by branch as follows:

- United States Army: 300,000
- United States Navy: 179,000
- United States Air Force: 175,000
- United States Marine Corps: 20,000
- United States Coast Guard: 7,000

82.2 Veterans

According to a March 2016 report by the National Center for Veterans Analysis and Statistics of the U.S. Department of Veterans Affairs (www.va.gov), there are 17.8

million veterans, of which 1.6 million are women. This represents 7.1% of the adult population. The median age among male and female veterans is 64 and 49, respectively. The number of veterans has declined from 12.7% of the adult population, or 26.4 million veterans in 2000.

Service among veterans is distributed as follows:

- Vietnam War: 36%
- Gulf Wars: 26%
- Peacetime service: 23%
- Korean Conflict: 10%
- World War II: 5%

82.3 Buying Power

Soldiers, sailors, and Marines receive average compensation of $122,263 per person. Military compensation – an average of $70,168 in pay and $52,095 in benefits – includes the value of housing, medical care, pensions, hazardous-duty incentives, enlistment bonuses, and combat pay in war zones.

The U.S. military provides housing, medical care, schools, and other social services to the spouses and children of active duty service members.

Military spending has helped boost cities and towns across the U.S. Of the 18 metros with the highest income gains during the past decade, 13 are military towns. They are as follows:

- Cheyenne, WY: Warren Air Force Base
- Clarksville, TN: Fort Campbell (Army)
- Columbus, GA: Fort Benning (Army)
- Crestview-Fort Walton Beach-Destin, FL: Eglin Air Force Base
- El Paso, TX: Fort Bliss (Army)
- Fayetteville, NC: Fort Bragg (Army); Pope Air Force Base
- Hanford-Corcoran, CA: Lemoore Naval Air Station
- Hinesville-Fort Stewart, GA: Fort Stewart (Army)
- Jacksonville, NC: Camp Lejeune (Marines)
- Killeen-Temple-Fort Hood, TX: Fort Hood (Army)
- Las Cruces, NM: Fort Bliss (Army); Holloman Air Force Base
- Lawton, OK: Fort Sill (Army)
- Manhattan, KS: Fort Riley (Army)

82.4 The Military Exchange System

The Military Exchange System (MES) serves all of the U.S. Armed Forces with a combined 4,028 stores. MES annual retail sales are approximately $14 billion.

The largest component of the MES is the Army and Air Force Exchange Service

(AAFES), with $8.8 billion in annual sales. During its 111 years of operation, AAFES has evolved from a purveyor of discounted basic necessities to a multichannel retailer with over 3,000 stores and restaurants and movie theaters, as well as catalogs and a growing Internet site. A survey found its prices are just 2.5% higher than Walmart's, but shoppers get the added benefit of forgoing sales taxes.

Within the U.S., AAFES stores, also called the PX for 'post exchange,' serve as de facto community centers for 11.5 million active or retired military service members and their families. Overseas, AAFES stores give troops the chance to connect with American culture and commerce through their broad selection of DVDs and electronics in addition to basic drugstore goods.

For grocery shopping, military personnel, including retirees, turn to a network of 281 stores (including about 95 overseas) operated by the Defense Commissary Agency (DeCA, www.commissaries.com). With annual sales of about $5 billion, DeCA generates revenues roughly equivalent to a conventional supermarket chain. Federal law does not allow the agency to make a profit, however, and products are sold at only a 5% markup from cost.

83

PET OWNERS

83.1 Overview

The American Pet Products Association (APPA, www.americanpetproducts.org) estimates that 79.7 million U.S. households (65% of all households) own pets. For comparison, in 1988, 56% of U.S. households owned a pet. Some 46% of all households today own more than one pet.

Topping the list of most-owned pets in 2016, there are 95 million freshwater fish in 12.3 million U.S. homes. Cats, with 85.8 million felines owned by 42.9 million household, are the second-most-popular pets in the U.S. Owned by more households than any other pet, 77.8 million pet dogs are owned by 54.4 million households.

83.2 Pets Owner Demographics

The following percentages of adults have pets (source: The Harris Poll [www.theharrispoll.com]):

Gender
- Female: 64%
- Male: 56%

Age
- 18-to-35: 62%
- 35-to-47: 66%
- 48-to-66: 64%
- 67 and older: 19%

Race/Ethnicity
- Hispanic: 68%
- White: 63%
- African American: 40%

Income
- $34,999 or less: 56%
- $35,000 to $49,999: 65%
- $50,000 to $74,999: 60%
- $75,000 to $99,999: 66%
- $100,000 or more: 68%

Education

- High school or less: 59%
- Some college: 63%
- College graduate: 61%
- Post graduate: 54%

Region

- West: 68%
- Midwest: 61%
- South: 57%
- East: 56%

83.3 Pets As Family

In a recent Harris Poll, 92% of dog-owners and 91% of cat-owners said they consider their pet to be a member of the family. Fifty-seven percent (57%) of pet owners said they frequently let their pet sleep in the bed with them; 23% say they never do this.

One-third of pet owners (33%) frequently purchase holiday presents for their pet; 27% occasionally do so. Twenty percent (20%) of pet owners frequently buy their pets birthday presents; 17% do so occasionally.

83.4 Spending On Pets

According to the APPA, spending on pets has been as follows:

- 2004: $34.4 billion
- 2005: $36.3 billion
- 2006: $38.5 billion
- 2007: $41.2 billion
- 2008: $43.2 billion
- 2009: $45.5 billion
- 2010: $48.4 billion
- 2011: $50.8 billion
- 2012: $53.3 billion
- 2013: $55.7 billion
- 2014: $58.0 billion
- 2015: $60.3 billion
- 2016: $62.8 billion

The distribution of spending on pets in 2016 is estimated as follows:

- Food: $24.0 billion
- Veterinarian care: $15.9 billion
- Supplies and over-the-counter medicines: $15.0 billion
- Pet services, boarding, and grooming: $ 5.7 billion
- Live animal purchases: $ 2.1 billion

The yearly cost of buying, feeding, and caring for pets tops what Americans spend on movies, video games, and recorded music combined.

Pet owners spend a combined $2.6 billion on holiday gifts for their pets, according to the APPA. One quarter of pet-related expenditures occur between Thanksgiving and Christmas.

83.5 Market Resources

American Pet Products Association, 255 Glenville Road, Greenwich, CT 06831. (203) 532-0000. (www.americanpetproducts.org)

84

RETIREES

84.1 Profile

Eighteen percent (18%) of all U.S. adults are retired, a figure that has increased by 6% in the last five years and will further increase as Baby Boomers exit the workforce over the next few decades.

According to the Employee Benefit Research Institute (EBRI, www.ebri.org), about 72% of Americans expect to remain engaged in some type of work after they officially retire. Almost half (47%) said they left their jobs sooner than they had planned.

A study by EBRI based on data from the University of Michigan Institute for Social Research (ISR, http://home.isr.umich.edu/) found that only 14% of people retire as planned. Overall, 38% of older workers retire before the age they had planned, and 48% retire after the age they had planned.

> **"Before age 62, actual retirement is higher than expected retirement. But by age 65 the opposite is the case. Eighty-one percent (81%) of workers expect to retire before age 65, but only 64% actually do so."**
>
> EBRI

According to *Trends In Retirement Satisfaction In The United States*, published in May 2016 by the Employee Benefit Research Institute, 48.6% of retirees say their retirement is "very satisfying."

84.2 Retiree Consumers

International Demographics (www.themediaaudit.com) provides the following characteristics of retirees:

- Eighty-three percent (83%) of retired adults in the U.S. own their own home.
- Thirty percent (30%) of retired adults have stocks and CDs.
- Thirteen percent (13%) of new automobile purchasers are retired, compared with 11% five years ago. Eight percent (8%) of adults who have a car loan are retired, compared to 6% five years ago.
- Sixteen percent (16%) of adults who frequently stay in hotels are retired, compared to 14% five years ago.
- Adults who are retired are 6% more likely than the average U.S. adult to frequently dine out at a full-service restaurant; retirees now make up nearly 20% of all adults who frequently dine out.
- Fourteen percent (14%) of adults taking an ocean cruise are retired.
- Compared with the average U.S. adult, those who are retired spend nearly 30% more time watching broadcast television, 14% more time watching cable television, and 25% more time reading a daily newspaper.
- Retired adults spend only 89 minutes per day online, 26% less than the average U.S. adult.

Ranked by retirees as a percentage of community population, the largest retiree markets are as follows:

- Ocala, FL: 36%
- Fort Myers-Naples, FL: 34%
- Daytona Beach, FL: 33%
- West Palm Beach, FL: 31%
- Melbourne-Titusville-Cocoa, FL: 29%

The most affluent retirees can be found in larger markets such as Washington, D.C., where the average retired adult earns $64,000 in household income and investment returns. San Jose, Fort Myers-Naples, San Francisco, and Long Island follow with household incomes of more than $50,000.

84.3 Saving For Retirement

A study by the Center for Retirement Research (CRR) at Boston College (http://crr.bc.edu), published in the November 2015 issue of *The Journal of Retirement*, estimates 65% to 85% of pre-retirement income is a reasonable “replacement rate” for most retirees, depending on the type of household.

The CRR estimates that 52% of Americans may not be able to maintain their standard of living which it defines as having an income that falls no more than 10% below the replacement rate.

The biggest problems face those with no private pension at all: 68% of these Americans are expected to fall short. Those covered by defined-benefit plans – in which pensions are linked to a worker’s salary – have the least difficulty: only 20% are deemed at risk. Of those in defined-contribution plans, 53% likely will not reach the replacement rate.

84.4 Post-Retirement Spending

Change in Household Spending After Retirement, published in December 2015 by the Employee Benefit Research Institute, reports that in the first year or two of retirement, 46% of households spend more than during their working years.

By the sixth year of retirement, 33% are spending more than they had in their pre-retirement years. Post-retirement spending as a percentage of pre-retirement spending in the sixth year of retirement is as follows:

- Spending less than 80% of pre-retirement income: 53.1%
- Spending 80% to 100% of pre-retirement income: 13.4%
- Spending 100% to 120% of pre-retirement income: 10.0%
- Spending 120% or more of pre-retirement income: 23.4%

> **"Many households spend more rather than less after retirement."**
>
> Demo Memo, 12/1/15

84.5 Financial Security

Household incomes of retirees are distributed as follows (percent with such income, source: International Demographics):

- Under $50,000: 72%
- $50,000 and above: 28%
- $75,000 and above: 14%
- $100,000 and above: 7%

Social security provides, on average, about 40% of retirement income.

The percentage of retirees by amount of liquid assets is as follows:

- Less than $100,000: 70%
- $100,000 and above: 30%
- $250,000 and above: 14%

The Employee Benefit Research Institute put the gap between what Americans need for retirement and what they have saved at $4.6 trillion. If Social Security benefits were to be eliminated, the deficit would rise to $8.5 trillion.

84.6 Primary Influences On Age Of Retirement

Research shows that debt and health are primary influences that determine when people retire.

An assessment by the Center for Retirement Research at Boston College found that 33% of adults ages 62-to-69 without debt were still working, while 46% with debt were. The study also reported that the percentage of 62-to-69-year-olds with debt grew from 48% to 62% between 1998 and 2010. Among those with debt, the median amount owed was $32,130.

"Older Americans with debt are more likely to delay retirement, according to a study by the Center for Retirement Research at Boston College. The study finds a growing share of older Americans in debt and their debt load rising."

Demo Memo

A study by the National Bureau of Economic Research (www.nber.org) reported that among men age 62, the percentage who work full-time is 44% for those in good health, 39% for those in fair health, 18% for those in poor health, and 4% for those in terrible health. Conversely, the percentage of men age 62 and older who are fully retired rises from 41% for those in good health to 46% for those in fair health, 68% for those in poor health, and 87% for those in terrible health.

"Poor health leads to an earlier retirement and the National Bureau of Economic Research documents just how much health matters. The differences are striking."

Demo Memo

84.7 Trends in Retirement and Semi-Retirement

According to an April 2016 survey by Gallup (www.gallup.com), the average are U.S. workers anticipate they will retire is 66, up from 64 in 2006 and 60 in 1995. Retirement, however, does not suggest that people will no longer work – many will transition into semi-retirement employment or self-employment.

Thirty-one percent (31%) of non-retired U.S. adults foresee they will retire after age 67, the current minimum age for receiving full Social Security retirement benefits. Another 38% expect to retire between the ages of 62 and 67, spanning the existing Social Security age thresholds for benefits eligibility, while 23% expect to stop working before they turn 62 – that is, before becoming eligible for any Social Security retirement benefits.

Few plan to retire completely nowadays, and by age 65 many Baby Boomers will have already transitioned into semi-retirement. Many surveys suggest work will be routine during Baby Boomers' older years. An AARP (www.aarp.org) national poll of Boomers found that 80% intend to work at least part time during their 'retirement' years.

According to the Social & Demographic Trends Project at Pew Research Center (www.pewsocialtrends.com), 52% of working adults ages 40-to-64 say they may delay their retirement; an additional 16% say they expect never to stop working.

Most who choose to continue working after age 60, or even 65, will likely find a new source of income; relatively few will remain in their current jobs. In fact, many have already left their career jobs.

According to the Bureau of Labor Statistics (www.bls.gov), just 60% of 60 year-olds are currently employed. But according to the AARP, 16% of older Baby Boomers are self-employed, compared with 10% of the overall workforce.

Aside from a desire to stay active, there will be a wide variation in the lifestyles of retiring Boomers. According to Nancy Schlossberg, Ph.D., a professor emeritus of education at the University of Maryland and author of *Retire Smart, Retire Happy: Finding Your True Path in Life* (2005, APA Life Tools), most retirees fall into one of a half-dozen distinct categories. There are 'continuers,' who maintain work ties in their chosen fields; 'adventurers,' who strike out in entirely different career paths; and 'searchers,' who try one organization after another until they find their niche. A lesser number may become 'easy gliders,' who take each day as it comes, or 'retreaters,' who would rather sit on the couch and watch television.

"I believe the word 'retirement' in a decade will be a quaint, charming term that people used to use."

Larry Minnix, President
American Association of Homes
and Services for the Aging

84.8 Market Resources

AARP, 601 E Street NW, Washington DC 20049. (888) 687-2277. (www.aarp.org)

Center for Retirement Research, Boston College, 140 Commonwealth Avenue, Chestnut Hill, MA 02467. (617) 552-1677. (http://crr.bc.edu)

Employee Benefit Research Institute, 1100 13th Street NW, Suite 878, Washington, DC 20005. (202) 659-0670. (www.ebri.org)

Growing Older in America: The Health and Retirement Study, University of Michigan Institute for Social Research. (http://hrsonline.isr.umich.edu/)

The Journal of Retirement, 225 Park Avenue South, New York, NY 10003. (800) 437-9997. (www.iijournals.com/toc/jor/current)

85

SINGLE CONSUMERS

85.1 Overview

According to the U.S. Census Bureau (www.census.gov), there are 105 million unmarried people over age 18 in the U.S., representing about 45% of the adult population. Fifty-three percent (53%) of unmarried adults were women; 47% were men.

Among unmarried adults, 62% had never been married, 24% are divorced, and 14% are widowed.

America's Families and Living Arrangements, by the Census Bureau, reports the percentage of people ages 25-to-29 that have never married as follows:

Female
- 1960: 11%
- 1980: 21%
- 2000: 39%
- 2015: 54%

Male
- 1960: 21%
- 1980: 33%
- 2000: 52%
- 2015: 68%

"Never-married single people ages 25-to-34 now outnumber the married crowd by 46%, a stark reversal from just a decade ago when couples held a 20-point edge in that age group."

Advertising Age

Driven by several factors, the trend toward delaying marriage has emerged over several decades. Financial burdens, such as large college loan debt, have made it more difficult for those in their 20s to reach independence, forcing some to move back in with their parents. Also, an increasing number of young adults are preoccupied with their careers, and there are increasing numbers of cohabiting couples.

While almost a quarter of single-person households are made up of young people under the age of 35 who have never been married, many are financially independent singles.

85.2 Single-Person Households

The *Current Population Survey*, by the Census Bureau, reported 42.1 million non-family households, representing 33.8% of all U.S. households, at year-end 2015. There were 34.9 million single-person households, or 28.0% of all U.S. households.

The following are the demographics of single-person households:

Generation

- Millennials: 20%
- Generation X: 19%
- Baby Boomers: 30%
- Seniors: 49%

Race/Ethnicity

- African-American: 35%
- Asian-American: 18%
- Caucasian: 30%
- Hispanic: 17%

85.3 Cohabitation

According to the U.S. Census Bureau, the estimated number of unmarried couples living together is as follows:

- Opposite-sex couples: 7.5 million
- Same-sex couples: 620,000
- Total: 8.1 million

Couples who choose cohabitation over marriage cite several advantages to the arrangement. Studies show that never-married couples with the intention of living together permanently are just as likely to stay together as married couples.

"The question," says Andrew J. Cherlin, Ph.D., a professor of sociology at Johns Hopkins University, "is not why fewer people are getting married, but why are so many still getting married?"

"It's a mistake to think of all unmarried people as single. Lots are living with partners."

Prof. Andrew J. Cherlin, Ph.D.
Johns Hopkins University
The New York Times

A trend that is increasing among singles is that of "committed unmarrieds," so dubbed by one sociologist. More than five million such couples cohabit in the U.S., nearly eight times the number in 1970, according to *Time*. The family dynamic of committed unmarried with children is also on the rise. Households such as these challenge the perceptions of family, and the greater majority of marketers don't even identify the market.

85.4 Spending Power

According to the Bureau of Labor Statistics (www.bls.gov), singles spend $2.2 trillion annually, which is 35% of all consumer spending.

The average single-household income is approximately $1,400 greater than the average income of two-person households divided by two; the average one-person household has over $1,300 in discretionary income.

Despite their spending clout, singles are seldom targeted by advertisers.

"Some marketers are taking notice: More ads are featuring singles and some companies are reaching out to them. But for the most part marketers are only slowly adjusting to the new normal."

Advertising Age

A study from Packaged Facts (www.packagedfacts.com) points out that singles are more receptive to ad pitches than the general population.

85.5 Singles Geodemographics

Pew Research Social & Demographic Trends (www.pewsocialtrends.org) assesses the number of unmarried men and women ages 25-to-34 in metropolitan areas as follows:

	Men per 100 Women	Women per 100 Men
• Akron, OH:	100	100
• Albany-Schenectady-Troy, NY:	120	83
• Albuquerque, NM:	117	86
• Allentown-Bethlehem-Easton, PA-NJ:	117	85
• Amarillo, TX:	144	69
• Anchorage, AK:	117	85
• Ann Arbor, MI:	142	71
• Anniston-Oxford-Jacksonville, AL:	82	121
• Asheville, NC:	112	90
• Atlanta-Sandy Springs-Roswell, GA:	106	95
• Atlantic City-Hammonton, NJ:	107	94
• Auburn-Opelika, AL:	96	104
• Augusta-Richmond County, GA-SC:	89	112
• Austin-Round Rock, TX:	114	88
• Bakersfield, CA:	136	74
• Baltimore-Columbia-Towson, MD:	103	97
• Bangor, ME:	103	97
• Barnstable Town, MA:	117	86
• Baton Rouge, LA:	100	100
• Beaumont-Port Arthur, TX:	135	74
• Bellingham, WA:	135	74
• Bend-Redmond, OR:	108	92
• Binghamton, NY:	109	91
• Birmingham-Hoover, AL:	100	100
• Bismarck, ND:	110	91
• Blacksburg-Christiansburg-Radford, VA:	149	67
• Bloomington, IL:	113	89
• Bloomington, IN:	117	86
• Boise City, ID:	141	71
• Boston-Cambridge-Newton, MA-NH:	109	91
• Bremerton-Silverdale, WA:	145	69
• Bridgeport-Stamford-Norwalk, CT:	110	91
• Brownsville-Harlingen, TX:	90	111
• Buffalo-Cheektowaga-Niagara Falls, NY:	116	86
• Burlington, NC:	116	86
• Burlington-South Burlington, VT:	123	81
• Canton-Massillon, OH:	112	89
• Cape Coral-Fort Myers, FL:	110	91
• Champaign-Urbana, IL:	104	96
• Charleston, WV:	114	87

- Charleston-North Charleston, SC: 109 92
- Charlotte-Concord-Gastonia, NC-SC: 100 100
- Chattanooga, TN-GA: 120 83
- Chicago-Naperville-Elgin, IL-IN-WI: 108 92
- Chico, CA: 136 73
- Cincinnati, OH-KY-IN: 108 93
- Clarksville, TN-KY: 188 53
- Cleveland-Elyria, OH: 107 93
- Coeur d'Alene, ID: 143 70
- College Station-Bryan, TX: 116 86
- Colorado Springs, CO: 131 77
- Columbia, MO: 127 79
- Columbia, SC: 107 93
- Columbus, OH: 106 94
- Corpus Christi, TX: 127 79
- Dallas-Fort Worth-Arlington, TX: 109 92
- Daphne-Fairhope-Foley, AL: 117 86
- Dayton, OH: 109 91
- Decatur, AL: 106 94
- Decatur, IL: 100 100
- Deltona-Daytona Beach-Ormond Beach, FL: 107 93
- Denver-Aurora-Lakewood, CO: 121 83
- Des Moines-West Des Moines, IA: 110 91
- Detroit-Warren-Dearborn, MI: 103 97
- Dover, DE: 101 99
- East Stroudsburg, PA: 135 74
- Eau Claire, WI: 103 97
- El Centro, CA: 133 75
- Elkhart-Goshen, IN: 108 92
- El Paso, TX: 113 88
- Erie, PA: 138 73
- Eugene, OR: 123 81
- Fayetteville, NC: 105 96
- Fayetteville-Springdale-Rogers, AR-MO: 151 66
- Flagstaff, AZ: 105 96
- Florence, SC: 97 103
- Fort Collins, CO: 130 77
- Fort Wayne, IN: 121 83
- Fresno, CA: 124 81
- Gadsden, AL: 148 68
- Gainesville, FL: 120 83
- Gainesville, GA: 111 90
- Glens Falls, NY: 122 82
- Goldsboro, NC: 104 96

• Grand Junction, CO:	144	69
• Grand Rapids-Wyoming, MI:	106	94
• Greensboro-High Point, NC:	97	103
• Greenville, NC:	89	113
• Greenville-Anderson-Mauldin, SC:	110	91
• Gulfport-Biloxi-Pascagoula, MS:	127	79
• Hanford-Corcoran, CA:	236	42
• Harrisburg-Carlisle, PA:	126	80
• Harrisonburg, VA:	119	84
• Hartford-West Hartford-East Hartford, CT:	119	84
• Hickory-Lenoir-Morganton, NC:	142	70
• Hilton Head Island-Bluffton-Beaufort, SC:	103	97
• Homosassa Springs, FL:	102	98
• Honolulu (urban), HI:	141	71
• Houma-Thibodaux, LA:	110	91
• Houston-The Woodlands-Sugar Land, TX:	111	90
• Huntsville, AL:	130	77
• Indianapolis-Carmel-Anderson, IN:	112	89
• Iowa City, IA:	129	78
• Ithaca, NY:	140	71
• Jackson, MI:	153	65
• Jackson, MS:	85	117
• Jackson, TN:	103	97
• Jacksonville, FL:	103	97
• Janesville-Beloit, WI:	123	81
• Jefferson City, MO:	127	78
• Johnstown, PA:	128	78
• Joplin, MO:	139	72
• Kalamazoo-Portage, MI:	108	93
• Kankakee, IL:	94	106
• Kansas City, MO-KS:	101	99
• Knoxville, TN:	126	80
• La Crosse-Onalaska, WI-MN:	170	59
• Lafayette-West Lafayette, IN:	124	81
• Lafayette, LA:	99	101
• Lake Havasu City-Kingman, AZ:	147	68
• Lakeland-Winter Haven, FL:	117	85
• Lancaster, PA:	98	102
• Lansing-East Lansing, MI:	117	85
• Laredo, TX:	93	108
• Las Cruces, NM:	145	69
• Las Vegas-Henderson-Paradise, NV:	118	85
• Lawrence, KS:	118	85
• Lebanon, PA:	118	85

- Lewiston-Auburn, ME: 81 124
- Lima, OH: 101 99
- Lincoln, NE: 128 78
- Little Rock-North Little Rock-Conway, AR: 96 104
- Los Angeles-Long Beach-Anaheim, CA: 119 84
- Louisville/Jefferson County, KY-IN: 115 87
- Lubbock, TX: 126 79
- Lynchburg, VA: 106 94
- Madera, CA: 83 121
- Manchester-Nashua, NH: 138 72
- Mansfield, OH: 215 46
- McAllen-Edinburg-Mission, TX: 111 90
- Medford, OR: 96 105
- Memphis, TN-MS-AR: 93 108
- Merced, CA: 125 80
- Miami-Fort Lauderdale-West Palm Beach, FL: 109 92
- Michigan City-La Porte, IN: 184 54
- Midland, TX: 133 75
- Milwaukee-Waukesha-West Allis, WI: 104 96
- Minneapolis-St. Paul-Bloomington, MN-WI: 116 86
- Mobile, AL: 93 108
- Modesto, CA: 120 83
- Monroe, LA: 110 91
- Monroe, MI: 123 81
- Montgomery, AL: 95 106
- Morgantown, WV: 146 69
- Muncie, IN: 125 80
- Muskegon, MI: 111 90
- Myrtle Beach-Conway-North Myrtle Beach, SC-NC: 96 104
- Napa, CA: 118 85
- Naples-Immokalee-Marco Island, FL: 125 80
- Nashville-Davidson-Murfreesboro-Franklin, TN: 100 100
- New Haven-Milford, CT: 98 102
- New Orleans-Metairie, LA: 102 98
- New York-Newark-Jersey City, NY-NJ-PA: 109 92
- Niles-Benton Harbor, MI: 171 59
- North Port-Sarasota-Bradenton, FL: 119 84
- Norwich-New London, CT: 108 93
- Ocala, FL: 125 80
- Ocean City, NJ: 108 93
- Odessa, TX: 111 90
- Ogden-Clearfield, UT: 131 76
- Oklahoma City, OK: 122 82
- Olympia-Tumwater, WA: 129 78

- Omaha-Council Bluffs, NE-IA: 120 84
- Orlando-Kissimmee-Sanford, FL: 128 78
- Oshkosh-Neenah, WI: 133 75
- Owensboro, KY: 108 93
- Oxnard-Thousand Oaks-Ventura, CA: 128 78
- Palm Bay-Melbourne-Titusville, FL: 127 79
- Parkersburg-Vienna, WV: 81 124
- Pensacola-Ferry Pass-Brent, FL: 121 83
- Philadelphia-Camden-Wilmington, PA-NJ-DE-MD: 108 93
- Phoenix-Mesa-Scottsdale, AZ: 118 84
- Pittsburgh, PA: 124 81
- Pittsfield, MA: 119 84
- Portland-South Portland, ME: 108 92
- Portland-Vancouver-Hillsboro, OR-WA: 111 90
- Port St. Lucie, FL: 114 87
- Prescott, AZ: 126 79
- Providence-Warwick, RI-MA: 117 85
- Provo-Orem, UT: 129 77
- Pueblo, CO: 132 76
- Punta Gorda, FL: 144 69
- Racine, WI: 83 120
- Raleigh, NC: 99 101
- Reading, PA: 125 80
- Redding, CA: 146 69
- Reno, NV: 124 81
- Richmond, VA: 114 88
- Riverside-San Bernardino-Ontario, CA: 116 86
- Roanoke, VA: 96 104
- Rochester, NY: 118 85
- Rockford, IL: 93 108
- Rocky Mount, NC: 72 140
- Sacramento-Roseville-Arden-Arcade, CA: 116 86
- Saginaw, MI: 99 101
- St. George, UT: 133 75
- St. Joseph, MO-KS: 147 68
- St. Louis, MO-IL: 108 93
- Salinas, CA: 152 66
- Salisbury, MD-DE: 142 70
- Salt Lake City, UT: 117 86
- San Angelo, TX: 115 87
- San Antonio-New Braunfels, TX: 114 87
- San Diego-Carlsbad, CA: 129 77
- San Francisco-Oakland-Hayward, CA: 116 86
- San Jose-Sunnyvale-Santa Clara, CA: 141 71

- San Luis Obispo-Paso Robles-Arroyo Grande, CA: 154 65
- Santa Cruz-Watsonville, CA: 143 70
- Santa Fe, NM: 110 91
- Santa Maria-Santa Barbara, CA: 136 74
- Santa Rosa, CA: 115 87
- Scranton-Wilkes Barre-Hazleton, PA: 107 93
- Seattle-Tacoma-Bellevue, WA: 121 83
- Sebastian-Vero Beach, FL: 104 96
- Sheboygan, WI: 145 69
- Shreveport-Bossier City, LA: 105 95
- Spartanburg, SC: 99 101
- Spokane-Spokane Valley, WA: 130 77
- Springfield, IL: 109 92
- Springfield, MA: 90 111
- Springfield, MO: 134 75
- Springfield, OH: 99 101
- State College, PA: 155 65
- Stockton-Lodi, CA: 110 91
- Syracuse, NY: 115 87
- Tampa-St. Petersburg-Clearwater, FL: 109 92
- Toledo, OH: 125 80
- Topeka, KS: 118 85
- Trenton, NJ: 124 81
- Tucson, AZ: 121 82
- Tuscaloosa, AL: 107 93
- Tyler, TX: 118 85
- Utica-Rome, NY: 120 83
- Vallejo-Fairfield, CA: 129 77
- Virginia Beach-Norfolk-Newport News, VA-NC: 108 92
- Visalia-Porterville, CA: 98 102
- Waco, TX: 98 102
- Washington-Arlington-Alexandria, DC-VA-MD-WV: 107 94
- Wausau, WI: 107 94
- Wenatchee, WA: 90 111
- Wichita, KS: 124 81
- Wichita Falls, TX: 171 59
- Wilmington, NC: 129 78
- Winston-Salem, NC: 109 91
- Worcester, MA-CT: 128 78
- Yakima, WA: 107 94
- York-Hanover, PA: 125 80
- Youngstown-Warren-Boardman, OH-PA: 108 92
- Yuba City, CA: 110 91
- Yuma, AZ: 164 61

85.6 Market Resources

Unmarried Equality, 7149 Rivol Road, West Hills, CA 91307. (347) 987-1068. (www.unmarried.org)

Pew Research Social & Demographic Trends, 1615 L Street NW, Suite 700, Washington, DC 20036. (202) 419-4300. (www.pewsocialtrends.org)

PART XIII: GEODEMOGRAPHICS

86

MEGAPOLITAN REGIONS

86.1 Overview

Megapolitan regions, also called megaregions, are clustered networks of American cities characterized by high density populations, high growth, and, in some instances, blurring boundaries between cities.

Eleven (11) megapolitans have been defined by Metropolitan Institute at Virginia Tech (www.mi.vt.edu) and the America 2050 project at the Regional Plan Association (RPA, www.rpa.org). Megapolitan regions were first defined in 2005.

A map of the megapolitan regions, as defined by the America 2050 project, is presented online at www.america2050.org/pdf/2050_Map_Megaregions2008.pdf.

86.2 Megapolitan Regions Defined

Eighty-three (83) of the top 100 primary census statistical areas are included in the 11 megapolitan areas. Major cities in the regions are as follows:

Arizona Sun Corridor

- Phoenix, Tucson

Cascadia

- Portland, Seattle, Tacoma, Vancouver, Victoria

Florida

- Daytona Beach, Fort Lauderdale, Jacksonville, Miami, Orlando, St. Petersburg, Tampa, West Palm Beach

Front Range

- Albuquerque, Colorado Springs, Denver, Pueblo, Santa Fe

Great Lakes

- Akron, Buffalo, Chicago, Cincinnati, Cleveland, Columbus, Dayton, Detroit, Fort Wayne, Grand Rapids, Green Bay, Hamilton, Indianapolis, Kansas City, Louisville, Milwaukee, Pittsburgh, Rochester, St. Louis, Toledo, Toronto, Twin Cities (Minneapolis-Saint Paul)

Gulf Coast

- Baton Rouge, Corpus Christi, Houston, Mobile, New Orleans, Pensacola

Northeast

- Baltimore, Boston, Hampton Roads (Virginia Beach-Norfolk), Harrisburg, Hartford, Lehigh Valley (Allentown-Bethlehem), New York City, Philadelphia, Portland, Providence, Richmond, Washington, Worcester

Northern California

- Fresno, Modesto, Reno, Sacramento, San Francisco Bay Area (San Francisco-Oakland-San Jose), Stockton

Piedmont Atlantic

- Atlanta, Birmingham, Charlotte, Chattanooga, Columbia, Huntsville, Knoxville, Montgomery, Nashville, Piedmont Triad (Greensboro-Winston-Salem), Research Triangle (Raleigh-Durham), Upstate South Carolina (Greenville-Spartanburg)

Southern California

- Anaheim, Las Vegas, Long Beach, Los Angeles, Riverside, San Bernardino, San Diego

Texas Triangle

- Austin, Dallas-Fort Worth Metroplex (Dallas-Fort Worth-Arlington), Houston, Oklahoma City, San Antonio, Tulsa, Wichita

86.3 Regional GDP

The 11 regions account for 74% of the total U.S. GDP, or $13.42 trillion in 2015. The GDP of each region was as follows:

- Northeast: $3.79 trillion
- Gulf Coast: $3.02 trillion
- Southern California: $1.51 trillion
- Texas Triangle: $1.19 trillion
- Northern California: $ 909 billion
- Florida: $ 888 billion
- Great Lakes: $ 765 billion
- Piedmont Atlantic: $ 710 billion
- Cascadia: $ 491 billion
- Front Range: $ 334 billion
- Arizona Sun Corridor: $ 278 billion

86.4 Population Projections

Seventy-five percent (75%) of the U.S. population resides in the 11 megapolitan regions. The population of the megaregions is projected by the RPA to increase 18% from the 2010 Census through 2025; the rest of the U.S. is expected to rise 14% during that period.

Population projections for 2025 are as follows:

- Arizona Sun Corridor: 7,362,613
- Cascadia: 10,209,826
- Florida: 21,358,829
- Front Range: 6,817,462
- Gulf Coast: 15,832,117
- Great Lakes: 62,894,147
- Northeast: 58,124,740
- Northern California: 17,290,363
- Piedmont Atlantic: 30,351,698
- Southern California: 28,692,923
- Texas Triangle: 23,586,856

*Megapolitan America (*2011, APA Planners Press), by Arthur C. Nelson, Professor of City and Metropolitan Planning at the University of Utah, and Robert E. Lang, Professor of Sociology and the Director of Brookings Mountain West at the University of Nevada Las Vegas, predicts that by 2040 there will be 10 distinct clusters composed of 23 megapolitan areas that will work together to dominate the U.S. economy.

86.5 Market Resources

Regional Plan Association, 4 Irving Place, 7th Floor, New York, NY 10003. (212) 253-2727. (www.rpa.org)

Metropolitan Institute at Virginia Tech, 1021 Prince Street, Suite 100, Alexandria, VA 22314. (703) 706-8100. (www.mi.vt.edu)

87

METROPOLITAN STATISTICAL AREAS

87.1 Overview

The United States Office of Management and Budget (OMB, www.omb.gov) defines a Metropolitan Statistical Area (MSA) as one or more adjacent counties or county equivalents that have at least one urban core area with a population of at least 50,000, plus adjacent territory that has a high degree of social and economic integration with the core as measured by commuting ties.

There are 380 MSAs. A description of the regions included in each MSA is available at www.census.gov/population/www/metroareas/metrodef.html.

Population data is available from the U.S. Census Bureau (www.census.gov) at www.census.gov/popest/.

87.2 MSA Populations

The U.S. population in 2015 was 321,418,820; 275,252,217,000 (85.6%) lived in metropolitan statistical areas.

The 2015 population in each MSA, as estimated by the U.S. Census Bureau, was as follows:

- Abilene, TX: 169,578,000
- Akron, OH: 704,243,000
- Albany, GA: 153,526,000
- Albany, OR: 120,547,000
- Albany-Schenectady-Troy, NY: 881,830,000
- Albuquerque, NM: 907,301,000
- Alexandria, LA: 154,484,000
- Allentown-Bethlehem-Easton, PA-NJ: 832,327,000
- Altoona, PA: 125,593,000
- Amarillo, TX: 262,056,000
- Ames, IA: 96,021,000
- Anchorage, AK: 399,790,000
- Ann Arbor, MI: 358,880,000
- Anniston-Oxford-Jacksonville, AL: 115,620,000
- Appleton, WI: 233,007,000
- Asheville, NC: 446,840,000
- Athens-Clarke County, GA: 203,189,000

- Atlanta-Sandy Springs-Roswell, GA: 5,710,795,000
- Atlantic City-Hammonton, NJ: 274,219,000
- Auburn-Opelika, AL: 156,993,000
- Augusta-Richmond County, GA-SC: 590,146,000
- Austin-Round Rock, TX: 2,000,860,000
- Bakersfield, CA: 882,176,000
- Baltimore-Columbia-Towson, MD: 2,797,407,000
- Bangor, ME: 152,692,000
- Barnstable Town, MA: 214,333,000
- Baton Rouge, LA: 830,480,000
- Battle Creek, MI: 134,314,000
- Bay City, MI: 105,659,000
- Beaumont-Port Arthur, TX: 408,419,000
- Beckley, WV: 122,507,000
- Bellingham, WA: 212,284,000
- Bend-Redmond, OR: 175,268,000
- Billings, MT: 168,283,000
- Binghamton, NY: 246,020,000
- Birmingham-Hoover, AL: 1,145,647,000
- Bismarck, ND: 129,517,000
- Blacksburg-Christiansburg-Radford, VA: 181,747,000
- Bloomington, IL: 189,413,000
- Bloomington, IN: 165,577,000
- Bloomsburg-Berwick, PA: 85,229,000
- Boise City, ID: 676,909,000
- Boston-Cambridge-Newton, MA-NH: 4,774,321,000
    - Boston, MA: 1,984,537,000
    - Cambridge-Newton-Framingham, MA: 2,361,182,000
    - Rockingham County-Strafford County, NH: 428,602,000
- Boulder, CO: 319,372,000
- Bowling Green, KY: 168,436,000
- Bremerton-Silverdale, WA: 260,131,000
- Bridgeport-Stamford-Norwalk, CT: 948,053,000
- Brownsville-Harlingen, TX: 422,156,000
- Brunswick, GA: 116,003,000
- Buffalo-Cheektowaga-Niagara Falls, NY: 1,135,230,000
- Burlington, NC: 158,276,000
- Burlington-South Burlington, VT: 217,042,000
- California-Lexington Park, MD: 111,413,000
- Canton-Massillon, OH: 402,976,000
- Cape Coral-Fort Myers, FL: 701,982,000
- Cape Girardeau, MO-IL: 97,534,000
- Carbondale-Marion, IL: 126,828,000
- Carson City, NV: 54,521,000

- Casper, WY: 82,178,000
- Cedar Rapids, IA: 266,040,000
- Chambersburg-Waynesboro, PA: 153,638,000
- Champaign-Urbana, IL: 238,984,000
- Charleston, WV: 220,614,000
- Charleston-North Charleston, SC: 744,526,000
- Charlotte-Concord-Gastonia, NC-SC: 2,426,363,000
- Charlottesville, VA: 229,514,000
- Chattanooga, TN-GA: 547,776,000
- Cheyenne, WY: 97,121,000
- Chicago-Naperville-Elgin, IL-IN-WI: 9,551,031,000
    - Chicago-Naperville-Arlington Heights, IL: 7,340,454,000
    - Elgin, IL: 635,199,000
    - Gary, IN: 703,031,000
    - Lake County-Kenosha County, IL-WI: 872,347,000
- Chico, CA: 225,411,000
- Cincinnati, OH-KY-IN: 2,157,719,000
- Clarksville, TN-KY: 281,021,000
- Cleveland, TN: 120,864,000
- Cleveland-Elyria, OH: 2,060,810,000
- Coeur d'Alene, ID: 150,346,000
- College Station-Bryan, TX: 249,156,000
- Colorado Springs, CO: 697,856,000
- Columbia, MO: 174,974,000
- Columbia, SC: 810,068,000
- Columbus, GA-AL: 313,749,000
- Columbus, IN: 81,162,000
- Columbus, OH: 2,021,632,000
- Corpus Christi, TX: 452,422,000
- Corvallis, OR: 87,572,000
- Crestview-Fort Walton Beach-Destin, FL: 262,172,000
- Cumberland, MD-WV: 99,979,000
- Dallas-Fort Worth-Arlington, TX: 7,102,796,000
    - Dallas-Plano-Irving, TX: 4,707,151,000
    - Fort Worth-Arlington, TX: 2,395,645,000
- Dalton, GA: 143,781,000
- Danville, IL: 79,282,000
- Daphne-Fairhope-Foley, AL: 203,709,000
- Davenport-Moline-Rock Island, IA-IL: 383,606,000
- Dayton, OH: 800,909,000
- Decatur, AL: 152,680,000
- Decatur, IL: 107,303,000
- Deltona-Daytona Beach-Ormond Beach, FL: 623,279,000
- Denver-Aurora-Lakewood, CO: 2,814,330,000

- Des Moines-West Des Moines, IA: 622,899,000
- Detroit-Warren-Dearborn, MI: 4,302,043,000
    - Detroit-Dearborn-Livonia, MI: 1,759,335,000
    - Warren-Troy-Farmington Hills, MI: 2,542,708,000
- Dothan, AL: 148,171,000
- Dover, DE: 173,533,000
- Dubuque, IA: 97,125,000
- Duluth, MN-WI: 279,601,000
- Durham-Chapel Hill, NC: 552,493,000
- East Stroudsburg, PA: 166,397,000
- Eau Claire, WI: 165,636,000
- El Centro, CA: 180,191,000
- Elizabethtown-Fort Knox, KY: 148,604,000
- Elkhart-Goshen, IN: 203,474,000
- Elmira, NY: 87,071,000
- El Paso, TX: 838,972,000
- Erie, PA: 278,045,000
- Eugene, OR: 362,895,000
- Evansville, IN-KY: 315,693,000
- Fairbanks, AK: 99,631,000
- Fargo, ND-MN: 233,836,000
- Farmington, NM: 118,737,000
- Fayetteville, NC: 376,509,000
- Fayetteville-Springdale-Rogers, AR-MO: 513,559,000
- Flagstaff, AZ: 139,097,000
- Flint, MI: 410,849,000
- Florence, SC: 206,448,000
- Florence-Muscle Shoals, AL: 146,950,000
- Fond du Lac, WI: 101,973,000
- Fort Collins, CO: 333,577,000
- Fort Smith, AR-OK: 280,241,000
- Fort Wayne, IN: 429,820,000
- Fresno, CA: 974,861,000
- Gadsden, AL: 103,057,000
- Gainesville, FL: 277,163,000
- Gainesville, GA: 193,535,000
- Gettysburg, PA: 102,295,000
- Glens Falls, NY: 126,918,000
- Goldsboro, NC: 124,132,000
- Grand Forks, ND-MN: 102,449,000
- Grand Island, NE: 85,066,000
- Grand Junction, CO: 148,513,000
- Grand Rapids-Wyoming, MI: 1,038,583,000
- Grants Pass, OR: 84,745,000

- Great Falls, MT: 82,278,000
- Greeley, CO: 285,174,000
- Green Bay, WI: 316,519,000
- Greensboro-High Point, NC: 752,157,000
- Greenville, NC: 175,842,000
- Greenville-Anderson-Mauldin, SC: 874,869,000
- Gulfport-Biloxi-Pascagoula, MS: 389,255,000
- Hagerstown-Martinsburg, MD-WV: 261,486,000
- Hammond, LA: 128,755,000
- Hanford-Corcoran, CA: 150,965,000
- Harrisburg-Carlisle, PA: 565,006,000
- Harrisonburg, VA: 131,131,000
- Hartford-West Hartford-East Hartford, CT: 1,211,324,000
- Hattiesburg, MS: 148,839,000
- Hickory-Lenoir-Morganton, NC: 362,510,000
- Hilton Head Island-Bluffton-Beaufort, SC: 207,413,000
- Hinesville, GA: 80,198,000
- Homosassa Springs, FL: 141,058,000
- Hot Springs, AR: 97,177,000
- Houma-Thibodaux, LA: 212,297,000
- Houston-The Woodlands-Sugar Land, TX: 6,656,947,000
- Huntington-Ashland, WV-KY-OH: 361,580,000
- Huntsville, AL: 444,752,000
- Idaho Falls, ID: 139,747,000
- Indianapolis-Carmel-Anderson, IN: 1,988,817,000
- Iowa City, IA: 166,498,000
- Ithaca, NY: 104,926,000
- Jackson, MI: 159,494,000
- Jackson, MS: 578,777,000
- Jackson, TN: 129,682,000
- Jacksonville, FL: 1,449,481,000
- Jacksonville, NC: 186,311,000
- Janesville-Beloit, WI: 161,448,000
- Jefferson City, MO: 151,145,000
- Johnson City, TN: 200,648,000
- Johnstown, PA: 136,411,000
- Jonesboro, AR: 128,394,000
- Joplin, MO: 177,211,000
- Kahului-Wailuku-Lahaina, HI: 164,726,000
- Kalamazoo-Portage, MI: 335,340,000
- Kankakee, IL: 110,879,000
- Kansas City, MO-KS: 2,087,471,000
- Kennewick-Richland, WA: 279,116,000
- Killeen-Temple, TX: 431,032,000

- Kingsport-Bristol-Bristol, TN-VA: 307,120,000
- Kingston, NY: 180,143,000
- Knoxville, TN: 861,424,000
- Kokomo, IN: 82,556,000
- La Crosse-Onalaska, WI-MN: 136,985,000
- Lafayette, LA: 490,488,000
- Lafayette-West Lafayette, IN: 214,363,000
- Lake Charles, LA: 205,605,000
- Lake Havasu City-Kingman, AZ: 204,737,000
- Lakeland-Winter Haven, FL: 650,092,000
- Lancaster, PA: 536,624,000
- Lansing-East Lansing, MI: 472,276,000
- Laredo, TX: 269,721,000
- Las Cruces, NM: 214,295,000
- Las Vegas-Henderson-Paradise, NV: 2,114,801,000
- Lawrence, KS: 118,053,000
- Lawton, OK: 130,644,000
- Lebanon, PA: 137,067,000
- Lewiston, ID-WA: 62,153,000
- Lewiston-Auburn, ME: 107,233,000
- Lexington-Fayette, KY: 500,535,000
- Lima, OH: 104,425,000
- Lincoln, NE: 323,578,000
- Little Rock-North Little Rock-Conway, AR: 731,612,000
- Logan, UT-ID: 133,857,000
- Longview, TX: 217,781,000
- Longview, WA: 103,468,000
- Los Angeles-Long Beach-Anaheim, CA: 13,340,068,000
    - Anaheim-Santa Ana-Irvine, CA: 3,169,776,000
    - Los Angeles-Long Beach-Glendale, CA: 10,170,292,000
- Louisville/Jefferson County, KY-IN: 1,278,413,000
- Lubbock, TX: 311,154,000
- Lynchburg, VA: 259,950,000
- Macon, GA: 230,096,000
- Madera, CA: 154,998,000
- Madison, WI: 641,385,000
- Manchester-Nashua, NH: 406,678,000
- Manhattan, KS: 98,545,000
- Mankato-North Mankato, MN: 99,134,000
- Mansfield, OH: 121,707,000
- McAllen-Edinburg-Mission, TX: 842,304,000
- Medford, OR: 212,567,000
- Memphis, TN-MS-AR: 1,344,127,000
- Merced, CA: 268,455,000

- Miami-Fort Lauderdale-West Palm Beach, FL: 6,012,331,000
  - Fort Lauderdale-Pompano Beach-Deerfield Beach, FL: 1,896,425,000
  - Miami-Miami Beach-Kendall, FL: 2,693,117,000
  - West Palm Beach-Boca Raton-Delray Beach, FL: 1,422,789,000
- Michigan City-La Porte, IN: 110,884,000
- Midland, MI: 83,632,000
- Midland, TX: 166,718,000
- Milwaukee-Waukesha-West Allis, WI: 1,575,747,000
- Minneapolis-St. Paul-Bloomington, MN-WI: 3,524,583,000
- Missoula, MT: 114,181,000
- Mobile, AL: 415,395,000
- Modesto, CA: 538,388,000
- Monroe, LA: 179,238,000
- Monroe, MI: 149,568,000
- Montgomery, AL: 373,792,000
- Morgantown, WV: 138,176,000
- Morristown, TN: 116,642,000
- Mount Vernon-Anacortes, WA: 121,846,000
- Muncie, IN: 116,852,000
- Muskegon, MI: 172,790,000
- Myrtle Beach-Conway-North Myrtle Beach, SC-NC: 431,964,000
- Napa, CA: 142,456,000
- Naples-Immokalee-Marco Island, FL: 357,305,000
- Nashville-Davidson-Murfreesboro-Franklin, TN: 1,830,345,000
- New Bern, NC: 126,245,000
- New Haven-Milford, CT: 859,470,000
- New Orleans-Metairie, LA: 1,262,888,000
- New York-Newark-Jersey City, NY-NJ-PA: 20,182,305,000
  - Dutchess County-Putnam County, NY: 394,796,000
  - Nassau County-Suffolk County, NY: 2,862,937,000
  - Newark, NJ-PA: 2,511,493,000
  - New York-Jersey City-White Plains, NY-NJ: 14,413,079,000
- Niles-Benton Harbor, MI: 154,636,000
- North Port-Sarasota-Bradenton, FL: 768,918,000
- Norwich-New London, CT: 271,863,000
- Ocala, FL: 343,254,000
- Ocean City, NJ: 94,727,000
- Odessa, TX: 159,436,000
- Ogden-Clearfield, UT: 642,850,000
- Oklahoma City, OK: 1,358,452,000
- Olympia-Tumwater, WA: 269,536,000
- Omaha-Council Bluffs, NE-IA: 915,312,000
- Orlando-Kissimmee-Sanford, FL: 2,387,138,000
- Oshkosh-Neenah, WI: 169,546,000

- Owensboro, KY: 117,463,000
- Oxnard-Thousand Oaks-Ventura, CA: 850,536,000
- Palm Bay-Melbourne-Titusville, FL: 568,088,000
- Panama City, FL: 197,506,000
- Parkersburg-Vienna, WV: 92,332,000
- Pensacola-Ferry Pass-Brent, FL: 478,043,000
- Peoria, IL: 378,018,000
- Philadelphia-Camden-Wilmington, PA-NJ-DE-MD: 6,069,875,000
    - Camden, NJ: 1,252,628,000
    - Montgomery County-Bucks County-Chester County, PA: 1,962,570,000
    - Philadelphia, PA: 2,131,336,000
    - Wilmington, DE-MD-NJ: 723,341,000
- Phoenix-Mesa-Scottsdale, AZ: 4,574,531,000
- Pine Bluff, AR: 93,696,000
- Pittsburgh, PA: 2,353,045,000
- Pittsfield, MA: 127,828,000
- Pocatello, ID: 83,744,000
- Portland-South Portland, ME: 526,295,000
- Portland-Vancouver-Hillsboro, OR-WA: 2,389,228,000
- Port St. Lucie, FL: 454,846,000
- Prescott, AZ: 222,255,000
- Providence-Warwick, RI-MA: 1,613,070,000
- Provo-Orem, UT: 585,799,000
- Pueblo, CO: 163,591,000
- Punta Gorda, FL: 173,115,000
- Racine, WI: 195,080,000
- Raleigh, NC: 1,273,568,000
- Rapid City, SD: 144,134,000
- Reading, PA: 415,271,000
- Redding, CA: 179,533,000
- Reno, NV: 450,890,000
- Richmond, VA: 1,271,334,000
- Riverside-San Bernardino-Ontario, CA: 4,489,159,000
- Roanoke, VA: 314,560,000
- Rochester, MN: 213,873,000
- Rochester, NY: 1,081,954,000
- Rockford, IL: 340,663,000
- Rocky Mount, NC: 148,069,000
- Rome, GA: 96,504,000
- Sacramento-Roseville-Arden-Arcade, CA: 2,274,194,000
- Saginaw, MI: 193,307,000
- St. Cloud, MN: 194,418,000
- St. George, UT: 155,602,000
- St. Joseph, MO-KS: 126,880,000

- St. Louis, MO-IL: 2,811,588,000
- Salem, OR: 410,091,000
- Salinas, CA: 433,898,000
- Salisbury, MD-DE: 395,300,000
- Salt Lake City, UT: 1,170,266,000
- San Angelo, TX: 119,659,000
- San Antonio-New Braunfels, TX: 2,384,075,000
- San Diego-Carlsbad, CA: 3,299,521,000
- San Francisco-Oakland-Hayward, CA: 4,656,132,000
    - Oakland-Hayward-Berkeley, CA: 2,764,960,000
    - San Francisco-Redwood City-South San Francisco, CA: 1,629,951,000
    - San Rafael, CA 261,221,000
- San Jose-Sunnyvale-Santa Clara, CA: 1,976,836,000
- San Luis Obispo-Paso Robles-Arroyo Grande, CA: 281,401,000
- Santa Cruz-Watsonville, CA: 274,146,000
- Santa Fe, NM: 148,686,000
- Santa Maria-Santa Barbara, CA: 444,769,000
- Santa Rosa, CA: 502,146,000
- Savannah, GA: 379,199,000
- Scranton-Wilkes-Barre-Hazleton, PA: 558,166,000
- Seattle-Tacoma-Bellevue, WA: 3,733,580,000
    - Seattle-Bellevue-Everett, WA: 2,889,626,000
    - Tacoma-Lakewood, WA: 843,954,000
- Sebastian-Vero Beach, FL: 147,919,000
- Sebring, FL: 99,491,000
- Sheboygan, WI: 115,569,000
- Sherman-Denison, TX: 125,467,000
- Shreveport-Bossier City, LA: 443,708,000
- Sierra Vista-Douglas, AZ: 126,427,000
- Sioux City, IA-NE-SD: 169,069,000
- Sioux Falls, SD: 251,854,000
- South Bend-Mishawaka, IN-MI: 320,098,000
- Spartanburg, SC: 325,079,000
- Spokane-Spokane Valley, WA: 547,824,000
- Springfield, IL: 211,156,000
- Springfield, MA: 631,982,000
- Springfield, MO: 456,456,000
- Springfield, OH: 135,959,000
- State College, PA: 160,580,000
- Staunton-Waynesboro, VA: 120,221,000
- Stockton-Lodi, CA: 726,106,000
- Sumter, SC: 107,480,000
- Syracuse, NY: 660,458,000
- Tallahassee, FL: 377,924,000

- Tampa-St. Petersburg-Clearwater, FL: 2,975,225,000
- Terre Haute, IN: 171,019,000
- Texarkana, TX-AR: 149,769,000
- The Villages, FL: 118,891,000
- Toledo, OH: 605,956,000
- Topeka, KS: 233,791,000
- Trenton, NJ: 371,398,000
- Tucson, AZ: 1,010,025,000
- Tulsa, OK: 981,005,000
- Tuscaloosa, AL: 239,908,000
- Tyler, TX: 222,936,000
- Urban Honolulu, HI: 998,714,000
- Utica-Rome, NY: 295,600,000
- Valdosta, GA: 142,875,000
- Vallejo-Fairfield, CA: 436,092,000
- Victoria, TX: 99,913,000
- Vineland-Bridgeton, NJ: 155,854,000
- Virginia Beach-Norfolk-Newport News, VA-NC: 1,724,876,000
- Visalia-Porterville, CA: 459,863,000
- Waco, TX: 262,813,000
- Walla Walla, WA: 64,282,000
- Warner Robins, GA: 188,149,000
- Washington-Arlington-Alexandria, DC-VA-MD-WV: 6,097,684,000
    - Silver Spring-Frederick-Rockville, MD: 1,285,438,000
    - Washington-Arlington-Alexandria, DC-VA-MD-WV: 4,812,246,000
- Waterloo-Cedar Falls, IA: 170,612,000
- Watertown-Fort Drum, NY: 117,635,000
- Wausau, WI: 135,868,000
- Weirton-Steubenville, WV-OH: 120,512,000
- Wenatchee, WA: 116,178,000
- Wheeling, WV-OH: 144,198,000
- Wichita, KS: 644,610,000
- Wichita Falls, TX: 150,780,000
- Williamsport, PA: 116,048,000
- Wilmington, NC: 277,969,000
- Winchester, VA-WV: 133,836,000
- Winston-Salem, NC: 659,330,000
- Worcester, MA-CT: 935,536,000
- Yakima, WA: 248,830,000
- York-Hanover, PA: 442,867,000
- Youngstown-Warren-Boardman, OH-PA: 549,885,000
- Yuba City, CA: 170,955,000
- Yuma, AZ: 204,275,000

88

METROPOLITAN ECONOMIC PROFILES

88.1 Overview

Pew Research Center (www.pewresearch.org) defines middle-income adults as those that live in households with incomes two-thirds to double the national median size-adjusted household income, about $42,000 to $125,000 annually in 2014 for a three-person household. Lower-income households have incomes less than two-thirds of the median, and upper-income households have incomes that are more than double the median. Household incomes are adjusted for the cost of living in metropolitan areas.

88.2 Income Tiers By Metro

A May 2016 report by Pew Research Center assessed the distribution of adults in lower-, middle-, and upper income households as follows:

	Lower	Middle	Upper
• Akron, OH:	24.5%	54.6%	20.9%
• Albany-Schenectady-Troy, NY:	20.2%	55.1%	24.8%
• Albuquerque, NM:	33.0%	50.7%	16.3%
• Allentown-Bethlehem-Easton, PA-NJ:	25.2%	55.7%	19.1%
• Amarillo, TX:	27.4%	52.6%	20.0%
• Anchorage, AK:	20.3%	55.5%	24.2%
• Ann Arbor, MI:	25.6%	49.3%	25.1%
• Anniston-Oxford-Jacksonville, AL:	33.6%	50.5%	16.0%
• Atlanta-Sandy Springs-Roswell, GA:	27.0%	50.5%	22.6%
• Atlantic City-Hammonton, NJ:	30.1%	52.8%	17.0%
• Auburn-Opelika, AL:	38.5%	43.0%	18.5%
• Augusta-Richmond County, GA-SC:	29.3%	52.7%	18.0%
• Austin-Round Rock, TX:	23.4%	52.5%	24.1%
• Bakersfield, CA:	41.5%	43.6%	14.9%
• Baltimore-Columbia-Towson, MD:	23.0%	51.3%	25.7%
• Bangor, ME:	32.6%	54.2%	13.3%
• Barnstable Town, MA:	17.7%	52.1%	30.3%
• Baton Rouge, LA:	26.2%	52.5%	21.3%
• Beaumont-Port Arthur, TX:	32.2%	50.8%	17.0%
• Bellingham, WA:	32.1%	51.8%	16.1%
• Bend-Redmond, OR:	29.1%	51.1%	19.8%

- Binghamton, NY: 28.8% 53.9% 17.4%
- Birmingham-Hoover, AL: 29.9% 49.6% 20.5%
- Blacksburg-Christiansburg-Radford, VA: 34.3% 50.7% 15.0%
- Bloomington, IL: 24.5% 50.2% 25.3%
- Boise City, ID: 29.6% 54.8% 15.6%
- Boston-Cambridge-Newton, MA-NH: 21.7% 48.6% 29.6%
- Bremerton-Silverdale, WA: 23.1% 57.1% 19.8%
- Bridgeport-Stamford-Norwalk, CT: 22.5% 45.6% 32.0%
- Brownsville-Harlingen, TX: 46.9% 42.7% 10.4%
- Buffalo-Cheektowaga-Niagara Falls, NY: 26.2% 52.8% 20.9%
- Burlington, NC: 34.1% 51.8% 14.1%
- Burlington-South Burlington, VT: 24.5% 51.5% 24.0%
- Canton-Massillon, OH: 25.3% 58.6% 16.2%
- Cape Coral-Fort Myers, FL: 28.4% 54.2% 17.4%
- Champaign-Urbana, IL: 35.9% 44.4% 19.7%
- Charleston-North Charleston, SC: 26.2% 53.4% 20.5%
- Charlotte-Concord-Gastonia, NC-SC: 27.5% 52.1% 20.4%
- Chattanooga, TN-GA: 29.2% 53.3% 17.5%
- Chicago-Naperville-Elgin, IL-IN-WI: 27.4% 51.1% 21.5%
- Chico, CA: 40.0% 46.9% 13.1%
- Cincinnati, OH-KY-IN: 22.6% 52.3% 25.2%
- Clarksville, TN-KY: 32.2% 55.7% 12.1%
- Cleveland-Elyria, OH: 25.5% 52.3% 22.3%
- Colorado Springs, CO: 23.5% 54.8% 21.7%
- Columbia, MO: 28.4% 53.9% 17.7%
- Columbus, OH: 23.6% 51.6% 24.9%
- Corpus Christi, TX: 29.9% 52.3% 17.8%
- Dallas-Fort Worth-Arlington, TX: 27.6% 50.4% 22.0%
- Daphne-Fairhope-Foley, AL: 27.4% 50.2% 22.4%
- Dayton, OH: 26.9% 52.7% 20.4%
- Decatur, AL: 27.2% 56.1% 16.7%
- Decatur, IL: 25.8% 53.6% 20.6%
- Deltona-Daytona Beach-Ormond Beach, FL: 34.4% 53.1% 12.5%
- Denver-Aurora-Lakewood, CO: 22.4% 53.0% 24.6%
- Detroit-Warren-Dearborn, MI: 28.1% 51.4% 20.5%
- Dover, DE: 23.2% 57.5% 19.3%
- East Stroudsburg, PA: 23.3% 60.0% 16.7%
- Eau Claire, WI: 22.6% 61.2% 16.2%
- El Centro, CA: 42.1% 44.7% 13.3%
- Elkhart-Goshen, IN: 23.1% 61.4% 15.5%
- El Paso, TX: 43.5% 45.6% 10.9%
- Erie, PA: 30.5% 52.3% 17.2%
- Eugene, OR: 34.7% 52.0% 13.3%
- Fayetteville, NC: 33.3% 52.2% 14.6%

- Fayetteville-Springdale-Rogers, AR-MO: 28.9% 51.2% 20.0%
- Flagstaff, AZ: 35.2% 47.0% 17.8%
- Fort Collins, CO: 26.2% 55.7% 18.1%
- Fort Wayne, IN: 26.9% 58.7% 14.4%
- Fresno, CA: 43.2% 44.3% 12.5%
- Gadsden, AL: 32.6% 55.6% 11.8%
- Gainesville, FL: 35.6% 47.2% 17.2%
- Gainesville, GA: 28.1% 54.1% 17.8%
- Glens Falls, NY: 27.2% 58.1% 14.6%
- Goldsboro, NC: 40.9% 47.8% 11.4%
- Grand Junction, CO: 28.0% 52.0% 20.0%
- Grand Rapids-Wyoming, MI: 24.8% 56.8% 18.4%
- Greensboro-High Point, NC: 31.3% 52.8% 15.9%
- Greenville, NC: 39.4% 46.3% 14.3%
- Greenville-Anderson-Mauldin, SC: 33.4% 50.2% 16.4%
- Gulfport-Biloxi-Pascagoula, MS: 33.5% 53.7% 12.7%
- Hanford-Corcoran, CA: 39.2% 49.1% 11.8%
- Harrisburg-Carlisle, PA: 21.3% 57.7% 21.1%
- Hartford-West Hartford-East Hartford, CT: 21.0% 49.3% 29.7%
- Hickory-Lenoir-Morganton, NC: 35.2% 54.3% 10.4%
- Hilton Head Island-Bluffton-Beaufort, SC: 23.1% 56.1% 20.9%
- Honolulu (urban), HI: 21.6% 63.0% 15.3%
- Houma-Thibodaux, LA: 32.5% 52.6% 14.9%
- Houston-The Woodlands-Sugar Land, TX: 28.5% 48.5% 23.0%
- Huntsville, AL: 25.5% 50.1% 24.4%
- Indianapolis-Carmel-Anderson, IN: 24.4% 54.8% 20.8%
- Jackson, MI: 30.3% 56.4% 13.3%
- Jackson, TN: 29.2% 55.3% 15.5%
- Jacksonville, FL: 28.2% 52.9% 18.9%
- Janesville-Beloit, WI: 19.5% 65.2% 15.4%
- Johnstown, PA: 25.2% 56.0% 18.8%
- Joplin, MO: 30.3% 56.8% 13.0%
- Kalamazoo-Portage, MI: 31.0% 52.5% 16.5%
- Kankakee, IL: 23.3% 62.1% 14.6%
- Kansas City, MO-KS: 23.0% 54.8% 22.2%
- Knoxville, TN: 32.5% 50.1% 17.5%
- Lafayette, LA: 28.2% 49.8% 22.1%
- Lake Havasu City-Kingman, AZ: 42.6% 47.6% 9.8%
- Lakeland-Winter Haven, FL: 33.5% 55.2% 11.3%
- Lancaster, PA: 24.1% 57.0% 18.8%
- Lansing-East Lansing, MI: 28.4% 55.1% 16.6%
- Laredo, TX: 46.9% 44.2% 8.9%
- Las Cruces, NM: 45.3% 45.5% 9.3%
- Las Vegas-Henderson-Paradise, NV: 29.0% 55.9% 15.0%

- Lebanon, PA: 21.2% 62.8% 15.9%
- Lewiston-Auburn, ME: 25.6% 53.2% 21.1%
- Lincoln, NE: 23.9% 56.1% 20.0%
- Little Rock-North Little Rock-Conway, AR: 26.9% 55.4% 17.6%
- Los Angeles-Long Beach-Anaheim, CA: 37.2% 46.5% 16.3%
- Louisville/Jefferson County, KY-IN: 25.4% 54.1% 20.5%
- Lubbock, TX: 33.6% 51.8% 14.6%
- Lynchburg, VA: 29.1% 54.9% 16.0%
- Madera, CA: 38.5% 51.3% 10.2%
- Manchester-Nashua, NH: 21.2% 56.2% 22.7%
- Mansfield, OH: 32.6% 54.4% 13.1%
- McAllen-Edinburg-Mission, TX: 46.1% 45.0% 8.9%
- Medford, OR: 33.8% 53.4% 12.8%
- Memphis, TN-MS-AR: 31.8% 49.5% 18.7%
- Merced, CA: 43.0% 47.4% 9.5%
- Miami-Fort Lauderdale-West Palm Beach, FL: 36.7% 48.5% 14.8%
- Michigan City-La Porte, IN: 27.1% 57.0% 15.9%
- Midland, TX: 20.7% 42.6% 36.8%
- Milwaukee-Waukesha-West Allis, WI: 25.5% 52.6% 22.0%
- Minneapolis-St. Paul-Bloomington, MN-WI: 20.1% 54.6% 25.4%
- Mobile, AL: 30.7% 53.3% 16.0%
- Modesto, CA: 36.5% 49.4% 14.1%
- Monroe, LA: 38.7% 41.8% 19.5%
- Monroe, MI: 24.0% 58.1% 17.9%
- Montgomery, AL: 30.5% 50.7% 18.8%
- Morgantown, WV: 37.7% 46.0% 16.3%
- Muncie, IN: 34.0% 53.0% 13.1%
- Muskegon, MI: 31.5% 56.1% 12.4%
- Napa, CA: 25.1% 51.5% 23.5%
- Naples-Immokalee-Marco Island, FL: 26.7% 51.5% 21.8%
- Nashville-Davidson-Murfreesboro-Franklin, TN: 26.5% 53.7% 19.8%
- New Haven-Milford, CT: 27.7% 50.0% 22.3%
- New Orleans-Metairie, LA: 30.3% 49.2% 20.6%
- New York-Newark-Jersey City, NY-NJ-PA: 30.9% 48.1% 21.0%
- Niles-Benton Harbor, MI: 31.6% 46.4% 22.0%
- North Port-Sarasota-Bradenton, FL: 26.6% 54.0% 19.4%
- Norwich-New London, CT: 18.6% 52.8% 28.7%
- Ocala, FL: 31.5% 55.8% 12.8%
- Ocean City, NJ: 28.6% 52.8% 18.7%
- Odessa, TX: 24.2% 54.8% 21.0%
- Ogden-Clearfield, UT: 18.9% 62.6% 18.5%
- Oklahoma City, OK: 26.5% 52.9% 20.6%
- Olympia-Tumwater, WA: 22.6% 56.0% 21.5%
- Omaha-Council Bluffs, NE-IA: 21.9% 56.0% 22.2%

- Orlando-Kissimmee-Sanford, FL: 32.7% 51.6% 15.7%
- Owensboro, KY: 27.7% 58.5% 13.8%
- Oxnard-Thousand Oaks-Ventura, CA: 26.4% 53.2% 20.4%
- Palm Bay-Melbourne-Titusville, FL: 27.1% 56.3% 16.6%
- Pensacola-Ferry Pass-Brent, FL: 26.1% 57.4% 16.5%
- Philadelphia-Camden-Wilm., PA-NJ-DE-MD: 27.0% 50.6% 22.4%
- Phoenix-Mesa-Scottsdale, AZ: 29.1% 52.3% 18.6%
- Pittsburgh, PA: 23.6% 54.6% 21.9%
- Portland-South Portland, ME: 22.1% 57.0% 21.0%
- Portland-Vancouver-Hillsboro, OR-WA: 25.0% 53.7% 21.3%
- Port St. Lucie, FL: 29.8% 54.9% 15.4%
- Prescott, AZ: 32.9% 52.8% 14.4%
- Providence-Warwick, RI-MA: 25.5% 52.3% 22.2%
- Provo-Orem, UT: 28.0% 58.3% 13.8%
- Pueblo, CO: 37.1% 51.2% 11.7%
- Punta Gorda, FL: 28.8% 54.0% 17.3%
- Racine, WI: 23.3% 55.1% 21.6%
- Raleigh, NC: 24.7% 50.4% 25.0%
- Reading, PA: 25.0% 56.9% 18.0%
- Redding, CA: 32.5% 53.2% 14.3%
- Reno, NV: 30.4% 52.8% 16.8%
- Richmond, VA: 21.6% 54.2% 24.2%
- Riverside-San Bernardino-Ontario, CA: 35.7% 51.0% 13.4%
- Rochester, NY: 25.2% 56.7% 18.0%
- Rockford, IL: 28.2% 53.7% 18.2%
- Rocky Mount, NC: 36.0% 51.7% 12.3%
- Sacramento-Roseville-Arden-Arcade, CA: 29.4% 48.9% 21.7%
- Saginaw, MI: 26.7% 58.5% 14.9%
- St. Louis, MO-IL: 22.5% 52.8% 24.7%
- Salinas, CA: 34.0% 50.6% 15.4%
- Salisbury, MD-DE: 23.1% 54.3% 22.5%
- Salt Lake City, UT: 24.1% 58.2% 17.8%
- San Angelo, TX: 28.0% 56.6% 15.5%
- San Antonio-New Braunfels, TX: 29.1% 52.6% 18.3%
- San Diego-Carlsbad, CA: 31.3% 50.4% 18.2%
- San Francisco-Oakland-Hayward, CA: 24.2% 47.7% 28.1%
- San Jose-Sunnyvale-Santa Clara, CA: 20.4% 48.5% 31.1%
- San Luis Obispo-Paso Robles-Arroyo G., CA: 29.8% 51.3% 18.9%
- Santa Cruz-Watsonville, CA: 30.1% 50.5% 19.5%
- Santa Fe, NM: 29.4% 49.3% 21.3%
- Santa Maria-Santa Barbara, CA: 33.8% 46.3% 19.9%
- Santa Rosa, CA: 27.0% 54.0% 19.1%
- Scranton-Wilkes Barre-Hazleton, PA: 28.5% 55.7% 15.8%
- Seattle-Tacoma-Bellevue, WA: 21.3% 52.6% 26.2%

- Sheboygan, WI: 18.2% 63.2% 18.7%
- Shreveport-Bossier City, LA: 32.8% 49.4% 17.9%
- Spartanburg, SC: 32.7% 50.1% 17.2%
- Spokane-Spokane Valley, WA: 32.1% 52.1% 15.8%
- Springfield, IL: 24.8% 49.3% 25.9%
- Springfield, MA: 28.8% 51.0% 20.2%
- Springfield, MO: 33.3% 53.8% 12.9%
- Springfield, OH: 32.3% 55.0% 12.8%
- State College, PA: 35.3% 49.4% 15.3%
- Stockton-Lodi, CA: 34.5% 50.6% 14.9%
- Syracuse, NY: 25.9% 54.9% 19.2%
- Tampa-St. Petersburg-Clearwater, FL: 31.8% 52.5% 15.7%
- Toledo, OH: 28.7% 53.1% 18.2%
- Trenton, NJ: 23.8% 48.1% 28.1%
- Tucson, AZ: 33.4% 49.4% 17.2%
- Tyler, TX: 34.4% 49.3% 16.4%
- Utica-Rome, NY: 28.5% 56.6% 14.9%
- Vallejo-Fairfield, CA: 26.6% 57.4% 16.0%
- Virginia Beach-Norfolk-Newport News, VA-NC: 23.8% 56.1% 20.1%
- Visalia-Porterville, CA: 46.1% 44.6% 9.3%
- Waco, TX: 32.7% 54.0% 13.3%
- Washington-Arlington-Alex., DC-VA-MD-WV: 18.9% 49.5% 31.6%
- Wausau, WI: 18.2% 67.2% 14.6%
- Wichita, KS: 26.1% 56.2% 17.7%
- Wichita Falls, TX: 30.1% 56.2% 13.7%
- Winston-Salem, NC: 30.9% 53.2% 16.0%
- Worcester, MA-CT: 23.7% 52.8% 23.5%
- Yakima, WA: 35.3% 52.3% 12.3%
- York-Hanover, PA: 22.8% 57.4% 19.7%
- Youngstown-Warren-Boardman, OH-PA: 26.8% 60.2% 12.9%
- Yuba City, CA: 37.3% 50.7% 12.0%
- Yuma, AZ: 43.7% 46.8% 9.5%

88.3 Market Resources

Pew Research Center, 1615 L Street NW, Suite 700, Washington, DC 20036. (202) 419-4300. (www.pewresearch.org)

89

MICROPOLITAN STATISTICAL AREAS

89.1 Overview

The United States Office of Management and Budget (OMB, www.omb.gov) defines a Micropolitan Statistical Area (µSA) as an urban area based around a core city or town with a population of 10,000 to 49,999.

There are 770 µSAs. The Census Bureau's description of the regions included in each µSA is available at www.census.gov/population/www/metroareas/metrodef.html.

Population data is available from the U.S. Census Bureau (www.census.gov) at www.census.gov/popest/.

89.2 µSA Populations

The U.S. population in 2015 was 321,418,820; 27,260,617 (8.5%) lived In micropolitan statistical areas.

The 2015 population in each µSA as estimated by the U.S. Census Bureau was as follows:

- Aberdeen, SD: 42,784,000
- Aberdeen, WA: 71,122,000
- Ada, OK: 38,194,000
- Adrian, MI: 98,573,000
- Alamogordo, NM: 64,362,000
- Albemarle, NC: 60,714,000
- Albert Lea, MN: 30,613,000
- Albertville, AL: 94,725,000
- Alexandria, MN: 37,075,000
- Alice, TX: 41,382,000
- Alma, MI: 41,540,000
- Alpena, MI: 28,803,000
- Altus, OK: 25,574,000
- Americus, GA: 35,947,000
- Amsterdam, NY: 49,642,000
- Andrews, TX: 18,105,000
- Angola, IN: 34,372,000
- Arcadia, FL: 35,458,000
- Ardmore, OK: 48,689,000

- Arkadelphia, AR: 22,633,000
- Arkansas City-Winfield, KS: 35,788,000
- Ashland, OH: 53,213,000
- Ashtabula, OH: 98,632,000
- Astoria, OR: 37,831,000
- Atchison, KS: 16,398,000
- Athens, OH: 65,886,000
- Athens, TN: 52,639,000
- Athens, TX: 79,545,000
- Auburn, IN: 42,589,000
- Auburn, NY: 78,288,000
- Augusta-Waterville, ME: 119,980,000
- Austin, MN: 39,116,000
- Bainbridge, GA: 27,174,000
- Baraboo, WI: 63,642,000
- Bardstown, KY: 45,126,000
- Barre, VT: 58,612,000
- Bartlesville, OK: 52,021,000
- Bastrop, LA: 26,395,000
- Batavia, NY: 58,937,000
- Batesville, AR: 37,052,000
- Bay City, TX: 36,770,000
- Beatrice, NE: 21,900,000
- Beaver Dam, WI: 88,502,000
- Bedford, IN: 45,495,000
- Beeville, TX: 32,874,000
- Bellefontaine, OH: 45,386,000
- Bemidji, MN: 45,672,000
- Bennettsville, SC: 27,494,000
- Bennington, VT: 36,317,000
- Berlin, NH-VT: 37,375,000
- Big Rapids, MI: 43,067,000
- Big Spring, TX: 38,521,000
- Big Stone Gap, VA: 58,772,000
- Blackfoot, ID: 44,990,000
- Bluefield, WV-VA: 104,063,000
- Blytheville, AR: 43,738,000
- Bogalusa, LA: 46,371,000
- Boone, IA: 26,643,000
- Boone, NC: 52,906,000
- Borger, TX: 21,734,000
- Bozeman, MT: 100,739,000
- Bradford, PA: 42,412,000
- Brainerd, MN: 92,134,000

- Branson, MO: 85,535,000
- Breckenridge, CO: 30,257,000
- Brenham, TX: 34,765,000
- Brevard, NC: 33,211,000
- Brookhaven, MS: 34,649,000
- Brookings, OR: 22,483,000
- Brookings, SD: 33,897,000
- Brownwood, TX: 37,896,000
- Bucyrus, OH: 42,306,000
- Burley, ID: 43,967,000
- Burlington, IA-IL: 47,050,000
- Butte-Silver Bow, MT: 34,622,000
- Cadillac, MI: 47,906,000
- Calhoun, GA: 56,574,000
- Cambridge, MD: 32,384,000
- Cambridge, OH: 39,258,000
- Camden, AR: 29,587,000
- Campbellsville, KY: 25,420,000
- Cañon City, CO: 46,692,000
- Canton, IL: 35,699,000
- Carlsbad-Artesia, NM: 57,578,000
- Cedar City, UT: 48,368,000
- Cedartown, GA: 41,524,000
- Celina, OH: 40,968,000
- Centralia, IL: 38,339,000
- Centralia, WA: 75,882,000
- Charleston-Mattoon, IL: 63,419,000
- Chillicothe, OH: 77,170,000
- Claremont-Lebanon, NH-VT: 216,923,000
- Clarksburg, WV: 93,802,000
- Clarksdale, MS: 24,620,000
- Clearlake, CA: 64,591,000
- Cleveland, MS: 33,322,000
- Clewiston, FL: 39,119,000
- Clinton, IA: 47,768,000
- Clovis, NM: 50,398,000
- Coffeyville, KS: 33,314,000
- Coldwater, MI: 43,664,000
- Columbus, MS: 59,710,000
- Columbus, NE: 32,847,000
- Concord, NH: 147,994,000
- Connersville, IN: 23,434,000
- Cookeville, TN: 108,191,000
- Coos Bay, OR: 63,121,000

- Cordele, GA: 22,881,000
- Corinth, MS: 37,388,000
- Cornelia, GA: 43,996,000
- Corning, NY: 97,631,000
- Corsicana, TX: 48,323,000
- Cortland, NY: 48,494,000
- Coshocton, OH: 36,569,000
- Craig, CO: 12,937,000
- Crawfordsville, IN: 38,227,000
- Crescent City, CA: 27,254,000
- Crossville, TN: 58,229,000
- Cullman, AL: 82,005,000
- Cullowhee, NC: 41,265,000
- Danville, KY: 54,272,000
- Danville, VA: 104,276,000
- Dayton, TN: 32,526,000
- Decatur, IN: 34,980,000
- Defiance, OH: 38,352,000
- Del Rio, TX: 48,988,000
- Deming, NM: 24,518,000
- DeRidder, LA: 36,462,000
- Dickinson, ND: 32,154,000
- Dixon, IL: 34,584,000
- Dodge City, KS: 34,536,000
- Douglas, GA: 43,108,000
- Dublin, GA: 57,387,000
- DuBois, PA: 80,994,000
- Dumas, TX: 22,255,000
- Duncan, OK: 44,581,000
- Dunn, NC: 128,140,000
- Durango, CO: 54,688,000
- Durant, OK: 44,884,000
- Dyersburg, TN: 37,893,000
- Eagle Pass, TX: 57,706,000
- Easton, MD: 37,512,000
- Edwards, CO: 53,605,000
- Effingham, IL: 34,371,000
- El Campo, TX: 41,486,000
- El Dorado, AR: 40,144,000
- Elizabeth City, NC: 63,578,000
- Elk City, OK: 23,768,000
- Elkins, WV: 29,126,000
- Elko, NV: 53,951,000
- Ellensburg, WA: 43,269,000

- Emporia, KS: 33,339,000
- Enid, OK: 63,569,000
- Enterprise, AL: 51,211,000
- Escanaba, MI: 36,377,000
- Española, NM: 39,465,000
- Eureka-Arcata-Fortuna, CA: 135,727,000
- Evanston, WY: 20,822,000
- Fairfield, IA: 17,555,000
- Fairmont, WV: 56,925,000
- Fallon, NV: 24,200,000
- Faribault-Northfield, MN: 65,400,000
- Farmington, MO: 66,520,000
- Fergus Falls, MN: 57,716,000
- Fernley, NV: 52,585,000
- Findlay, OH: 75,573,000
- Fitzgerald, GA: 17,403,000
- Forest City, NC: 66,390,000
- Forrest City, AR: 26,589,000
- Fort Dodge, IA: 37,071,000
- Fort Leonard Wood, MO: 53,221,000
- Fort Madison-Keokuk, IA-IL-MO: 60,433,000
- Fort Morgan, CO: 28,360,000
- Fort Polk South, LA: 50,803,000
- Frankfort, IN: 32,609,000
- Frankfort, KY: 72,354,000
- Fredericksburg, TX: 25,963,000
- Freeport, IL: 45,749,000
- Fremont, NE: 36,706,000
- Fremont, OH: 59,679,000
- Gaffney, SC: 56,194,000
- Gainesville, TX: 39,229,000
- Galesburg, IL: 51,441,000
- Gallup, NM: 76,708,000
- Garden City, KS: 41,074,000
- Gardnerville Ranchos, NV: 47,710,000
- Georgetown, SC: 61,298,000
- Gillette, WY: 49,220,000
- Glasgow, KY: 53,479,000
- Glenwood Springs, CO: 75,882,000
- Gloversville, NY: 53,992,000
- Grants, NM: 27,329,000
- Great Bend, KS: 27,103,000
- Greeneville, TN: 68,580,000
- Greenfield Town, MA: 70,601,000

- Greensburg, IN: 26,521,000
- Greenville, MS: 48,130,000
- Greenville, OH: 52,076,000
- Greenwood, MS: 41,242,000
- Greenwood, SC: 94,770,000
- Grenada, MS: 21,578,000
- Guymon, OK: 21,489,000
- Hailey, ID: 27,955,000
- Hannibal, MO: 39,076,000
- Harrison, AR: 45,135,000
- Hastings, NE: 31,587,000
- Hays, KS: 29,029,000
- Heber, UT: 29,161,000
- Helena, MT: 78,063,000
- Helena-West Helena, AR: 19,513,000
- Henderson, NC: 44,568,000
- Hereford, TX: 18,952,000
- Hermiston-Pendleton, OR: 87,721,000
- Hillsdale, MI: 45,941,000
- Hilo, HI: 196,428,000
- Hobbs, NM: 71,180,000
- Holland, MI: 114,625,000
- Hood River, OR: 23,137,000
- Houghton, MI: 38,548,000
- Hudson, NY: 61,509,000
- Huntingdon, PA: 45,668,000
- Huntington, IN: 36,630,000
- Huntsville, TX: 85,101,000
- Huron, SD: 18,372,000
- Hutchinson, KS: 63,718,000
- Hutchinson, MN: 35,932,000
- Indiana, PA: 86,966,000
- Indianola, MS: 27,005,000
- Ionia, MI: 64,223,000
- Iron Mountain, MI-WI: 30,252,000
- Jackson, OH: 32,596,000
- Jackson, WY-ID: 33,689,000
- Jacksonville, IL: 39,920,000
- Jacksonville, TX: 51,542,000
- Jamestown, ND: 21,103,000
- Jamestown-Dunkirk-Fredonia, NY: 130,779,000
- Jasper, IN: 55,055,000
- Jefferson, GA: 63,360,000
- Jesup, GA: 29,534,000

- Junction City, KS: 37,030,000
- Juneau, AK: 32,756,000
- Kalispell, MT: 96,165,000
- Kapaa, HI: 71,735,000
- Kearney, NE: 55,448,000
- Keene, NH: 75,909,000
- Kendallville, IN: 47,733,000
- Kennett, MO: 30,895,000
- Kerrville, TX: 50,955,000
- Ketchikan, AK: 13,709,000
- Key West, FL: 77,482,000
- Kill Devil Hills, NC: 39,733,000
- Kingsville, TX: 32,264,000
- Kinston, NC: 58,106,000
- Kirksville, MO: 29,814,000
- Klamath Falls, OR: 66,016,000
- Laconia, NH: 60,641,000
- La Grande, OR: 25,790,000
- LaGrange, GA: 69,763,000
- Lake City, FL: 68,348,000
- Lamesa, TX: 13,520,000
- Laramie, WY: 37,956,000
- Las Vegas, NM: 27,967,000
- Laurel, MS: 84,784,000
- Laurinburg, NC: 35,509,000
- Lawrenceburg, TN: 42,564,000
- Lebanon, MO: 35,473,000
- Levelland, TX: 23,433,000
- Lewisburg, PA: 44,954,000
- Lewisburg, TN: 31,552,000
- Lewistown, PA: 46,500,000
- Lexington, NE: 25,859,000
- Liberal, KS: 23,152,000
- Lincoln, IL: 29,494,000
- Lock Haven, PA: 39,441,000
- Logan, WV: 34,707,000
- Logansport, IN: 37,979,000
- London, KY: 127,953,000
- Los Alamos, NM: 17,785,000
- Ludington, MI: 28,783,000
- Lufkin, TX: 88,255,000
- Lumberton, NC: 134,197,000
- Macomb, IL: 31,333,000
- Madison, IN: 32,416,000

- Madisonville, KY: 46,222,000
- Magnolia, AR: 24,114,000
- Malone, NY: 50,660,000
- Malvern, AR: 33,426,000
- Manitowoc, WI: 79,806,000
- Marietta, OH: 61,112,000
- Marinette, WI-MI: 64,432,000
- Marion, IN: 67,979,000
- Marion, NC: 44,989,000
- Marion, OH: 65,355,000
- Marquette, MI: 67,215,000
- Marshall, MN: 25,673,000
- Marshall, MO: 23,258,000
- Marshall, TX: 66,746,000
- Marshalltown, IA: 40,746,000
- Martin, TN: 33,960,000
- Martinsville, VA: 65,526,000
- Maryville, MO: 22,810,000
- Mason City, IA: 50,586,000
- Mayfield, KY: 37,421,000
- Maysville, KY: 17,099,000
- McAlester, OK: 44,610,000
- McComb, MS: 52,530,000
- McMinnville, TN: 40,435,000
- McPherson, KS: 28,941,000
- Meadville, PA: 86,484,000
- Menomonie, WI: 44,497,000
- Meridian, MS: 104,499,000
- Merrill, WI: 27,980,000
- Mexico, MO: 26,096,000
- Miami, OK: 31,981,000
- Middlesborough, KY: 27,337,000
- Milledgeville, GA: 54,010,000
- Mineral Wells, TX: 27,895,000
- Minot, ND: 79,814,000
- Mitchell, SD: 23,243,000
- Moberly, MO: 25,104,000
- Montrose, CO: 40,946,000
- Morehead City, NC: 68,879,000
- Morgan City, LA: 52,810,000
- Moscow, ID: 38,778,000
- Moses Lake, WA: 93,259,000
- Moultrie, GA: 45,844,000
- Mountain Home, AR: 41,053,000

- Mountain Home, ID: 25,876,000
- Mount Airy, NC: 72,743,000
- Mount Pleasant, MI: 70,698,000
- Mount Pleasant, TX: 32,623,000
- Mount Sterling, KY: 46,194,000
- Mount Vernon, IL: 38,353,000
- Mount Vernon, OH: 61,061,000
- Murray, KY: 38,343,000
- Muscatine, IA: 43,011,000
- Muskogee, OK: 69,699,000
- Nacogdoches, TX: 65,664,000
- Natchez, MS-LA: 51,396,000
- Natchitoches, LA: 39,179,000
- Newberry, SC: 38,012,000
- New Castle, IN: 48,985,000
- New Castle, PA: 88,082,000
- New Philadelphia-Dover, OH: 92,916,000
- Newport, OR: 47,038,000
- Newport, TN: 35,162,000
- Newton, IA: 36,827,000
- New Ulm, MN: 25,313,000
- Nogales, AZ: 46,461,000
- Norfolk, NE: 48,184,000
- North Platte, NE: 36,908,000
- North Vernon, IN: 27,897,000
- North Wilkesboro, NC: 68,502,000
- Norwalk, OH: 58,469,000
- Oak Harbor, WA: 80,593,000
- Ogdensburg-Massena, NY: 111,007,000
- Oil City, PA: 53,119,000
- Okeechobee, FL: 39,469,000
- Olean, NY: 77,922,000
- Oneonta, NY: 60,636,000
- Ontario, OR-ID: 53,276,000
- Opelousas, LA: 83,848,000
- Orangeburg, SC: 89,208,000
- Oskaloosa, IA: 22,324,000
- Othello, WA: 19,254,000
- Ottawa, KS: 25,609,000
- Ottawa-Peru, IL: 150,564,000
- Ottumwa, IA: 43,942,000
- Owatonna, MN: 36,755,000
- Owosso, MI: 68,619,000
- Oxford, MS: 53,154,000

- Oxford, NC: 58,674,000
- Ozark, AL: 49,565,000
- Paducah, KY-IL: 97,312,000
- Pahrump, NV: 42,477,000
- Palatka, FL: 72,023,000
- Palestine, TX: 57,580,000
- Pampa, TX: 23,210,000
- Paragould, AR: 44,196,000
- Paris, TN: 32,147,000
- Paris, TX: 49,440,000
- Parsons, KS: 20,803,000
- Payson, AZ: 53,159,000
- Pecos, TX: 14,732,000
- Peru, IN: 35,862,000
- Picayune, MS: 55,191,000
- Pierre, SD: 21,935,000
- Pinehurst-Southern Pines, NC: 94,352,000
- Pittsburg, KS: 39,217,000
- Plainview, TX: 34,360,000
- Platteville, WI: 52,250,000
- Plattsburgh, NY: 81,251,000
- Plymouth, IN: 46,857,000
- Point Pleasant, WV-OH: 57,179,000
- Ponca City, OK: 45,366,000
- Pontiac, IL: 36,671,000
- Poplar Bluff, MO: 42,951,000
- Portales, NM: 19,120,000
- Port Angeles, WA: 73,486,000
- Port Clinton, OH: 40,877,000
- Port Lavaca, TX: 21,895,000
- Portsmouth, OH: 76,825,000
- Pottsville, PA: 144,590,000
- Price, UT: 20,479,000
- Prineville, OR: 21,630,000
- Pullman, WA: 48,177,000
- Quincy, IL-MO: 77,220,000
- Raymondville, TX: 21,903,000
- Red Bluff, CA: 63,308,000
- Red Wing, MN: 46,435,000
- Rexburg, ID: 51,092,000
- Richmond, IN: 67,001,000
- Richmond-Berea, KY: 104,766,000
- Rio Grande City, TX: 63,795,000
- Riverton, WY: 40,315,000

- Roanoke Rapids, NC: 72,882,000
- Rochelle, IL: 51,659,000
- Rockingham, NC: 45,437,000
- Rock Springs, WY: 44,626,000
- Rolla, MO: 44,794,000
- Roseburg, OR: 107,685,000
- Roswell, NM: 65,764,000
- Russellville, AR: 85,103,000
- Ruston, LA: 47,774,000
- Rutland, VT: 59,736,000
- Safford, AZ: 37,666,000
- St. Marys, GA: 52,102,000
- Salem, OH: 104,806,000
- Salina, KS: 61,666,000
- Sandpoint, ID: 41,859,000
- Sandusky, OH: 75,550,000
- Sanford, NC: 59,660,000
- Sault Ste. Marie, MI: 38,033,000
- Sayre, PA: 61,281,000
- Scottsbluff, NE: 38,309,000
- Scottsboro, AL: 52,419,000
- Searcy, AR: 79,161,000
- Sedalia, MO: 42,255,000
- Selinsgrove, PA: 40,444,000
- Selma, AL: 41,131,000
- Seneca, SC: 75,713,000
- Seneca Falls, NY: 34,833,000
- Sevierville, TN: 95,946,000
- Seymour, IN: 44,069,000
- Shawano, WI: 45,877,000
- Shawnee, OK: 71,875,000
- Shelby, NC: 96,879,000
- Shelbyville, TN: 47,183,000
- Shelton, WA: 61,023,000
- Sheridan, WY: 30,009,000
- Show Low, AZ: 108,277,000
- Sidney, OH: 48,901,000
- Sikeston, MO: 39,008,000
- Silver City, NM: 28,609,000
- Snyder, TX: 17,615,000
- Somerset, KY: 63,782,000
- Somerset, PA: 75,522,000
- Sonora, CA: 53,709,000
- Spearfish, SD: 24,827,000

- Spencer, IA: 16,507,000
- Spirit Lake, IA: 17,111,000
- Starkville, MS: 49,800,000
- Statesboro, GA: 72,651,000
- Steamboat Springs, CO: 24,130,000
- Stephenville, TX: 41,122,000
- Sterling, CO: 22,036,000
- Sterling, IL: 57,079,000
- Stevens Point, WI: 70,408,000
- Stillwater, OK: 80,850,000
- Storm Lake, IA: 20,493,000
- Sturgis, MI: 61,018,000
- Sulphur Springs, TX: 36,223,000
- Summerville, GA: 24,922,000
- Summit Park, UT: 39,633,000
- Sunbury, PA: 93,246,000
- Susanville, CA: 31,345,000
- Sweetwater, TX: 15,107,000
- Tahlequah, OK: 48,447,000
- Talladega-Sylacauga, AL: 91,586,000
- Taos, NM: 32,907,000
- Taylorville, IL: 33,642,000
- The Dalles, OR: 25,775,000
- Thomaston, GA: 26,368,000
- Thomasville, GA: 45,063,000
- Tiffin, OH: 55,610,000
- Kingsville, TX: 32,264,000
- Kinston, NC: 58,106,000
- Kirksville, MO: 29,814,000
- Klamath Falls, OR: 66,016,000
- Laconia, NH: 60,641,000
- La Grande, OR: 25,790,000
- LaGrange, GA: 69,763,000
- Lake City, FL: 68,348,000
- Lamesa, TX: 13,520,000
- Laramie, WY: 37,956,000
- Las Vegas, NM: 27,967,000
- Laurel, MS: 84,784,000
- Laurinburg, NC: 35,509,000
- Lawrenceburg, TN: 42,564,000
- Lebanon, MO: 35,473,000
- Levelland, TX: 23,433,000
- Lewisburg, PA: 44,954,000
- Lewisburg, TN: 31,552,000

- Lewistown, PA: 46,500,000
- Lexington, NE: 25,859,000
- Liberal, KS: 23,152,000
- Lincoln, IL: 29,494,000
- Lock Haven, PA: 39,441,000
- Logan, WV: 34,707,000
- Logansport, IN: 37,979,000
- London, KY: 127,953,000
- Los Alamos, NM: 17,785,000
- Ludington, MI: 28,783,000
- Lufkin, TX: 88,255,000
- Lumberton, NC: 134,197,000
- Macomb, IL: 31,333,000
- Madison, IN: 32,416,000
- Madisonville, KY: 46,222,000
- Magnolia, AR: 24,114,000
- Malone, NY: 50,660,000
- Malvern, AR: 33,426,000
- Manitowoc, WI: 79,806,000
- Marietta, OH: 61,112,000
- Marinette, WI-MI: 64,432,000
- Marion, IN: 67,979,000
- Marion, NC: 44,989,000
- Marion, OH: 65,355,000
- Marquette, MI: 67,215,000
- Marshall, MN: 25,673,000
- Marshall, MO: 23,258,000
- Marshall, TX: 66,746,000
- Marshalltown, IA: 40,746,000
- Martin, TN: 33,960,000
- Martinsville, VA: 65,526,000
- Maryville, MO: 22,810,000
- Mason City, IA: 50,586,000
- Mayfield, KY: 37,421,000
- Maysville, KY: 17,099,000
- McAlester, OK: 44,610,000
- McComb, MS: 52,530,000
- McMinnville, TN: 40,435,000
- McPherson, KS: 28,941,000
- Meadville, PA: 86,484,000
- Menomonie, WI: 44,497,000
- Meridian, MS: 104,499,000
- Merrill, WI: 27,980,000
- Mexico, MO: 26,096,000

- Miami, OK: 31,981,000
- Middlesborough, KY: 27,337,000
- Milledgeville, GA: 54,010,000
- Mineral Wells, TX: 27,895,000
- Minot, ND: 79,814,000
- Mitchell, SD: 23,243,000
- Moberly, MO: 25,104,000
- Montrose, CO: 40,946,000
- Morehead City, NC: 68,879,000
- Morgan City, LA: 52,810,000
- Moscow, ID: 38,778,000
- Moses Lake, WA: 93,259,000
- Moultrie, GA: 45,844,000
- Mountain Home, AR: 41,053,000
- Mountain Home, ID: 25,876,000
- Mount Airy, NC: 72,743,000
- Mount Pleasant, MI: 70,698,000
- Mount Pleasant, TX: 32,623,000
- Mount Sterling, KY: 46,194,000
- Mount Vernon, IL: 38,353,000
- Mount Vernon, OH: 61,061,000
- Murray, KY: 38,343,000
- Muscatine, IA: 43,011,000
- Muskogee, OK: 69,699,000
- Nacogdoches, TX: 65,664,000
- Natchez, MS-LA: 51,396,000
- Natchitoches, LA: 39,179,000
- Newberry, SC: 38,012,000
- New Castle, IN: 48,985,000
- New Castle, PA: 88,082,000
- New Philadelphia-Dover, OH: 92,916,000
- Newport, OR: 47,038,000
- Newport, TN: 35,162,000
- Newton, IA: 36,827,000
- New Ulm, MN: 25,313,000
- Nogales, AZ: 46,461,000
- Norfolk, NE: 48,184,000
- North Platte, NE: 36,908,000
- North Vernon, IN: 27,897,000
- North Wilkesboro, NC: 68,502,000
- Norwalk, OH: 58,469,000
- Oak Harbor, WA: 80,593,000
- Ogdensburg-Massena, NY: 111,007,000
- Oil City, PA: 53,119,000

- Okeechobee, FL: 39,469,000
- Olean, NY: 77,922,000
- Oneonta, NY: 60,636,000
- Ontario, OR-ID: 53,276,000
- Opelousas, LA: 83,848,000
- Orangeburg, SC: 89,208,000
- Oskaloosa, IA: 22,324,000
- Othello, WA: 19,254,000
- Ottawa, KS: 25,609,000
- Ottawa-Peru, IL: 150,564,000
- Ottumwa, IA: 43,942,000
- Owatonna, MN: 36,755,000
- Owosso, MI: 68,619,000
- Oxford, MS: 53,154,000
- Oxford, NC: 58,674,000
- Ozark, AL: 49,565,000
- Paducah, KY-IL: 97,312,000
- Pahrump, NV: 42,477,000
- Palatka, FL: 72,023,000
- Palestine, TX: 57,580,000
- Pampa, TX: 23,210,000
- Paragould, AR: 44,196,000
- Paris, TN: 32,147,000
- Paris, TX: 49,440,000
- Parsons, KS: 20,803,000
- Payson, AZ: 53,159,000
- Pecos, TX: 14,732,000
- Peru, IN: 35,862,000
- Picayune, MS: 55,191,000
- Pierre, SD: 21,935,000
- Pinehurst-Southern Pines, NC: 94,352,000
- Pittsburg, KS: 39,217,000
- Plainview, TX: 34,360,000
- Platteville, WI: 52,250,000
- Plattsburgh, NY: 81,251,000
- Plymouth, IN: 46,857,000
- Point Pleasant, WV-OH: 57,179,000
- Ponca City, OK: 45,366,000
- Pontiac, IL: 36,671,000
- Poplar Bluff, MO: 42,951,000
- Portales, NM: 19,120,000
- Port Angeles, WA: 73,486,000
- Port Clinton, OH: 40,877,000
- Port Lavaca, TX: 21,895,000

- Portsmouth, OH: 76,825,000
- Pottsville, PA: 144,590,000
- Price, UT: 20,479,000
- Prineville, OR: 21,630,000
- Pullman, WA: 48,177,000
- Quincy, IL-MO: 77,220,000
- Raymondville, TX: 21,903,000
- Red Bluff, CA: 63,308,000
- Red Wing, MN: 46,435,000
- Rexburg, ID: 51,092,000
- Richmond, IN: 67,001,000
- Richmond-Berea, KY: 104,766,000
- Rio Grande City, TX: 63,795,000
- Riverton, WY: 40,315,000
- Roanoke Rapids, NC: 72,882,000
- Rochelle, IL: 51,659,000
- Rockingham, NC: 45,437,000
- Rock Springs, WY: 44,626,000
- Rolla, MO: 44,794,000
- Roseburg, OR: 107,685,000
- Roswell, NM: 65,764,000
- Russellville, AR: 85,103,000
- Ruston, LA: 47,774,000
- Rutland, VT: 59,736,000
- Safford, AZ: 37,666,000
- St. Marys, GA: 52,102,000
- Salem, OH: 104,806,000
- Salina, KS: 61,666,000
- Sandpoint, ID: 41,859,000
- Sandusky, OH: 75,550,000
- Sanford, NC: 59,660,000
- Sault Ste. Marie, MI: 38,033,000
- Sayre, PA: 61,281,000
- Scottsbluff, NE: 38,309,000
- Scottsboro, AL: 52,419,000
- Searcy, AR: 79,161,000
- Sedalia, MO: 42,255,000
- Selinsgrove, PA: 40,444,000
- Selma, AL: 41,131,000
- Seneca, SC: 75,713,000
- Seneca Falls, NY: 34,833,000
- Sevierville, TN: 95,946,000
- Seymour, IN: 44,069,000
- Shawano, WI: 45,877,000

- Shawnee, OK: 71,875,000
- Shelby, NC: 96,879,000
- Shelbyville, TN: 47,183,000
- Shelton, WA: 61,023,000
- Sheridan, WY: 30,009,000
- Show Low, AZ: 108,277,000
- Sidney, OH: 48,901,000
- Sikeston, MO: 39,008,000
- Silver City, NM: 28,609,000
- Snyder, TX: 17,615,000
- Somerset, KY: 63,782,000
- Somerset, PA: 75,522,000
- Sonora, CA: 53,709,000
- Spearfish, SD: 24,827,000
- Spencer, IA: 16,507,000
- Spirit Lake, IA: 17,111,000
- Starkville, MS: 49,800,000
- Statesboro, GA: 72,651,000
- Steamboat Springs, CO: 24,130,000
- Stephenville, TX: 41,122,000
- Sterling, CO: 22,036,000
- Sterling, IL: 57,079,000
- Stevens Point, WI: 70,408,000
- Stillwater, OK: 80,850,000
- Storm Lake, IA: 20,493,000
- Sturgis, MI: 61,018,000
- Sulphur Springs, TX: 36,223,000
- Summerville, GA: 24,922,000
- Summit Park, UT: 39,633,000
- Sunbury, PA: 93,246,000
- Susanville, CA: 31,345,000
- Sweetwater, TX: 15,107,000
- Tahlequah, OK: 48,447,000
- Talladega-Sylacauga, AL: 91,586,000
- Taos, NM: 32,907,000
- Taylorville, IL: 33,642,000
- The Dalles, OR: 25,775,000
- Thomaston, GA: 26,368,000
- Thomasville, GA: 45,063,000
- Tiffin, OH: 55,610,000
- Tifton, GA: 40,764,000
- Toccoa, GA: 25,586,000
- Torrington, CT: 183,603,000
- Traverse City, MI: 148,334,000

- Troy, AL: 33,046,000
- Truckee-Grass Valley, CA: 98,877,000
- Tullahoma-Manchester, TN: 102,048,000
- Tupelo, MS: 139,817,000
- Twin Falls, ID: 105,189,000
- Ukiah, CA: 87,649,000
- Union City, TN-KY: 36,877,000
- Urbana, OH: 38,987,000
- Uvalde, TX: 27,245,000
- Valley, AL: 34,123,000
- Van Wert, OH: 28,562,000
- Vermillion, SD: 13,964,000
- Vernal, UT: 37,928,000
- Vernon, TX: 13,027,000
- Vicksburg, MS: 56,635,000
- Vidalia, GA: 36,192,000
- Vincennes, IN: 37,927,000
- Vineyard Haven, MA: 17,299,000
- Wabash, IN: 32,138,000
- Wahpeton, ND-MN: 22,798,000
- Wapakoneta, OH: 45,876,000
- Warren, PA: 40,396,000
- Warrensburg, MO: 53,951,000
- Warsaw, IN: 78,620,000
- Washington, IN: 32,906,000
- Washington, NC: 47,651,000
- Washington Court House, OH: 28,679,000
- Watertown, SD: 27,939,000
- Watertown-Fort Atkinson, WI: 84,559,000
- Wauchula, FL: 27,502,000
- Waycross, GA: 54,473,000
- Weatherford, OK: 29,744,000
- West Plains, MO: 40,117,000
- Whitewater-Elkhorn, WI: 102,804,000
- Williston, ND: 35,294,000
- Willmar, MN: 42,542,000
- Wilmington, OH: 41,917,000
- Wilson, NC: 81,714,000
- Winnemucca, NV: 17,019,000
- Winona, MN: 50,885,000
- Wisconsin Rapids-Marshfield, WI: 73,435,000
- Woodward, OK: 21,559,000
- Wooster, OH: 116,063,000
- Worthington, MN: 21,770,000

- Yankton, SD: 22,702,000
- Zanesville, OH: 86,290,000
- Zapata, TX 14,374,000

90

STATE POPULATION PROFILES

90.1 Overview

The population of the United States was counted in the 2010 Census at 308,745,538, an increase of 27,323,632, or 9.7%, from the 2000 census.

This chapter provides the population counts, median age, and racial/ethnic distributions for each state.

90.2 State Populations

The 2015 population in each state, as estimated by the U.S. Census Bureau, and change from the 2010 Census, is as follows:

	2015	2010	Change
• Alabama:	4,858,979	4,780,127	1.6%
• Alaska:	738,432	710,249	4.0%
• Arizona:	6,828,065	6,392,307	6.8%
• Arkansas:	2,978,204	2,915,958	2.2%
• California:	39,144,818	37,254,503	5.1%
• Colorado:	5,456,574	5,029,324	8.5%
• Connecticut:	3,590,886	3,574,118	0.4%
• Delaware:	945,934	897,936	5.3%
• District of Columbia:	672,228	601,767	11.7%
• Florida:	20,271,272	18,804,623	6.7%
• Georgia:	10,214,860	9,688,681	5.4%
• Hawaii:	1,431,603	1,360,301	5.2%
• Idaho:	1,654,930	1,567,652	5.6%
• Illinois:	12,859,995	12,831,549	0.2%
• Indiana:	6,619,680	6,484,229	2.1%
• Iowa:	3,123,899	3,046,869	2.5%
• Kansas:	2,911,641	2,853,132	2.0%
• Kentucky:	4,425,092	4,339,349	2.0%
• Louisiana:	4,670,724	4,533,479	3.0%
• Maine:	1,329,328	1,328,361	0.0%
• Maryland:	6,006,401	5,773,785	4.0%
• Massachusetts:	6,794,422	6,547,817	3.8%
• Michigan:	9,922,576	9,884,129	0.4%
• Minnesota:	5,489,594	5,303,925	3.5%

- Mississippi: 2,992,333 2,968,103 0.8%
- Missouri: 6,083,672 5,988,927 1.6%
- Montana: 1,032,949 989,417 4.3%
- Nebraska: 1,896,190 1,826,341 3.8%
- Nevada: 2,890,845 2,700,691 7.0%
- New Hampshire: 1,330,608 1,316,466 1.1%
- New Jersey: 8,958,013 8,791,936 1.9%
- New Mexico: 2,085,109 2,059,192 1.3%
- New York: 19,795,791 19,378,087 2.1%
- North Carolina: 10,042,802 9,535,692 5.3%
- North Dakota: 756,927 672,591 12.5%
- Ohio: 11,613,423 11,536,725 0.6%
- Oklahoma: 3,911,338 3,751,616 4.3%
- Oregon: 4,028,977 3,831,073 5.1%
- Pennsylvania: 12,802,503 12,702,887 0.8%
- Rhode Island: 1,056,298 1,052,931 0.4%
- South Carolina: 4,896,146 4,625,401 5.8%
- South Dakota: 858,469 814,191 5.4%
- Tennessee: 6,600,299 6,346,275 4.0%
- Texas: 27,469,114 25,146,105 9.2%
- Utah: 2,995,919 2,763,888 8.3%
- Vermont: 626,042 625,745 0.0%
- Virginia: 8,382,993 8,001,045 4.8%
- Washington: 7,170,351 6,724,543 6.6%
- West Virginia: 1,844,128 1,853,011 -0.4%
- Wisconsin: 5,771,337 5,687,289 1.5%
- Wyoming: 586,107 563,767 4.0%

The fastest-growing states were as follows:

- North Dakota: 12.5%
- District of Columbia: 11.7%
- Texas: 9.2%
- Colorado: 8.5%
- Utah: 8.3%
- Florida: 6.7%
- Nevada: 7.0%
- Arizona: 6.8%
- Washington: 6.6%
- South Carolina: 5.8%

The following states had the least growth:

- West Virginia: -0.4%
- Maine: 0.0%
- Vermont: 0.0%
- Illinois: 0.2%
- Connecticut: 0.4%
- Rhode Island: 0.4%
- Massachusetts: 0.4%

90.3 Median Age

The median age for each state and the District of Columbia in 2014 (most recent data available) and 10-year (2005-2014) change were as follows (source: Census Bureau):

State	Median	Change
Alabama:	38.6	1.2%
Alaska:	33.3	-0.6%
Arizona:	36.9	2.4%
Arkansas:	37.8	0.8%
California:	36.0	1.6%
Colorado:	36.3	1.6%
Connecticut:	40.5	1.2%
Delaware:	39.6	1.7%
District of Columbia:	33.8	-2.1%
Florida:	41.6	2.1%
Georgia:	36.1	1.8%
Hawaii:	38.1	-0.4%
Idaho:	35.9	1.3%
Illinois:	37.5	1.9%
Indiana:	37.4	1.3%
Iowa:	38.2	-0.4%
Kansas:	36.2	0.1%
Kentucky:	38.5	1.0%
Louisiana:	36.1	0.7%
Maine:	44.1	2.9%
Maryland:	38.3	1.2%
Massachusetts:	39.4	1.2%
Michigan:	39.6	2.7%
Minnesota:	37.8	1.1%
Mississippi:	36.7	1.2%
Missouri:	38.5	1.1%
Montana:	39.6	-0.6%
Nebraska:	36.2	0.0%
Nevada:	37.4	2.2%
New Hampshire:	42.5	3.0%
New Jersey:	39.4	1.4%
New Mexico:	37.2	1.0%
New York:	38.2	0.7%
North Carolina:	38.3	2.1%
North Dakota:	35.1	-4.0%
Ohio:	39.4	1.8%
Oklahoma:	36.2	-0.3%
Oregon:	39.3	2.3%
Pennsylvania:	40.7	1.0%
Rhode Island:	39.8	1.4%
South Carolina:	38.8	1.7%
South Dakota:	36.6	-0.4%
Tennessee:	38.6	1.3%
Texas:	34.3	1.1%
Utah:	30.5	2.0%
Vermont:	42.8	2.1%
Virginia:	37.7	0.5%
Washington:	37.5	0.8%
West Virginia:	41.9	1.2%
Wisconsin:	39.2	1.3%
Wyoming:	36.6	-2.5%

90.4 Racial and Ethnic Distributions

Census 2010 reported distributions by race and ethnicity as follows:

Alabama

Race

- White: 68.5%
- Black: 26.2%
- Asian: 1.1%
- American Indian: 0.6%
- Native Hawaiian: 0.1%
- Two or more: 1.5%
- Other: 2.0%

Ethnicity

- Non-Hispanic: 96.1%
- Hispanic: 3.9%

Alaska

Race

- White: 66.7%
- American Indian: 14.8%
- Asian: 5.4%
- Black: 3.3%
- Native Hawaiian: 1.0%
- Two or more: 7.3%
- Other: 1.6%

Ethnicity

- Non-Hispanic: 94.5%
- Hispanic: 5.5%

Arizona

Race

- White: 73.0%
- American Indian: 4.6%
- Black: 4.1%
- Asian: 2.8%
- Native Hawaiian: 0.2%
- Two or more: 3.4%
- Other: 11.9%

Ethnicity

- Non-Hispanic: 70.4%
- Hispanic: 29.6%

Arkansas

Race

- White: 77.0%
- Black: 15.4%
- Asian: 1.2%
- American Indian: 0.8%
- Native Hawaiian: 0.2%
- Two or more: 2.0%
- Other: 3.4%

Ethnicity

- Non-Hispanic: 93.6%
- Hispanic: 6.4%

California

Race

- White: 57.6%
- Asian: 13.0%
- Black: 6.2%
- American Indian: 1.0%
- Native Hawaiian: 0.4%
- Two or more: 4.9%
- Other: 17.0%

Ethnicity

- Non-Hispanic: 62.4%
- Hispanic: 37.6%

Colorado

Race

- White: 81.3%
- Black: 4.0%
- Asian: 2.8%
- American Indian: 1.1%
- Native Hawaiian: 0.1%
- Two or more: 3.4%
- Other: 7.2%

Ethnicity

- Non-Hispanic: 79.3%
- Hispanic: 20.7%

Connecticut

Race

• White:	77.6%
• Black:	10.1%
• Asian:	3.8%
• American Indian:	0.3%
• Native Hawaiian:	0.0%
• Two or more:	2.6%
• Other:	5.6%

Ethnicity

• Non-Hispanic:	86.6%
• Hispanic:	13.4%

Delaware

Race

• White:	68.9%
• Black:	21.4%
• Asian:	3.2%
• American Indian:	0.5%
• Native Hawaiian:	0.0%
• Two or more:	2.7%
• Other:	3.4%

Ethnicity

• Non-Hispanic:	91.8%
• Hispanic:	8.2%

District of Columbia

Race

• White:	38.5%
• Black:	50.7%
• Asian:	3.5%
• American Indian:	0.3%
• Native Hawaiian:	0.1%
• Two or more:	2.9%
• Other:	4.1%

Ethnicity

• Non-Hispanic:	90.9%
• Hispanic:	9.1%

Florida

Race

• White:	75.0%
• Black:	16.0%
• Asian:	2.4%
• American Indian:	0.4%
• Native Hawaiian:	0.1%
• Two or more:	2.5%
• Other:	3.8%

Ethnicity

• Non-Hispanic:	77.5%
• Hispanic:	22.5%

Georgia

Race

• White:	59.7%
• Black:	30.5%
• Asian:	3.2%
• American Indian:	0.3%
• Native Hawaiian:	0.1%
• Two or more:	2.1%
• Other:	4.0%

Ethnicity

• Non-Hispanic:	91.2%
• Hispanic:	8.8%

Hawaii

Race

• Asian:	38.6%
• White:	24.7%
• Native Hawaiian:	10.0%
• Black:	1.6%
• American Indian:	0.3%
• Two or more:	23.6%
• Other:	1.2%

Ethnicity

• Non-Hispanic:	91.1%
• Hispanic:	8.9%

Idaho

Race

- White: 89.1%
- American Indian: 1.4%
- Asian: 1.2%
- Black: 0.6%
- Native Hawaiian: 0.1%
- Two or more: 2.5%
- Other: 5.1%

Ethnicity

- Non-Hispanic: 88.8%
- Hispanic: 11.1%

Illinois

Race

- White: 71.5%
- Black: 14.5%
- Asian: 4.6%
- American Indian: 0.3%
- Native Hawaiian: 0.0%
- Two or more: 2.3%
- Other: 6.7%

Ethnicity

- Non-Hispanic: 84.2%
- Hispanic: 15.8%

Indiana

Race

- White: 84.3%
- Black: 9.1%
- Asian: 1.6%
- American Indian: 0.3%
- Native Hawaiian: 0.0%
- Two or more: 2.0%
- Other: 2.7%

Ethnicity

- Non-Hispanic: 94.0%
- Hispanic: 6.0%

Iowa

Race

- White: 91.3%
- Black: 2.9%
- Asian: 1.7%
- American Indian: 0.4%
- Native Hawaiian: 0.1%
- Two or more: 1.8%
- Other: 1.8%

Ethnicity

- Non-Hispanic: 95.0%
- Hispanic: 5.0%

Kansas

Race

- White: 83.8%
- Black: 5.9%
- Asian: 2.4%
- American Indian: 1.0%
- Native Hawaiian: 0.1%
- Two or more: 3.0%
- Other: 3.9%

Ethnicity

- Non-Hispanic: 89.5%
- Hispanic: 10.5%

Kentucky

Race

- White: 87.8%
- Black: 7.8%
- Asian: 1.1%
- American Indian: 0.2%
- Native Hawaiian: 0.1%
- Two or more: 1.7%
- Other: 1.3%

Ethnicity

- Non-Hispanic: 96.9%
- Hispanic: 3.1%

Louisiana

Race

• White:	62.6%
• Black:	32.0%
• Asian:	1.5%
• American Indian:	0.7%
• Native Hawaiian:	0.0%
• Two or more:	1.6%
• Other:	1.5%

Ethnicity

• Non-Hispanic:	95.8%
• Hispanic:	4.2%

Maine

Race

• White:	95.2%
• Black:	1.2%
• Asian:	1.0%
• American Indian:	0.6%
• Native Hawaiian:	0.0%
• Two or more:	1.6%
• Other:	0.3%

Ethnicity

• Non-Hispanic:	98.7%
• Hispanic:	1.3%

Maryland

Race

• White:	58.2%
• Black:	29.4%
• Asian:	5.5%
• American Indian:	0.4%
• Native Hawaiian:	0.1%
• Two or more:	2.9%
• Other:	3.6%

Ethnicity

• Non-Hispanic:	91.8%
• Hispanic:	8.2%

Massachusetts

Race

• White:	80.4%
• Black:	6.6%
• Asian:	5.3%
• American Indian:	0.3%
• Native Hawaiian:	0.0%
• Two or more:	2.6%
• Other:	4.7%

Ethnicity

• Non-Hispanic:	90.4%
• Hispanic:	9.6%

Michigan

Race

• White:	78.9%
• Black:	14.2%
• Asian:	2.4%
• American Indian:	0.6%
• Native Hawaiian:	0.0%
• Two or more:	2.3%
• Other:	1.5%

Ethnicity

• Non-Hispanic:	95.6%
• Hispanic:	4.4%

Minnesota

Race

• White:	85.3%
• Black:	5.2%
• Asian:	4.0%
• American Indian:	1.1%
• Native Hawaiian:	0.0%
• Two or more:	2.4%
• Other:	1.9%

Ethnicity

• Non-Hispanic:	95.3%
• Hispanic:	4.7%

Mississippi

Race

- White: 59.1%
- Black: 37.0%
- Asian: 0.9%
- American Indian: 0.5%
- Native Hawaiian: 0.0%
- Two or more: 1.1%
- Other: 1.3%

Ethnicity

- Non-Hispanic: 97.3%
- Hispanic: 2.7%

Missouri

Race

- White: 82.8%
- Black: 11.6%
- Asian: 1.6%
- American Indian: 0.5%
- Native Hawaiian: 0.1%
- Two or more: 2.1%
- Other: 1.3%

Ethnicity

- Non-Hispanic: 96.5%
- Hispanic: 3.5%

Montana

Race

- White: 89.4%
- American Indian: 6.3%
- Asian: 0.6%
- Black: 0.4%
- Native Hawaiian: 0.1%
- Two or more: 2.5%
- Other: 0.6%

Ethnicity

- Non-Hispanic: 97.1%
- Hispanic: 2.9%

Nebraska

Race

- White: 86.1%
- Black: 4.5%
- Asian: 1.8%
- American Indian: 1.0%
- Native Hawaiian: 0.1%
- Two or more: 2.2%
- Other: 4.3%

Ethnicity

- Non-Hispanic: 90.8%
- Hispanic: 9.2%

Nevada

Race

- White: 66.2%
- Black: 8.1%
- Asian: 7.2%
- American Indian: 1.2%
- Native Hawaiian: 0.6%
- Two or more: 4.7%
- Other: 12.0%

Ethnicity

- Non-Hispanic: 73.5%
- Hispanic: 26.5%

New Hampshire

Race

- White: 93.9%
- Asian: 2.2%
- Black: 1.1%
- American Indian: 0.2%
- Native Hawaiian: 0.0%
- Two or more: 1.6%
- Other: 0.9%

Ethnicity

- Non-Hispanic: 97.2%
- Hispanic: 2.8%

New Jersey
Race
- White: 68.6%
- Black: 13.7%
- Asian: 8.3%
- American Indian: 0.3%
- Native Hawaiian: 0.0%
- Two or more: 2.7%
- Other: 6.4%

Ethnicity
- Non-Hispanic: 82.3%
- Hispanic: 17.7%

New Mexico
Race
- White: 68.4%
- American Indian: 9.4%
- Black: 2.1%
- Asian: 1.4%
- Native Hawaiian: 0.1%
- Two or more: 3.7%
- Other: 15.0%

Ethnicity
- Non-Hispanic: 53.7%
- Hispanic: 46.3%

New York
Race
- White: 65.7%
- Black: 15.9%
- Asian: 7.3%
- American Indian: 0.6%
- Native Hawaiian: 0.0%
- Two or more: 3.0%
- Other: 7.4%

Ethnicity
- Non-Hispanic: 82.4%
- Hispanic: 17.6%

North Carolina
Race
- White: 68.5%
- Black: 21.5%
- Asian: 2.2%
- American Indian: 1.3%
- Native Hawaiian: 0.1%
- Two or more: 2.2%
- Other: 4.3%

Ethnicity
- Non-Hispanic: 91.6%
- Hispanic: 8.4%

North Dakota
Race
- White: 90.0%
- American Indian: 5.4%
- Black: 1.2%
- Asian: 1.0%
- Native Hawaiian: 0.0%
- Two or more: 1.8%
- Other: 0.5%

Ethnicity
- Non-Hispanic: 98.0%
- Hispanic: 2.0%

Ohio
Race
- White: 82.7%
- Black: 12.2%
- Asian: 1.7%
- American Indian: 0.2%
- Native Hawaiian: 0.0%
- Two or more: 2.1%
- Other: 1.1%

Ethnicity
- Non-Hispanic: 96.9%
- Hispanic: 3.1%

Oklahoma

Race

- White: 72.2%
- American Indian: 8.8%
- Black: 7.4%
- Asian: 1.7%
- Native Hawaiian: 0.1%
- Two or more: 5.9%
- Other: 4.1%

Ethnicity

- Non-Hispanic: 91.1%
- Hispanic: 8.9%

Oregon

Race

- White: 83.6%
- Asian: 3.7%
- Black: 1.8%
- American Indian: 1.4%
- Native Hawaiian: 0.3%
- Two or more: 3.8%
- Other: 5.3%

Ethnicity

- Non-Hispanic: 88.3%
- Hispanic: 11.7%

Pennsylvania

Race

- White: 81.9%
- Black: 10.8%
- Asian: 2.7%
- American Indian: 0.2%
- Native Hawaiian: 0.0%
- Two or more: 1.9%
- Other: 2.4%

Ethnicity

- Non-Hispanic: 94.3%
- Hispanic: 5.7%

Rhode Island

Race

- White: 81.4%
- Black: 5.7%
- Asian: 2.9%
- American Indian: 0.6%
- Native Hawaiian: 0.1%
- Two or more: 3.3%
- Other: 6.0%

Ethnicity

- Non-Hispanic: 87.6%
- Hispanic: 12.4%

South Carolina

Race

- White: 66.2%
- Black: 27.9%
- Asian: 1.3%
- American Indian: 0.4%
- Native Hawaiian: 0.1%
- Two or more: 1.7%
- Other: 2.5%

Ethnicity

- Non-Hispanic: 94.9%
- Hispanic: 5.1%

South Dakota

Race

- White: 85.9%
- American Indian: 8.8%
- Black: 1.3%
- Asian: 0.9%
- Native Hawaiian: 0.0%
- Two or more: 2.1%
- Other: 0.9%

Ethnicity

- Non-Hispanic: 97.3%
- Hispanic: 2.7%

Tennessee

Race

- White: 77.6%
- Black: 16.7%
- Asian: 1.4%
- American Indian: 0.3%
- Native Hawaiian: 0.1%
- Two or more: 1.7%
- Other: 2.2%

Ethnicity

- Non-Hispanic: 95.4%
- Hispanic: 4.6%

Texas

Race

- White: 70.4%
- Black: 11.8%
- Asian: 3.8%
- American Indian: 0.7%
- Native Hawaiian: 0.1%
- Two or more: 2.7%
- Other: 10.5%

Ethnicity

- Non-Hispanic: 62.4%
- Hispanic: 37.6%

Utah

Race

- White: 86.1%
- Asian: 2.0%
- American Indian: 1.2%
- Black: 1.1%
- Native Hawaiian: 0.9%
- Two or more: 2.7%
- Other: 6.0%

Ethnicity

- Non-Hispanic: 87.0%
- Hispanic: 13.0%

Vermont

Race

- White: 95.3%
- Asian: 1.3%
- Black: 1.0%
- American Indian: 0.4%
- Native Hawaiian: 0.0%
- Two or more: 1.7%
- Other: 0.3%

Ethnicity

- Non-Hispanic: 98.5%
- Hispanic: 1.5%

Virginia

Race

- White: 68.9%
- Black: 19.4%
- Asian: 5.5%
- American Indian: 0.4%
- Native Hawaiian: 0.1%
- Two or more: 2.9%
- Other: 3.2%

Ethnicity

- Non-Hispanic: 92.1%
- Hispanic: 7.9%

Washington

Race

- White: 77.3%
- Asian: 7.2%
- Black: 3.9%
- American Indian: 1.5%
- Native Hawaiian: 0.6%
- Two or more: 4.7%
- Other: 5.2%

Ethnicity

- Non-Hispanic: 88.8%
- Hispanic: 11.2%

West Virginia

Race

- White: 93.9%
- Black: 3.4%
- Asian: 0.7%
- American Indian: 0.2%
- Native Hawaiian: 0.0%
- Two or more: 1.5%
- Other: 0.3%

Ethnicity

- Non-Hispanic: 98.8%
- Hispanic: 1.2%

Wisconsin

Race

- White: 86.2%
- Black: 6.3%
- Asian: 2.3%
- American Indian: 1.0%
- Native Hawaiian: 0.0%
- Two or more: 1.8%
- Other: 2.4%

Ethnicity

- Non-Hispanic: 94.1%
- Hispanic: 5.9%

Wyoming

Race

- White: 90.7%
- American Indian: 2.4%
- Asian: 0.8%
- Black: 0.8%
- Native Hawaiian: 0.1%
- Two or more: 2.3%
- Other: 3.0%

Ethnicity

- Non-Hispanic: 91.1%
- Hispanic: 8.9%

90.5 Diversity

Based on the data of Census 2010, *USA Today* assessed diversity using a Diversity Index, defined as the probability that two people chosen randomly from a state will have different ethnic or racial backgrounds. The Diversity Index is a 0-to-100 score; a score of 50 means there is a 50% chance two randomly chosen people are of a different ethnicity or race.

The Diversity Indices are as follows:

- Hawaii: 81
- California: 73
- New Mexico: 67
- Texas: 66
- Nevada: 65
- District of Columbia: 63
- New York: 62
- Maryland: 61
- Arizona: 60
- New Jersey: 60
- Florida: 59
- Georgia: 59
- Alaska: 57
- Illinois: 55
- Delaware: 53
- Louisiana: 53
- Mississippi: 53
- Virginia: 53
- North Carolina: 52
- Oklahoma: 51
- South Carolina: 51
- Alabama: 48
- Colorado: 48
- Connecticut: 47
- Washington: 46
- Arkansas: 42
- Massachusetts: 41
- Rhode Island: 41
- Tennessee: 40
- Michigan: 39
- Kansas: 38
- Oregon: 38
- Pennsylvania: 36
- Utah: 35
- Indiana: 33
- Missouri: 33
- Ohio: 33
- Nebraska: 32
- Minnesota: 31
- Wisconsin: 30
- Idaho: 29
- South Dakota: 28
- Wyoming: 27
- Kentucky: 25
- Montana: 23
- Iowa: 22
- North Dakota: 21
- New Hampshire: 15
- West Virginia: 13
- Maine: 11
- Vermont: 11

91

STATE ECONOMIC PROFILES

91.1 Median Household Income

According to the U.S. Census Bureau (www.census.gov), U.S. median household income in 2014 (most recent data available)was $50,502. Median household income by state and rank were as follows:

	Median Income	Rank
• Alabama:	$41,415	47
• Alaska:	$69,825	2
• Arizona:	$46,709	31
• Arkansas:	$38,758	49
• California:	$67,458	3
• Colorado:	$55,387	16
• Connecticut:	$65,753	4
• Delaware:	$57,954	12
• District of Columbia:	$65,124	5
• Florida:	$44,299	38
• Georgia:	$46,007	34
• Hawaii:	$62,814	9
• Idaho:	$43,341	41
• Illinois:	$53,234	19
• Indiana:	$46,438	32
• Iowa:	$49,427	25
• Kansas:	$48,964	27
• Kentucky:	$41,141	48
• Louisiana:	$41,734	45
• Maine:	$46,033	33
• Maryland:	$70,004	1
• Massachusetts:	$64,859	6
• Michigan:	$45,981	35
• Minnesota:	$61,814	10
• Mississippi:	$36,919	51
• Missouri:	$45,247	37
• Montana:	$44,222	39
• Nebraska:	$50,296	23
• Nevada:	$48,927	28
• New Hampshire:	$64,712	7

- New Jersey: $60,287 11
- New Mexico: $41,963 44
- New York: $55,246 17
- North Carolina: $43,916 40
- North Dakota: $51,704 21
- Ohio: $45,749 36
- Oklahoma: $43,225 42
- Oregon: $46,816 30
- Pennsylvania: $50,228 24
- Rhode Island: $53,636 18
- South Carolina: $42,367 43
- South Dakota: $48,321 29
- Tennessee: $41,693 46
- Texas: $49,392 26
- Utah: $55,869 15
- Vermont: $52,776 20
- Virginia: $62,881 8
- Washington: $57,835 13
- West Virginia: $38,482 50
- Wisconsin: $50,395 22
- Wyoming: $56,322 14

91.2 Personal Income

Personal income in first quarter 2016 was as follows (source: Bureau of Economic Analysis [www.bea.gov]):

- Alabama: $ 193.3 billion
- Alaska: $ 41.5 billion
- Arizona: $ 274.7 billion
- Arkansas: $ 119.7 billion
- California: $2.11 trillion
- Colorado: $ 282.1 billion
- Connecticut: $ 246.6 billion
- Delaware: $ 46.2 billion
- District of Columbia: $ 49.2 billion
- Florida: $ 922.5 billion
- Georgia: $ 426.8 billion
- Hawaii: $ 70.3 billion
- Idaho: $ 63.3 billion
- Illinois: $ 653.0 billion
- Indiana: $ 279.7 billion
- Iowa: $ 143.4 billion
- Kansas: $ 136.1 billion
- Kentucky: $ 177.6 billion

- Louisiana: $ 204.5 billion
- Maine: $ 58.0 billion
- Maryland: $ 347.4 billion
- Massachusetts: $ 428.8 billion
- Michigan: $ 436.4 billion
- Minnesota: $ 283.1 billion
- Mississippi: $ 108.4 billion
- Missouri: $ 267.3 billion
- Montana: $ 43.0 billion
- Nebraska: $ 92.0 billion
- Nevada: $ 125.6 billion
- New Hampshire: $ 76.0 billion
- New Jersey: $ 548.4 billion
- New Mexico: $ 81.4 billion
- New York: $1.17 trillion
- North Carolina: $ 420.9 billion
- North Dakota: $ 40.4 billion
- Ohio: $ 520.1 billion
- Oklahoma: $ 174.6 billion
- Oregon: $ 179.0 billion
- Pennsylvania: $ 648.4 billion
- Rhode Island: $ 54.4 billion
- South Carolina: $ 192.6 billion
- South Dakota: $ 39.2 billion
- Tennessee: $ 286.8 billion
- Texas: $1.30 trillion
- Utah: $ 121.1 billion
- Vermont: $ 30.7 billion
- Virginia: $ 448.5 billion
- Washington: $ 378.9 billion
- West Virginia: $ 68.8 billion
- Wisconsin: $ 270.6 billion
- Wyoming: $ 32.0 billion

91.3 Unemployment Rate

The national unemployment rate in May 2016 was 4.7%. For each state, the unemployment rate was as follows (sources: Bureau of Labor Statistics [www.bls.gov] and National Conference of State Legislatures [www.ncsl.org]):

- Alabama: 6.1%
- Alaska: 6.7%
- Arizona: 5.6%
- Arkansas: 3.8%
- California: 5.2%
- Colorado: 3.4%
- Connecticut: 5.7%
- Delaware: 4.1%
- District of Columbia: 6.1%
- Florida: 4.7%

- Georgia: 5.3%
- Hawaii: 3.2%
- Idaho: 3.7%
- Illinois: 6.4%
- Indiana: 5.0%
- Iowa: 3.9%
- Kansas: 3.7%
- Kentucky: 5.1%
- Louisiana: 6.3%
- Maine: 3.5%
- Maryland: 4.5%
- Massachusetts: 4.2%
- Michigan: 4.7%
- Minnesota: 3.8%
- Mississippi: 5.8%
- Missouri: 4.3%
- Montana: 4.2%
- Nebraska: 3.0%
- Nevada: 6.1%
- New Hampshire: 2.7%
- New Jersey: 4.9%
- New Mexico: 6.2%
- New York: 4.7%
- North Carolina: 5.1%
- North Dakota: 3.2%
- Ohio: 5.1%
- Oklahoma: 4.7%
- Oregon: 4.5%
- Pennsylvania: 5.5%
- Rhode Island: 5.4%
- South Carolina: 5.6%
- South Dakota: 2.5%
- Tennessee: 4.1%
- Texas: 4.4%
- Utah: 3.8%
- Vermont: 3.1%
- Virginia: 3.8%
- Washington: 5.8%
- West Virginia: 6.2%
- Wisconsin: 4.2%
- Wyoming: 5.6%

APPENDIX A

ACADEMIC RESEARCH CENTERS

Bowling Green State University, Center for Family and Demographic Research, Five Williams Hall, Bowling Green, OH 43403. (419) 372-7279 (www.bgsu.edu/arts-and-sciences/center-for-family-demographic-research.html)

Carnegie Mellon University, Center for Behavioral Decision Research, Tepper School of Business, 5000 Forbes Avenue, Pittsburgh, PA 15213. (412) 268-2268. (www.cbdr.cmu.edu)

Columbia University, Behavioral Research Lab, Graduate School of Business, 3022 Broadway, New York, NY 10027. (212) 854-5553. (http://www8.gsb.columbia.edu/behaviorlab/)

Duke University, Fuqua School of Business, 100 Fuqua Drive, Box 90120, Durham, NC 27708. (919) 660-7700. (www.fuqua.duke.edu)

Duquesne University, Palumbo-Donahue School of Business, 600 Forbes Avenue, Pittsburgh, PA 15282. (www.duq.edu/academics/schools/business#/1)

Eastern Illinois University, Family and Consumer Sciences, 1032 Klehm Hall, 600 Lincoln Avenue, Charleston, IL 61920. (www.eiu.edu/famsci/)

Elon University, Imagining The Internet Center, School of Communications, Elon, NC 27244. (336) 278-2000. (www.imaginingtheinternet.org)

Georgia State University, Center for Mature Consumer Studies, J. Mack Robinson College of Business, 35 Broad Street NW, Atlanta, GA 30303. (http://marketing.robinson.gsu.edu/research-centers-roundtables/cmcs)

Georgetown University, Institute for Consumer Research, McDonough School of Business, Rafik B. Hariri Building, Georgetown University, Washington, DC 20057. (202) 687-0111. (http://consumerresearch.georgetown.edu)

Golden Gate University, Edward S. Ageno School of Business, 536 Mission Street, San Francisco CA, 94105. (800) 448-4968. (www.ggu.edu/programs/business-and-management)

Harvard Business School, Bloomberg Center, 25 Harvard Way, Boston, MA 02163. (www.library.hbs.edu/guides/demographicsconsumerbehavior.html)

Kansas State Olathe, Sensory & Consumer Research Center, 22201 W. Innovation Drive, Olathe, KS 66061. (913) 307-7354. (http://olathe.k-state.edu/centers-institutes/consumer-research/index.html)

New Mexico State University, Consumer Behavioral Research Lab, Business Complex Room 246, Las Cruces, NM, 88003. (http://cobelab.nmsu.edu)

NYU Stern, Henry Kaufman Management Center, 44 West Fourth Street, New York, NY 10012. (212) 998-0100. (www.stern.nyu.edu)

Rochester Institute of Technology, E. Philip Saunders College of Business, 105 Lomb Memorial Drive, Rochester, NY 14623. (http://saunders.rit.edu)

Saint Joseph University, Center For Consumer Research, Erivan K. Haub School Of Business, 5600 City Avenue, Philadelphia, PA 19131. (610) 660-1645. (www.sju.edu/academics/centers/ccr/index.html)

Stanford University, Behavioral Lab, Graduate School of Business, Knight Management Center, 655 Knight Way, Stanford, CA 94305. (www.gsb.stanford.edu/faculty-research/labs/behavioral-lab)

University of California Davis, Center for Consumer Research, Davis, CA 95616. (530) 752-2774. (http://ccr.ucdavis.edu/)

University of California Los Angeles (UCLA), Interdisciplinary Group in Behavioral Decision Making, Anderson School of Management, Box 951481, Los Angeles, CA 90095. (310) 825-0003. (www.anderson.ucla.edu/x2271.xml)

University of Chicago, Center for Decision Research, Booth School of Business, 5807 South Woodlawn Avenue, Chicago, IL 60637. (773) 702-4877. (http://research.chicagobooth.edu/cdr/)

University of Chicago, National Opinion Research Center, 1155 E. 60th Street, 3rd Floor, Chicago, IL 60637. (773) 256-6000. (www.norc.org)

University of Georgia, Selig Center for Economic Growth, 110 East Clayton Street, Suite 608, Athens, GA 30602. (706) 542-4085. (www.terry.uga.edu/selig/)

University of Massachusetts Dartmouth Center for Marketing Research, 285 Old Westport Road, North Dartmouth, MA 02747. (508) 999-8000. (www.umassd.edu/cmr)

University of Michigan, Stephen M. Ross Business School, 701 Tappan Street, Ann Arbor, MI 48109. (734) 615-9700. (www.bus.umich.edu)

University of Minnesota, Carlson School of Management, 321 19th Avenue South, Minneapolis, MN 55455. (612) 625-0027. (www.csom.umn.edu)

University of Minnesota, Population Center, 50 Willey Hall 225, 19th Avenue South, Minneapolis, MN 55455. (612) 624-5818. (www.pop.umn.edu/)

University of North Carolina Chapel Hill, Center for Decision Research, Kenan-Flagler Business School, 300 Kenan Center Drive, Chapel Hill, NC 27599. (http://c4dr.unc.edu)

University of Pennsylvania, Customer Analytics Initiative, Wharton School of Business, Jon M. Huntsman Hall, 3730 Walnut Street, Philadelphia, PA 19104. (215) 898-6183. (http://wcai.wharton.upenn.edu)

University of Pittsburgh, Joseph M. Katz Graduate School of Business and College of Business Administration, Mervis Hall, Pittsburgh, PA 15260. (412) 648-1700. (www.business.pitt.edu)

University of Rochester, Simon Graduate School of Business, 305 Schlegel Hall, Rochester, NY 14627. (www.simon.rochester.edu)

University of Southern California, Center for the Digital Future, Annenberg School for Communication and Journalism, 11444 West Olympic Boulevard, Suite 120, Los Angeles, CA 90064. (www.digitalcenter.org)

Vanderbilt University, Owen Graduate School of Management, 401 21st Avenue South, Nashville, TN 37203. (www.owen.vanderbilt.edu)

Washington State University, Center for Behavioral Business Research, Carson College of Business, P.O. Box 644750, Pullman, WA 99164. (http://business.wsu.edu/research-faculty/centers/behavioral-business-research)

Washington University in St. Louis, CB Research Lab, Olin Business School, One Brookings Drive, Campus Box 1133, St. Louis, MO 63130. (http://research.olin.wustl.edu/res/cbresearch/Index.html)

Yale University, Center for Customer Insights, School of Management, 135 Prospect Street, Box 208200, New Haven, CT 06520. (203) 432-6069. (www.cci.som.yale.edu)

APPENDIX B

ANALYSTS

ABI Research, 249 South Street, Oyster Bay, NY 11771. (516) 624-2500. (www.abiresearch.com)

American Customer Satisfaction Index (ACSI), 625 Avis Drive, Ann Arbor, MI 48108. (734) 913-0788. (www.theacsi.org)

America's Research Group, 810 Travelers Boulevard, Suite G-1, Summerville, SC 29485. (843) 695-0090. (www.americasresearchgroup.com)

Belden Russonello Strategists, 1724 20th Street NW, Suite 201, Washington DC 20009. (202) 822-6090. (www.brspoll.com)

BIA/Kelsey, 14150 Parkeast Circle, Chantilly, VA 20151. (703) 818-2425. (www.biakelsey.com)

Boston Consulting Group, Exchange Place, 31st Floor, Boston, MA 02109. (617) 973-1200. (www.bcg.com)

Brand Keys, 115 East 57th Street, 11th Floor, New York, NY 10022. (212) 532-6028. (www.brandkeys.com)

Brookings Institution, 1775 Massachusetts Avenue NW, Washington, DC 20036. (202) 797-6000. (www.brookings.org)

Chadwick Martin Bailey, 179 South Street, 3rd Floor, Boston, MA 02111. (617) 350-8922. (www.cmbinfo.com)

Concentric Marketing, 101 Worthington Avenue, Suite 190, Charlotte, NC 28203. (704) 731-5100. (www.getconcentric.com)

Economic Analysis Associates, 5 Glen Court, Greenwich, CT 06830. (203) 869-9667. (www.eaaresearch.com)

eMarketer, 11 Times Square, New York, NY 10036. (212) 376-5291. (www.emarketer.com)

Envirosell Inc., 907 Broadway, 2nd, 3rd & 7th Floors, New York, NY 10010.
(212) 673-9100. (www.envirosell.com)

Experian Marketing Services, 475 Anton Boulevard, Costa Mesa, CA 92626.
(888) 246-2804. (www.experian.com/marketing-services/about.html)

First Research, 5800 Airport Boulevard, Austin, TX 78752. (866) 788-9389.
(www.firstresearch.com)

ForeSee Results, 2500 Green Road, Suite 400, Ann Arbor, MI 48105. (800) 621-2850.
(www.foreseeresults.com)

Forrester Research, 60 Acorn Park Drive, Cambridge, MA 02140. (617) 613-5730.
(www.forrester.com)

Frost & Sullivan, 7550 IH 10 West, Suite 400, San Antonio, TX 78229.
(877) 463-7678. (www.frost.com)

GfK MRI, 200 Liberty Street, 4th Floor, New York, NY 10281. (212) 884-9200.
(www.gfkmri.com)

The Harris Poll, a Nielsen Company, 60 Corporate Woods, Rochester, NY 14623.
(585) 272-8400. (www.theharrispoll.com)

Horowitz Research, 270 North Avenue, Suite 805, New Rochelle, NY 10801.
(914) 834-5999. (www.horowitzresearch.com)

IEG, 350 North Orleans Street, Suite 1200, Chicago, IL 60654. (800) 834-4850.
(www.sponsorship.com)

International Demographics, 10333 Richmond Avenue, Suite 200, Houston, TX 77042.
(713) 626-0333. (www.themediaaudit.com)

Ipsos Marketing, 1271 Avenue of the Americas, 15th Floor, New York, NY 10020. (212)
265-3200. (www.ipsos.com/marketing)

IRI, 150 North Clinton Street, Chicago, IL 60661. (312) 726-1221.
(www.iriworldwide.com)

J.D. Power and Associates, 3200 Park Center Drive, 13th Floor, Costa Mesa, CA 92626.
(714) 621-6200. (www.jdpower.com)

Javelin Strategy & Research, 6 High Ridge Park, Stamford, CT 06905. (203) 629-1200.
(www.javelinstrategy.com)

Kantar Retail, 585 S. Front Street, Suite 50, Columbus, OH 43215. (614) 355-4000. (www.kantarretail.com)

Luxury Institute, 115 East 57th Street, 11th Floor, New York, NY 10022. (646) 792-2669. (www.luxuryinstitute.com)

MediaPost Communications, 15 East 32nd Street, 7th Floor, New York, NY 10006. (212) 204-2000. (www.mediapost.com)

New Strategist, 26 Austin Avenue, P.O. Box 635, Amityville, NY 11701. (800) 848-0842. (www.newstrategist.com)

ORC International, 902 Carnegie Center, Suite 220, Princeton, NJ 08540. (800) 444-4672. (www.orcinternational.com)

Paramount Market Publishing, 950 Danby Road, Suite 136, Ithaca, NY 14850. (607) 275-8100. (www.paramountbooks.com)

Parks Associates, 15950 N. Dallas Parkway Suite 575, Dallas, TX 75248. (972) 490-1113. (www.parksassociates.com)

Pew Research Center, 1615 L Street NW, Suite 700, Washington, DC 20036. (202) 419-4300. (www.pewresearch.org)

Prosper Business Development, 400 West Wilson Bridge, Suite 200, Worthington, OH 43085. (614) 846-0146. (www.goprosper.com)

Richard K. Miller & Associates, 4132 Atlanta Highway, Suite 110, Loganville, GA 30052. (888) 928-7562. (www.rkma.com)

Riedel Marketing Group, 5327 East Pinchot Avenue, Phoenix, AZ 85018. (602) 840-4948. (www.4rmg.com)

Sentier Research, 8 Mayo Avenue, Annapolis, MD 21403. (703) 764-0249. (www.sentierresearch.com)

Service Management Group, 1737 McGee Street, Kansas City, MO 64108. (800) 764-0439. (www.smg.com)

Shapiro+Raj, 153 West Ohio Street, Suite 300, Chicago, IL 60654. (312) 321-8111. (www.ljs.com)

Technavio, 110 E. Schiller, Suite 208, Elmhurst, IL 60126. (630) 333-9501. (www.technavio.com)

Temkin Group, 48 White Oak Road, Waban, MA 02468. (617) 916-2075. (www.temkingroup.com)

The Conference Board, 845 Third Avenue, New York, NY 10022. (212) 759-0900. (www.conference-board.org)

The Demand Institute, 845 Third Avenue, New York, NY 10022. (212) 339-0220. (www.demandinstitute.org)

The Futures Company, 1300 Environ Way, Chapel Hill, NC 27517. (919) 932-8858. (www.thefuturescompany.com)

The Gallup Organization, 901 F Street NW, Washington, DC 20004. (202) 715-3030. (www.gallup.com)

The Nielsen Company, 85 Broad Street, New York, NY 10004. (212) 708-7500. (www.nielsen.com)

The NPD Group, 900 West Shore Road, Port Washington, NY 11050. (516) 625-0700. (www.npd.com)

Unity Marketing, 206 E. Church Street, Stevens, PA 17578. (717) 336-1600. (www.unitymarketingonline.com)

Urban Institute, 2100 M Street NW, Washington, DC 20037. (202) 833-7200. (www.urban.org)

Urban Land Institute, 1025 Thomas Jefferson Street NW, Suite 500 West, Washington, DC 20007. (202) 624-7000. (www.uli.org)

WSL Strategic Retail, 307 Seventh Avenue, Suite 1707, New York, NY 10001. (212) 924-7780. (www.wslstrategicretail.com)

YouGov, 38 West 21st Street, 5th Floor, New York, NY 10010. (646) 537-9818. (www.yougov.com)

APPENDIX C

ASSOCIATIONS

American Association of Advertising Agencies, 1065 Avenue of the Americas, 16th Floor, New York, NY 10018. (212) 682-2500. (www.aaaa.org)

American Marketing Association, 311 S. Wacker Drive, Suite 5800, Chicago, IL 60606. (312) 542-9000. (www.ama.org)

AARP, 601 E Street NW, Washington DC 20049. (888) 687-2277. (www.aarp.org)

American Planning Association, 205 N. Michigan Avenue, Suite 1200, Chicago, IL 60601. (312) 431-9100. (www.planning.org)

Association for Consumer Research, c/o Labovitz School of Business & Economics, University of Minnesota Duluth, 11 East Superior Street, Suite 210, Duluth, MN 55802. (218) 726-7853. (www.acrwebsite.org)

Retail Gift Card Association, 529 14th Street NW, Suite 750, Washington, DC 20045. (202) 591-2454. (www.thergca.org)

Society for Consumer Psychology, c/o American Psychological Association, 750 First Street NE, Washington, DC 20002. (800) 374-2721. (www.myscp.org)

Society for New Communications Research, 2625 Middlefield Road, Suite 662, Palo Alto, CA 94306. (408) 825-9288. (www.sncr.org)

Sports & Fitness Industry Association, 8505 Fenton Street, Suite 211, Silver Spring, MD 20910. (301) 495-6321. (www.sfia.org)

Urban Land Institute, 1025 Thomas Jefferson Street NW, Suite 500 West, Washington, DC 20007. (202) 624-7000. (www.uli.org)

APPENDIX D

BLOGS

Behavioral Research Blog (Noldus; http://info.noldus.com)

Bentley University Consumer Behavior Blog (http://bentleyuniversityconsumerbehaviorblog.blogspot.com/)

Beyond The Purchase (Ryan T. Howell and Ravi Iyer; www.beyondthepurchase.org/blog/)

Big Consumer Blog (BIGinsight; https://bigconsumerblog.wordpress.com/category/consumer-behavior-trends/)

Consumer Behavior (Forrester Research; http://blogs.forrester.com/category/consumer_behavior)

Consumer Behavior (JWT; www.jwt.com/blog/tag/consumer-behavior/)

Consumer Behavior (Mohamed Nassar; http://nassar-consumerbehavior.blogspot.com/)

Consumer Behavior (*The New York Times*; http://topics.nytimes.com/top/reference/timestopics/subjects/c/consumer_behavior/index.html)

Consumer Behavior & Psychology Blog (Christopher Lee; http://christopherlee.com/blog/)

Consumer Behavior Blog (Diego Campos; http://diegoacampos.blogspot.com/)

Consumer Behavior Blog (Lyndsie Berens; http://lberens.blogspot.com)

Consumer Insights (JWT; www.jwt.com/blog/category/consumer_insights/)

Consumer Insights (WWP; http://www.wpp.com/wpp/marketing/consumerinsights/)

Dan Ariely Blog (http://danariely.com)

Disruptive Demographics (Joseph F. Coughlin; http://bigthink.com/blogs/disruptive-demographics)

Demo Memo (Cheryl Russell; www.demomemo.blogspot.com)

Demographics (Brookings Institution; www.brookings.edu/research/topics/demographics)

Demographics (World Bank; http://blogs.worldbank.org/category/tags/demographics)

Federal Reserve Bank of Atlanta Blog (www.frbatlanta.org/research/blogs.aspx)

Federal Reserve Bank of Chicago Blog (www.chicagofedblogs.org)

Federal Reserve Bank of San Francisco Blog (www.frbsf.org/community-development/blog/)

Gerd's Consumer Behavior Blog (Gerd Sumer; https://gerdsumer.wordpress.com/)

Inside The Consumer Mind (*Psychology Today*; www.psychologytoday.com/blog/inside-the-consumer-mind)

Kit Yarrow Blog (www.kityarrow.com)

Liberty Street Economics (Federal Reserve Bank of New York; http://libertystreeteconomics.newyorkfed.org)

Marketing: Consumer Behavior (Harvard Business School; http://hbswk.hbs.edu/topics/consumerbehavior.html)

Marketing Forward - Consumer Insights (Experian; www.experian.com/blogs/marketing-forward/category/consumer/)

Master in Market Research & Consumer Behavior Blog (IE School of Social and Behavior Sciences; http://mrcb.blogs.ie.edu/)

On The Economy (Federal Reserve Bank of St. Louis; www.stlouisfed.org/on-the-economy/)

Perspectives On Consumer Behavior (Francisco Teixeira; (http://innovationthroughconsumerinsights.wordpress.com)

Philip Graves Blog (http://philipgraves.net/blog/)

Power Your Instinct (Tip Tap Lab; http://blog.tiptaplab.com)

Urban Demographics (Rafael Pereira; http://urbandemographics.blogspot.com)

APPENDIX E

GOVERNMENT AGENCIES

Bureau of Economic Analysis, 1441 L Street NW, Washington, DC 20230. (202) 606-9900. (www.bea.gov)

Bureau of Labor Statistics, U.S. Department of Labor, 2 Massachusetts Avenue NE, Washington, DC 20212. (202) 691-5200. (www.bls.gov)

Bureau of Transportation Statistics, U.S. Department of Transportation, 1200 New Jersey Avenue SE, Washington, DC 20590. (800) 853-1351. (www.bts.gov)

Congressional Research Service, c/o The Library of Congress, 101 Independence Avenue SE, Washington, DC 20540. (202) 707-5000. (www.loc.gov/crsinfo/about/)

Federal Reserve Board, 20th Street and Constitution Avenue NW, Washington, DC 20551. (www.federalreserve.gov)

National Center for Health Statistics, 3311 Toledo Road, Room 5419, Hyattsville, MD 20782. (800) 232-4636. (www.cdc.gov/nchs)

U.S. Census Bureau, 4600 Silver Hill Road, Washington, DC 20233. (800) 923-8282. (www.census.gov)

USDA Economic Research Service, 1400 Independence Avenue SW, Mail Stop 1800, Washington, DC 20250. (202) 694-5100. (www.ers.usda.gov)

APPENDIX F

MARKET RESEARCH SOURCES

F.1 Consumer Surveys and Opinion Polls

Surveys and polls are popular tools for identifying consumer attitudes, preferences, and behaviors relating to a broad spectrum of interests. There are a host of firms that specialize in this field; some of the major survey firms in the U.S. are as follows:

- Gallup Inc. (www.gallup.com)
- GfK MRI (www.gfkmri.com)
- Harris Poll (www.theharrispoll.com)
- Ipsos (www.ipsos.com)
- J.D. Power and Associates (www.jdpower.com)
- Kantar Retail (www.kantarretail.com)
- Nielsen Local (www.scarborough.com)
- ORC International (www.orcinternational.com)
- Prosper Business Development (www.goprosper.com)
- Shapiro+Raj (www.ljs.com)

F.2 Consumer-Focused Market Studies

The following firms publish market research reports assessing consumer market segments and market characteristics:

- America's Research Group (www.argconsumer.com)
- CBRE Global Research and Consulting (www.cbre.com/EN/research/Pages/default.aspx)
- Datamonitor (www.datamonitor.com)
- Euromonitor International (www.euromonitor.com)
- GfK North America (www.gfk.com)
- Mintel (www.mintel.com)
- MMGY Global (www.mmgyglobal.com)
- New Strategist Publications (www.newstrategist.com)
- Packaged Facts (www.packagedfacts.com)
- Paramount Market Publishing (www.paramountbooks`.com)
- Parks Associates (www.parksassociates.com)
- Prosper Business Development (www.goprosper.com)
- Richard K. Miller & Associates (www.rkma.com)

- STR Global (www.strglobal.com)
- The Futures Company (www.thefuturescompany.com)
- The NPD Group (www.npd.com)
- The Yankee Group (www.yankeegroup.com)
- Unity Marketing (www.unitymarketingonline.com)
- WSL Strategic Retail (www.wslstrategicretail.com)

F.3 Geodemographic Segmentation

Information about consumers based on where they live guides companies in siting their new stores. The data is also used to guide direct marketing campaigns as well as the placement of local spot ads. Various geodemographic segmentation tools, primarily based on geographic information system (GIS) technology, are available for this type of analysis. The following are companies specializing in this field:

- Acxiom (www.acxiom.com)
- Applied Geographic Solutions (www.appliedgeographic.com)
- ESRI (www.esri.com)
- Nielsen SiteReports (www.nielsen.com)
- Phoenix Marketing International (www.phoenixmi.com)
- Pitney Bowes Software (www.pbinsight.com)

F.4 Media Consumption Research

Several specialized companies offer survey-based data on consumer use of various media. This data is used by advertisers to guide marketing campaigns and ad placements. The following are leading companies in this field:

- Audience Research & Analysis (www.audienceresearch.com)
- IHS Technology (https://technology.ihs.com/Industries/450465/media-intelligence)
- Kantar Media (www.kantarmedia.com)
- Media Management, Inc. (www.mediaaudit.com)
- PQ Media (www.pqmedia.com)
- Screen Digest (www.screendigest.com)
- The Nielsen Company (www.nielsen.com)

F.5 Online Activities

Several companies track consumers' online activities, and the assessments are used by marketers to guide the placement of online ads and promotions. They also provide insight into consumers' ever-changing habits as they surf the net or shop online. The following are some market research firms specializing in online tracking:

- Compete (www.compete.com)
- ComScore (www.comscore.com)
- Experian Hitwise (www.experian.com/hitwise)

- Forrester Research (www.forrester.com)
- Juniper Research (www.juniperresearch.com)
- Quantcast (www.quantcast.com)
- Shop.org of the National Retail Federation (www.shop.org)
- The Nielsen Company (www.nielsen.com)

F.6 Retail Sales Reporting

Many companies develop comprehensive retail analyses based on sales data provided to them by major retail chains. Reporting companies provide data as varied as products that consumers purchase as well as how much they spend. In addition to receiving a fee for their data, retailers gain access to information that includes their competitors' sales figures. A few retailers, including Walmart, do not release sales data.

Companies that provide point-of-sale market research data include the following:

- Experian (www.experian.com/marketing-services/marketing-services.html)
- IRI Group (www.iriworldwide.com)
- Market Decisions (www.marketdecisions.com)
- SportScanINFO (www.sportscaninfo.com)
- The Nielsen Company (www.nielsen.com)
- The NPD Group (www.npd.com)

Such companies also develop retail market data based on statistical-sample monitoring of households. This approach (e.g., sampling and projecting) was the norm in the data gathering industry before scanner data became available.

APPENDIX G

PERIODICALS

Journal of Consumer Psychology, published by Elsevier Publishing Co. (www.elsevier.com) and Society for Consumer Psychology (www.myscp.org)

Journal of Consumer Research, P.O. Box 180078, Chicago, IL 60618. (www.ejcr.org)

Knowledge@Wharton, published online by Wharton School of the University of Pennsylvania. (http://knowledge.wharton.upenn.edu/)

MIT Sloan Management Review, published by Massachusetts Institute of Technology. One Charles Park, EE20-600 6th Floor, Cambridge, MA 02142. (www.sloanreview.mit.edu)

Multicultural Marketing News, Multicultural Marketing Resources, Inc., 150 W 28th Street, Suite 1501, New York, NY 10001. (212) 242-3351. (www.multicultural.com)

Research Brief, Center for Media Research, MediaPost Communications, 15 East 32nd Street, 7th Floor, New York, NY 10016. (www.mediapost.com/publications/research-brief/)

The Media Audit FYI, The Media Audit, 10333 Richmond Avenue, Suite 200, Houston, TX 77042. (713) 626-0333. (www.themediaaudit.com/press/archived-newsletters)

APPENDIX H

RESEARCH STUDIES & SURVEYS

Affluent Market Tracking Study, American Affluence Research Center. (www.affluenceresearch.org)

American Community Survey, Census Bureau. (www.census.gov/acs/www/)

American Customer Satisfaction Index, ForeSee Results. (www.theacsi.org)

American Housing Survey, Census Bureau. (www.census.gov/housing/ahs/data/national.html)

American Lifestyles 2016, Mintel. (www.mintel.com/american-lifestyles-2016)

American Time Use Survey Results, Bureau of Labor Statistics. (www.bls.gov/news.release/atus.nr0.htm)

Consumer Comfort Index, Bloomberg. (www.bloomberg.com/consumer-comfort-index/).

Consumer Confidence Index, The Conference Board. (www.conference-board.org)

Consumer Expenditures, Bureau of Labor Statistics. (www.bls.gov/news.release/cesan.nr0.htm)

Consumer Price Index Summary, Bureau of Labor Statistics. (www.bls.gov/cpi)

Current Population Survey, Census Bureau. (www.census.gov/cps/)

Customer Loyalty Engagement Index, Brand Keys. (www.brandkeys.com)

Eating Patterns In America, The NPD Group. (www.npd.com/latest-reports/eating-patterns-america-consumer-consumption-behavior/)

EquiTrend, Harris Poll. (www.theharrispoll.com/equitrend-information/)

General Social Survey, University of Chicago. (http://www3.norc.org/GSS+Website/)

Household Income Trends, Sentier Research. (www.sentier.com)

Housing Vacancies and Homeownership, Census Bureau. (www.census.gov/housing/hvs/)

Income and Poverty In The United States, Census Bureau. (www.census.gov/hhes/www/income/income.html)

Index of Consumer Sentiment, University of Michigan's Institute for Social Research and Thomson Reuters. (www.sca.isr.umich.edu/)

Luxury and Affluence Monthly Pulse Shullman Research Center. (www.shullman.net)

Market-By-Market Study, GfK MRI. (www.gfkmri.com/Products/MarketbyMarket.aspx)

Mendelsohn Affluent Survey, Ipsos. (www.ipsos-na.com)

Migration/Geographic Mobility, Census Bureau. (www.census.gov/hhes/migration/)

National Consumer Study, Experian Marketing Services. (www.experian.com/consumer-insights/consumer-study.html)

Panel Study of Income Dynamics, University of Michigan. (http://psidonline.isr.umich.edu/)

State of the Nation's Housing, Joint Center for Housing Studies at Harvard University. (www.jchs.harvard.edu/research/state_nations_housing)

Stress In American, American Psychological Association. (www.apa.org/news/press/releases/stress/)

Survey Of Consumer Expenditures, Bureau of Labor Statistics. (www.bls.gov/cex/)

Survey of Consumer Finances, Federal Reserve. (www.federalreserve.gov/econresdata/scf/scfindex.htm)

The Survey Of The American Consumer, GfK MRI. (www.gfkmri.com/Products/TheSurveyoftheAmericanConsumer.aspx)

REFERENCES

Chapter 2: Consumer Income & Wealth
DeNavas-Walt, Carmen, and Bernadette D. Proctor, *Income and Poverty In The United States 2014*, Census Bureau, September 2015.

Chapter 3: Consumer Debt
Birth, Allyssa, *Student Loans Continue To Delay Spending Dreams*, October 14, 2015.

Debt Styles By Age And Over Time, Urban Institute, November 2015.

Quarterly Report On Household Debt and Credit, Federal Reserve Bank of New York, February 2016.

Chapter 4: Households & Housing
Characteristics Of New Housing, Census Bureau, 2016.

Current Population Survey, Census Bureau, 2016.

Housing Vacancies and Homeownership, Census Bureau, 2016.

State of the Nation's Housing 2016, by the Joint Center for Housing Studies at Harvard University, June 2016.

Chapter 5: Communities
City and Town Totals: Vintage 2014, Census Bureau, May 2015.

Two-Thirds of U.S. Non-Metro Counties Lost Population Over 2010-2014, USDA Economic Research Service, June 2015.

Chapter 6: Urban & Rural Populations
Badger, Emily, "New Census Data: Americans Are Returning To The Far-Flung Suburbs," *The Washington Post*, March 26, 2015.

Frey, William H., "Migration To The Suburbs And Sun Belt Picks Up, Brookings Institution, April 8, 2015.

Kotkin, Joel, "So Much For The Death Of Sprawl: America's Exurbs Are Booming," *Forbes*, November 3, 2015.

Chapter 7: Where People Want To Live
Shannon-Missal, Larry, "Moving Motivations: What Make Americans Consider Uprooting To Another State?" The Harris Poll, January 6, 2016.

Shannon-Missal, Larry, "The Beach Beckons: Florida, California, Hawaii Top States Where Americans Want To Live," The Harris Poll, December 16, 2015.

Chapter 9: Personal Life
Report on the Economic Well-Being of U.S. Households in 2015, Federal Reserve, May 2016.

Chapter 10: Personal Well-Being
Witters, Dan, "Hawaii Reclaims Top Spot In U.S. Well-Being," Gallup, January 28, 2016.

Chapter 14: Use Of Time
American Time Use Survey - 2015 Results, Bureau of Labor Statistics, June 24, 2016.

Chapter 15: Use Of Media & The Internet
2015 Digital Future Project, Center for the Digital Future, University of Southern California, Annenberg School for Communication, December 2015.

Anderson, Monica, *Technology Device Ownership*, Pew Research Center, October 29, 2015.

Digital Democracy Survey, Tenth Edition, Deloitte, March 2016.

"Growth In Time Spent With Media Is Slowing," eMarketer, June 6, 2016.

Horrigan, John B. and Maeve Duggan, *Home Broadband 2015*, Pew Research Center, December 21, 2015.

Perrin, Andrew, *American's Internet Access: 2000-2015*, Pew Research Center, June 26, 2015.

Smith, Aaron and Dana Page, *U.S. Smartphone Use In 2015*, Pew Research Center, April 1, 2015.

Chapter 21: Use Of Technology
18th Annual Household CE Ownership and Market Potential Study, Consumer Technology Association, April 28, 2016.

Anderson, Monica, *Technology Device Ownership*, Pew Research Center, October 29, 2015.

Birth, Allyssa, “More Than 7 in 10 Americans Think Technology Has Become Too Distracting And Is Creating a Lazy Society,” The Harris Poll, November 4, 2015.

Digital Democracy Survey, Tenth Edition, Deloitte, March 2016.

Loechner, Jack, “Technology Impact On Our Lives: Distracts Or Improves,” *Research Brief*, Center for Media Research, November 23, 2015.

Perrin, Andrew, *American's Internet Access: 2000-2015*, Pew Research Center, June 26, 2015.

Smith, Aaron and Dana Page, *U.S. Smartphone Use In 2015*, Pew Research Center, April 1, 2015.

U.S. Consumer Technology Sales and Forecasts, Consumer Technology Association, January 4, 2016.

Chapter 25: Mobile Shopping

Chamberlain, Lauryn, “Mobile Will Drive $689 Billion In Store Sales During 2016,” Geomarketing, December 8, 2015.

“M-Commerce's Rapid Growth Is Primarily Coming From Smartphones,” eMarketer, May 4, 2016.

“Most Digital Buyers Will Make Purchases Via A Smartphone By 2017,” eMarketer, February 16, 2016.

“Why Don't Consumers Buy More Via Mobile?” eMarketer, February 5, 2016.

Chapter 26: Peer-To-Peer Shopping

“How Do Consumers Feel About The Sharing Economy?” eMarketer, May 27, 2016.

“How Much More Can Ride-Sharing Services Grow In The U.S.?” eMarketer, May 17, 2016.

“Is The Sharing Economy A Retail Disruptor?” eMarketer, November 12, 2015.

“Millennials Are More On Board With The Sharing Economy,” eMarketer, October 13, 2015.

Steinmetz, Katy, “The Way We Work. A New Poll Reveals The Size Of The Peer-To-Peer Revolution,” *Time*, January 18, 2016.

Chapter 27: Omnichannel Shopping
17th Annual Customer Engagement Survey, Boston Retail Partners, January 18, 2016.

"Are Retailers Providing A Consistent Omnichannel Experience?" eMarketer, January 28, 2016.

"Consumers Like To Shop Digitally, Pick Up In-Store," eMarketer, April 21, 2016.

"Gen Zers, Millennials Say Brands Should Have Physical Stores," eMarketer, April 14, 2016.

"In-Store Pickups Account For Significant E-Commerce Sales," eMarketer, January 25, 2016.

The State of Retail 2016, TimeTrade, January 2016.

"What Retailers Are Focusing On In 2016," eMarketer, January 26, 2016.

"Which Omnichannel Retailing Services Need Improvement," eMarketer, April 28, 2016.

Chapter 28: Brand Loyalty
How Consumers Evaluate Brands, Spring, July 28, 2015.

Loechner, Jack, "What Are They Really Thinking?" *Research Brief*, Center for Media Research, October 26, 2015.

Chapter 29: Buying American-Made
Walker, Rob, "A Guide To Made In America," *Bloomberg Businessweek*, November 7, 2015, pp 44-45.

Chapter 30: Buying Local
Birth, Allyssa, "Americans Split On Importance Of Buying Local At The Grocery Store," Harris Poll, December 8, 2015.

Chapter 33: Ethically Conscious Consumerism
2015 Millennial CSR Study, Cone Communications, September 2015.

2016 Edelman Trust Barometer, Edelman, January 2016.

"Do Company Ethics Affect Purchase Decisions?" eMarketer, December 10, 2015.

The Ethical Consumer U.S., Mintel and Lightspeed GMI, November 18, 2015.

Chapter 34: Gift Giving
Danziger, Pam, *Gifting Report 2015*, Unity Marketing, May 2015.

Loechner, Jack, "Better To Give Than To Receive," *Research Brief*, Center for Media Research, December 1, 2015.

Loechner, Jack, "Gifts Without A Price Tag," *Research Brief*, Center for Media Research, December 14, 2015.

Chapter 35: Loyalty Program Participation
"Loyalty Program Memberships Climb, But Participation Wanes," eMarketer, February 10, 2016.

"Rewards, Offers Keep Loyalty Program Participation Going," eMarketer, November 3, 2015.

"Would Loyal Customers Pay For Rewards?" eMarketer, July 16, 2015.

Chapter 36: Payment Preferences
"Fewer Digital Wallet Users Are Making Payments," eMarketer, November 20, 2015.

"For Retail Purchases, Credit Card Swipes Are Quickest," eMarketer, November 30, 2015.

"Mobile Payments Will Triple In The U.S. In 2016," eMarketer, October 26, 2015.

"Plastic Dominates For Holiday Payment," eMarketer, December 17, 2015.

Chapter 38: Privacy Issues
2016 Identity Fraud Study, Javelin Strategy & Research, February 2, 2016.

Madden, Mary and Lee Rainie, *Americans' Attitudes About Privacy, Security, And Surveillance*, Pew Research Center, May 20, 2015.

"Mobile App Users Reluctant To Share Location," eMarketer, November 25, 2015.

Chapter 39: Purchase Decision Making
2015 Digital Consumer Preferences Survey, BrandShop, April 2015.

"How Do Shoppers Decide Between Brick-and-Mortar Retailers?" eMarketer, August 6, 2015.

"How Retailers Are Marketing Via Influencers," eMarketer, December 24, 2015.

Loechner, Jack, "Brands Must Provide The Whole Magillah," *Research Brief*, Center for Media Research, October 14, 2015.

"Millennials Admit To Impulse Shopping," eMarketer, January 19, 2016.

Chapter 41: Response To Customer Service

Customer Service Survey, Onestop, February 22, 2016.

"How to Win At Customer Service," eMarketer, October 15, 2015.

"Q1 2016 Consumer Benchmark Survey," Temkin Research, March 3, 2016.

"Sales Associates Improve Shipping For Men, Women Alike," eMarketer, July 27, 2015.

"Will A Poor Customer Experience Affect Future Purchases?" eMarketer, March 18, 2016.

Chapter 43: Response To Visuals

Birt, Nate, "How Visual Content Affects Your Brain (and Improves Sales!)," *Content Marketing*, June 4, 2015.

Loechner, Jack, "The Eyes Have It ... From The Customer's Point Of View," *Research Brief*, Center for Media Research, January 19, 2016.

Loechner, Jack, "What You See Is What You Get," *Research Brief*, Center for Media Research, January 28, 2016.

Styles, Mia, "What Is Color Psychology Marketing and How It Affects Your Brand," My Evideo, August 19, 2015.

Chapter 44: Shopping Research

2015 Connected Shopper Report, Harris Poll, November 19, 2015.

"Internet Users Research Prices Online Before In-Store Shopping," eMarketer, December 11, 2015.

"When Do Digital Buyers Research Products?" eMarketer, January 8, 2016.

Chapter 46: Theme Appeal

Global Trust in Advertising: Winning Strategies for an Evolving Media Landscape, Nielsen, September 2015.

Chapter 47: Affluence Profile

Affluent Market Tracking Study, American Affluence Research Center, 2016.

Chapter 48: Population Centers Of U.S. Affluence
2015 United States Wealth Report, Capgemini, 2015.

Schiffman, Betsy, "Full List: America's Most Expensive ZIP Codes 2015," *Forbes*, November 10, 2015.

Swanson, Ana, "The Wealthiest ZIP Codes In America," *The Washington Post*, May 8, 2015.

U.S. Affluent & HNW Markets - 2015 Market Sizing Update & Millionaires By State Ranking, Phoenix Marketing International, June 2015.

Chapter 49: Affluence E-Commerce
Global Luxury E-tailing Market 2015-2019, Technavio, February 2016.

Jones, Sarah, "Luxury Online Retail Market To Reach $41.8 Billion by 2019," *Luxury Daily*, February 29, 2016.

Chapter 51: Defining The Middle Class
Cohen, Patricia, "Middle Class, Or So They Think," *The New York Times*, April 11, 2015.

Chapter 52: Middle Class Falling Behind
Kochhar, Rakesh and Richard Fry, *America's Shrinking Middle Class: A Close Look At Changes Within Metropolitan Areas*, Pew Research Center, May 11, 2016.

Kochhar, Rakesh and Richard Fry, *The American Middle Class Is Losing Ground*, Pew Research Center, December 9, 2015.

Chapter 53: Income & Wealth Inequality
In It Together: Why Less Inequality Benefits All, Organization for Economic Cooperation and Development, 2015.

Ingraham, Christopher, "If You Thought Income Inequality Was Bad, Get A Load Of Wealth Inequality," *The Washington Post*, May 21, 2015.

Chapter 56: Customer Experience
Temkin, Bruce, *2016 Temkin Experience Ratings*, Temkin Group, March 2016.

Chapter 59: Reputation Ranking
"Annual Reputation Rankings For The 100 Most Visible Companies In The U.S.," The Harris Poll, February 18, 2016.

Chapter 60: African-American Consumers
Anderson, Monica, "A Rising Share Of The U.S. Black Population Is Foreign Born," Pew Research Center, April 9, 2015.

Consumer Expenditure Survey 2014, U.S. Bureau of Labor Statistics, September 2015.

Loechner, Jack, "African-Americans Top Media Users," *Research Brief*, Center for Media Research, February 23, 2015.

"Multicultural Consumers By The Numbers," *Advertising Age*, April 6, 2015, p. 20.

Toppo, Greg, "Immigrants Alter Black Statistics," *USA Today*, April 10, 2015.

Chapter 62: Asian-American Consumers
Consumer Expenditure Survey 2014, U.S. Bureau of Labor Statistics, September 2015.

"Multicultural Consumers By The Numbers," *Advertising Age*, April 6, 2015, p. 20.

"The Model Minority Is Losing Patience," *The Economist*, October 3, 2015, pp 23-26.

Chapter 63: Hispanic & Latino-American Consumers
"Bicultural Hispanics: Who Are They and Why Should Marketers Be Paying Attention?" eMarketer, December 24, 2015.

Consumer Expenditure Survey 2014, U.S. Bureau of Labor Statistics, September 2015.

Krogstad, Jens Manuel, "English Proficiency On The Rise Among Latinos," Pew Research Center, May 12, 2015.

"Most Hispanics Speak English Proficiently," Demo Memo, May 18, 2015.

"Multicultural Consumers By The Numbers," *Advertising Age*, April 6, 2015, p. 20.

"U.S. Hispanic Millennials More Receptive To Mobile Ads," eMarketer, June 16, 2015.

Chapter 66: Native-American Consumers
Facts for Features: American Indian and Alaska Native Heritage, U.S. Census Bureau, November 2015.

"Of Slots And Sloth," *The Economist*, January 17, 2016.

Chapter 68: Male Consumers
"A Father's Place," *The Economist*, May 16, 2016.

"Change Is Afoot In Fatherhood As Millennials Become Prime Parenting Generation," eMarketer, April 6, 2016.

College Enrollment and Work Activity of 2015 High School Graduates, Bureau of Labor Statistics, May 2016.

Chapter 69: Generational Comparison
"Generations In A Mirror: How They See Themselves," Pew Research Center, September 5, 2015.

Chapter 70: Seniors
"65-Plus Who Work Full Time," Demo Memo, November 5, 2015.

A Look at the End-of-Life Financial Situation in America, Employee Benefit Research Institute, May 2015.

Chapter 73: Millennial Consumers
Fry, Richard, "More Millennials Living With Family Despite Improved Job Market," Pew Research Center, July 29, 2015.

General Social Survey, Census Bureau, November 2015.

Chapter 74: Generation Z
Lenhart, Amanda, *Teens, Social Media & Technology*, Pew Research Center, April 9, 2015.

Steinmetz, Katy, "Move Over Millennials," *Time*, January 4, 2016, p. 134.

Taking Stock With Teens - Spring 2016, Piper Jaffrey, April 2016.

Chapter 81: Married Couples
Families and Living Arrangements, U.S. Census Bureau, 2015.

National Longitudinal Survey of Youth 1997, Bureau of Labor Statistics, April 2016.

Chapter 82: Military Consumers
Profile of Veterans: 2014, National Center for Veterans Analysis and Statistics, March 2016.

Chapter 84: Retirees
"Age May Well Wither Them," *The Economist*, November 7, 2015.

Change in Household Spending After Retirement, Employee Benefit Research Institute, December 2015.

Munnell, Alicia, Wenliang Hou and Anthony Webb, “National Retirement Readiness Index (NRRI) Shows Half of Working Age Americans Still Falling Short,” *The Journal of Retirement*, November 2015.

Saad, Lynda, “Three In 10 U.S. Workers Foresee Working Past Retirement Age,” Gallup Poll, April 6, 2016.

Schieber, Sylvester, “U.S. Retirement Policy Considerations for the Twenty-First Century,” *The Journal of Retirement*, November 2015.

Trends In Retirement Satisfaction In The United States, Employee Benefit Research Institute, May 2016.

Chapter 85: Single Consumers

America’s Families and Living Arrangements, Census Bureau, 2016.

Current Population Survey, Census Bureau, 2016.

Chapter 88: Metropolitan Economic Profiles

Kochhar, Rakesh and Richard Fry, *America’s Shrinking Middle Class: A Close Look At Changes Within Metropolitan Areas*, Pew Research Center, May 11, 2016.